REA

ALLEN COUNTY PUBLIC LIBRARY

3 1833 01533 9267

Y0-DFW-719

306.85 T72f v.2
Tremblay, Helene
Families of the world

**DO NOT REMOVE
CARDS FROM POCKET**

ALLEN COUNTY PUBLIC LIBRARY

FORT WAYNE, INDIANA 46802

You may return this book to any agency, branch, or bookmobile of the Allen County Public Library.

DEMCO

FAMILIES OF THE WORLD

FAMILIES OF THE WORLD

Family Life at the Close of the Twentieth Century

Volume 2

East Asia, Southeast Asia, and the Pacific

HÉLÈNE TREMBLAY

Script Editor Pat Capon

FARRAR, STRAUS AND GIROUX

NEW YORK

Allen County Public Library
Ft. Wayne, Indiana

Copyright © 1990 by Famo Ltd.
All rights reserved
Printed in the United States of America
Designed by Helen Barrow
First edition, 1990

LIBRARY OF CONGRESS CATALOGING-IN-PUBLICATION DATA
Tremblay, Hélène.
    Families of the world, vol. 2
    Contents: v. 1. The Americas and the Caribbean—
v. 2. East Asia, Southeast Asia, and the Pacific.
      1. Family—Cross-cultural studies. 2. Family—
History—20th century. I. Capon, Pat. II. Title.
HQ518.T6813   1990   306.8′5   88-7106

CREDITS

CARTOGRAPHY AND GRAPHICS
    Barbara Mullin,
    Department of Geology and Geography,
    Hunter College, New York City

RESEARCH ASSISTANTS
    Jeanette Farrell and Noemie Terzian
    Patricia Farr

PHOTO EDITOR
    Lauren Stockbower

ACKNOWLEDGMENTS

It is with immense gratitude that I must first acknowledge the steadfast and continuing support of the following institutions which have provided financial and logistic assistance in the making of this volume. Without their backing, I would not feel truly assured today that this collection will eventually be completed. I sincerely thank:

> The Canadian International Development Agency (CIDA)
> The United Nations Children's Fund (UNICEF)
> The United Nations Development Programme (UNDP)
> Canada Save the Children
> The United Nations Fund for Population Activities (UNFPA)
> The United Nations Department of Public Information
> The Olympus Corporation, Consumer Products Group, USA

I am deeply grateful to the following institutions which have added their support in the making of this volume:

> The United Nations Fund for Women in Development (UNIFEM)
> The Asia Society, New York
> The American Forum (Education in a Global Age)

It is important to mention the crucial support I have received from all those who believed in the project and always gave me time to draw on their professional advice and help in so many essential ways: Tony Hewett, Jan Ralph, Mehri Hekmati, André Champagne, Jamie Cloud.

All those who know me will understand if I once again thank Jean Tetrault: for having stood continuously by my side as a friend, but also for his precious insights and feedback. Sharing our complementary knowledge of the world has always been a true pleasure of this quest.

My deep-felt thanks to Noemie Terzian, whose unfailing energy, faith, and good humor have made her a very special collaborator. I thank Jeanette Farrell, who has so smoothly invested herself in this collaborative effort with her talents as writer, researcher, and assistant, thereby allowing Noemie to give birth to Pauline and I to turn in this volume to my publishers.

I very warmly thank Pat Capon. Between sitters and baby naps, we have gone word by word and step by step into the details of daily life on two continents. Sharing our thoughts and reactions about all we learned through these exercises has made an adventure of our working hours.

And because my quest is to learn, and I cannot do so without the help of others, I give special acknowledgment to the many individuals in every country who helped me to discover, understand, and get a sense of their people. I thank those who guided me and introduced me to the families and those who, when there were language barriers, interpreted so warmly the words of others. And with great emotion, I think of those who so kindly opened their doors and welcomed me into the warmth of their homes and honored me with their friendship: *the families.*

PREFACE

In the introduction to the first volume of Families of the World, *Hélène Tremblay asks, "What could be easier than to introduce one family to another?" I am delighted to know she thinks it is so easy, because that means other volumes will follow these first two magnificent books. It has not been easy for Hélène. To pay extended visits to more than sixty countries is hardly an everyday affair. To be able to meet new people in each country, to enter into their lives and become their friend, and then to have to leave again—that is something which only an exceptional woman could undertake.*

When I first met Hélène Tremblay, I was very impressed by the enthusiasm with which she explained her reasons for embarking on this difficult project. She did not have to convince me of the importance of the subject. I have always thought of the family as a crucial institution. We consider our development efforts successful when they contribute to the well-being and happiness of the family. Indeed, whether one is concerned with education, health, employment, the environment, population, or children, one is thinking of individuals who belong to a family.

Families of the World *breathes life into our repeated statements, in the UN building, concerning the family; that we share one world, that we are, in the last analysis, part of each other's destiny. Out of these vivid pictures and the lively descriptions of ordinary people's lives comes a powerful and very complex message. The book reminds us of the differences, the gaps, between us and our perceptions of the world. It is Hélène Tremblay's mission and her gift to us to make those gaps a little smaller and to remind us that what divides us is less important than what unites us.*

I hope the book will contribute to a greater awareness and understanding of the daily problems which confront families throughout the world, and so lead to a greater acceptance of the diverse cultures to which these families belong.

Families of the World *has been years in the making. It shows what one person can do if she has the will. Hélène Tremblay has the will, and she has certainly found the way.*

NAFIS SADIK
EXECUTIVE DIRECTOR
UNITED NATIONS POPULATION FUND

CONTENTS

INTRODUCTION xi
AUTHOR'S NOTE xv

EAST ASIA
People's Republic of China 2
Japan 22
Republic of Korea* 30
Mongolian People's Republic 38

SOUTHEAST ASIA
Brunei Darussalam 48
Indonesia 56
Democratic Kampuchea 78
Lao People's Democratic Republic 86
Malaysia 94
Union of Myanmar (Burma) 102
Philippines 110
Singapore 124
Thailand 132
Socialist Republic of Vietnam 146
Refugees and Displaced Persons 154

THE PACIFIC
Australia 164
Republic of Fiji 172
Kiribati 186
Nauru 194
New Zealand 202
Papua New Guinea 210
Solomon Islands 224
Kingdom of Tonga 232
Tuvalu 240
Vanuatu 248
Western Samoa 256

KEY TO SOURCE NOTES 267
SOURCES 269

* See page xvi for note on Democratic People's Republic of Korea.

INTRODUCTION

The desire to know the world, its peoples, and the thousands of ways we lead our daily lives is one shared by all of humankind. When I visited the Pacific islands, I brought photographs of families I had visited in East and Southeast Asia. Witnessing the islanders' discovery of other cultures was as fascinating for me as discovering the Pacific countries. First, everyone searched for similarities. In Fiji, I sat in the chief's house with a dozen villagers. They came to the conclusion that the houses in Kampuchea looked very much like their own traditional houses; that clothing in Brunei was similar to theirs; and, added the boys, that the girls were really beautiful. They were also fascinated by the differences. "Look how well they use bamboo in Laos!" said the chief, explaining that bamboo grew generously in their country but that Fijians did not know how to make use of it anymore. In Kiribati, the whole village made an incredible discovery when they looked at the Mongolian family: "There are places without any trees. And cow and horse dung is used for cooking!" I often wondered if their desire and curiosity to know the world and all its people would ever be satisfied.

Family life is the one social experience that is common to all humankind, and sharing this experience among other families all over the world is the most powerful force for international understanding among "ordinary" people that I have ever witnessed.

There is a particularly urgent need to strengthen international communication about the family today when it is feeling the impact of the hurricane of change that is sweeping through the world. Everywhere I have found that families are wondering where the forces of change are taking them and whether these forces will bring them better lives.

When asked about their beliefs and traditions, young people invariably exclaim, "Oh, Grandmother used to do this or think that, but it is not so anymore." And everywhere grandmothers say with regret, "Things are not as they used to be."

Young people are impatient to master every piece of information that comes their way. The old feel sad and powerless when they see the young turn their backs on traditional culture. In between these two groups there is a generation of people in their late thirties and early forties who act as a buffer and try to ensure that young and old live happily side by side and communicate with each other.

Satisfying both groups, however, does not entail the same responses. The old want the pattern of their daily lives to be unchanged. They want to feel that their beliefs are shared. To keep them happy, new ideas must often be filtered and their impact softened. Meanwhile, the deepest concern of the world's parents is how to satisfy the young.

In the developing countries these forces are far more manifest than in the industrial countries, but families have fewer resources to cope with them. To satisfy the aspirations of today's young people, the buffer generation must find more and more cash.

The first priority, I have found everywhere, is education, including school clothes, equipment, and transport. Young people are also pushing their parents out of the subsistence economy in a process which may start in an apparently trivial way, with a desire for jeans and T-shirts with a slogan, the universal uniform of youth. Young people are hungry for the new universal music and for the foreign products that transnational advertising, television, and video offer as daily temptations. They become dissatisfied with the stillness of village life, and the attraction of the city starts to break the spell of the extended community.

For millions of people living in societies that have known a regular, predictable, unchanging way of life for centuries, today is a time of tumult. They feel with alarm that their lives are spiraling out of the control of their community and coming under the influence of a new, international "paramount chief," who is motivated by cash and materialism rather than by spirit and soul.

Meanwhile, as societies and individuals try to understand what is happening, the daily round continues. Children must be fed, roofs must be repaired before the rainy season, and water must be fetched. Gardens and fields must be planted, weeded, and harvested, rents paid, debts met. And whatever may be happening to the old cultures and values, every man and woman who wakes up to start a new day shares with unknown millions elsewhere in the world the same desire to live through it in dignity and faith. How much stronger they would feel in face of the new doubts, if they knew they shared this desire, for I find that most people feel lonely, thinking that their own worries are the worst.

I must restate how privileged I feel to have the opportunity, while doing this project, to become acquainted with the world. And since access to information is so limited on a global scale, the fact that you have access to this book indicates how privileged you are. If the people of this world are to know with whom they share this planet, this knowledge should be considered a basic human need, not a privilege. Through my discovery of the unknown, my goal has become clear. I would like to think I am contributing, in my own modest way, to the realization of a world encounter.

I have come to life on this planet. The idea of one day dying without having known where I have dwelled is very disturbing to me. As far as I am concerned, there is nothing more inspiring than to discover the planet and meet those I share it with. How great is the feeling of simply breathing when the energy comes from beyond the borders set by our society, culture, and often ourselves. The sunset is friendlier when it chills you if you are aware that it is sliding to warm friends down under.

INTRODUCTION xiii

In my travels, I have grown to respect farmers deeply. As a first gesture in the morning, every farmer or fisherman looks up at the sky and understands it. If he is someone who prays, he prays for nature to be clement. And, in a way, the farmer's prayers are for all humankind, as he is the one who feeds us. Farmers unite the world.

So many times I have felt that we are one. For every individual and every parent, the struggle is similar: to provide ourselves and our children with shelter from the cold and the heat, to secure our daily food and keep those we love protected and alive. Yet we are characterized by our cultural, geographical, social, and economic differences and find different ways to assure these basic needs.

The travel and research for Volume 2 were done in three phases, between April 1986 and May 1988. I began with East Asia, then went on to Southeast Asia and the Pacific. From the beginning, I had to be very sensitive to each country's differences. Even sitting down was not done in the same manner everywhere. I often wondered if I was doing anything wrong; if I was shocking my host or being impolite. Upon leaving, I would apologize for anything I had done that was improper. The polite Asians would, in turn, apologize for anything they could have done to displease me.

While putting together Volume 1, I often questioned my own background, trying to understand what made it possible for me to share the lives of different people so easily. In more than one situation, I thought that as a French Canadian I had much in common with the people of Latin America. I have experienced differences more sharply as I traveled through Asia and the Pacific.

On the Asian continent, every gesture taught to me by my culture was challenged. I had always believed that I was basically the product of a society, a culture, and a family. This has now been confirmed, and I know that if I had been born in some other country in a different culture, the manner in which I express my pain, my love, my convictions would be somewhat different.

Our emotions and the way we express them are certainly culturally rooted. The pain expressed by parents who have lost a child is but one example. Love and care is another. In Asia and the Pacific, I discovered that through foreign films and videos the Western way of expressing those emotions is seriously influencing people. Nearly all the parents in Volume 2 were in some kind of arranged marriage. All of them said that they would let their children choose their own partners. In Japan, a woman told me: "I ask my husband to tell me he loves me, but Japanese men don't say things like that." The Indian couple in Fiji, who are in their early thirties, also had an arranged marriage. They told me they had learned to care for each other. But "it is not the same," they said. "We would like to try marrying for love." That notion of "love" was for them, I felt, a new concept (or Western product) to experience.

In the industrialized world, our lives have to some extent become based on packaged ideas. Travel companies have brought us the concept of paradise on earth: the sandy beaches, the palm trees leaning toward a turquoise sea. I remember one day in particular. I was with Agnes Fihu in the Solomon Islands. We were going to one of the family gardens. First we had to row the pirogue along the seashore. The sea was calm and crystal-clear. The mountain next to us was lush, waterfalls rushing noisily into the sea. We were singing to keep the rhythm of our paddles. This is paradise, I thought. Just like so many people's dream of escaping the rushed world we live in. After a while, my shoulder started to hurt a little. I knew that Agnes's shoulder did not hurt. We had to row for more than one hour. Then a small motorboat went by at full speed, and Agnes said: "When we know how fast and easy it is to get from one point to another, we don't want to row anymore." This was not a holiday paradise; this was not an adventure. This woman was going to her garden to collect food. She had two to three hours of traveling every day to feed her family. If she had the possibility of cutting this time in half, she would do so. I would do likewise.

After we finished rowing, we had to go up the mountain. It was during the rainy season and the ground was muddy and slippery. Climbing up was fine, since my toes could grab the muddy ground, but coming down was another story. I was convinced I would end up sliding on my back. Agnes, who had the garden produce on her back, held by a string over her forehead, turned to take my heavy camera bag. I refused. She not only insisted; she grabbed it and threw it as if it was a feather on the top of her load and climbed down as if she were on solid terrain. How little I felt, but how great and strong she was, I thought. She has, like many other people I have met, all my admiration.

After the publication of Volume 1, I was often asked why I had not involved myself more personally in the texts. What did I think and feel in the course of such unusual adventures? From the beginning, I thought it would be impossible to contribute personal comments on 160 countries. As I write *Families of the World*, I constantly question myself and the world we live in. I am personally growing and my knowledge and understanding of global issues increase and evolve in the process. My opinions might be quite different when all this is over.

Moreover, my personal opinions might stop you from forming your own. Does it really matter how I felt? Your feelings, as you discover those with whom you share the planet, are more important. If ever you experience warmth and understanding for the families in this book, despite their differences from you, I would feel that I had brought you more than a book, more than information: the adventure would also be yours.

As I write these lines, I am traveling and doing research for Volume 3: *Europe*. In the West I have heard people say: "Beside my very close family and one or two friends, I don't know and don't wish to know anyone else." Yet every day I see, hear, and read about how Eastern Europe is opening its borders to millions of people who express their impatience to discover their neighbors. How will these people meet? What will I discover in Europe? I am eager to contribute to a world encounter that is drawing closer with events in Eastern Europe today.

H.T.

AUTHOR'S NOTE

I have been very fortunate to establish contacts in every country through the exceptional support of the United Nations Fund for Children (UNICEF) and the United Nations Development Programme (UNDP). Their personnel was always available to discuss my choices and guide me in my search for the family. It is difficult to imagine getting into some countries, and actually living with a family, without such contacts. There are no words strong enough to express my deep-felt appreciation for this support.

The families in this book were chosen from detailed statistical profiles and accurately reflect the characteristics of each country. If the majority of a country's population is rural, the family chosen to represent it is rural. The family earns the average national income and has the number of children that corresponds to the national average. I have tried to choose couples in similar age groups because the changes between generations are extreme in many countries. The family's home also had to be representative of the country's architecture and the predominant standard of living.

Other factors also influence life-styles: access to electricity, to safe and piped water, to roads. A country's major problems must also be taken into consideration: deforestation, overpopulation, migration to the cities, the inequalities of the social classes. Looking at a map is very different when you try to imagine who lives where, and what the climate and geography are like. Life varies in high altitudes, on the seashore, in the desert, in countries with a monsoon, in villages, in cities of 10,000, 100,000, or one million inhabitants. And the choice of a representative family is made even more difficult when half the population is rural and the other half is urban.

During my travels I also gather the data for the statistical pages. Percentages and averages change every year, so I always take into consideration when the data were compiled, as well as the country's present and future social and economic trends. I really dislike writing, "No data." In Western Samoa, the statistical office informed me that they had no information on teenage pregnancy and births out of wedlock. I asked them what questions they asked on their birth registrations.

"We ask the mother's age, whether the mother is married, and the name of the father," they said.

"Well, then you have the answers to my questions."

"We have to compile the information," the statistician said. There are approximately five thousand births in Samoa in one year; I decided I could manage to compile the information myself. I won't describe the look I got from the statistician, but I did get the birth registrations. They came with one of the wonderful smiles that only the Pacific people know the secret of.

From the beginning, the inclusion of statistical pages in this volume has been somewhat controversial. Are they really necessary? Are people interested? Doesn't it make the book look too serious? Indeed, statistical information is mostly found in unattractive books, but that doesn't mean that the information itself is unattractive. Data tell a lot about a country and its inhabitants' living conditions. When I find myself in a country where, for instance, there are no statistics available on how many sixteen-year-olds are in school, at work, or unemployed, because research has not been done or compiled, I can only ask myself: What are they doing for their young people?

When all the information I have gathered

takes me to a particular region, the personnel of the United Nations establishes contacts with local professionals working at the grass-roots level. Group sessions are often required to define the family's main features and to locate someone who knows the community intimately enough to knock on a family's door and introduce me. That is how I discovered the incredible work women's organizations are doing. Their work is often voluntary or very poorly paid, but the time and energy I have seen them give to their communities has more than once amazed me. It is through these people that initial contact with a family is made possible. If the person I am with when the time comes to knock on doors is someone whom everyone trusts, then I benefit more readily from such trust. This is a crucial element, since, in general, families are not notified of my coming. The only exceptions to this rule were China, Mongolia, Vietnam, and Laos. These were also the only countries where my interpreters had to stay with me constantly.

When I need interpreters, I ask them to come one or two hours a day, leaving me alone with the family the rest of the time. There are always high-school students around who are only too happy to practice their English, and the struggle to understand each other always brings special moments. Even if the interpreters are from the same country, I often feel that they provoke more unease in the families than my own presence. Moreover, I have noticed that city people, as the interpreters generally are, often feel they cannot live comfortably in the simplicity of a rural environment, even their own. But I will never forget Mrs. Daijinnyam, who accompanied me in Mongolia. She was an extraordinary woman and made our stay in the family very special. I also remember the long hours spent in the train with Chen Lin in China after we had spent nearly a month together. A genuine intimacy had settled between us.

I must have seemed demanding to those who were kind enough to help me in my search. I often insisted that the family have one more or one less child, a larger or smaller house, or that the heads of the households have different occupations, in order to correspond adequately to the ideal statistical profile. And, no concessions were made on major features. In that respect, all the essays are as faithful a depiction of each country as possible, so that readers who are part of the mainstream in their own country can reflect: If I had been born there, that is how I would live. When, for some reason or another, the family enjoys a standard of living above the average, I always mention it in the text.

In each country there are minority groups, and I am always asked to present them. There are always mixed feelings about the minorities. People may be proud, may want to show them off to tourists. But when you really look into it, few minority groups are given the chance to grow within the national culture with equal opportunities. Minorities are a subject in themselves. It would be very difficult to write about them without being political. I would like to do so at a later stage perhaps, but that is not within the present objectives of *Families of the World*.

I have made a few exceptions to these basic criteria. As it was an important feature of the country, and as the Pacific is trying to retain traditional customs alongside development, I chose to represent the traditional groups in Vanuatu. I also thought it was important to add a chapter on the numerous minorities of Southeast Asia grouped in a region known to us as the Golden Triangle. That is why the Akha family in Thailand has been included.

Despite numerous requests from several United Nations Agencies, I was refused entry into the Democratic People's Republic of Korea. If permission is ever granted, I would be happy to include this country in future editions of Volume 2.

FAMILIES OF THE WORLD

EAST ASIA

People's Republic of China

The Zhou Family

Zhou Yugen, age 45 (1)
Gong Chaolian, 41 (2)
Zhou Xinzhi, 22 (3)*
Zhou Xingeng, 19 (4)
Zhou Xinzhi, 17 (5)
Zhou Xinyao, 15 (6)
Zhou Xinmin, 12 (7)
Xu Shulan (Nai Nai), 92 (8)
Yan Gengying (daughter-in-law), 20 (9)
Zhou Guangyan, 3 months, (10)

2 pigs
15 chickens

* Zhou Xinzhi does not share his sister's name. The two names are written in different characters and pronounced in a different tone.

An Le Village, Sichuan Province

APRIL 20

6:45 A roaring noise bursts from the speaker in the inner courtyard just a few feet from the ears of the sleeping Zhou family. It's time for the national news, broadcast over the village radio and wired into each An Le home. Nobody in the Zhou family moves at the sound of the local Communist Party secretary, at the daily advice on field management, the summaries of the country's total production, and the dates for children's medical checkups.

7:00 A Niang (Aunty) gets up. She has come to take her sister-in-law's place while Gong Chaolian visits her sick brother a three-hour bus ride away in Sichuan Province. At her heels is Nai Nai (Granny), her mother.

At ninety-two, Nai Nai is as strong as the beam holding up the four-bedroom farmhouse, and her lively spirit is the sunshine of the Zhou family. Nai Nai lives the moments as they come. The present ones are the most peaceful of her life. She has lived through four major upheavals: the fall of the Empire in 1911; the 1927 civil war between the Communists and the Nationalists; the Communist Revolution of 1949; and in 1967, the Cultural Revolution. More recently, with China's modernization, Nai Nai has seen sweeping social and agrarian reforms transform her way of life yet again. She was born a peasant during the Qin Dynasty, a time when the peasants of her province were so poor they had to beg heartless landlords for something to eat. It was during those years that Nai Nai had her feet bound to restrict growth, as was then the style. Farmers' daughters were not obliged to follow the trend, but young peasant girls wanted to feel as beautiful as the women in the Emperor's court. That was many years, children, and revolutions ago. When asked her name, Nai Nai laughs. "I don't have a name anymore," she says. "I have been Mama and Nai Nai for much too long."

Sitting behind the immense earthen-brick stove, Grandmother stokes the fire with coal and dry grass while A Niang cuts the vegetables and gets the rice ready for breakfast. Outside, Zhou Yugen checks the irrigation in the rice fields. The planting is over and there is nothing to do until it's time to weed. Zhou Yugen has contracted from the government 0.8 mu [1 mu = ⅕ hectares] of land for each member of his family. On these 6 mu, they cultivate all the rice, wheat, potatoes, cabbage, and green vegetables they need. The family pays its taxes with a portion of the harvest, and sells about two percent of it for cash. The rest they eat.

Sichuan has fertile land and a temperate climate, and the peasants live well here. The province is known as the "breadbasket of China." When agricultural reforms were necessary, Sichuan Province became the site of government experiments. Collective farming started in the fifties, and peasants jointly worked one government-owned plot and shared the harvest equally. But this provided no incentive for hard work, and as the uninspired workers slacked off, China was still not growing enough to feed its expanding population. Since 1983, under the new "responsibility system," families work individual plots of land. Peasants who have fulfilled their production quota can dispose of the surplus in any way they wish, and are also free to devote themselves to a non-farming industry of their choice. Three years ago, the Zhou family went into noodle making. Zhou Yugen borrowed money at the bank (the only type of loan possible in China), cemented over the back yard, built a shed, and bought the equipment. Now every night, because often there is no electricity during the day, the family works together making noodles. One of the shops in the village buys everything they produce.

8:00

After breakfast, the two youngest girls, Zhou Xinyao and Xinmin, leave for school, heading out into the dense traffic on the rural road in front of the house. It is market day at the Ping Luo township. Peasants sell all they can to supplement their farming income. People hurry by with handwoven carpets balanced on their heads; others, with poles balanced on their shoulders, carry dangling baskets overflowing with ducks or vegetables. Still others on bicycles pull wheelbarrows loaded with coal or a few pigs. Anyone who sells a pig today will go home with full pockets.

Daughter-in-law Yan Gengying prepares the basin for her baby's bath. She seems happy to be alone for a minute during the quiet morning to make a fuss over her baby. In the afternoon, after classes, and at night, there are just too many people in this cheerful, loving family that want to take the infant girl away from her mother.

Zhou Xingeng refills the house's thermos with the hot water to be kept ready for tea or washing. Zhou Xingeng and her seventeen-year-old sister have finished their schooling and have agreed to help in the noodle business until they are twenty, the legal marriage age. This morning the nineteen-year-old sweeps the house's cement floor in the inner courtyard. The family home is fifty years old, a new building in this two-thousand-year-old town. The house originally had only two bedrooms but was enlarged after Yan Gengying became pregnant and Zhou Xinzhi, the Zhous' only son, had to marry her. An unfortunate accident: unmarried parents are not allowed in China and births

In front of the Zhous' house, rice has just been planted in the irrigated field that separates the house from the road leading to the village.

are not encouraged before a woman's twenty-eighth birthday. But Zhou Xinzhi's marriage was happily celebrated and the coming of the first grandchild was a joyful event. In the courtyard the wedding decorations and congratulatory poems still adorn the windows. Now six doors open onto the courtyard from the surrounding rooms: the kitchen, Zhou Xinzhi and his wife's bedroom, the four girls' two bedrooms, and the two small storage rooms which hold the year's grain harvest.

9:45 Grandmother hoses down the cement pig stall between the kitchen and the toilet. She does this at least three times a day. For the past eight years, the Zhou family has used methane gas, produced by fermenting manure in a pit, as an energy source. It is cheap, clean, and efficient. The solid waste of a family of four plus one pig provides enough gas for all the family cooking. After the feces have decomposed past the point of producing methane, they are stored until hygienically safe to use as fertilizer. Everywhere in urban and rural China, night soil (human feces) is collected and used as compost.

Zhou Yugen and his son spend the morning cleaning the noodle-making machine parts. The machine must be kept clean to run well, and the owner of the store that buys their noodles comes regularly to check on sanitary conditions. A neighbor who is building a new house and doesn't have a water tap yet comes to fill pails of water, and sits to chat about the work he is doing. Everywhere in Qiang Lai county, construction is booming. The country's goal is to reduce the difference in the standard of living between the rural areas and the cities. The road into the county is also under construction, as it is the only road to Tibet and an important truck route.

11:00 Behind the house, next to the river, is the vegetable garden where A Niang and Nai Nai, still following her daughter around, pick cabbage and potatoes to cook with eggs for lunch. The clouds that bring the spring rains have already obscured the terraced mountains just beyond the rice paddies. A Niang's two older nieces have in the meantime finished laying the noodles made the night before to dry in the sun. Now she gives them cooking chores.

3:00 After lunch and an afternoon nap, the family turns its attention to the noodle business, while the schoolgirls slip off with their friends.

4:45 Zhou Xinmin crosses the yard, shouting. She has seen her mother coming across the ridges between the rice fields. After a week's absence, Gong Chaolian receives a great welcome. She brings fruits and vegetables from the south that are not growing here yet, and, of course, she has other little presents. The first one is for Zhou Guangyan, her granddaughter: a nice pink outfit with a hat to match. Then sweet and salt candies, a special one for Nai Nai. Instinctively, the old woman slips the treat into her blue apron pocket, with a sideways glance to check that no one saw her. This is what Nai Nai has learned to do with luxuries after a long hard life.

It takes only a few minutes for Gong Chaolian to take over her household. She puts on her apron, which doesn't come off until bedtime, and starts

Nai Nai stokes the stove with coal and dry grass. Gong Chaolian prefers cooking on deep traditional iron cauldrons over her earthen-brick coal stove, but she uses a two-burner stove and methane gas to boil water and for fast cooking.

preparing dinner. To continue the homecoming celebration, it will be a special treat: pork and fresh homemade tofu.

8:00   A few neighbors, and the two younger girls, pull the kitchen table chairs up in front of the television to watch a serial. Under a bare light bulb in the shed out back, the rest of the family works quietly, making noodles until late into the night.

People's Republic of China

The Hu Family

Hu Buzhong, age 34 (1)
Wang Xi'an, 34 (2)
Hu Xiaoxian, 16 (3)
Hu Xiaochui, 12 (4)
Hu Xiaosan, 9 (5)
Hu Yansai, 4 (6)
Wang Shengxiu, 70 (7)
Gao Jinlian, 60 (8)

1 sow and piglets
1 dog
1 cat

Xu Jia Gou Village, Yan'an Province

APRIL 10

6:30 A loud donkey brays in the village; a sow grunts in the yard. Grandmother Gao Jinlian is the first to brave this chilly spring morning. Her rustling as she opens the door wakes up her daughter Wang Xi'an, sleeping in the next cave with her husband and their son. She goes out to the yard to chop up small pieces of coal for the day's first fire. Like most villages of the municipality of Yan'an, Xu Jia Gou is carved out of a hillside. In the misty morning air, black smoke drifts from all the villagers' fires, seeming to come from the mountainside itself.

Hu Buzhong is washing his face in the basin when Hu Xiaochui jumps out from under her cotton comforter. In a wink she is back in the warmth of yesterday's clothes left piled up at her feet the night before. Her two sisters, still cuddled up like spoons, have no choice but to get up when Xiaochui pulls off their blankets. She piles the covers neatly against the wall. The *kang* where they slept has become the table.

A hot fire is now burning under the two-burner kitchen stove. Wang Xi'an puts corn soup on and heats up the millet. Xiaochui serves herself a bowl of soup and eats outside on the brick wall that borders the courtyard, looking out over the valley and the trees' green spring buds. Xiaochui gulps her soup and hurries back in to finish her homework: a paper on her "goal in life." She writes that she wants to be a teacher, but adds that her real dream is to become a great artist like her mother.

Wang Xi'an makes elaborate paper cuttings. With swift snips of her scissors, she turns thin red folded papers into delicate animals, faces, and intricate patterns. The township art school sells her work, but she makes very little money, so Wang Xi'an does not want her daughters to be artists. Neither she nor her husband finished primary school, and they remember their hard life as peasants. They dream of seeing their children graduate from the university. "Art is very nice, but it does not bring bread to the table," she says.

Nevertheless, it is not money but Wang Xi'an's artistic touch that has made her home more pleasant than her neighbors'. Her work decorates the cave walls, along with pictures of their family and their ancestors. A poster of a laughing Mao standing in the midst of children hangs on the wall as well. Everyone here is proud that their region gave birth to the Communist Revolution. In one of these caves Mao found shelter at the end of the Long March.

Hu Buzhong has already made six trips down the slippery and narrow path to the river which runs past the house in a deep gorge. He will need a couple more trips to fill up the earthen water jar that sits in the kitchen with the jars of flour, millet, and pickled vegetables.

8:20 Standing behind her younger sister, Xiaoxian tries to peer in the mirror above the desk to tie red ribbons around her ponytails. When finished, the two hop on their one bicycle for their twenty-minute ride to school.

9:00 After slopping the pigs, Wang Xi'an and her mother spend the rest of the morning turning the cement millstone in the yard to grind buckwheat flour for the evening's noodles. When the school bell rings, they can see Hu Xiaosan and her friends line up singing as they walk into their classroom.

11:00 Wang Xi'an is preparing a bottle of sugar water for her son. She does not buy milk anymore because she cannot afford to give it to all her children. Hu Yansai is a little old to drink from a bottle, but as the only son, he can be spoiled. To have him, she disobeyed the government's one-child policy (established after she had her three daughters). Traditionally, girls go and live in their husband's home. A couple without a son will have no one to help them work the land and care for them in their old age. For Wang Xi'an, a son was even more important, as there were only girls in her family for the last four generations. "I knew that I was making a son when I made that child," says Hu Buzhong. Two years later the government population controllers came into the village and as punishment sent Hu Buzhong, who was employed in a factory, back to work as a peasant in the fields for six months. Wang Xi'an had to pay a fine from the profit of her art. "It was worth it," they say. "We have our son."

Wang Xi'an and Hu Buzhong laugh easily and often tease each other. They were introduced by their parents, who thought they would make a good couple. "They were right. It was love at first sight. We were made for each other," says Wang Xi'an.

1:00 Wang Shengxiu is sitting by himself, hunchbacked in his customary corner of the yard. Unlike his daughter's, his marriage was arranged, and his wife is a distant woman who hardly even speaks to him. Wang Shengxiu is animated only when another old man of the village comes to have tea with him.

In the storage room, Gao Jinlian chops green vegetables for lunch. In the other cave, Wang Xi'an prepares bread dough. The two women are always very creative with the few ingredients they have. In this part of the country, rice does not grow and is not part of the everyday diet. Potatoes, millet corn,

PEOPLE'S REPUBLIC OF CHINA

Because of the dire need for land to farm in this cold and arid country and for protection from the terrific sandstorms brought with the western winds, the people here choose to live in caves. Depending on their financial means and family size, each family has one or more caves.

and wheat are the basic foods, supplemented by whatever green vegetable is in season.

Back from school, the hungry teenagers run in to get a bowl of soup. Their father returns from his job as a buyer at a soybean-processing plant. With his sociable personality, he is more suited to this work than to toiling in the fields.

There are now few families in the country who don't have at least one family member employed in something other than farming. "It was hard before I started to work at the factory," says Hu Buzhong. "When my wife was pregnant, she had to stay in bed, so I had to work the fields alone."

3:00 While the grandparents have their afternoon nap, Wang Xi'an goes to Zhen Wu Dong government hospital. "Women's problems," she says. On her way home, she stops at the market to get green vegetables. It is planting season in Ansai county, so all the vegetables at the market have been brought in from other parts of the country.

5:00 With grandson in hand, Grandfather goes up the mountain to a Buddhist temple tended by a monk who lives nearby in a small cave. Only the old remember how to pray. Grandfather goes to the temple, burns incense, and prostrates himself before a statue of Buddha. His grandson, who will not be taught this religion, laughs as he imitates his grandfather.

5:30 Women's problems or not, Wang Xi'an walks to the field with her husband. Luckily, a cousin is visiting today, and tradition has it that visiting relatives must help the family. He has come at the right time; the Hu family is late plowing their field and planting potatoes and corn. "We live better since the agrarian reform of 1983," Wang Xi'an says. "Now we can plant what we want, when we want, and how we want, as long as we meet our quotas."

Hu Buzhong gets his neighbor's bulls. He will help his neighbor later, in exchange for their use. As he works, Hu Buzhong is very careful to plow to the exact limits of his piece of land. If he plows himself short, he will plant less crop, and if he plows onto his neighbor's land, there will be a fight in the village.

The minute her parents head out to the field, Xiaoxian leaves her younger sister to help Grandmother with the evening meal, and runs down the hill to the small shop. There is a television there and she likes to watch a serial about the days before liberation. Her mother says of Xiaoxian, "If we don't tell her what to do, this one does not do a thing."

8:00 Since Monday, clocks have been set to summer time, giving the peasants longer days to work. Hu Buzhong sings as he comes back home with his wife and cousin: "The sun shines, we go to the mountains with our donkeys, the bells on their heads sparkle in the sun and ring to the music we sing."

"It is the tradition of our county to come down the mountain singing,"

The chimney from the stove runs under the kang, *the platform at the rear of the cave, warming the family as they eat and sleep. The family has three caves. One serves as a kitchen and the girls' bedroom; another, as the parents' room, the living and working room; the third is for Wang Xi'an's parents, and storage. But the old couple prefer to sleep with their granddaughters.*

he says, adding, "But it's not that way in the next municipality. People there don't sing."

11:00 After a late dinner of soup made with Grandmother's noodles and the leftovers from lunch, Wang Xi'an spreads out the comforters again. Hu Yansai, who has fallen asleep, is carried to his parents' *kang*. Wang Xi'an covers him lovingly and prepares a feeding bottle for the night. Wang Xi'an admits that, of all her children, she prefers her son. Hu Buzhong bends over Hu Yansai now, gazes at him with admiration and tenderness, and kisses him. "It is impossible for a father to love his son more than I love mine," he says.

People's Republic of China

The Liang Family

Liang Yuqun, age 63 (1)
Liang Yannian, 38 (2)
Jin Yong (daughter-in-law), 37 (3)
Liang Yu, 10 (4)

Liang Yanyi, 36 (5)
Fu Zeng (daughter-in-law), 33 (absent)
Liang Hong, 6 (6)

Liang Yanghou, 31 (7)
Kang Xiao Mei (daughter-in-law), 30 (8)

3 cats
8 pet fish

Beijing

JULY 17

5:00   Liang Yannian unlocks the gates and jogs down the street. Except for a few other exercisers, the city's *hutongs* (alleys) are almost deserted. As Yannian passes the workers' stadium, an instructor leads a group of mostly old people in the tai chi exercises. "Only they have the patience to practice the slow movements of tai chi," says Yannian. A group of young people are doing the Jane Fonda workout in the park.

    Yannian's father, Liang Yuqun, takes a broom out to the stone courtyard at the center of his three sons' houses. A creaking wooden door opens and slams, and then another, as each member of each family heads out of the courtyard to the public toilets across the *hutong*. Jin Yong, holding her family's night chamber pot, stands behind her neighbors in the women's line. Six women can squat at once in each malodorous room. When finished, she returns to the yard and fills a basin at the family's courtyard water tap to wash dishes. She greets her sister-in-law, who is fetching water for her morning tea. Liang Yuqun's three sons and their families live very close together, and he considers it a great happiness that they all live in harmony. "Family unity is a most important thing, but it is very difficult to achieve," he says.

    In 1967, the Red Guards took over the house and all the family's belongings. Liang Yuqun's two older sons were taken out of school and sent to do farmwork in Inner Mongolia, and Liang Yuqun, his wife, and his father had to move to a small room with their younger son. He and his sons have difficulty speaking about those terrible times. In 1978, the dark "eleven years" were over and the family moved back. What Liang Yuqun regrets the most is that his father and his wife died before the happy homecoming.

    The Liang family knows how fortunate they are to have this much space of their own, and a garden, and nearly no rent to pay. With six salaries among the three families, and Liang Yuqun's pension, they are a comfortable "middle-class" family.

7:00   The color of the sky portends rain, lightning, and thunder. Schoolbag on his back and umbrella under his arm, Liang Yu leaves the house first. The boy's father covers himself with plastic and climbs on his bicycle for his fifteen-minute ride to work. Jin Yong takes her umbrella and joins the bus commuters clogging the sidewalks at the stops. Roaring cars, trucks, and buses bursting with people move slowly on the main boulevards. On special side lanes, thousands of skilled cyclists pedal attentively.

Liang Yannian works as an accountant in a Mercedes-Benz repair shop, a good job but not good enough for him ever to own a Mercedes. Those cars are reserved for officials and for the new millionaires who have been springing up in the last seven years. Liang Yannian and his family hope for a new small Fiat, made in Poland and imported to China. "If we save carefully and wait patiently while our name travels up the waiting list, maybe in six or seven years we will get one," says Yannian, adding, "Now everything seems possible in China."

Liang Yanghou comes to the yard to get the floor mop and clean the gray cement floor of his two rooms. The Liang men do not need to be badgered into sharing household duties. Men and women were officially declared equal in 1949, and the brothers appreciate that their wives work and share the costs of living.

In his house, Liang Yanyi covers his bed neatly with a bedspread, shakes the buckwheat-filled pillows, folds the blanket, places it on the pillows, and covers it with a towel to keep it free of the eternal Beijing dust and soot.

8:15 Before leaving for his job as a Holiday Inn taxi driver, Liang Yanyi has breakfast with his six-year-old daughter, Liang Hong. His wife, Fu Zeng, is in the hospital for a tubal ligation. The government allows each family only one child. The Liang couples don't agree with this law but have no intention of breaking it. They see the overcrowding in their city and are aware of the expense of supplying the entire population with adequate education and medical security. "But having only one child is hard on the parents, and on the character of the child, who needs a brother or sister to share with," say the Liang sons. Already Liang Hong is called "the Little Empress." Her parents don't know how to deny her anything. "She is the only child we will ever have, how could we possibly not spoil her," says Liang Yanyi.

Liang Yanghou and his wife, Kang Xiao Mei, are not in a hurry to have their child. "Next year, maybe," says Liang Yanghou. "When we have all we need in our home." Their two rooms are already quite well equipped; the bedroom with a television, stereo, and fan, and the living room with a couch, refrigerator, and washing machine. Liang Yanghou has had the great privilege of graduating from the Industrial University of Beijing and works as assistant engineer in a water-pollution treatment plant. Kang Xiao Mei works as a secretary. When the couple are ready to have their child, Kang Xiao Mei will have to inform the authorities at her work unit. Each work unit has a yearly quota of mothers out on leave. Kang Xiao Mei's name will be put on a list with other prospective mothers. When her name comes up, it will be her turn to conceive, and her job will be kept for her.

The Little Empress has been brought to kindergarten by Shen Fupin, the live-in maid. In China it is the grandmother's duty to take care of the house

Many typical Beijing courtyard houses have been destroyed to make room for apartment buildings. But the Liang family's neighborhood was declared historic and their house is now safe. They are fortunate to have so much space. Most of the millions of workers in the big capital must be content with overcrowded apartments.

and the children. With no grandmother, Liang Yanyi's family needed a maid. Once all the adults are at work, Shen Fupin cleans the house and shops for the noon meal just around the corner at the free market, where peasants come from surrounding farms to sell their goods, and at the Bai Huo Pu (government-run store), which takes her family's coupons. All state workers receive food rations of rice, flour, and cooking oil according to the size and composition of the family.

11:30 Shen Fupin fetches her charge from kindergarten and serves her a lunch of rice, green vegetables, and chicken. Liang Yanyi and his wife do not consider the school food nutritious, so they bring Liang Hong home for a good meal. Liang Yuqun lunches with his granddaughter. As a retiree, he was lucky to be able to keep a part-time advisory position at the state bank.

1:00 Liang Yuqun brings his granddaughter back to kindergarten, where the Empress becomes just another student. Discipline is strict. From kindergarten on, children are taught obedience, honesty, sharing, and respect for their elders. Yuqun then withdraws to spend the hot hours in his tiny room.

5:00 The children and workers are back. Life has returned to the courtyard. Liang Hong plays alone. Her cousin Liang Yu has a cup of tea, then goes into his house. He has at least two hours of homework a day. Chinese writing is not easy to learn. Each character has a different meaning. Just to read the newspaper, one must be able to recognize two thousand different characters. Liang Yannian encourages his son to study; only a small percentage of secondary-school graduates get into a university. But Liang Yu wants to be a taxi driver like his Uncle Liang Yanyi. "That is the best way to make money," he says.

In 1967, the house was divided among six other families. Walls were taken down, rooms divided, and, as a "bourgeois concept," the private bathrooms destroyed. In 1978, Liang Yuqun was given back his home.

Whoever comes home first, husband or wife, starts the evening meal. As the main meal, it requires the most organization. Very often, each family prepares one dish to share with the others.

6:30   In each of the three houses, the table stored along the wall has been unfolded. The families eat separately, coming together only for special occasions. Liang Yuqun rotates among the households. This week he takes his meals with his eldest son. In China, not only tradition but law requires children to care for their aged parents.

7:30   Liang Yanyi dresses the Little Empress in a beautiful frilly dress to visit her mother in the hospital. Once again, the streets and park are overflowing with people walking; fathers bicycling with their children; people fishing in the park ponds; old men carrying their caged songbirds to sing together in concert. The homes are small, so socializing is done in public.

9:00   In the three couples' bedrooms, the television sets are on. There is a Japanese serial that no one wants to miss. When there is nothing interesting on television, they use the VCR. Liang Yanyi, who earns the most, has bought the equipment and Liang Yanghou, the engineer, has wired it so that they can all watch the same film from their beds. When a good videocassette comes in from Hong Kong or Taiwan, the Liangs are sure to see it.

9:30   "Come to bed," says Liang Yuqun to his grandson. The old man does not like to sleep alone. Liang Yu grudgingly obeys. The couples turn down the TV to let the two other generations sleep.

The Chinese

THE NAME: In Chinese, the name is *Zhongguo* (Middle Country). The name China originated in the Qin (Ch'in) Dynasty, during which the country was unified.

GEOGRAPHY
Three major topographic regions: southwest: Tibetan Plateau, averaging over 4,000 m. (13,000 ft.) above sea level, surrounded by high mountain ranges; northwest: Mountain ranges separated by extensive basins; east: River valleys and low intervening hills. The two major rivers, the Yellow River and the Chang Jiang (Yangtze), both run generally west to east.
  Max. altitude: 8,825 m. (29,028 ft.) (Mt. Everest, the highest point in the world)
Area: 9,631,600 sq. km. (3,718,783 sq. mi.)
Density: 112 pers./sq. km. (291 pers./sq. mi.) (1988)
Arable land: 10% (1985)
Forest: 14%
Climate: The north is generally dry, with extreme temperature variation between summer and winter. The south receives abundant rain and has more moderate temperatures, although July and August are hot and humid.

CAPITAL: Beijing, pop. 5,860,000 (metropolitan area, pop. 6,450,000) (1985 est.)

LANGUAGE: Chinese or Putonghua (Mandarin) (official)
  There are many regional dialects of Chinese, as well as non-Sinitic languages, which are spoken by minority groups. China has had a written language for two thousand years.

RELIGION: Buddhism, Daoism (Taoism), Islam
  Under the government of Deng Xiaoping, restrictions on religious practices have been relaxed.

POPULATION: Total—1,103,983,000 (1988)
  Annual growth: 0.9% (9,535,698) (1985)
  Doubling time: 49 yrs.
  Urban: 21% (1985) (est. for year 2000: 25%)
  Rural: 79%

AGE GROUPS (1982)
  9% under 5 yrs.   29% from 20 to 39
  33% under 15   17% from 40 to 59
  46% under 20   8% 60 yrs. and over

ETHNIC GROUPS
  Han: 93%
  Zhuang: 1%
  Other: 6% (as many as 56 groups)

HISTORY
Chinese civilization begins to develop near the Yellow River at least ten thousand years ago
1766–1122 B.C.: Shang, the first fully historical dynasty
1122–221 B.C.: Zhou (Chou) Dynasty, characterized by a sharply divided class society and wars between contending states. Beginnings of Confucianism and Taoism in the latter half of this period
221–206 B.C.: Qin (Ch'in) Dynasty unifies China
207 B.C.–A.D. 220: Han Dynasty achieves great cultural and technological advances
220–581: Prolonged disunity follows the fall of the Han; foreign influences are incorporated, including Buddhism from India
618–907: Following the brief Sui Dynasty, the Tang (T'ang) rules a reunified China and institutes important governmental reforms, including the civil service system
960: Song (Sung) Dynasty brings technological advances such as printing, expansion of trade, and a flowering of the arts
1271: Mongols conquer China and establish the Yuan Dynasty
1368: Ming Dynasty begins, a period of social stability and hostility to foreign influences
1644: Qing (Ch'ing) Dynasty established by Manchus. The empire reaches its greatest extent and prospers until the nineteenth century
1840: Opium War with Britain introduces an era of European imperialism in China, with the opening of several ports to foreign powers
1912: Republic of China proclaimed under the leadership of Sun Yat-sen; war-lord era ensues, during which Chiang Kai-shek rises to power
1927: Chiang establishes Nationalist government in Nanjing

1934–35: Chinese Red Army undertakes its 6,000 mile "Long March" from Tiangxi to Yanan

1937: Following another conquest of Manchuria, Japan launches a full-scale invasion of China. Troops remain until the end of WWII

Oct. 1, 1949: Civil War ends with proclamation of the People's Republic of China. Chiang and his Nationalist forces flee to Taiwan

1958: The Great Leap Forward, an effort to modernize the economy, contributes to a severe famine

1966: Mao Zedong proclaims the Cultural Revolution, which ends with his death in 1976

1977: Deng Xiaoping comes to power and begins to lay the foundation for economic and social reform

FAMILY

Marital status, for females 15 yrs. + (1981)
Single: 28%
Married: 64%
Widowed: 7%
Divorced: 0.5%

Female head of household: no data

Fertility rate: 2.3 (1987)

Teenage births: 2.5% / Teenage fertility rate: 8.7/1,000 (1982)

Births out of wedlock: 0% (1982)
It is illegal and considered criminal to have sexual relationships outside of wedlock.

Contraception: 74% (1986)

Abortion: 49/100 live births (1984)

Government's position on family planning: Curbing population growth is a top priority. Government encourages women to pledge to have only one child. Those who do are given priority for housing, monthly subsidies, higher pensions, and free education. Those who sign the pledge and have more than one child are fined. Exceptions to the one-child policy are made for some minority nationalities, immigrants from Hong Kong and Taiwan, and rural couples when one parent is an only child. In some provinces, if the first child is female, the couple may have a second. Bride price, concubinage, and polygamy are illegal. The minimum age of marriage is 20 for women and 22 for men. Abortion and sterilization are legally available.

SOCIAL INDICATORS

Life expectancy: 69 yrs. (male: 68; female: 70) (1986)

Infant mortality: 33/1,000 births (1987)

Crude birth rate: 21/1,000 pop. (1987)

Crude death rate: 7/1,000

HEALTH

Access to health services: no data
Births attended by trained health personnel: no data

HOUSING

Persons per household: 4.4 (1982)

Electricity: no data

Access to safe water: urban: 85% (1987); rural: 30% (1985)

Source of water: no data

Toilet facilities (1985 est.)
Urban latrine systems (communal and individual): 90%
Night soil collected in rural areas: 90%

Construction materials: Timber and brick, with tile for roofs, are traditional and most common. Adobe used in rural areas. Other housing includes the felt tents of Inner Mongolia and northwest China, cave dwellings carved from the porous yellow soil of north-central China, and the bamboo-and-thatch huts of some southern minorities.

EDUCATION

Literacy: 69% (male: 82%; female: 56%) (1985)

Gross enrollment ratio (1985)
First level: 124% (completing in 1980–86: 66%)
Second: 39%
Third: 17%

Educational attainment for pop. 25 yrs. + (1982)
None: 44%   Second: 22%
First level: 33%   Third: 1%

ECONOMIC ACTIVITY

Economically active population: 51% (male: 56%; female: 46%) (1982)

Agriculture: 61% act. pop.; 25% of GDP

Mines: 5% act. pop.; 9% of GDP

Industry: 17% act. pop.; 41% of GDP

Services: 17% act. pop.; 25% of GDP

Per capita GNP: US$300 (1986)

Population in absolute poverty
rural: 10% (1985)

National currency: yuan

Principal resources: Coal, rice, wheat, corn

COMMUNICATIONS

Radio
Transmitters: 571 (1985)
Receivers: 113/1,000 pop. (1985)

Television
Transmitters: 5,400 (1985)
Receivers: 9.4/1,000 pop. (1985)

Newspapers (1984)
Dailies: 60
Circulation: 30,000,000 (29/1,000 pop.)

People's Republic of China

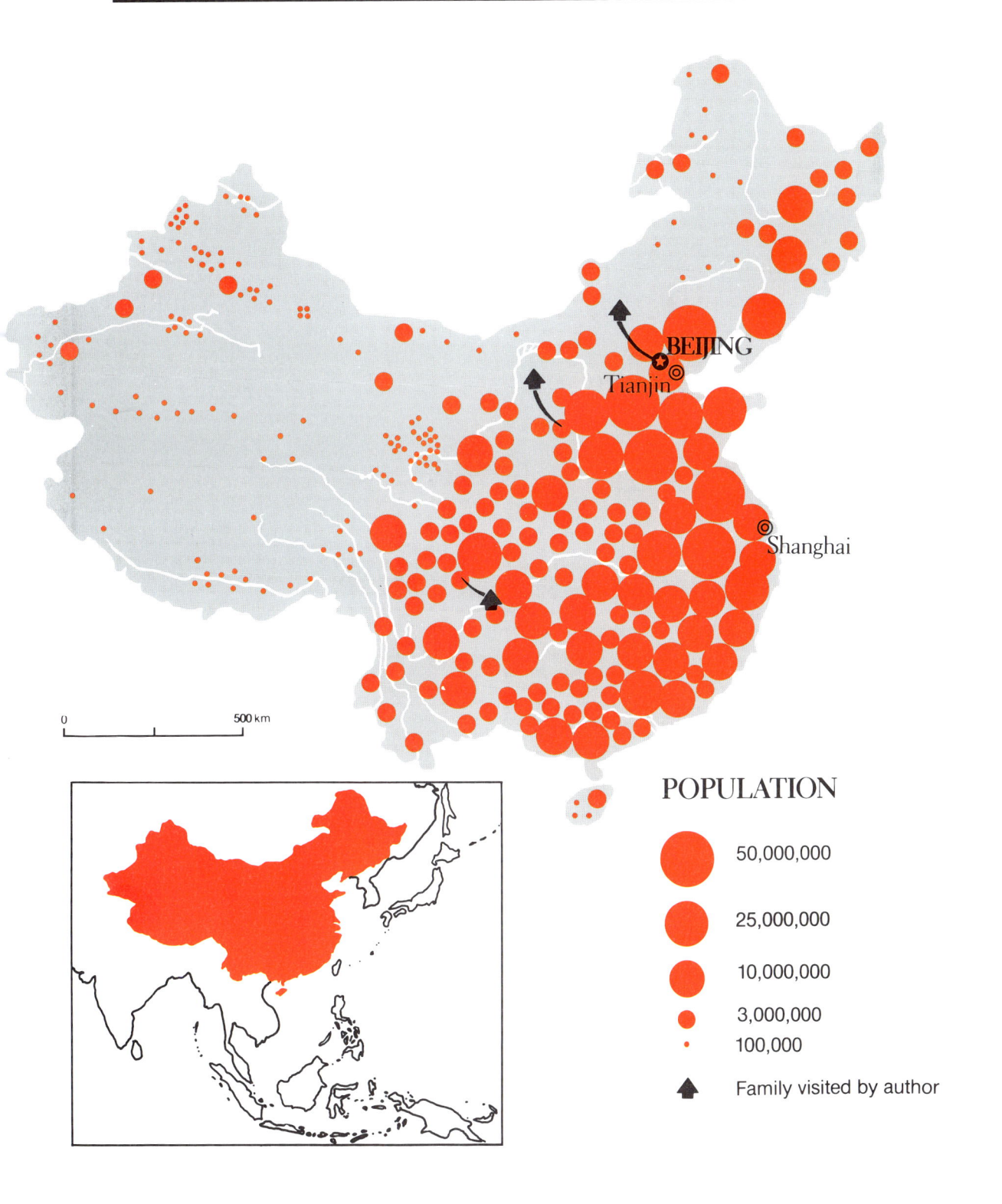

POPULATION

- 50,000,000
- 25,000,000
- 10,000,000
- 3,000,000
- 100,000

▲ Family visited by author

Japan

The Matsuo Family

Hisaharu Matsuo, age 35 (1)
Takako Matsuo, 33 (2)
Daisuke, 6 (3)
Hiroko, 5 (4)

Yokohama

JUNE 10

6:45 Takako gets up, dresses, and tiptoes quietly out of her tiny bedroom. She picks up the newspaper (which is delivered to her door twice a day), drops it on the kitchen table, and puts the kettle on to boil for the first of the many cups of coffee she will drink during the day. She lights a cigarette and reads the paper. When she was first married, Takako served breakfast to her husband, but soon he asked her to let him sleep as long as possible in the morning. Hisaharu's commitment to his work requires such an investment of time and energy that it leaves him little time for family life.

7:10 Takako's two children, still in their pajamas, join her. Daisuke, the older, lies on the carpet, while his sister, Hiroko, sits in a *zaisu*, a Japanese chair without legs. Takako's daily life revolves around the education of her children and her meetings with her five friends for tea and English classes. "All housewives don't have teatime, as we do. With the education of our children, we mothers are very busy. But the time spent with my friends discussing problems of the children and the home refreshes me," Takako explains.

This morning she listens patiently to her son's excited chatter as she prepares their breakfast of juice, toast, and jam. Takako feels responsible for her children's future, and she measures her worth by their success. She believes her nurturing and encouraging them will instill in her children the confidence and self-worth necessary to survive the rigors of their educational life. Takako sits down beside the children with a cup of coffee and her cosmetic bag. Her appearance is faultless. Throughout the day, she looks beautiful and fresh. "Women should be kind, gentle, and graceful," she says.

8:15 Takako wakes her husband. He cannot sleep one minute more. He showers, shaves, dresses, and ten minutes later rushes to the door, where the family's shoes are always left. Takako pushes Daisuke behind his father, tucking an umbrella under her son's arm. This morning, like every morning in June, it is raining.

Father and son go down in the elevator together and pass through the building's shopping arcade. They part at a footbridge which spans five rows of railroad tracks. Daisuke waves to his father as he heads toward school and Hisaharu squeezes into a packed train. In forty-five minutes, after traveling through sprawling city suburbs, Hisaharu will arrive in the center of Tokyo. Before entering the media department of the advertising company where he

Takako is content with her 70-square-meter apartment. Among the 148 families in the complex, she has made five particularly good friends. It is easier "to find people of quality in such a complex than when you are alone in a house," she says.

works, he will gulp down a bowl of noodle soup from a stand in the crowded train station. It was in this same building that Hisaharu met Takako nine years ago. Their marriage, which traditionally would have been arranged by their families, instead came through the matchmaking efforts of co-workers. Today the workplace is the social meeting ground for most Japanese.

8:30 Takako checks Hiroko's school uniform and helps her put on her raincoat. The elevator slowly descends the eleven floors. At each floor the children's voices grow louder as they pile in with their mothers. The pre-school is in the adjoining high-rise building next to the library, where, every Saturday, Takako chooses new books. The Japanese are among the most avid readers in the world, and the Matsuo children are no exception. But Hiroko does not read yet. In pre-school she learns the social skills needed for cooperative group living.

8:45 Takako pours another cup of coffee. She just has time to tidy up the apartment before her ballet-jazz class. In the room where the women gather for class, their infants and toddlers play. In Japan, children under the age of three rarely leave their mother's side.

11:45 As Takako opens the door, her telephone rings. Two of her neighbors want her to join them for lunch. The women will eat hastily. In nice weather, a pre-school teacher who lives in the building usually brings the children home, but with today's rain, the mothers have to pick them up.

12:30 Friday is a particularly busy day for Takako. The minute the children arrive from school, they change their school clothes for a sports uniform, eat a quick bowl of tofu soup, and leave with their mother for the sports center, where twice a week they have group swimming lessons.

Takako watches the progress of her children attentively, and like the teacher, she praises every improvement, encouraging them to go one step further, to do a little bit better, all the while being considerate to the other members of their team. She says good children must have persistence, confidence, and sensitive hearts.

3:30 Takako must leave early; she will not see all of today's progress. Daisuke and Hiroko will return with her friend Oshima. Daisuke pouts. A mama's boy, he is unhappy when his mother's eyes are not on him, but this month Takako is in charge of receiving the bulk delivery of food from her cooperative.

Like most women in Japan, Takako is responsible for her family's finances. After the house payment, the fees for primary school and swimming classes, and her husband's monthly allowance, there is hardly any money left. At bonus time, in December and July, she can buy clothing for the children and herself, purchase a few things for the house, and plan for the family's month-long holiday. But group buying with neighbors at wholesale prices is the only way she is able to stay within her monthly budget. Five other women and their children help Takako carry the load of groceries to her apartment. They push the kitchen table closer to the counter, put the other furniture in the tatami room, lay a large, thick plastic sheet over the carpet, and start emptying the contents of the boxes onto it. One woman with the distribution list calls out the items. Beside her, Takako checks the prices and ensures that everything that has been paid for is delivered. All the food ordered by the co-

The main room of the Matsuos' apartment, bought five years ago, serves as both kitchen and family room. In addition, they have two bedrooms, one bathroom, and a tatami, a room of woven mats, kept for guests.

operative is chemically untreated. As the children come back from school and swimming classes, they gather in Daisuke and Hiroko's bedroom. The small apartment is now crowded and very noisy.

5:30 The apartment is quiet. Daisuke finishes his homework and writing drills under his mother's gentle supervision. When he is finished, Takako asks the children to clean up their room. They protest heartily. "Complain as much as you want, there will be no cartoons until that room is clean," says their mother. Plush animals have been thrown into the hall, blocks are strewn all over. Takako helps and they quickly finish the task. Fifteen minutes later, in front of the television, Daisuke sits on the floor and his sister lies down with her head on his lap. Takako starts to prepare potatoes and meat croquettes for dinner.

7:30 Takako removes the cover from the bathtub. The water she ran one hour before is still hot. After she and the two children shower, they will sit in the tub to relax and talk. This daily ritual (part of a relationship the Japanese call "skinship") will last until the children reach puberty and their teenage shyness prevails. In hot water up to their necks, Takako and her children chat. "Closer to the body, closer to the soul," explains Takako. She adds, "Often, children have worries which are difficult for them to talk about. When we are all naked in the bath, what they feel in their hearts comes out." Their father used to bathe with them, but he has had a promotion and is expected to work overtime. With a patient smile, Takako quietly remarks, "My husband has to socialize and drink with his clients and his colleagues and gets home every night at eleven-thirty."

Takako leaves the television on, so the sound will help the children fall asleep. Then she washes the dishes, cleans up the kitchen, and puts away the leftovers. She always has something ready in the refrigerator in case Hisaharu comes home hungry.

10:30 The evening is getting on. Now Takako can't help being conscious of the trains' bells. They are fifteen minutes apart, and each time one rings, she looks up from her evening paper to the clock. With luck, Hisaharu might come home early. Takako admits that she would like her husband to share time with her and the children. Except for the holidays, they hardly do anything together. On weekends, Hisaharu plays golf when he can afford it, watches TV, or sleeps.

11:15 The bells ring. This time Takako goes out on the balcony to see the train arrive. She watches the passengers as they cross the bridge, but her husband is not among them. She is certain Hisaharu will be on the next train. It is the last.

The Japanese

THE NAME: In Japanese, the name is Nippon or Nihon. The name Japan is from the Chinese *Ji-pen-kuo* or "land of the rising sun."

GEOGRAPHY
An archipelago consisting of several volcanic ranges forming four main islands and thousands of smaller islands which lie in an arc 3,800 km. long; forest-covered rugged highlands alternate with narrow strips of lowland and plains; frequent volcanic eruptions and earthquake activity.
Max. altitude: 3,776 m. (12,395 ft.) (Mt. Fuji)
Area: 377,801 sq. km. (145,870 sq. mi.)
Density: 324 pers./sq. km. (839 pers./sq. mi.) (1988)
Arable land: 11% (1985)
Forest: 67%
Climate: Generally mild, although temperatures in the north are considerably lower than in the south. The winter monsoon brings rain and snow to the east and wind to the west coast; the summer monsoon brings destructive typhoons to the Pacific Coast.

CAPITAL: Tokyo, pop. 8,353,674 (metropolitan area, pop. 27,700,000) (1985)

LANGUAGE: Japanese

RELIGION: Shintoism and Buddhism
The religions are not exclusive; many Japanese are married in Shinto shrines but have Buddhist rites at their funeral.

POPULATION: Total—122,424,000 (1988)
Annual growth: 0.4% (489,696) (1988)
Doubling time: 133 yrs.
Urban: 76% (1985) (est. for year 2000: 79%)
Rural: 24%

AGE GROUPS (1985)
7% under 5 yrs.   30% from 20 to 39
22% under 15   27% from 40 to 59
30% under 20   15% 60 yrs. and over

ETHNIC GROUPS
Great majority, Japanese. Small minorities of Koreans and Chinese. Very small number of Ainu, an indigenous people

HISTORY
Evidence of human habitation thirty thousand years ago
660 B.C.: Reputed accession of the first emperor, Jimmu
4th cent. A.D.: First unified Japanese state, ruled by the Yamato court
710–784: Buddhism flourishes
794–1185: Heian period
1192: First military government, or shogunate, established
1573–1867: Period of warring states leads to Tokugawa shogunate; gradual political unification
1868–1912: Meiji Restoration begins Japan's modernization; first constitution
1909: Annexation of Korea
1923: Great Tokyo earthquake
1926–1989: Showa period. Truly constitutional government achieved
1931: Japan seizes control of Manchuria
1937: Japanese armies invade China
1941–45: As one of the Axis Powers in WWII, Japan invades most of Southeast Asia and establishes military bases on many Pacific islands
1945: First two atomic bombs dropped on Hiroshima and Nagasaki by U.S.A.; Japan surrenders
1945–52: U.S.A. occupies Japan
1947: New constitution vests sovereign power in the people, guarantees fundamental human rights, renounces war
1952 to present: Dramatic recovery makes Japan one of the world's great economic powers

FAMILY
Marital status, for females 15 yrs. + (1980)
Single: 21%
Married: 64%
Widowed: 12%
Divorced: 2%

JAPAN

Female head of household: 15.2% (1985)
Fertility rate: 1.7 (1987)
Teenage births: 12% (1985) / **Teenage fertility rate:** 4.1/1,000 (1985)
Births out of wedlock: 1.0% (1986)
Contraception: 64% (1985)
Government's position on family planning: Population growth and fertility rate are satisfactory. Child-bearing considered a matter of individual choice. Supports family-planning education. Hormonal birth-control pills illegal for health reasons. Abortion is legal; sterilization is legal under certain circumstances. Minimum age of marriage is 16.

SOCIAL INDICATORS
Life expectancy: 78 yrs. (male: 75; female: 81) (1985–90)
Infant mortality: 6/1,000 births (1986)
Crude birth rate: 12/1,000 pop. (1986)
Crude death rate: 7/1,000

HEALTH (1984)
Access to health services: 100%
Births attended by trained health personnel: 99.6%

HOUSING
Persons per household: 3.2 (1980)
Electricity: It can be assumed entire population has access to electricity.
Access to safe water: 99% (1985)
Source of water (1978)
   Piped inside or out: 93%
   Without piped water: 7%
Toilet facilities (1978)
   Flush: 46%
   Other: 54%

Construction materials (1983)
   Wood: 46%
   Wood, fireproofed: 31%
   Reinforced concrete: 20%
   Concrete block: 2%
   Other: 1%

EDUCATION
Literacy: 99% (male: 99%; female: 99%) (1970)
Gross enrollment ratio (1985)
   First level: 102% (completing in 1980–86: 100%)
   Second: 96%
   Third: no data
Educational attainment for pop. 25 yrs. + (1980)
   None: under 1%   Second: 40%
   First level: 45%   Third: 14%

ECONOMIC ACTIVITY
Economically active population: 49% (male: 61%; female: 39%) (1985)
Agriculture: 9% act. pop.; 3% of GDP
Mines: 1% act. pop.; 0.5% of GDP
Industry: 34% act. pop.; 40% of GDP
Services: 56% act. pop.; 56% of GDP
Per capita GNP: US$12,840 (1986)
National currency: yen
Principal resources: Rice, fish, manufacturing

COMMUNICATIONS
Radio
   Transmitters: 1,134 (1985)
   Receivers: 787/1,000 pop. (1985)
Television
   Transmitters: 13,119 (1985)
   Receivers: 580/1,000 pop. (1985)
Newspapers (1984)
   Dailies: 125
   Circulation: 67,380,000 (562/1,000 pop.)

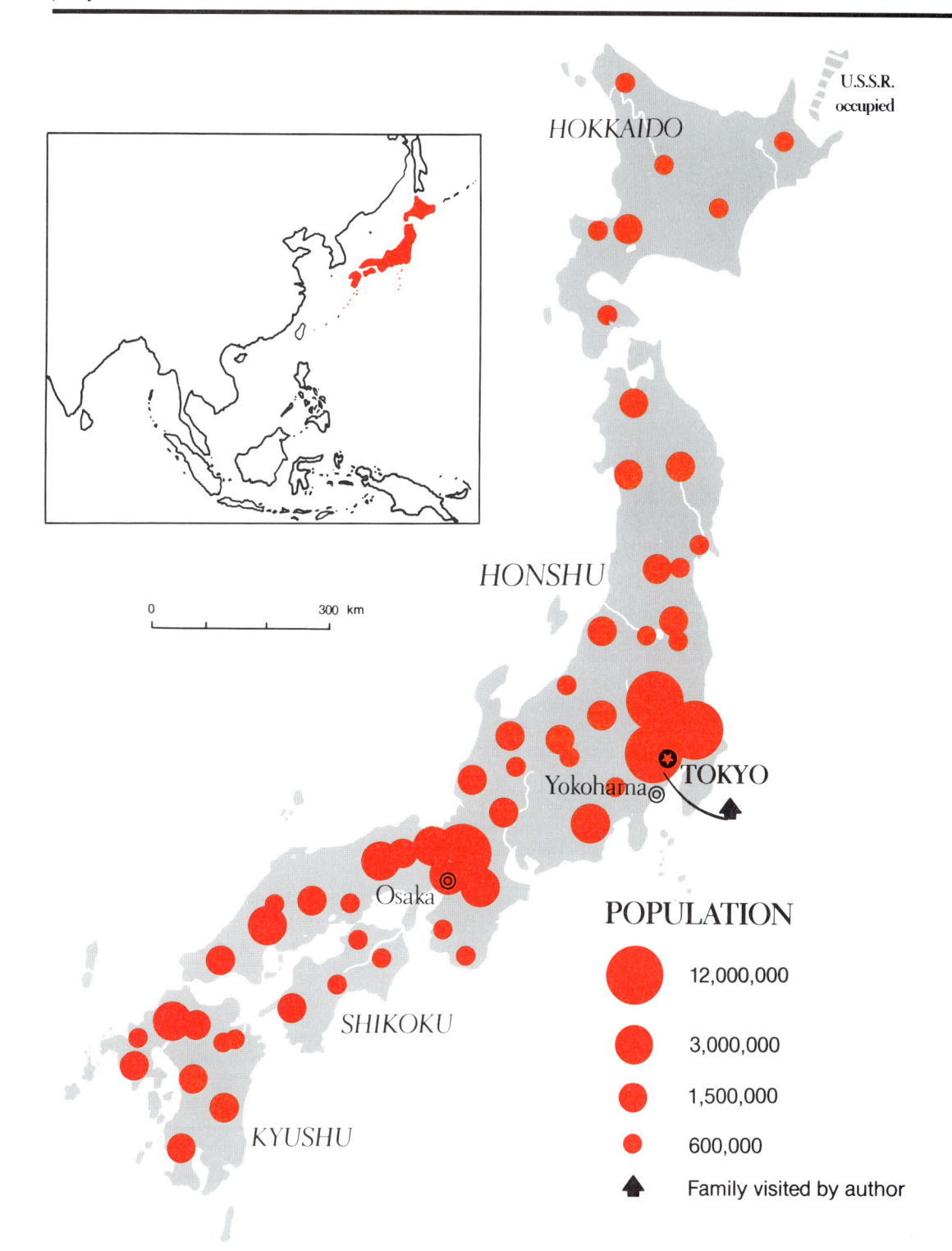

Japan

HOKKAIDO

U.S.S.R. occupied

HONSHU

Yokohama

TOKYO

Osaka

SHIKOKU

KYUSHU

POPULATION

- 12,000,000
- 3,000,000
- 1,500,000
- 600,000
- ▲ Family visited by author

Republic of Korea

The Cho Family

Cho Hee Sim, age 45 (1)
Swang Ill Sun, 40 (2)
Cho Min Su, 16 (3)
Cho Kuk Nam, 14 (4)
Cho Siem Su, 11 (5)

1 dog

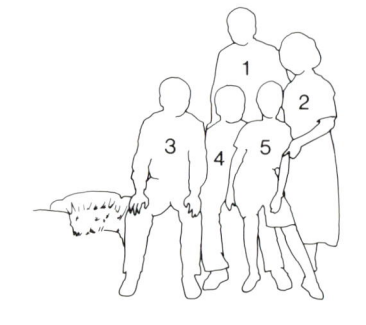

Taegu

MAY 26

5:00 Ill Sun climbs the stairs to the second floor of her spacious brick house. Passing the rooms of her two youngest children, she stops at the last door and knocks. Then she gently opens it, to encourage her elder son, Min Su, to get up.

In the family room where she has slept, Ill Sun sits on the floor at a small low table and opens one of the books she signed out of the library the day before. This one is on popular psychology, one of her favorite subjects. All is silent as the lamplight plays on the mother-of-pearl inlay on the dark wood furniture. Ill Sun hears Min Su's footsteps as he walks to his desk. She reads for pleasure, but he is studying seriously to try to get into the university. A Korean saying goes: "If a student sleeps three hours a night, he has a chance to enter the university; if he sleeps, four, he has none."

5:30 The young maid arrives, and Ill Sun goes with her to the kitchen to prepare breakfast and lunches. Breakfast is the largest meal of the day, as Ill Sun considers it healthy to eat the most in the morning. There are small dishes of beef, seaweed with rice, well-spiced and pickled vegetables, fish soup, mushrooms, and salad. When the Chos were young, food was not so abundant and meat was eaten only on holidays. But in the last twenty years the economy has so improved that meat is eaten more regularly. Hee Sim's sons, like most young Koreans, are five to six inches taller than their parents. The people of Hee Sim's generation take pride in any sign of improvement. They live to be better, to succeed.

5:45 Hee Sim is sitting cross-legged beside his daughter, who is lying on her mother's *yo*, a simple cotton pallet. Her husband has built a bedroom with a Western-style double bed, but Ill Sun prefers her old *yo* on the floor and lets her husband sleep alone. Father and daughter watch the morning news on television. The two boys gather their schoolbags, with one eye on the clock, to make sure they won't miss their bus. Min Su dresses in a camouflage-patterned military-training outfit. Three hours of military training a week is compulsory for all secondary-school students, and at nineteen Min Su will begin three years of mandatory military service.

Hee Sim has his three children's future planned. His sons will go into the liberal professions: Min Su will be a doctor; Kuk Nam, a lawyer; and his daughter, Siem Su, a pianist. Hee Sim does not ask his children what they want to be. If he did, he would find that Min Su prefers mathematics and

Kuk Nam science. The only one content with her father's decision is Siem Su.

7:00 Hee Sim leaves to drive into the industrial section of Taegu to his lumber import business. His father was in the same business and worked hard to put Hee Sim, the oldest of eight, through teachers college. Afterwards, Hee Sim taught, and paid for the studies of his brothers and his sisters. However, a teacher's salary was not enough when, after three years of marriage, he decided to leave his parents' home for a house of his own. He left teaching to go into his father's field. He sold wood as an employee, and eventually he borrowed money to start his own enterprise. Today Hee Sim imports wood from Malaysia, the U.S.A., and Canada, and has fifteen employees.

Hee Sim considers himself lucky to have children who learn easily. Since the Yi Dynasty in the year 1392, Koreans have held knowledge in high esteem. Hee Sim has decided that his sons will have that respect, and he has given his life to achieve it.

8:45 Siem Su walks to school through the alley between the high courtyard walls that hide the houses within. The Korean home is a very private place.

At home, Ill Sun sits cross-legged on a cushion in front of the mirror. She combs her hair and puts a little color on her lips, as the maid sweeps up. The house is so spotless one can walk in stocking feet and sit right on the floor. "It is normal to have a maid when your parents are dead and cannot help you," says Ill Sung. The house is mostly silent, and what conversation there is is conducted in quiet, confidential tones.

The maid has quite a big house to clean. This is the home Hee Sim has worked toward for years. The family has lived in five houses altogether, two rented and three that Hee Sim built, each one bigger than the last. "You can't get credit on a twenty-year loan here," he says. "I always had to pay cash. Luckily, I don't drink and I don't smoke."

Hee Sim says he needs these 250 square meters to receive the fifty members of his family that come to mourn their dead parents four times a year. As he is the oldest of his family, it is traditional for him to host the gathering, and for his house to be the largest among those of his siblings.

10:20 Ill Sun leaves the house to catch the bus. Along with other well-educated middle-class women, she is taking government training to do volunteer social work. Her ten-day course trains workers to combat delinquency, a problem that emerged after the Korean War as Korea became more Westernized. A university professor is instructing these well-to-do women in how to conduct an interview with teenage rebels. Ill Sun is told that a delinquent youth can only bring about a delinquent society, and that the problem has to be solved.

The house has another extension, not seen in this picture. With the country's spectacular economic progress, people like Cho Hee Sim, who are called "nouveau riche," can gain influence through the money they earn and their material possessions. But in Korea it is a degree from a fine university that commands real respect.

12:00　Siem Su's primary school serves the children a warm lunch. She ties a white apron around her waist and puts her white scarf over her head. With an aluminum tray in her hand, she lines up in the hall where the older boys have brought the cauldrons of rice, soup, eggs, bread, and barley tea. She eats at her desk, hurrying a little so she has time to play jump rope outside.

　　At the lumberyard, Hee Sim and his employees have gathered with their lunch boxes on a drying pile of wood. In one corner of the yard, hidden by piles of timber, is the second house Hee Sim built for his family. It is now rented to three employees.

4:00　The bus drops Ill Sun off at the corner. She has just stepped in the door and taken off her shoes when Siem Su walks in. Immediately the young girl sits down and starts her homework. Like her brothers, she is serious, and that pleases her mother. The two boys spend long hours at school and the father at work, so the mother and daughter are often alone together working side by side or talking quietly. Once in a while Siem Su comes to rest her head on her mother's back to get the love all hard workers need.

　　Leaving her daughter to her studies, Ill Sun takes a taxi to the supermarket for the pre-chopped vegetables and fresh meat that are basic to Korean cuisine.

5:00　Siem Su's violin teacher arrives, and the girl and the teacher go into the music room. The room is Siem Su's domain and contains her sheet music, her violin, and the piano she has been playing since the age of six. Ill Sun helps the maid with dinner.

On her kitchen balcony, Ill Sun can choose from many clay urns of marinated sauces, pickles, and spices to give her meals their scorching-hot Korean flavor.

6:30   Dinner is ready, but the men are not home yet. Ill Sun goes to her bedroom and washes. She does not shower. Only during the coldest months of winter does the Cho family use the water-heating system. It would be too expensive to use all year round. Tomorrow Ill Sun will go to the public bath, a traditional place to socialize, where there is plenty of hot water.

7:20   Kuk Nam arrives from school, where he stayed late to study with a tutor. Families that wanted their children to succeed used to pay tutors at home. The expense was tremendous and the tutors often took advantage of the anxious parents. In 1980, the government passed a law that made home tutoring illegal and punishable by imprisonment for parents and tutors. The school now employs tutors, and students are invited to stay after classes and study if they wish.

7:30   Hee Sim finally gets home. As long as he can remember, he has put in twelve-hour workdays. His employees work as hard, except on some of the coldest days in the winter, when they will work only eight hours. Now the family can sit down to dinner. Ill Sun sets up the low folding table in the center of the family room, and they sit cross-legged on the floor around it.

10:00   Min Su's day at school is over, but not his work. He goes into the kitchen, grabs a bite, sits a few minutes with his parents, who are watching television, and goes up to his room. Besides a game of soccer or baseball here and there, getting into the university is all this young man has on his mind. He will study for another hour or two before catching the few short hours of sleep his ambitions allow him.

The Koreans

THE NAME: Meaning "high and clear." Derived from the "Koryo" Dynasty, which reunited the country in the tenth century

GEOGRAPHY
A mountainous peninsula and 3,418 contiguous islands. A chain of mountains extends along the east coast; plains form the central region. In the south, foothills slope gradually to the sea. Max. altitude: 1,950 m. (6,398 ft.) (Mt. Halla)
Area: 98,484 sq. km. (38,025 sq. mi.)
Density: 428 pers./sq. km. (1,108 pers./sq. mi.) (1988)
Arable land: 20% (1985)
Forest: 66%
Climate: Four distinct seasons: winters are cold and dry, and summers hot and humid. Summer monsoons bring most of the rainfall.

CAPITAL: Seoul, pop. 9,645,932 (1985)

LANGUAGE: Korean

RELIGION
    Buddhist: 37%   Catholic: 5%
    Protestant: 26%   Other: 14.5%
    Confucian: 17.5%

POPULATION: Total—42,621,000 (1985)
    Annual growth: 1.2% (1988)
    Doubling time: 52 yrs.
    Urban: 65% (1985) (est. for year 2000: 80%)
    Rural: 35%

AGE GROUPS (1986)
    10% under 5 yrs.
    30% under 15
    41% under 20
    35% from 20 to 39
    18% from 40 to 59
    7% 60 yrs. and over

ETHNIC GROUPS
    Korean; the world's most ethnically homogeneous nation

HISTORY
Evidence of being inhabited from early Paleolithic times
2333 B.C.: Legendary King Tangun, to whom Korea traces its origin, ascends the throne
5th cent. A.D.: Height of Three Kingdoms: Silla, Koguryo, and Paekche
668: Peninsula unified under Silla
936: Koryo kingdom established
1259: Conquest by the Mongols
1392–1910: Yi Dynasty, with Confucianism as the official creed. Impressive scientific and cultural development
17th cent.: After successive Chinese invasions, Korea retreats from foreign contact, earning the name "Hermit Kingdom"
1910–1945: Japan annexes Korea. After Japanese surrender in WWII, Korea partitioned, with Soviet troops occupying the north and American troops the south
Sept. 9, 1948: Proclamation of Republic of Korea in the south and Democratic People's Republic of Korea in the north
1950: North Korea invades South Korea, UN troops under American command support the south
1953: Border reestablished at the 38th parallel
1956: Syngman Rhee elected president
1961: National uprising leads to Rhee's resignation; Park Chung Hee's military forces take control
1979: Martial law declared, following Park's assassination
1981: General Chun Doo Hwan becomes president
1987: Roh Tae Woo elected to replace Chun

FAMILY
Marital status, for females 15 yrs. + (1980)
    Single: 29%
    Married: 57%
    Widowed: 13%
    Divorced: 0.6%
Female head of household: 14.7% (1985)
Fertility rate: 1.9 (1987)
Teenage births: 3% / Teenage fertility rate: 11.7/1,000 (1983)
Births out of wedlock: 0.5% (1983)
Contraception: 70% (1985)

REPUBLIC OF KOREA

Government's position on family planning: After a 50% decline from 1950 to 1985, fertility rate is considered satisfactory. Targets 1.86 by 1991. Continues to encourage the one-child family through medical care, housing, and education incentives. Government directly supports family-planning programs.

SOCIAL INDICATORS
Life expectancy: 69 yrs. (male: 65; female: 72) (1985)
Infant mortality: 26/1,000 births (1987)
Crude birth rate: 20/1,000 pop. (1985)
Crude death rate: 6/1,000

HEALTH
Access to health services: 80% (1983)
Births attended by trained health personnel: 75% (1983)

HOUSING
Persons per household: 4.5 (1980)
Electricity: 30% without (1986)
Access to safe water: 78% (urban: 86%; rural: 61%) (1980–83)
Source of water (1980)
    Piped inside or out: 58%
    Pumped: 25%
    Other safe sources: 2%
Toilet facilities (1980)
    Flush: 18%
    Other: 80%
    None: 2%
Construction materials (1980)
    Wood: 38%
    Cement bricks: 25%
    Brick or stone: 11%
    Reinforced concrete: 11%
    Earth or earth bricks: 11%
    Other: 4%

EDUCATION
Literacy: 92% (male: 96%; female: 88%) (1986)
Gross enrollment ratio (1986)
    First level: 94% (completing in 1980–86: 94%)
    Second: 95%
    Third: 33%
Educational attainment for pop. 25 yrs. + (1980)
    None: 20%
    First level: 35%
    Second: 37%
    Third: 9%

ECONOMIC ACTIVITY
Economically active population: 38% (male: 46%; female: 29%) (1985)
Agriculture: 28% act. pop.; 12% of GDP
Mines: 1% act. pop.; 1% of GDP
Industry: 28% act. pop.; 30% of GDP
Services: 43% act. pop.; 57% of GDP
Per capita GNP: US$2,370 (1986)
    The fastest growing GNP in the world ($90 per capita in 1962)
Population in absolute poverty: urban: 18%; rural: 11% (1977–86)
National currency: won
Principal resources: Forestry, rice, fish, manufacturing

COMMUNICATIONS
Radio
    Transmitters: 214 (1985)
    Receivers: 936/1,000 pop. (1985)
Television
    Transmitters: 144 (1985)
    Receivers: 187/1,000 pop. (1985)
Newspapers (1986)
    Dailies: 35
    Circulation: 8,654,000

Republic of Korea

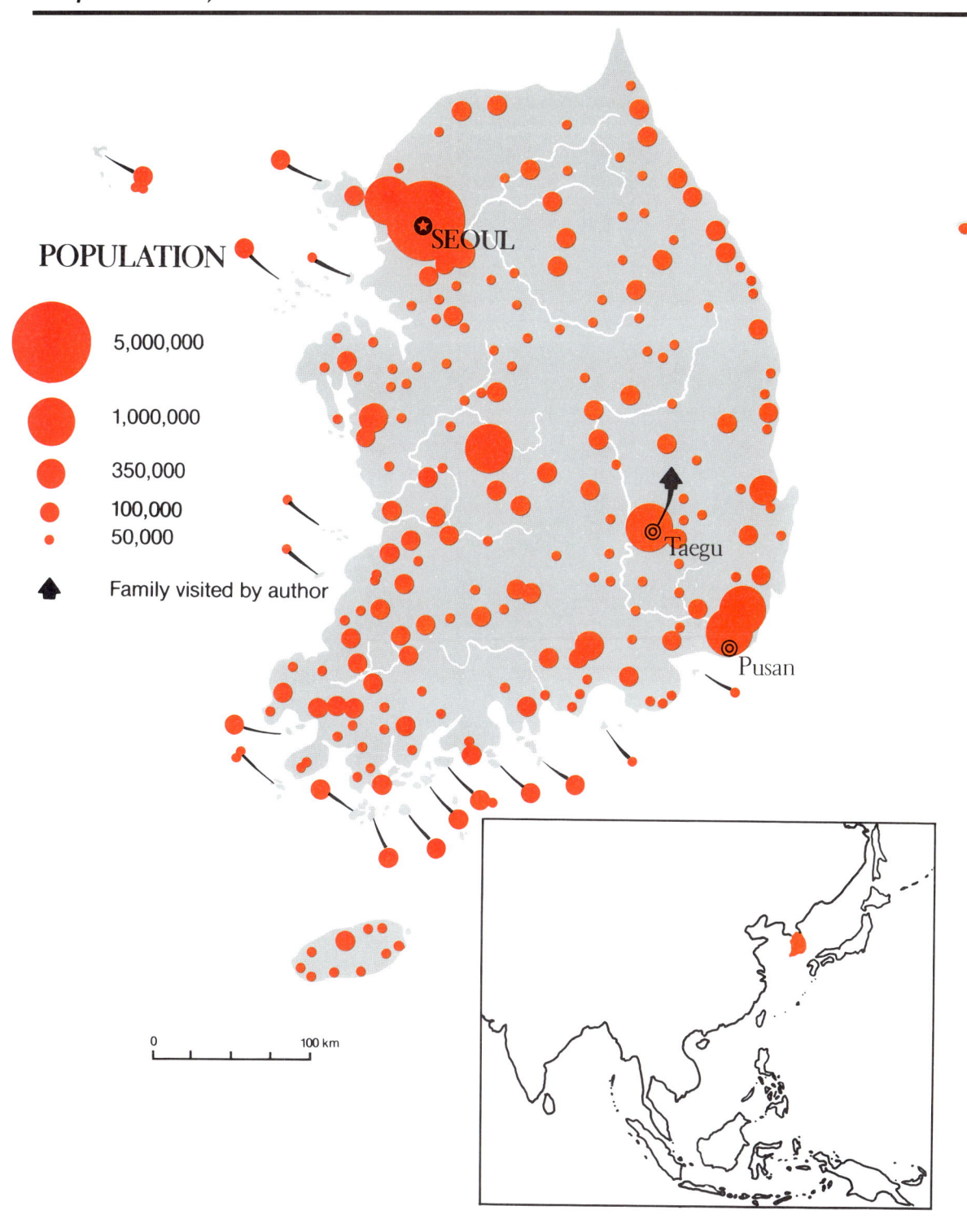

POPULATION

- 5,000,000
- 1,000,000
- 350,000
- 100,000
- 50,000

▲ Family visited by author

SEOUL

Taegu

Pusan

0   100 km

Mongolian People's Republic

Sereeter's Family

    Sereeter Choindongiin, age 36 (1)
    Ayushjav Dorjiin, 32 (2)
    Narankhuu Sereeteryn, 13 (3)
    Gantsetseg, 10 (4)
    Naransambuu, 8 (5)
    Narantsetseg, 7 (6)

    1,000 sheep owned by the cooperative
    25 horses and colts
    15 cows and calves
    52 sheep
    14 goats
    2 dogs

Bayantuul Brigade

AUGUST 7

6:30   Ayushjav has finished washing near the river. She calls to her children in a soft but firm voice: *"Minee huu serere! Minee ohin sereree!"* (Wake up, my sons! Wake up, my daughters!) She needs her daughters to help her milk the cows, and her husband, Sereeter, needs his sons to tie up the colts. Gantsetseg, as diligent as her mother, gets up immediately, followed by Narantsetseg, her younger sister. Their mother's voice is too gentle; the boys have not heard her call.

7:30   Sereeter returns home across the large open pasturelands with his horses, which at night wander freely in the immensity of the Mongolian steppe. It is Sereeter's first task to fetch them every morning. Retrieving the young animals is difficult, and takes time, so his patience is strained when he sees that his older son is not awake to help tie up the colts. When he bends down to put his head through the door, there is no gentleness in his voice. The boys reluctantly lift the thick woolen blankets and face the glacial morning air. It is summer now in Mongolia, but the northern country nights are always cold. The boys put on pants and their *deel*, the traditional tunic worn by men and women, and wrap their feet with strips of cotton cloth before pulling on their boots. Narankhuu, the older, takes two saddles from beside the door and walks to the horses. Every member of the family has a horse. They are vital to existence in a country with great distances between sparsely populated areas.

    The two boys are off to take the sheep out on the steppe, as they do every day during their two-month school holiday. These thousand sheep are part of one of the vast, government-maintained sheep cooperatives. After a ewe is weaned, Sereeter and his wife are responsible for the first year of its life. Their work is assessed by the kilos of wool the sheep produce in a year. Sereeter must keep track of every single sheep, checking for weight loss or disease and paying special attention to them throughout the winter, with its strong winds and temperatures as low as $-50°$ C.

8:00   Ayushjav has finished milking the cows and now lights the horse-dung fire, so the milk can be put on to boil. Gantsetseg is still in the field making up packs of fresh cow dung, which is also used as fuel. The shovel the young girl uses is too big for her, so she often uses her hands to combine the piles of dung. She flattens the packs and leaves them to dry, then walks barefoot to the river to wash her hands.

    Already a little mother, Gantsetseg walks back into the *ger** and tells Nar-

---

* *Ger* is the Mongolian name for their felt tents, which are now made of canvas. They are referred to as *yurt* by all foreigners.

antsetseg that she is lazy and that the floor she is cleaning is not clean enough. Narantsetseg makes a face. She wishes she were with her brothers on her horse. When the others are at boarding school and she is alone with her parents, she is the one who helps her father gather the sheep. This year, Narantsetseg will also leave for school. Her parents know they will be lonely, but sending the children away to school is the only way to educate them. They could have another child. The Mongolian government encourages large families; the country has vast resources and not enough people to tap them. A woman with five children is awarded her pension at an early age and receives two weeks of paid vacation a year in one of the many spas located throughout the country. But, for now, these benefits are not attractive enough for Ayushjav to consider having another baby.

As elegant as a princess, Ayushjav walks toward her husband, carrying two milk pails. During the summer months, their children's assistance with the sheep is essential, as Sereeter and Ayushjav's life revolves around the milking of the mares, which takes place every two hours. Sereeter has caught the colts and tied them to a rope rail. Once the babies are tied up, the mares will not leave. Sereeter brings the first mare's colt to her and lets it drink for a few seconds. He needs all his strength to pull its mouth away while still holding the colt's body against its mother's. Hurriedly, Ayushjav bends to take the colt's place, making the mare believe that her colt is still sucking. Ayushjav's fingers are strong and she rapidly empties the two teats.

Mare's milk, available only during the two summer months, is one of the great pleasures of Mongolian cuisine. Once fermented, it is called *airag*. Some is kept for the winter season, but most of the forty-five liters produced each day are used up without difficulty. The family drink countless bowls of *airag*, and visitors can help themselves freely. Mongolia's hospitality is proportional to its solitude. A *ger* is open to all who wander by, with the expectation that a visitor will share news of his region.

9:00 The boys have left the sheep to graze. Their empty stomachs send them galloping over the flat plain to a breakfast of salted milk-tea and yogurt. They leave the *ger* the minute they are finished eating, taking a happy Narantsetseg with them. The sheep have to be herded farther away. If they graze too long in one place, the grass will die and not grow again.

In two or three days, Sereeter's family will move to an ungrazed area of the steppe, about three kilometers away. Moving is a fact of life—something they do over twenty times a year. It takes them less than one hour to prepare. The house separates into six collapsible parts; the furniture is also made to break down easily. The choice of a place to settle is important. There must be water and good grass. The grasses vary, depending on the winds and the temperature. Cows like long grass; sheep like it short. Sereeter has to see to every-

In half the time it takes his horse, Sereeter's motorcycle gets him to Shireet Sum, the closest administrative center serving the three thousand people who have their ger *in the area. Now it's only an hour's trip to the hospital and the boarding school.*

one's happiness. From November to February, the family hide in the mountains out of the bitter winds of winter.

11:00 The mares have been milked a second time. Now there is a moment to relax. Ayushjav stands in front of the mirror to comb and braid her long black hair. She does the same for her older daughter. Always adding beauty and grace to her well-organized household, she ties huge colorful bows on Gantsetseg's braids.

12:00 Ayushjav sits down in front of her stove, to make the bread that will be served with yogurt, cheese, and a bowl of mare's milk. In two hours, when her children return, lunch will be ready.

2:30 The sheep are safe for the afternoon and everyone feels like a nap. The boys lie in one bed, the girls in another. Sereeter and Ayushjav talk softly in their bed. As a bonus for their herdmanship, the couple have been offered a two-week holiday to visit the region of Uvur Hangai. They cannot decide whether to go. Sereeter is not particularly social and prefers simply going to a sanatorium for a checkup. He is a worrier and has stomach trouble, which makes him appear angry and severe. "He may have a menacing look, but he is very gentle," Ayushjav says, adding, "He would not be able to live without me."

3:30 The children are off across the field to pick up horse dung. Like all Mongolians on the steppe, the family use everything connected with their animals: the dung, the skins, the meat, and the milk. Ayushjav and her husband milk the mares; then Ayushjav sits in front of her house to make *aaruul*, another staple of the family's diet. She fills a cotton bag with yogurt and presses out the water. She then spreads the moist yogurt on plates and sets them on the roof of her house, where the sun quickly dries the yogurt into a cheese that kept a long time. Along with milk products, meat is central to the family diet, but when an animal is killed, it is shared with friends, relatives, and people who pass by the *ger*.

6:30 Narankhuu and Naransambuu leave to fetch the herd of sheep. Ayushjav milks the cows once more, and Sereeter frees the mares for the night. Inside the *ger*, the mare's milk sits in a tall plastic jar. It is one of the children's tasks to beat the *airag* with a long, flat-ended stick. The milk needs five thousand strokes to ferment. Gantsetseg starts counting. When she gets to five hundred, she passes the stick to her sister, who makes another face at this daily chore.

8:30 Once the sheep herd has settled beside the *ger*, Sereeter walks around inspecting every sheep. He gauges their contentment by the way each chews its cud. Satisfied that they are all well, he goes inside, always ready to run back out if he senses the herd getting excited or annoyed.

It is dusk and everyone is sitting near the stove in semi-darkness. Torches and fat-oil lamps are used for light, even though a small Honda generator can provide electricity. It is used mainly for emergencies. "It has changed our life, but using it every evening would mean too many trips to the center for fuel," explains Ayushjav.

In the dim light, the *ger* looks like a house in a fairy tale. The colors of the embroidered furnishings add to the warmth of the stove, so that it seems the coldest winds of winter could not penetrate. But for now it is summer and the evening stars twinkle through the open roof flap. A perfect setting for the best of dreams.

In this country of vast steppe and little forest, dung is used for cooking and to warm the colorful home. Ayushjav embroiders to decorate the house and nothing is left unadorned: pillowcases and walls alike. She also sews the family clothing and, with her husband, works the animal skin and fur for their winter clothes.

The Mongolians

THE NAME: From Mongol, the tribe of Chinggis (Genghis) Khan. Upon conquering the other major tribes of the steppes, he decreed that all "dwellers of felt tents" be called Mongols.

GEOGRAPHY
Three major topographic zones: in the north and west, fingerlike mountain ridges; to the east, vast hilly steppe plains; and in the south, the Gobi plateau of grasslands and desert.
Max. altitude: 4,374 m. (14,351 ft.) (Tavan Bogdo)
Area: 1,565,000 sq. km. (604,250 sq. mi.)
Density: 1.2 pers./sq. km (3.1 pers./sq.mi.) (1986) (lowest density in the world)
Arable land: 0.8% (1985) (83% of the land is steppe and suitable for grazing)
Forest: 9%
Climate: Characterized by extreme variations in temperature and very low precipitation. Winters cold and sunny; summers short, with sudden downpours. The center of the world's maximum atmospheric pressure, it has an average of 230 to 260 clear sunny days a year.

CAPITAL: Ulan Bator, pop, 488,200 (1985 est.)

LANGUAGE: Mongol (official), of which the Khalkha dialect is most prevalent.
Kazakh (Turkic language) also spoken

RELIGION: Mongolian culture has been heavily influenced by Tibetan Buddhism (Lamaism). Since the 1921 revolution, religion is separate from state and school, and today there are few practicing adherents.

POPULATION: Total—2,092,000 (1988)
Annual growth: 2.7% (51,516) (1985)
Doubling time: 26 yrs.
Urban: 51% (1985) (est. for year 2000: 55%)
Rural: 49%

AGE GROUPS (1985 est.)
29% under 10 yrs.	32% from 20 to 45
41% under 15	12% from 45 to 65
52% under 20	3% 65 yrs. and older

ETHNIC GROUPS (about 20 different groups)
Khalkha Mongol: 78%
Kazakh: 5%
Durbet: 3%
Bayat: 2%
Other: 12%

HISTORY
Inhabited since Lower Paleolithic times (between 100,000 and 500,000 years ago)
3rd century B.C.: The Huns emerge as the first powerful united tribe among many pastoral nomadic peoples
A.D. 552–840: Turk and Uighur empires rule Mongolia
1204: Chinggis (Genghis) Khan conquers the major tribes of Mongolia to create a powerful confederation which goes on to invade great areas of Asia and Europe
1279: Qubilai (Kublai), grandson of Chinggis, establishes the Yuan Dynasty after conquering China
1368: Yuan Dynasty falls, and Mongol power begins to decline
16th cent.: Lama Buddhism, introduced to Mongolia from Tibet, begins to flourish
17th cent.: Internal strife leaves Mongolia vulnerable to the Manchus, leaders of China's Qing (Ch'ing) Dynasty
mid-18th cent.: Manchus integrate Inner Mongolia with China, and dominate Outer Mongolia. Russia controls Buryat-Mongolia (in Siberia)
1911: Mongolia shifts to the Russian orbit until the 1917 Revolution, when it reverts to Chinese
1921: Mongolia, with the help of Russian troops, drives the Chinese out of Outer Mongolia
Nov. 4, 1924: Proclamation of the Mongolian People's Republic in Outer Mongolia. Inner Mongolia remains part of China

FAMILY
Marital status: no data
Female head of household: no data
Fertility rate: 5.3 (1987)
Teenage births: no data
Births out of wedlock: no data
Contraception: no data

Government's position on family planning: In a reversal of position, as of 1986 fertility rate is considered too high. Government supports family planning and maternal and child health-care services. Abortion and sterilization are available only for health reasons.

SOCIAL INDICATORS
Life expectancy: 64 yrs.
Infant mortality: 46/1,000 births (1986)
Crude birth rate: 35/1,000 pop. (1986)
Crude death rate: 8/1,000

HEALTH
Access to health services: 100%
At some times of the year, accessibility within an hour is not feasible and mobile units are relied on. (1984)
Births attended by trained health personnel: 100% (1984)

HOUSING
Persons per household: no data
Electricity: no data. It can be assumed the majority of the rural population are without electricity.
Access to safe water: 100% (urban: 100%; rural: 100%) (1983)
Source of water: no data. It can be assumed the majority of the rural population get water from wells and rivers.
Toilet facilities (1983)
Sanitation facilities: 50%
Construction materials: no data. The majority have canvas *ger* (yurts).

EDUCATION
Literacy: 93% (male: 95%; female: 90%) (1984–85)
Gross enrollment ratio (1984)
First level: 105% (completing in 1978: 95%)
Second: 88%
Third: no data
Educational attainment for pop. 10 yrs. + (1979)
None: no data
First level: 37%
Second: complete 7%; incomplete 23% (specialized secondary: 6%)
Third: 5%

ECONOMIC ACTIVITY
Economically active population: 37% (male: 50%; female: 25%) (1985 est.)
Agriculture: 36% act. pop.; 29% of GDP
Mines: 6% act. pop.; 12% of GDP
Industry: 24% act. pop.; 25% of GDP
Services: 34% act. pop.; 34% of GDP
Per capita GNP: US$780 (1979)
National currency: tugrik
Principal resources: Livestock, coal, iron ore, tin, semi-precious stones, gold, tungsten, oil, uranium

COMMUNICATIONS
Radio
Transmitters: 22 (1985)
Receivers: 131/1,000 pop. (1985)
Television
Transmitters: 20 (1985)
Receivers: 31/1,000 pop. (1985)
Newspapers (1984)
Dailies: 1
Circulation: 156,000 (84/1,000 pop.)

Mongolian People's Republic

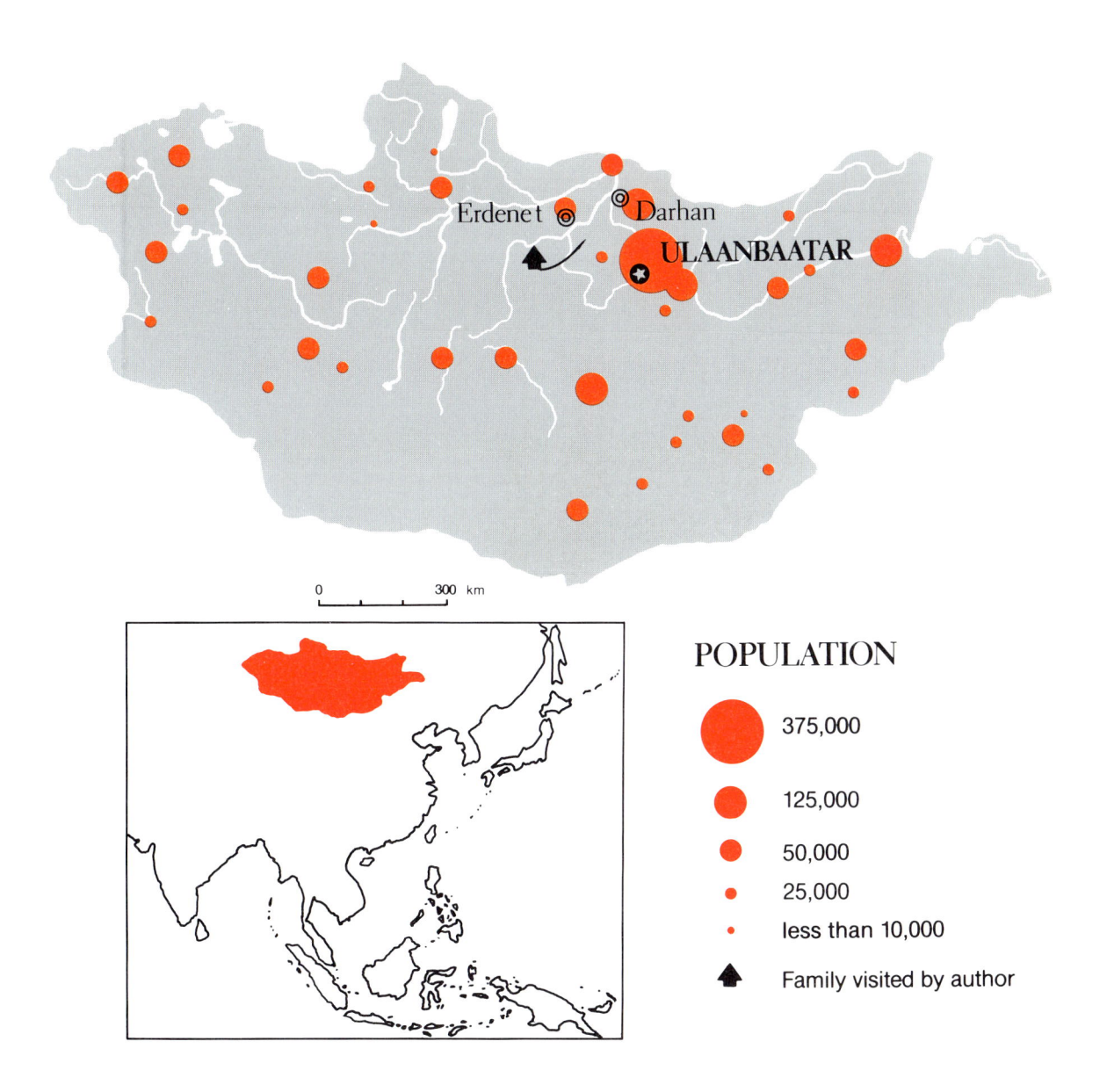

POPULATION

- 375,000
- 125,000
- 50,000
- 25,000
- less than 10,000
- Family visited by author

SOUTHEAST ASIA

Brunei Darussalam

Ahmad's Family*

Ahmad bin Haji Abdul Ghafar, age 42 (1)
Amnah binti Haji Ludin, undetermined (2)
Hazimah binti Haji Awang Ahmad (Zimah), 18 (3)
Mohammed Zahurin bin Haji Awang Ahmad (Rin), 17 (4)
Ernawati binti Haji Awang Ahmad (Wati), 16 (5)
Mohammed Yazmin bin Haji Awang Ahmad (Min), 15 (6)

* The honorific title *Haji* indicates that a person has been on a pilgrimage, or *haji*, to Mecca in Saudi Arabia, the most holy place in the Muslim faith. *Bin* means "son of"; *binti*, "daughter of."

Jalan Muara

FEBRUARY 5

5:30 Amnah Haji goes down the stairs to the kitchen to cut pieces of *bingka dakak* (rice cake) and fill the *ringis* (rolls stuffed with potato and meat curry). She has a contract with two government schools that offer a snack to the students at recess, as well as with the Ministry of Culture, Youth and Sports, where Ahmad Haji, her husband, works. She turns on the radio for the morning prayer broadcast.

As her father washes and returns to his room for the *subuh*, the first of the five prayers Muslims say each day, Zimah dresses and goes to the kitchen to prepare coffee.

6:30 Wati is the last one in the shower. After her prayers, she hurries to put on her school uniform. First the blue *kin* sarong, a long skirt, and over that the *bajuku rung*, a knee-length blouse that will hide her young girl's shape. She wraps a *tudund rung*, a head scarf, over her hair, bringing the material across her forehead just above her eyebrows so not a hair shows. With several pins, she fastens the scarf so it will stay tight to her head for the whole day. She hastily drinks a cup of coffee and joins her brothers waiting in the family car. Min is always the first one in the car. He can't wait until he is old enough to drive. For now he must satisfy himself with starting the Nissan and backing it up a little. His mother loads her food tray, and then her family is off.

Fabulous oil wealth has flooded the capital with cars; the traffic is dense at this time of morning. Public transportation is inadequate, and each student is brought to school in the family car. After dropping the children off, Ahmad Haji takes the expressway to the center of Bandar Seri Begawan, the country's capital.

Zimah has stayed home. She has completed the O-level exam, taken halfway through secondary school, and waits for the result. If she passes, she will need two more years, and a passing mark on the A-level exam, to be eligible for a government scholarship. As the country's population is too small to support a broad university curriculum and Zimah wants to specialize in science, she will be sent overseas. She is looking forward to this, but for now her favorite subject is the study of Islam and the *fiqueh*, a text that explains how to incorporate religion into everyday life.

8:30 Amnah Haji squats in her combination bath and laundry room in front of her daily washing. During school holidays this is usually Zimah's work, but her daughter has studied hard and her mother lets her rest.

10:30 Amnah Haji is now squatting in her kitchen. The large room is equipped with Western-style counters and appliances, but Amnah Haji prefers the traditional Malay way, working on the floor. The room looks like a restaurant kitchen. In the cabinets, more than a hundred glasses and plates are neatly aligned; there are two full-service china sets, three mixers, three toasters, three stoves, and two ovens.

Both husband and wife have eight brothers and sisters, all of whom are married and have growing families. In the rest of the house, there is no longer enough space for them all. The downstairs living room, overflowing with china knickknacks of all kinds, with bronze antiques and porcelain vases perched upon lace doilies, can hardly seat twenty people.

Ahmad plans to enlarge the 150-square-meter house. In five years his first loan will be paid off and he will take out another for an addition to the living room. For him, a bigger house is not an impossible dream. The government can provide free medical care and free education for all and also makes special low-interest (half a percent) building loans available to most of its citizens. With such loans, nearly every young couple can have a house.

11:30 Zimah comes into the room, squats, and starts cutting onions, while her mother dips the pieces of chicken in curry for lunch. Amnah, whose world is within her house and among the women in her family, listens attentively to her daughter's excited chatter about the pre-engagement party at Ahmad's father's house tonight.

12:35 The midday prayer broadcast on the radio tells everyone it's time for lunch. Ahmad Haji parks in front of the school, waiting behind other cars. Since none of his family drives, he is responsible for everyone's movements. Between the family visits and the religious and traditional activities, it is impossible for him to stay home one day without having to chauffeur people around. "I drive at least a thousand miles a month," says Ahmad.

1:00 Father and children leave their shoes at the door. Ahmad Haji changes from his pants, shirt, and tie to a T-shirt and a sarong. Then he goes to the bathroom and, as he washes his face, says a prayer. Another is said as he puts water on his head, and a final one while cleaning his feet and knees. Now he is prepared to kneel on his prayer carpet and pray, always facing Mecca.

The meal is abundant: rice, fragrantly spiced chicken, fish, and vegetables. Ahmad dominates the conversation. A socially open and exuberant man, Ahmad contrasts sharply with his children, who are quiet and less talkative. Lunch over, the girls cover the leftovers with a straw basket and wash the dishes. Ahmad Haji is going back to work, where he will attend a rehearsal of the country's dance company. With his colleagues, Ahmad Haji is preparing

A big house is traditional and almost necessary in Brunei—the most wealthy Asian country, and one of the last countries with a sultanate government—but now Ahmad's house is nearly too small.

the troupe for the Asian Festival of Performing Arts. They have only two months to prepare the young amateur dancers for this big event. The troupe is small. Most young people are more interested in rock music than in traditional dances, and because of religious beliefs, many families do not permit women to perform publicly. It is Ahmad's job to make sure that the dances and the women's costumes are not irreverent. It is not an easy job, but he likes the challenge.

2:30 Wati is sitting at her desk in her room, reading an English book and writing a report. She has studied English since her first year in school, and many of her classes—physics, engineering, science, and math—are taught in English. The official language when Brunei was a British protectorate, English is still a necessary part of education and work.

The house is quiet. In the boys' room Rin reads the newspaper and does not resist the temptation to nap before starting his homework. Amnah and her children often spend their afternoons at Ahmad's parents' house: it is the hangout of the extended family and the place where both Amnah and Ahmad grew up. She is her husband's cousin, and the marriage was arranged by Ahmad's father. "We have been educated never to doubt our father's decisions," says Ahmad Haji. Marriages within extended families are common, but, more and more, young people want to choose their own mate.

4:30 Min has said his afternoon prayers and now mows the yard in front of the house. The phone rings, and the quiet and shy Amnah Haji is suddenly transformed. It's her sister-in-law on the line. The two women speak for over twenty minutes, with great animation. After hanging up, Amnah Haji calls her husband to ask him to buy some cooking oil on his way home. Amnah

The kitchen is equipped to receive at least a hundred guests. There are prayer ceremonies for every special occasion, which gather together family and friends, the essence of Bruneian social life.

Haji entrusts everything to her husband, from the administration of the household to her own personal papers. Amnah does not even know her age or her birthday. She only knows she was born during the Japanese invasion. At that time, people lived shut up in their homes, without paying much attention to the date.

5:00 A steady stream of cars flows down the suburban streets; all offices are now closed. Ahmad comes in and repeats the same ritual as at lunchtime. Once his prayers are finished, he goes down to practice the piano.

7:00 The sun has gone down, dinner is finished, and everyone is lining up for the shower. The girls choose their outfits carefully for their cousin's pre-engagement party.

The terms of the marriage have been discussed, and tonight uncles, aunts, and other family members on both sides are meeting to get to know each other. There are cars everywhere on the street. As socializing is done separately, women are led to the second floor's living room, and the men are seated in the main floor's. The women in Ahmad's family have been cooking for two days in preparation for this gathering. The minute they arrive, Amnah and her daughters join them on the kitchen floor to help out. They will spend their evening serving food and coffee for the nearly one hundred guests.

11:00 Home again, everyone gets back into a comfortable sarong. The students are off to bed. Zimah goes into her parents' room to watch TV with her father, while, alone in her kitchen, Amnah prepares rice, cakes, and rolls to meet her government contract for another day.

The Bruneians

THE NAME: From Malay *berunai*, meaning "plant," and *Darussalam*, "abode of peace"

GEOGRAPHY
Brunei lies on the northwest coast of the island of Borneo. Part of Malaysia divides Brunei into two enclaves: the western enclave consists of three river valleys; and the eastern enclave, of one. Forested hills, becoming mountainous toward the southeast, surround the valleys. Along the northwest coast is a narrow coastal plain. Max. altitude: 1,850 m. (6,070 ft.) (Birkit Pagon)
Area: 5,765 sq. km. (2,226 sq. mi.)
Density: 43 pers./sq. km. (112 pers./sq. mi.) (1988)
Arable land: 5% (1985)
Forest: 47%
Climate: Tropical, characterized by constant high humidity and heavy rainfall

CAPITAL: Bandar Seri Begawan, pop. 63,868 (1981)

LANGUAGE: Malay (official)
English is the effective lingua franca; Chinese also used
Of the literate citizens nine years of age and older, half are bilingual.

RELIGION
 Muslim: 64%
 Buddhist: 14%
 Christian: 10%
 Freethinker: 9%
 Other: 3%

POPULATION: Total—249,000 (1988)
 Annual growth: 1.9% (4,256) (1985)
 Doubling time: 25 yrs.
 Urban: 58% (1985) (est. for year 2000: 59%)
 Rural: 42%

AGE GROUPS (1984)
 14% under 5 yrs.
 37% under 15
 47% under 20
 35% from 20 to 39
 13% from 40 to 59
 5% 60 yrs. and over

ETHNIC GROUPS (1981)
 Malay: 65%   Chinese: 21%
 Other indigenous: Indian: 3%
 8%   Other: 4%

HISTORY
Earliest settlers, probably Austronesian-speaking, joined over ten thousand years ago by peoples who migrated from the Asian mainland
6th cent.: Serves as a trading center, especially for China
13–15th cent.: Vassal of the Javanese Majapahit Empire
15th cent.: Converts to Islam and becomes a sultanate
16th cent.: Brunei becomes a major Southeast Asian power, presiding over most of Borneo as well as parts of the Philippines, until the Dutch, Spanish, and Portuguese diminish its power
early 19th cent.: After centuries of encroachment by foreign powers, and intense internal rivalry, Brunei begins to look toward Britain for help
1841: English adventurer James Brooke is appointed governor (or rajah) of Sarawak
1888: Brunei becomes a British Protectorate
1929: Discovery of large oil fields transforms the economy
1941–45: Japanese occupation
1959: Full internal self-government and constitution
Jan. 1, 1984: Independence from Great Britain

FAMILY
Marital status, for females 15 yrs. + (1981)
 Single: 34%   Widowed: 6%
 Married: 59%   Divorced: 0.8%
Female head of household: no data
Fertility rate: 3.6 (1988)
Teenage births: 6% / **Teenage fertility rate:** 38.7/1,000 (1984)
Births out of wedlock: no data
Contraception: no data
Government's position on family planning: Population growth and fertility are satisfactory. No explicit policy to modify fertility. Society has strong pro-family values. Government supports program to advise women on spacing births for health reasons only. Abortion is legal only if the woman's life is threatened.

BRUNEI DARUSSALAM

SOCIAL INDICATORS
Life expectancy: 71 yrs. (male: 69; female: 70) (1984)

Infant mortality: 12/1,000 births (1987)

Crude birth rate: no data

Crude death rate: no data

HEALTH
Access to health services: 96% (1984)

Births attended by trained health personnel: 85.3% (1982)

(100% of women had at least three visits for prenatal care.)

HOUSING
Persons per household: 5.8 (1981)

Electricity: no data. It can be assumed the majority have access to electricity.

Access to safe water: 90% (1984)

Source of water: no data. It can be assumed the majority have water piped inside.

Toilet facilities (1984)
Flush: 80%
Other: no data

Construction materials: Most housing is of durable materials.

EDUCATION
Literacy: male: 85%; female: 69% (1985)

Educational attainment for pop. 25 yrs. + (1981)
None: 32%
First level: 28%
Second: 30%
Third: 9%

ECONOMIC ACTIVITY
Economically active population: 37% (male: 52%; female: 19%) (1981)

Agriculture: 3% act. pop.; 1% of GDP

Mines: 2% act. pop.; 50% of GDP

Industry: 23% act. pop.; 10% of GDP

Services: 72% act. pop.; 39% of GDP

Per capita GNP: US$15,400 (1986)

National currency: Brunei dollars

Principal resources: Petroleum, natural gas

COMMUNICATIONS
Radio
Transmitters: 4 (1983)
Receivers: 216/1,000 pop. (1985)

Television
Transmitters: 2 (1983)
Receivers: 151/1,000 pop. (1985)

Newspapers (1984)
Believed to have no general-interest dailies

Brunei Darussalam

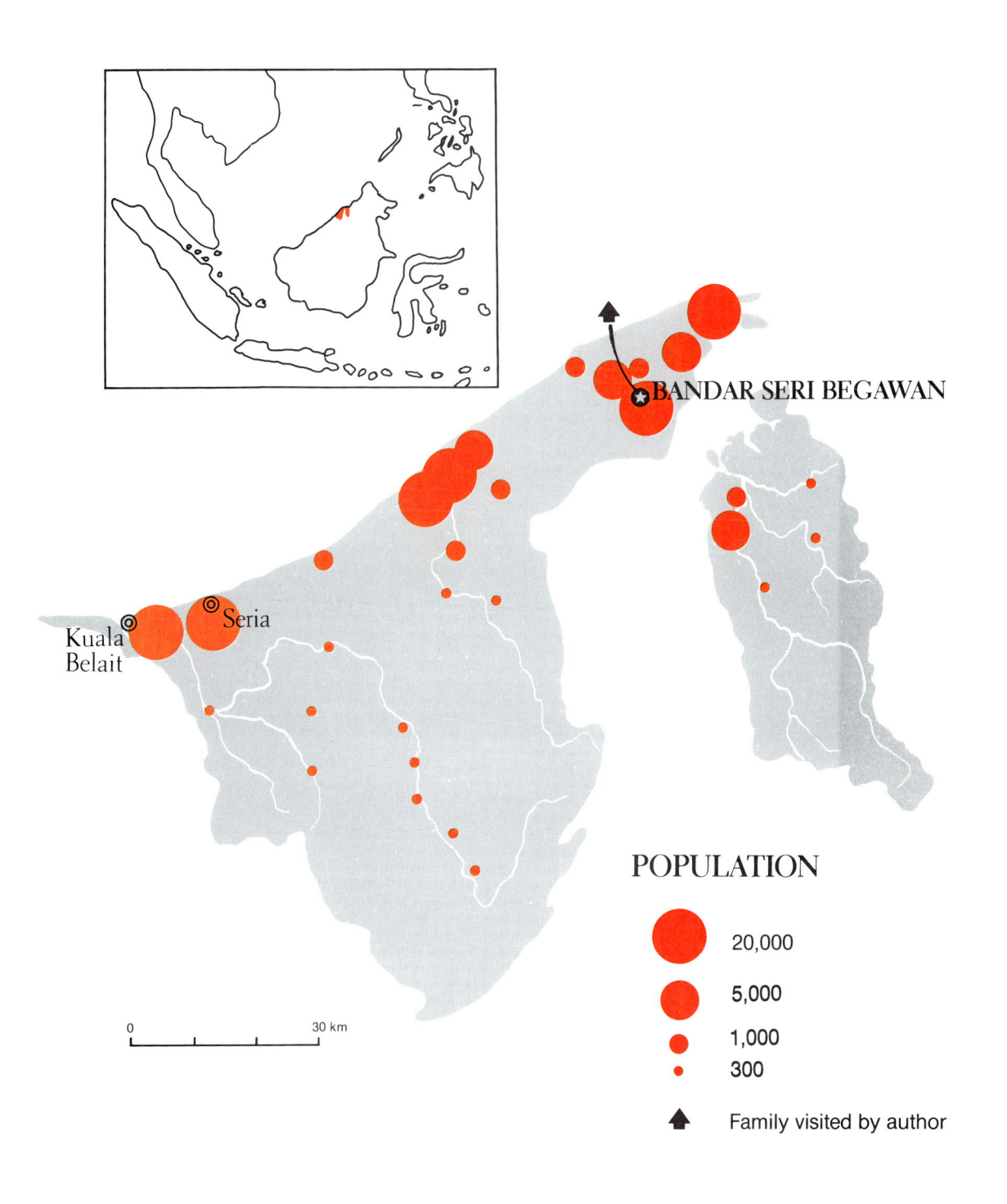

POPULATION

- 20,000
- 5,000
- 1,000
- 300

⬆ Family visited by author

Kuala Belait

Seria

BANDAR SERI BEGAWAN

0   30 km

Indonesia

Amin bin Karta's Family

Amin bin Karta, age 56 (1)
Tasem, 47 (2)
Suparsi, 27 (absent)
Carmina, 22 (absent)
Ojok, 19 (absent)
Casdpin, 17 (3)
Alisa, 15 (4)
Kurnaisih, 14 (5)
Kusnadi, 13 (6)
Taryono, 8 (7)
Dadi bin Amin (son-in-law), 22 (8)

1 bull
5 sheep
100 *bebek* (ducks)
2 other ducks and ducklings
1 rooster
4 hens and chicks

Kampung Cikundang, Java

JANUARY 1

4:00   The gentle sound of the scattered drops from last night's rain falling from the trees is suddenly drowned out by the voice of the *baduk* calling the *uduk* (Muslim morning prayers). Tasem gets up and goes to the semi-attached red brick shed that serves as kitchen. She squats on the dirt floor in front of the fire and lights dry branches. The oil lamps are already lit in the neighboring houses where two of her married daughters live. The family starts work early during rice-planting season, when they are all employed by a farmer. Suparsi and Carmina leave with their husbands to work in the rice paddies. Their fifteen-year-old sister, Alisa, who lives at her parents' with her husband, quickly swallows a bowl of cold rice in the kitchen before following her sisters.

Tasem's nineteen-year-old daughter, Ojok, is the only absentee. Now divorced for the third time, Ojok is away, training to work as a family maid in Saudi Arabia. She is the only child Tasem and Amin are a little worried about. There are all kinds of stories about workers who have never been heard of after going abroad.

Amin bin Karta comes out into the wet muddy yard, lighting his way to the well with a torch. He draws a pail of water to shower before his morning prayers. Back in the house's main room, he covers half his body with a white sarong and his head with a prayer cap, and kneels beside the bed where his eight-year-old grandson, Taryono, is sleeping. Taryono is his daughter Suparsi's son from a first marriage. When the boy's mother remarried four years ago and moved next door with her new husband, Taryono did not want to move. Amin bends his head down to the floor, facing Mecca, and repeats the words he has said since he learned the *uduk* as a child. Then he sits on his bed, rolls tobacco in a palm-tree leaf, lights his cigarette, and calls to his two sons Kusnadi and Casdpin sleeping in the bunk beds adjacent to his. Kusnadi quickly performs his ablutions at the well, returns, and kneels to repeat the same words as he bends his head to the prayer carpet.

5:00   The light of day is rising, and Tasem is tossing rice on her woven tray to sort out the bad grains. Around her, the four hens and their chicks are hoping for some spills. It's not clumsiness but her desire to make the animals happy that sends some grains to the ground.

6:00 Kurnaisih attends school in the afternoon, so she helps her mother with morning household chores. Her older brother Casdpin walks to the road to catch the bus to school. With a sure-footed step, he traverses the muddy ridges of two rice fields. His step mirrors his confident attitude about his future. He has enrolled in the Agricultural High School to study farm technology and mechanization. His father says dryly: "Rice will always be hand-made."

Amin leaves home with his hoe on his shoulder. Today he will flood some of his paddies by damming the small dirt canals that crisscross the fields, to divert water onto his land. This irrigation permits him to harvest two crops a year. In the course of many years, Amin has managed to buy 1.4 acres of land, which he has divided in twenty *petak* (square partitions) bordered by the elevated ridges of the canals. But this small amount of land is not enough to meet the family's needs, and so Amin also hires himself out as a farmhand. His sons-in-law have no land because there is no more land available, and they, too, must work for other farmers.

The island of Java is one of the most densely populated regions in the world. The roads are lined with houses like a never-ending city. Beyond the buildings are rice fields. This morning they are full of people. Men drive skinny bulls pulling plows or toss bunches of rice shoots into the paddies for the women to plant, bent over in the water, a bobbing row of straw hats. Men and women both work in mud and water up to their knees.

Indonesia is a country of 13,667 islands. Sixty percent of the population live on Java and Bali, where the land is best. The government would like people to move and colonize other still-forested islands under a resettlement program. But for Amin's daughters and sons-in-law that is a bold step: it means choosing to separate from family and from community, to cut through the dense jungle and risk attack from herds of elephants, wild pigs, bears, tigers, and snakes. For now, Amin's daughters will stay near their parents. And Suparsi and Carmina are strong-willed enough to influence their husbands.

Kusnadi goes off with his hundred *bebek* (a type of duck) and five sheep. Unlike his brother Casdpin, he is a school dropout. His father did not question his decision. "If he prefers to work, let him work," says Amin. And he works very well. He started with just five *bebek*, sold their eggs, saved the money, and bought more ducks. Now his little business is prospering. Amin refuses the money Kusnadi offers him, and encourages his son to invest more. Kusnadi can be seen all morning happily walking his *bebek* along the fields. The feathered creatures follow each other and hunt for snails. At night, Kusnadi will give them *menir*, fine broken bits of rice left after the threshing.

After coffee and rice with a spicy sauce on the side, Tasem, like everyone else, will spend her morning in the fields. She wanders along the ridges, cut-

Amin bin Karta's typical Javanese tile-roofed house is densely populated, like Java itself. His son raises ducks, so many that the vegetable garden has to be spiked to keep them out.

ting long grass to feed the bull, laying the bundles on the ridges. Later Amin will come with two baskets balanced on his shoulders and collect the grass. After feeding the bull, he will take its dung back to use as fertilizer in the fields.

12:00   After cutting the grass and weeding one *petak*, Tasem comes back home, collecting papayas along the way from one of the numerous fruit trees that grow around their land. There are exotic fruits such as rambutan, durian, *kedong-*

INDONESIA

Both men and women work with bullocks in the muddy rice paddies to prepare each square for planting. Lunch—rice and fish with a spicy sauce—is taken squatting on the ridge of the canal from which they will flood the fields.

dong, as well as the more familiar coconut, banana, and pineapple—all good supplements to the daily diet of rice and seasonal vegetables.

When Tasem gets home, her daughter Alisa is sitting on the courtyard's bench. Most workers sit on the ridges to have their lunch, but Alisa was not far and preferred to come home. She washes, prays, sits down on the floor with a bowl of rice and vegetables, and is off again. This afternoon she will weed instead of plant.

In the kitchen, Kurnaisih has eaten some rice and is preparing to go to her afternoon classes. With some trepidation, Tasem heads off to the mill to buy rice chaff to feed the animals. At the mill she walks in silently, staying close to the wall. Tasem does not have money to buy the chaff and she will offer the millkeeper eggs instead of cash. She knows he will yell at her. "Everybody wants to give me eggs, I need cash, too"; but finally he will agree.

"This is the last time," he always says. The proud Tasem would rather not go through this humiliation.

2:00 The afternoon rain has started. Tasem takes down the clothes that have been drying for the last two days. With luck they will be dry tomorrow. She then squats in the kitchen and starts preparing food for the evening meal. With a pumpkin, ground coconut, and strong peppers, she makes the accompaniment for the rice. Now there is always rice, and chicken and meat more and more often. It was not always so. Amin and Tasem remember the days when eating one little piece of meat was one of the great events of the year. Then the country did not even produce enough rice to feed the whole population. Amin's sons eat better than he did, and he is proud to see them growing strong and tall.

4:00 The rain has stopped. After a nap, Amin goes back to plow his small cassava garden. Before sunset, he stops in a *petak* to weed a row of rice. As he walks back home, he checks his crops, looking for that first shaft of rice. The farmers say the harvest comes forty days after its appearance.

6:30 Tasem and Kusnadi must feed the ducks rice gruel and grass, so they are the last to sit down at the eating mat. There is not much dinner conversation: everyone listens to a government program on the radio giving advice to farmers. This year the rice harvest is threatened by an insect that may destroy half the country's production. Kurnaisih steps out and goes to the village to watch television in one of the two homes in Kampung Cikundang that have a set. People here cannot afford the installation of electricity, let alone a television.

8:45 With no electricity—just two small oil lamps to light the entire house—and with the morning prayers coming so soon, everybody goes to sleep as the battery-operated radio plays. An oil lamp stays lit in one corner to keep the ghosts away.

Indonesia

Napsiah bin Moktar's Family

Napsiah bin Moktar, age 35 (1)
Rabiah, 32 (2)
Samsiah bin Napsiah, 14 (3)
Sanusi, 12 (4)
Rabiin, 10 (5)
Mani, 7 (6)
Mati, 5 (7)
Sansudin, 2½ (8)

Kampung Pondok Pratie, Lombok

DECEMBER 22

12:00 *Ponkok oh! oh! oh! Ponkok oh! oh! oh!* The rhythmic chant of the fishermen returning at midnight from night fishing joins the breaking of the surf, as they help each other haul the first boats to shore. Behind them, the sea is dotted with the glow of oil lanterns on the sailboats heading into land.

Samsiah and Sanusi wait on the beach with four other young boys. Traditionally, the fishermen give a small fish to the children who wait for them. Napsiah's sons sell their fish and get a few rupiah as pocket money, with which they'll buy shrimp chips or pieces of sugarcane.

Two hours later, when all the fishermen are in, Samsiah comes back and lies down alongside his family on the cement floor of the one-room bamboo house. His brother Sanusi prefers to stay on the beach to wait for the next fleet of returning fishermen, and lies down on the damp sand with three other boys, using his sarong as cover against the cold and bugs. The night is never silent; the villagers sleep to the sound of knives chopping off fish heads and cleaning the fish for the morning market.

4:30 The Muslim morning prayers blare from the speakers at the village mosque. The first one up, little Mani, walks about in the house, holding her sarong under her arm, impatient for the day to begin. Napsiah gets up, grabs his plastic tobacco box, and rolls a cigarette before leaving to fish with his oldest son, Samsiah. Rabiah sits on the doorstep with the crying Sansudin, pulling up her T-shirt to give him her breast.

Sansudin's cries have awakened Mati, who, in her turn, starts crying. She gets up and runs to the kitchen, but as she sees her mother busy comforting her little brother, her cries lose momentum and she stops. She walks out of the house, her sad, pretty face looking for something to cheer her up.

The baby has had diarrhea for the last two days and is still not feeling well this morning, and his parents are worried. They cannot help thinking about last year's epidemic, when fifteen children from the *kampung* (village) died, five in one day. They don't have the money to go to the doctor or to buy medication. Rabiah hopes that this afternoon she will be able to talk with the health worker. His second wife lives here in the *kampung*, and it is his day to visit her. Today the Islamic law that obliges a man who has more than one wife to give them equal shelter and time might just help Rabiah.

6:30 This morning, the children will have a breakfast of fish soup that their grandfather is cooking next door. Leaving the baby with her older children, Rabiah takes the washing, crosses the street, and enters one of the small alleyways that meander between the crowded houses of Kampung Pondok Pratie. While she washes at the public well, other women talk to her from their doorstep. Rabiah listens, responding shyly but attentively. As one is never alone in the crowded *kampung*, it is essential to be in harmony with the community. One never knows when neighbors will be needed to lend food or to rebuild a roof after a cyclone.

8:00 By the time Rabiah comes back home, Rabiin has left for school. He is the only one getting an education. The girls are still too young, and his brother Sanusi left after first grade. He was not doing very well, so his teacher sat him with the girls. Humiliated, Sanusi refused to go back. Napsiah tried to force him with numerous beatings, but, to escape the beatings, Sanusi would start walking to school and then run and hide somewhere on the seaside. Finally Napsiah stopped bothering. Sanusi's parents are sad and upset. They know they won't be able to count on him in their old age.

The couple hope that at least one of their children will make it to advanced studies. Samsiah, their oldest boy, never even passed the state exam for secondary school. The exam, prepared in the capital, is too difficult for those educated on the outlying islands like Lombok. The exam must be selective, as there are not enough places for all the students in the state classrooms. The only other paths to a higher education are private secondary schools, whose reputation is not as good, or bribes. Both require money. So higher education is only for the extremely bright or for the financially privileged—and for those as ambitious as Rabiah's youngest brother, who goes fishing at night to pay for his studies during the day.

One type of education Napsiah doesn't have to force on his children is Islamic studies. They eagerly attend the free classes at the village mosque, where they learn to incorporate the precepts of their religion into their daily life.

9:30 Mati becomes a little cleaning whirlwind. With a branch broom, she sweeps her family's yard, her grandfather's yard, and starts in on the neighbors'. But when two other little girls call her to play, she runs down to the beach. Most children who play on the beach have a rash of small itchy pimples on their faces. The sub-district health center has told the people that the skin disease is the result of the beach's being used as a toilet and has urged that a pit latrine

INDONESIA

When Napsiah's father put up his bamboo hut on the beach, there were only seven other fishermen. Now there are three hundred. The villagers are being pressured to leave by an oil company that is building storage tanks on the beach. Napsiah's family doesn't want to move inland. "We are fishermen," Napsiah says. "We must live beside the sea."

be built. But no one listens. The beach is still a toilet, and the dogs and the chickens spread the filth everywhere.

11:00 *Ponkok oh! oh! oh!* A fisherman with a motorboat pulls Napsiah's boat to shore. There is no wind and no fish today. Napsiah, like the other fishermen, can tell by the color of the sea and the sky, and by the winds, if there will be fish or not. These days, Napsiah feels blessed by Allah if he catches enough to sell at the market. Today Napsiah brings home enough fish to eat, but no more.

From the middle of January to the middle of March, the surf is so rough that the men cannot go out at all. Women and children move farther inside the *kampung*, while the men fish on the other side of the island. They settle on the beach, sheltering under palm leaves, and come back every two weeks to bring money and fish to their families.

1:30 The lunch, fish and rice, is finished. The women lie down on their sarongs, children clinging to their breasts. Some women sleep; others sit and talk as they pick lice out of each other's hair. There is nothing to do but wait for the afternoon heat to pass. There was a time when women made baskets to sell, but now there is no one to buy them. They would like to have a project that might generate income and are hoping someone will come from outside and give them an idea. "What could we do, with a child at our breast, another in our womb, and another hanging on our sarong?" say the women.

The men are beside them, slowly repairing their fishing nets and talking among themselves. In the back of the house, in the shade of the trees, Napsiah paints the new boat he has carved out of a tree trunk.

5:00 Rabiah prepares dinner, and Napsiah makes about fifteen trips to the well with his pail to fill the water jars and the basin for his baby's bath. While Sansudin relaxes in the water, Napsiah pours a pail of water over Mati. But when the time comes to put panties on her, Mati runs and her father cannot catch her. The little girl does not like clothing. Napsiah gives up and places Sansudin, relaxed and smiling, in a sarong that he has draped from his shoulder like a sling. The baby falls asleep as the sun sets, and Napsiah brings him into the house and lays him down in his *ayun-ayun* (hammock). He then goes back to the seashore, where the night fishermen are preparing their boats.

7:00 Rabiah calls him when the rice and fish are ready. The sea glows with the tiny lights of the fishermen's boats. After emptying her plate, Rabiah sweeps her house for the third and last time before turning the floor into a bed.

7:25 Mati walks naked toward her mother, dragging her sarong in her hands. She draws her sarong over her head and throws herself in her mother's arms. Her dress has become her blanket. Rabiah caresses her little girl and lies down on the floor beside her, still stroking her softly. In three minutes, Mati is asleep.

Rabiah helps her husband pour some kerosene from the big fishing lantern into a bottle, and carefully transfer it to a little oil lamp. Soon there will be no more fuel, but, whatever the expense, they will not sleep in the dark,

Napsiah gives all he earns to his wife, and it is usually just enough for kitchen firewood, rice, salt, coconut oil, chili, and the petrol for the lamp. By saving diligently, they manage to buy nineteen-meter sails for the boat each year. Today Napsiah brings home enough fish to eat, but none to sell.

for fear of ghosts. As the light spreads softly, one of the mosque staff members comes to collect the expected monthly donation. He sits to chat for a while, and a neighbor or two join in.

9:30 The small children lie in a row on the tarp that protects them from the cement floor. Rabiah lies between Mati and Sansudin, to whom she gives her breast. Napsiah sits between Rabiin and Mani, his back against the wall. The children are restless. It is hot and the mosquitoes irritate them. Rabiah turns to caress Mati, who grumbles. Napsiah fans his family with a sarong, until they are all asleep.

Indonesia

Anak Agung Ngurah Gde Manik's Family*

Anak Agung Ngurah Gde Manik, age 40 (1)
Anak Agung Sagung Suryaningsih, 33 (2)
Anak Agung Sagung Ratna, 10 (3)
Anak Agung Ngurah Gde Damar, 9 (4)
Anak Agung Sagung Mas, 7 (5)
Anak Agung Ngurah Kertagama, 2 (6)

2 monkeys   1 eagle
100 birds   10 fighting roosters
2 dogs   aquarium fish
2 cats

* The title *Anak Agung* is used in Bali with the names of members of the Brahmanic caste. *Ngurah* is an additional title for men of that caste; *Sagung*, for women; *Gde* precedes the name of the firstborn son.

Denpasar, Bali

DECEMBER 24

4:30 Beo, the family parrot, has been calling the names of every family member for some time, and with the *clicli* and the *toutou* birds and the roosters now joining in, the wild menagerie of sounds gives a sleeper the impression of being in the jungle. But this is the center of the city of Denpasar, the capital of the island of Bali, in the inner courtyard of the palace of Anak Agung Ngurah Gde Manik.

Anak Agung Sagung Suryaningsih puts on one of her simplest dresses. There is no need to look like a queen; she is only going to the market. Anak Agung Suryaningsih trusts no one but herself with this important job. Not counting the hundred gods of the temple, she must feed six of the eight wives of her late father-in-law, eight of his twenty-one children, fifteen servants, and her own four children.

With a maid carrying an empty basket on her head, Anak Agung Suryaningsih stops first at the flower merchant. She needs flowers for the altar of the *pura*, the adjacent temple. The market is vast and lively, and fresh fruits, vegetables, meat, and fish abound. She negotiates briefly, knowing the prices she should pay, and leaves. The maid will pick up the purchases.

5:00 An old woman, the first wife of the late patriarch Ida Cokorda Ngurah Gde Pemecutan, crosses the terrace on her way to the bathroom. In front of the rooms where the six older wives live, seven- and nine-year-old Mas and Damar sit beside a large aquarium, drinking glasses of milk, while watching the rare, bright-colored fish. They nod to their father, who is on his way to play tennis, as he does three times a week.

6:00 Anak Agung Suryaningsih is back, and the three servants in charge of the prayer temple are at work in the special kitchen, preparing the food for the gods. With baskets of food, flowers, and incense, they cross the palace's five acres, making offerings to each of the gods' shrines. From the god Penunggun Karan, sitting at the front door protecting the palace, to Sanggah Kumulan, to whom an altar was built before the house's construction even began, each of the one hundred gods is honored daily. "Everything we do for ourselves is done first for the gods, as a sign of gratitude for what they have given us," says Anak Agung Ngurah Gde Manik.

Ngurah Gde Manik will soon assume the title of religious leader of the

Hindus of Bali, inherited eight months ago, when his ninety-year-old father died. His father held the title of king as well as that of religious leader, but his son will decline that honor. "I believe in democracy," he says, "and the title of king is not fitting anymore." This worldly aristocrat is not in a hurry to be elected to his religious position. The moment the title becomes official, his life will be completely ruled by tradition. Where he sits; where, when, and what he eats; whom he receives—all will be dictated by Hindu laws.

7:00 The driver waits outside to bring Ngurah Gde Manik to the Regency Municipal Legislative Council, of which he is chairman, but today there won't be much work. The Ministry of Sports has declared Friday a "day of fitness." From seven to nine, the government employees do gymnastics; then they clean up the streets around their office buildings. Those who are Muslim are given time to pray at their mosque, as Friday is their holy day. All offices close at two.

Anak Agung Suryaningsih has had a cup of coffee with cake and has gone up to her immediate family's apartments, where she and her husband each have bedrooms, and a large open-air living room. She showers and chooses a colorful sarong and *kebaya*, the traditional skirt and blouse, from her extensive wardrobe.

8:00 Mama Sitri is feeding little Kertagama while the three other children play on the cool terrace tiles. Mama Sitri is the third wife of Ngurah Gde Manik's father, and his real mother. The two first wives could not have children, so when Mama Sitri conceived, the child in her womb was ceremoniously named the child of the first wife and was raised by her. Ngurah Gde Manik did not learn who his biological mother was until he was in his teens, but he was taught to consider both women his mother, and he is respectful and responsible to all his father's wives. Times have changed, however, and he himself cannot afford eight wives. His only wife, Suryaningsih, prefers it that way.

8:45 An elegantly dressed Anak Agung Suryaningsih descends the stairs with a careful, stately pace, bound for a cousin's son's marriage ceremony. The children don't seem to mind that their parents come and go. With six grandmothers, fifteen maids, and their cousins who live in the palace grounds, they are never alone. Home on school holidays, they seem content with the quiet, intricate palace routine. When hungry, they will be fed; when hurt, they will be comforted. Confident that these needs are being satisfied, their parents can concentrate on their education.

The family house of Anak Agung Ngurah Gde Manik, religious leader of Bali and heir to its ancient royal throne, is inside spacious palace grounds where offerings are given at the shrines of a hundred Hindu gods every day.

10:00 The heat is now intense. No one can be seen, but voices and music come from Ngurah Gde Manik's brothers' apartments, mixing with the sounds of hammers from the family-owned hotel adjacent to the palace. Ngurah Gde Manik has built a simple and inexpensive hotel. Not being beside the sea, it does not interest the tourists, but it is busy with Balinese customers, and he is adding more rooms. In addition to the income from the hotel, he has his salary as a government employee, and the profit from 127 hectares (313 acres) of farmland that he rents to peasants, who give him half of what they make. He says this is hardly enough for him to meet the responsibilities that go with his title. As Ida Cokorda, he is responsible for all living family members of his line. His is the eleventh generation, so he does not know how many people this represents. They are dispersed throughout Indonesia and throughout the world, and they all have the right to come to him when in need. Unless they (like his sister) have married someone of a lower caste and have been disowned by the family.

11:00 Anak Agung Suryaningsih showers and changes again, before she and her husband attend the cremation of a high-class Brahman. The ceremony is spectacular. Thousands follow the coffin, dressed in their best traditional clothing. First come the women carrying offerings on their heads, then the musicians, and then a wooden bull in which the dead man will be burned. Tourists with cameras follow, in scant summer clothing. Later the local people complain about this lack of respect; they would like tourists restricted from going into the streets and the temples in improper dress. But the authorities are reluctant; they fear such a law would hurt tourism, Bali's main income.

2:00 Once again, the couple just have time to refresh themselves and put on new outfits, and they are off to another part of their cousin's wedding ceremony, *pemadikan*, when the groom comes to carry away his bride from her parents' house.

5:00 This is the time when Ngurah Gde Manik sits on the terrace and is available to members of his huge family. Tonight an old man and his son have come. The old man possesses only a plot of land he thought too small to be taxed; nevertheless, he has received a bill and is anxious, wanting to know who is right. Ngurah Gde Manik will defend him if necessary.

At the other end of the terrace, a maid has put out tea with milk for the children. It is now humid and hot, and Mama Sitri has filled a basin with water for the youngest. She rests, watching him play. The old lady has carried so many babies on her hip, it now juts permanently to one side.

6:00 For the third time today, Ngurah Gde Manik and his wife leave for the temple, with a basket holding coffee, rice cakes, and flowers. Tonight they pray to Pemerajan, the god who links them to their ancestors, asking for protection for themselves, their children, and the young bridegroom.

Mama Sitri is chasing Kertagama with a handful of rice and meat ready to shove in his mouth when she catches him. The others eat in the kitchen.

7:00 Daughter Ratna's dancing teacher has arrived. With attractive costumes and quick fluid movements of the body and hands, Balinese dance was originally

Daughter Ratna snacks on the cool terrace, in front of the beautifully colored rare fish in the aquarium. With six grandmothers and fifteen maids living in the palace grounds, she and her siblings are never neglected when their parents are out on their ceremonial duties.

created for royal children, with the idea that the physical and social demands of the dance would strengthen the character. Ngurah Gde Manik is serious about both his sons' and daughters' education, which includes dancing, combat horse riding, and other military skills. He wants them strong. All his ancestors, with the exception of his grandfather, have died in wars. The men of his line are disciplined, and they do not tolerate the weak and lazy. Ngurah Gde Manik has already started educating his older son for his future responsibilities.

8:00   Mama Sitri sits in the yard, making palm baskets for the god offerings. The children are all in their one room, two in the bunk beds, Ratna on a mattress on the floor, and Kertagama in his baby bed. Before falling asleep, they play or read, content in each other's company, while their parents go up to their apartments to prepare for an infrequent quiet evening at home.

The Indonesians

THE NAME: Indonesia combines the prefix form of India and the ancient Greek for islands. Ancestral name, Tanah Air, meaning "land and water." It has also been called Nusantara, meaning "archipelago."

GEOGRAPHY

The largest archipelago in the world, consisting of five main and over 13,667 smaller islands and islets, 6,000 of which are inhabited, forming a rough crescent between the Pacific and the Indian Ocean. The majority of islands are covered by thickly forested, rugged volcanic mountains, with a hundred active volcanoes.

Max. altitude: 5,030 m. (16,503 ft.) (Puncak Jaya)

Area: 1,919,443 sq. km. (741,101 sq. mi.)
Density: 90 pers./sq. km. (233 pers./sq. mi.) (1988)
Arable land: 8% (1985)
Forest: 64%. Deforestation: 0.5% (620,000 hectares) per year (1980s)
Climate: Equatorial. The climate changes every six months, rainy season and dry season. Weather greatly influenced by the mountains and the sea. High humidity; moderately high temperatures inland, higher along the coast

CAPITAL: Jakarta, pop. 6,503,449 (metropolitan area: pop. 7,000,000) (1980)

LANGUAGE: Bahasa Indonesia (official and lingua franca)
250 languages and dialects (spoken and written)
Main local languages: Acehnese, Batak, Javanese (spoken by 40% to 50% of the population), Sundanese (15%), Madurese, Sasak, Tetun, and Timor
Most Indonesians are bilingual.

RELIGION (1980)
Muslim: 88.1%
Protestant: 5.4%
Catholic: 2.5%
Hindu: 2.0%
Buddhist: 1.0%
Other: 1.0%

POPULATION: Total—174,951,000 (1988)
Annual growth: 2.2% (3,662,208) (1985)
Doubling time: 40 yrs.
Urban: 25% (1985) (est. for year 2000: 36%)
Rural: 75%

AGE GROUPS (1984)
14% under 5 yrs.
39% under 15
50% under 20
29% from 20 to 39
15% from 40 to 59
5% 60 yrs. and over

ETHNIC GROUPS

An estimated 300 ethnic groups, mostly of Malay descent

Due to the similar ancestry, the government has reclassified the population on the basis of their linguistic identities into four ethnic groups: the Melanesians, the Pro-Austronesians, the Polynesians, and the Micronesians.

Principal non-indigenous group: Chinese (2%)

HISTORY

Archaeological evidence of Australopithecine man 1.9 million years ago, and *Homo erectus* 400,000 to 600,000 years ago

40,000 B.C.: Evidence of *Homo sapiens*, resembling present-day inhabitants of New Guinea and Aboriginal Australia

3000–500 B.C.: Migrations of sub-Mongoloid people from Asia

1st cent. B.C.: Commercial relations with China begin; Hindu and Buddhist cultural influence from India; period of Hindu kingdoms, ruled by indigenous rajahs, lasts to 15th century A.D.

7th–13th cent.: Buddhist kingdom of Srivijaya flourishes in much of Indonesia

13th–15th cent.: Javanese Hindu Majapahit kingdom dominates the region, with dependencies as far as present-day North Vietnam and the Philippines

1292: Visit by Marco Polo, first European to reach Indonesia

INDONESIA

14th–16th cent.: Islam is brought to Sumatra by Gujarati and Persian traders and spreads to most of Indonesia

1511: Portuguese arrive in the Moluccas in pursuit of the spice trade, followed by the Spanish, Dutch, and British

1602: Dutch East India Company establishes a monopoly of the spice trade, leading to colonial control over Java, Sumatra, and the Moluccas. Indonesia is known as the Dutch East Indies until WWII

1825–30: Prince Diponegoro of Java leads long, bloody guerrilla war, one of many revolts against Dutch colonialism

1906, 1908: People of Bali launch suicidal charges against the Dutch fortifications

1908: Indonesian leaders unify against Dutch colonialism in the Indonesian national movement for independence

1927: Indonesia Nationalist Party (PNI) emerges under the leadership of Sukarno

1942–45: Japanese occupation drives Dutch off the islands

1945: Sukarno and Mohammad Hatta declare independence for Indonesia. Four years of fierce fighting ensue

1949: UN adopts cease-fire resolution; Holland recognizes sovereignty of Indonesia

Dec. 27, 1949: Proclamation of independent Federal Republic of Indonesia

1945–65: Sukarno struggles to unify the country and stabilize the economy. Communist Party (PKI) gains influence; attempts a coup, which is thwarted by the army under General Suharto. Chaos follows, with widespread massacres of alleged Communists; an estimated 750,000 are killed

1968: National Assembly elects Suharto president

FAMILY
Marital status, for females 15 yrs. + (1980)
  Single: 18%
  Married: 65%
  Widowed: 12%
  Divorced: 5%
Female head of household: 14% (1980)
Fertility rate: 3.7 (1986)
Teenage births: no data
Births out of wedlock: no data
Contraception: 40% (1985)

Government's position on family planning: Population growth and fertility are too high. Targets an annual growth rate of 1.5% and birth rate of 23 per 1,000 pop. by 1990. Promotes family-planning education and access to contraception. Abortion available for health reasons only. Sterilization is legal.

SOCIAL INDICATORS
Life expectancy: 56 yrs. (male: 54; female: 57) (1986)
Infant mortality: 76/1,000 births (1986)
Crude birth rate: 29/1,000 pop. (1986)
Crude death rate: 12/1,000

HEALTH
Access to health services: 75% (1986)
Births attended by trained health personnel: 43% (1984)

HOUSING
Persons per household: 4.8 (1980)
Electricity: 70% without (urban: 27%; rural: 84%) (1985)
Access to safe water: 36% (urban: 53%; rural: 29%) (1986)
Source of water (1985)
  Well: 54%
  Piped: 11% (urban: 32%; rural: 3%)
  Pump: 8%
  Other: 27%
Toilet facilities (1984)
  Sanitation facilities: 30% (urban: 30%; rural: 30%)
Construction materials: Most housing is of durable materials.

EDUCATION
Literacy: 74% (male: 83%; female: 65%) (1980)
Gross enrollment ratio (1984)
  First level: 118% (completing in 1980–86: 80%)
  Second: 39%
  Third: 7%
Educational attainment for pop. 25 yrs. + (1980)
  None: 41%
  First level: 32%
  Second: 10%
  Third: 0.8%

Indonesia

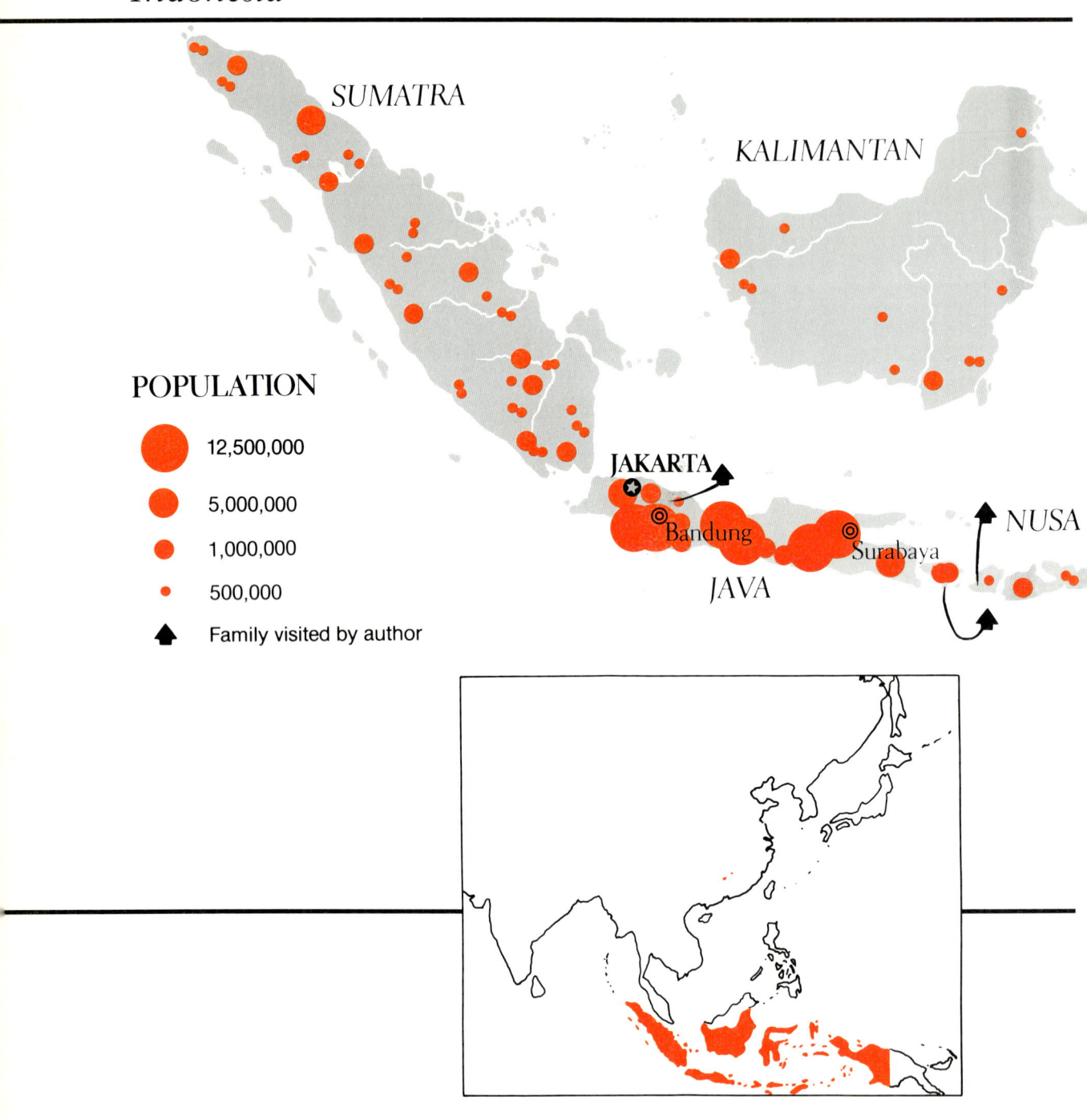

SUMATRA

KALIMANTAN

POPULATION

- 12,500,000
- 5,000,000
- 1,000,000
- 500,000
- ▲ Family visited by author

JAKARTA

Bandung

Surabaya

JAVA

NUSA

SULAWESI

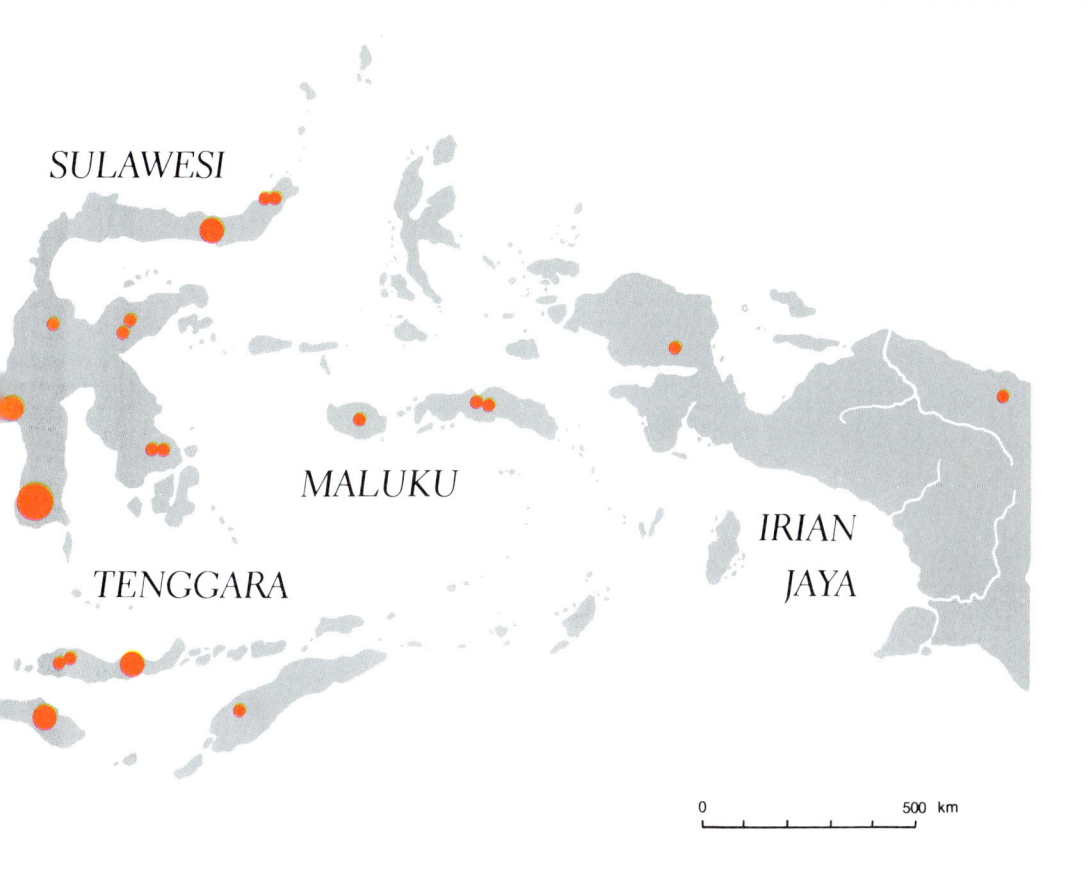

MALUKU

IRIAN JAYA

TENGGARA

0   500 km

ECONOMIC ACTIVITY
Economically active population: 36% (male: 48%; female: 24%) (1980)
Agriculture: 52% act. pop.; 28% of GDP
Mines: 1% act. pop.; 12% of GDP
Industry: 15% act. pop.; 14% of GDP
Services: 32% act. pop.; 46% of GDP
Per capita GNP: US$490 (1986)
Population in absolute poverty: urban: 26%; rural: 44% (1985)
National currency: rupiah
Principal resources: Rice, tin

COMMUNICATIONS
Radio
 Transmitters: 745 (1985)
 Receivers: 117/1,000 pop. (1985)
Television
 Transmitters: 207 (1985)
 Receivers: 39/1,000 pop. (1985)
Newspapers (1984)
 Dailies: 55
 Circulation: 2,878,000 (18/1,000 pop.)

Democratic Kampuchea

The Pann Family

Pann Dek, age 38 (1)
Nou Yong, 36 (2)
Pann Chanthan, 13 (3)
Pann Chanta, 8 (4)
Pann Chanrath, 5 (5)
Pann Ran, 3 (6)

3 bulls
1 dog
1 cat

Chrop Ampil Village

MARCH 26

4:30 The first, the second, and then the third rooster's crow echoes across the flat fertile lands of the Kien Svay district in the Kandal Province. Nou Yong and her husband, Pann Dek, get up, pack their garden vegetables in bundles on their backs, and walk to the rural road that follows the Mekong River as it flows toward the Tonkin Gulf. Everyone in the whole countryside seems to be on the road. Workers pedal nearly two hours to jobs in Phnom Penh, the capital city; bicycle-taxis carry their clients on a rack above the front tire; and motorbikes pull trailers full of people taking their harvests to market. Nou Yong boards one of these trailers and Pann Dek piles their garden's harvest on around her. As treasurer of the household, selling at the market is her business.

Pann Dek brings his bulls to pasture and waters his garden, while his oldest daughter takes care of the younger children. Since 1979, he has cultivated his rice communally with ten to fifteen other families. After a rice tax of about seven percent of the harvest, the rest is divided equally among the members of the group. Pann Dek's solidarity group works land thirty kilometers (nineteen miles) away from his home. The government is encouraging farmers to grow more and sell their surplus, but Pann Dek, like many other farmers, is not interested. The country is barely self-sufficient in rice, and this year has been particularly arid. He knows even before harvesting that there won't be enough to feed his family. Moreover, the state has been buying the rice at a very low price and, instead of money, giving coupons good only for government consumer goods, which are quite scarce.

Shy, silent Pann Dek prefers working his garden for cash. Quietly he carries water, bucket by bucket, to his plants. He will water three times today, thus assuring himself of some real money on the "parallel market."

6:20 The village's brick-factory bell rings, followed by a national radio news broadcast blaring from the factory's speakers. Eight-year-old Chanta leaves for school. Shortly afterwards comes the rattling sound of the loom in the bamboo lean-to beside the Panns' house. Nou Yong's sister is already at work making *krama*, a piece of woven cotton, usually red and white, used by the Khmer for just about everything. Men and women wear it around their necks and coil it around their heads for protection from the sun, or to shield their faces from the dust of passing vehicles, or to cover themselves when they wash at the well or the river. Until recently, weaving families could earn US$18 a year selling *krama*; now everybody is making *krama* to get some cash, and the prices are falling.

8:45 Nou Yong, already back from the city market, swiftly cleans a fish, while her husband cuts wood and starts a fire for breakfast. She has splurged at the market, buying a piece of watermelon. Chanrath and Ran crowd around her, laughing with joy. Oldest daughter Chanthan waits patiently to be served, her eyes staring at the fruit. This serious-looking young girl, who was born at the start of the Pol Pot regime, knows she is lucky not to have been one of the almost one million people who died of famine during that time.

Back from the field for the breakfast break, Pann Dek sits silently at the *krea* (a bamboo table), using an old school-notebook page to roll a cigarette, while his wife supervises the fire. Nou Yong cooks with as little wood as possible because it is becoming very scarce.

9:30 Pann Dek and his wife go back to the field, where they will spend the morning working quietly side by side.

While her parents are busy, thirteen-year-old Chanthan carries Ran in a *krama* sling from her shoulder like a mother. She seems older than her years. During the Pol Pot period, her father was sent away to work in the fields, but luckily, although she lost her grandfather and many uncles and cousins, she did not lose either of her parents. As peasants without education, they had a better chance of survival. No one who had as much as a high-school diploma survived, unless they fled or hid. By 1979, Kampuchea had lost ninety percent of its doctors; equipment in hospitals, universities, and schools was completely destroyed. After liberation, the country had to start all over again. Since Chanthan's father and mother were reunited, they have been very busy, like all parents in Kampuchea, rebuilding their lives and their country.

10:30 Having put her brother to sleep, Chanthan goes to pick fruit. Bananas, coconut, breadfruit, and mangoes grow around the house. It is mango season, and the trees sag under the weight. As she passes the house next door, where her aunt is starching the cotton to be woven, a cousin runs out to join Chanthan. The two girls happily take off into the countryside, but they are always close enough to run back home when Chanthan's brother wakes up.

12:30 The length of the house's shadow tells Nou Yong it is time for her oldest daughter to leave for afternoon school. Chanthan quickly pulls on her too tight school uniform, grabs the few coins her mother hands her for a rice-soup lunch, and pedals off on her bicycle toward the school, three kilometers away.

The Panns contribute as much as they can to their children's schooling and, along with their neighbors, rebuilt the village school. They buy pens and

The house shelters the rice, the bicycle, the family's few pieces of clothing, stored in a cement water jar, and the sleeping platform where the Panns sleep side by side. All food preparation, eating, and the midday nap take place on the krea *(bamboo table) beside the house.*

notebooks for their children, but they do not expect to be able to afford advanced studies, except perhaps for their son. Despite a current education drive, the country has a fifty-percent dropout rate after primary school, mostly among girls, whose education is considered less important. They have children and work on the looms.

Kampuchea lost seventy-five percent of its teachers. Now not one can be spared, and Chanthan's teacher has her own infant on her hip. A notebook for each student and a few textbooks are all that can be afforded in the classroom. But the children are taught the practical skills they will need in a country which is ninety percent rural. They work in the school's garden, planting rice and vegetables, and between harvests they learn cooking and sewing. The profit from their harvest will be used to buy more schoolbooks.

12:50 The factory's bell calls everyone back to work after lunch. Nou Yong sits at the *krea*, spinning cotton, with Ran beside her, but the moment her head is turned, he falls down off the table. She leaves her work, carries her crying child into the dark shade of the house, and tenderly coaxes him to sleep. Now that she has a son, Nou Yong does not want any more children. Knowing nothing about contraception, she just hopes luck will be on her side.

2:30 Pann Dek goes to the fields to move the tethered bulls to the shade. Leaving her spinning, Nou Young calls to Chanta, back from school, to bring Ran to her in the field when he wakes up, and with a *krama* on her head goes to tend to the vegetables for tomorrow's market.

4:00 As her husband waters the garden for the last time today, Nou Yong returns to the house, grabs yet another clean *krama*, and Chanrath and Ran, and crosses

Tonight's dinner is a simple one, but in two weeks the Panns will celebrate the new lunar year, the most important annual feast. On that day, nothing will be lacking. There will be tomatoes, cucumbers, pineapple, and mint.

the road to the well. Many wells are not used anymore, because thousands of dead bodies were thrown in them during the Pol Pot years. People walk very far to fetch their water from new wells. But this part of the village is new, and mainly formed by young families who had to spread out to find the 0.8 hectares (2 acres) of land the government allows them. Unfortunately, this push farther out into the country also pushes the peasants away from the river, the irrigated fields, the roads, and the markets where money can be earned.

Nou Yong pours a pailful of water on the children's heads, then wipes them with her hand to take the dust off their bodies. Soap is not available, and children often get skin rashes from the lack of hygiene. Ran wriggles away from his mother. She gently pulls him to her and asks him to behave. In the Khmer family, the husband has greater authority, being responsible for housing and feeding the family; but the mother is the teacher of social, ethical, and moral values. The three walk back home in the quiet of a country evening. The factory trucks are gone, the looms are silent.

6:30 Pann Dek brings in the bulls and ties them to the yard's fruit trees for the night. He sits at the *krea*, and Nou Yong serves the evening's fish, rice, cabbage, and green mangoes. With the cat at one corner of the *krea* and the dog underneath, not even the scraps that fall will be wasted. Before going to talk with her relatives, Nou Yong puts her younger children to bed. Pann Dek rolls a second cigarette and joins the men who have gathered across the road to help Nou Yong's brother take down his house and build a stronger one before the rainy season begins.

9:30 Children are sleeping when the curfew is announced, calling the men and women back into their homes. It is the nightly reminder that the country's relatively new peace is still very tenuous.

The Kampucheans

THE NAME: From Sanskrit *Kambuja*, "born of Kambu." Kambu is the mythical forefather of the Khmers.

GEOGRAPHY
Low-lying large central plains rimmed on the northeast and east by highlands and on the north and southwest by low mountain ranges. The Mekong River flows through the eastern part of the country.
Max. altitude: 1,771 m. (5,810 ft.) (Phnom Aural)
Area: 181,035 sq. km. (69,898 sq. mi.)
Density: 37 pers./sq. km. (95 pers./sq. mi.) (1988)
Arable land: 16% (1985)
Forest: 74%. Deforestation: 0.2% (30,000 hectares) per year (1980s)
Climate: Tropical, monsoon climate, with heaviest rainfall in the southwestern mountains. The wet season runs from May to October.

CAPITAL: Phnom Penh, pop. 400,000 (1981 est.)

LANGUAGE: Khmer (official)

RELIGION: A large majority practice Theravada Buddhism; others are Mahayana Buddhist, Taoist, Muslim, or followers of folk religions.

POPULATION: Total—7,869,000 (1988 est.)
Annual growth: 2.5% (1988 est.)
Doubling time: 28 yrs.
Urban: 11% (1985) (est. for year 2000: 14%)
Rural: 89%

AGE GROUPS (1962)
15% under 5 yrs.
44% under 15
53% under 20
27% from 20 to 39
14% from 40 to 59
5% 60 yrs. and over

ETHNIC GROUPS
Khmer: 85%
Chinese, Cham-Malay, Vietnamese, and Thai: 15%

HISTORY
Sometime before 200 B.C., Mon–Khmer people move from present-day Thailand to the Mekong Delta
3rd–6th cent. A.D.: Kingdom of Funan, influenced by Indian culture
6th–8th cent.: Chenla, another Hindu–Buddhist kingdom, succeeds Funan
802: Jayavarman II founds the Khmer kingdom of Kambuja, beginning the Angkor period, during which Khmer civilization fully develops. Temples of Angkor Wat built
1218: Death of Jayavarman VII, who had extended the empire. Decline of the Khmers begins
1863: Becomes French Protectorate
1941: The French install Prince Norodom Sihanouk's government as the legitimate authority
1941–45: Occupation by the Japanese, who leave the French Vichy administration in place
1969: Vietnam War carried to Cambodian territory
1970: Sihanouk deposed by General Lon Nol
1975: Supported by China, Communist Khmer Rouge under Pol Pot gain control of the country and proclaim it the Republic of Democratic Kampuchea. Massive executions; city dwellers are forced into rural areas. An estimated one million die
1979: Vietnamese troops occupy Phnom Penh and the People's Republic of Kampuchea is established under the leadership of Khmer Communist Party forces favorable to Vietnam
1987: Vietnamese government agrees to pull out troops by 1990
Sept. 1989: Vietnam removes its troops; search for a stable government begins

FAMILY
Marital status: no data
Female head of household: no data
Fertility rate: 4.6 (1987)
Teenage births: no data
Births out of wedlock: no data
Contraception: no data
Government's position on family planning: Population growth and fertility are too low to exploit natural resources and defend country's territorial integrity. Targets tripling population. Promotes prenatal care, restricts access to contraception

SOCIAL INDICATORS
Life expectancy: 49 yrs. (1987)
Infant mortality: 133/1,000 births (1987)
Crude birth rate: 43/1,000 pop. (1986)
Crude death rate: 17/1,000

HEALTH
Access to health services: 53% (urban: 80%; rural: 50%) (1987)
Births attended by trained health personnel: no data

HOUSING
Persons per household: 5.0 (1962)
Electricity: 85% without (15% to 20% "sometimes" have electricity) (est.)
Access to safe water: 3% (urban: 10%; rural: 2%) (1980–86)
Source of water (est.)
  Piped inside: 5%
  River: 25%
  Well: 25%
  Other: 35%
  Mixed: 10%
Toilet facilities: no data (majority without)
Construction materials: Bamboo or similar

EDUCATION
Literacy: 75% (male: 85%; female: 65%) (1985)
Gross enrollment ratio (1980–85)
  First level: 95% (completing primary: 50%)
  Second: 16%
  Third: no data (30% of secondary students continue with higher education)
Educational attainment: no data

ECONOMIC ACTIVITY
Economically active population: no data
Agriculture: 80% act. pop.; 60% of GDP
Mines: 0% act. pop.; 0% of GDP
Industry: 3% act. pop.; 5% of GDP
Services: 17% act. pop.; 35% of GDP
Per capita GNP: US$70 (1974)
National currency: riels
Principal resources: Rice, rubber, fish

COMMUNICATIONS
Radio
  Transmitters: 6 (1985)
  Receivers: 110/1,000 pop. (1985)
Television:
  Transmitters: 2 (1985)
  Receivers: 7.1/1,000 pop. (1985)
Newspapers (1984)
  Dailies: 10
  Circulation: no data

Democratic Kampuchea

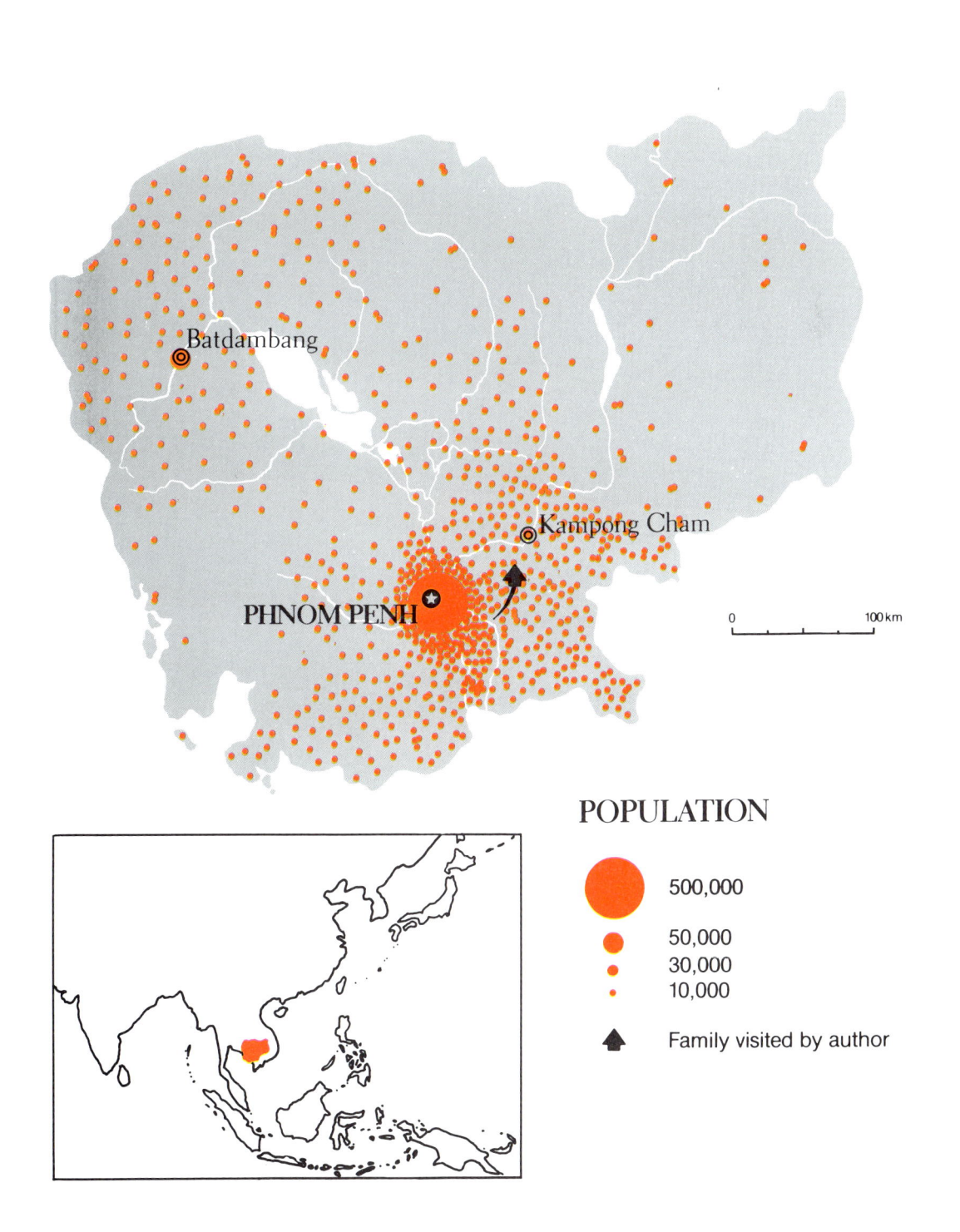

POPULATION

- 500,000
- 50,000
- 30,000
- 10,000

▲ Family visited by author

Lao People's Democratic Republic

Nang Noi's Family

Nang Noi, age 48 (1)
Thao Ky, 17 (2)
Thao Choy, 16 (3)
Nang Tia, 15 (4)
Thao Bounlot, 13 (5)
Nang La, 12 (6)
Nang Hieng, 12 (7)
Nang Xeune, 9 (8)
Thao Bang, 6 (9)

1 sow
3 ducks
6 chickens
2 dogs
1 cat

Ban Nong Pene

MARCH 20

5:30 The sun is already up by the time the sounds of morning filter through the bamboo walls of the houses in Ban Nong Pene Village. Throughout the month of March, there are festivals in every one of the country's thousands of wats (temples), and that means many late nights for the villagers. Last night, there was a marionette show at the local wat, from which Thao Choy, Nang Tia, and Thao Bounlot returned only an hour ago.

But having gone to a festival is no excuse for not getting the day's work done. Last night's dishes have to be washed. As there is no electricity and night falls suddenly, this work is always left for fifteen-year-old Nang Tia when she gets up.

Nang Noi starts the fire and grills some fish, working slowly but steadily as she squats on her kitchen floor. There are plenty of fish in the nearby pond in the forest, but vegetables are scarce this late in the dry season. For the last few weeks there has been only "mango rain." It softens the hot air but is too light and brief to moisten the earth for planting.

Last year Nang Noi's husband died of liver disease. She admits she is worried about how she is going to raise her children, but she does not complain about being alone, without any nearby relatives to help her. "Nothing has changed," she says. "I keep on working in the fields and gardens, cooking and feeding the children and animals." A quiet, introverted woman, who reveals nothing but a sad smile, Nang Noi is familiar with death. Of the thirteen children she carried, two were born dead, and three died from fever, most likely caused by malaria, the foremost cause of child mortality in Laos. Since her last stillbirth, Nang Noi has not felt well herself, but doesn't know to whom to turn. In rural areas especially, medicine is lacking, and trained nurses and doctors are scarce.

While their mother and sister are busy in the kitchen, Thao Bounlot and the twins bundle up the mosquito nets and pile the sleeping mats in one corner of the house's only large room. Then they hang their clothes on a rope stretched across the room.

7:00 Thao Ky leaves on his bicycle for the district secondary school where this year he will finish his first three years. Nang Noi, who does not know how to read and write, counts on her children's education and hopes that they will not be among the many who drop out after primary school. "I am old now," she says, "and I hope that soon my children will be taking care of me." Her twin

In this country, bamboo is used with great ingenuity: for the walls and floors of houses, for fish traps, baskets, cradles, and tables.

girls are the best students; Nang Noi hopes they will be chosen to be members of the government youth organization, the Pioneers. As Pioneers, they would be given priority in education and employment.

On any other day, the twins and their younger sister and brother would be leaving for the village shed that serves as primary school. But today a bride and groom have borrowed all the tables and chairs for their wedding guests. As this is the wedding season, many such school holidays can be expected in March.

9:30 Nang Noi's children, not too stimulated by their barren classroom and ill-equipped teacher, wander from house to house to watch the wedding preparations. Their mother helps a neighbor with the cooking. The youngsters eagerly anticipate the food and music and dancing to come.

Nang Noi is from the t'ai Dam tribe, one of the many minority groups that live in Laos's mountainous north. She came south into the lowlands when she was ten years old to live with an aunt because her own family could not afford to feed her. Nang Noi was her husband's third wife. Both her and her husband's families, along with many other t'ai, fled the country during the 1953 war of independence from French colonial rule. The few t'ai that are left live together in villages like Nang Noi's, and their children are becoming assimilated to the Lao way of life. Largely forested and sparsely populated, Laos is extremely underdeveloped, and most of its limited resources are underexploited. The internal transportation system is inadequate, and the government is encouraging more and more mountain people to come to live in the fertile Mekong Valley, where eight percent of the country's agricultural land is located and where government facilities are more accessible.

12:00 Lunchtime. Nang Tia takes the steaming basket off the fire and turns the rice over on a bamboo plate. She fluffs it to allow it to breathe, then spoons it into the small bamboo baskets that serve as plates. She covers and places them on a low bamboo table, which she pulls out onto the house's open terrace. The steamed rice is "sticky rice," a short-grain variety which the children and their mother roll into rice balls and dip in fish sauce. They sit in a silence as heavy as the heat that hangs so oppressively during this season. The food baskets are emptied in a wink.

When the meal is over, the twins wash the dishes in a pot of water and rinse them in a basin on the windowsill. Nang Noi takes a second batch of rice off the fire, briskly fluffs it and puts it behind a mosquito screen on the kitchen's only shelf, for the evening meal.

The rice fields Nang Noi and her children once worked never produced enough rice for their consumption. Luckily, the Ban Nong Pene Village district, not far from the capital and accessible by road, has been used for pilot agricultural projects. Since 1983, Australian foreign aid has sponsored the production of a wild grass whose seeds may be used as fertilizer. It grows early in the dry sandy earth, and Nang Noi's family can process it, using the same methods as rice. With the profit, they buy rice instead of growing it. Nang Noi also raises chickens, pigs, and green vegetables from her garden to earn cash. Growing the grain fertilizer is still experimental, and she and the other peasants are not totally confident that it will serve as a continued means of income.

1:30 When the food and dishes are put away, Nang Noi and her daughters go out into the shadow of the house to thresh the new crop, as they have threshed

Tonight the family will join the villagers for a local wedding. A Laotian celebration requires lots of good food, and, as this is a marriage of poor people, sharing is a must. Nang Noi has given two of her chickens.

their rice for hundreds of years. Nang Noi takes small bundles of the grass and places them on a stone in a depression in the ground. Hanging from a seesaw-like contraption is a large wooden pole. Nang Tia and her twin sisters stand barefoot on one end of the thresher to bring the heavy pole up above the grain, then they step off, allowing it to drop. With each vibrating thud, the pole separates the grains from the stalk. After it rises, Nang Noi takes the grass and shakes the seeds free. She and her daughters work steadily for two hours. When the sun becomes unbearable, they rest under the house, and then begin again.

3:30 Nang Noi's daughters start making the trips to the well. They take turns carrying the water in two small, tightly woven baskets slung from a pole which balances easily on their shoulders. Her day's work finished, Nang Noi goes to the well in her bathing sarong to rinse off the dust of threshing. There was a time when she could use her own well, but many seasons of drought have dried it up. There is now only one well left for the whole village.

5:00 Under the house, the sow makes terrible grunts, so Nang Tia feeds her one more time. Soon she will have piglets, and Nang Noi is worried about finding food for them.

The chickens slowly gather and find their favorite tree for the night. The birds and crickets sing loudly in the calm countryside and the children get dressed. Everyone will follow the boy groom in parade from his house to his new bride's home. It is said: "Bring a woman inside the house of a man and you bring in the plague, but bring a man into a woman's house and you bring an attic full of rice."

8:00 Everyone comes bearing food, making the traditional *wai* greeting with hands flat and joined, the younger bowing especially low to the elders. A villager who has declared himself disc jockey hangs the tiny speakers and takes charge of the worn cassettes that play everyone's favorite songs. The kerosene lantern that hangs from a tree in the middle of the yard barely lights the few shy dancers. Timid young girls line up on a school bench in the dark, while the boys stand under the house, drinking for courage to approach them. Only then will the festivities really begin. And only then does the sadness leave Nang Noi's face.

The Laotians

THE NAME: Originally Lan Xang, meaning "land of a million elephants." Named Laos by the French, after the Lao people

GEOGRAPHY
Landlocked country dominated by dense jungle and rugged mountains, with a vast drainage basin in the center and alluvial plains in the west along the Mekong River.
Max. altitude: 2,820 m. (9,252 ft.) (Phou Bia)
Area: 236,800 sq. km. (91,429 sq. mi.)
Density: 16 pers./sq. km. (42 pers./sq. mi.)
Arable land: 4% (1985)
Forest: 56%. Deforestation: 1% (130,000 hectares) per year (1980s)
Climate: Sub-equatorial, monsoonal, with a wet season from May to October and a dry season from November to April. High humidity most of the year

CAPITAL: Vientiane, pop. 150,000 (1985)

LANGUAGE: Lao Lum (official), spoken by about half the population. The various ethnic groups speak many other languages.

RELIGION: A large majority practice Theravada Buddhism.
Animism is common among the mountain tribes.

POPULATION: Total—3,874,000 (1988)
Annual growth: 2.5% (89,850) (1985)
Doubling time: 28 yrs.
Urban: 16% (1985) (est. for year 2000: 25%)
Rural: 84%

AGE GROUPS (1985)
17% under 5 yrs.
44% under 15
54% under 20
26% from 20 to 39
13% from 40 to 59
6% 60 yrs. and over

ETHNIC GROUPS
Estimated 68 ethnic groups, divided into three main groups:
Lao Lum (lowland Lao): about half the population
Lao Sung (highland Lao): about one-third
Lao Theung (high-plateau Lao): the rest

HISTORY
8 cent. B.C.: Lao people develop along the Yangtze River in what is now southern China
8 cent. A.D.: The Lao arrive in Laos, displacing indigenous tribes of Mon-Khmer origin
1353: Unification of Laos under King Fa Ngum. His kingdom of Lan Xang covers much of present-day Thailand as well as Laos, and establishes Buddhism as the state religion
1700: Territory splits into three separate kingdoms: Luang Prabang, Vientiane, and Champassak
1778: Siam invades Vientiane; the three kingdoms become colonies of Siam, ruled by Lao kings
1886: With Siam's approval, French appoint vice-consul at Luang Prabang
1893: Franco–Siamese treaty establishes French control over Laos
1939–45: Japanese occupation drives out French
1945: Prince Phetsarath declares Laos an independent monarchy
1946: French rule restored
1947: First constitution
1949: Granted limited autonomy within the French Union. Pathet Lao, a patriotic front which later fights the French in the First Indochina War in the 1950s, is formed
1954: French defeated at Dien Bien Phu (Vietnam). Geneva Conference on Indochina negotiates full independence for Laos
1962: Vietnamese war carried onto Lao territory
1975: Lao People's Democratic Republic proclaimed under leadership of Pathet Lao and Laotian Communist Party

FAMILY
Marital status: no data

Female head of household: no data
Fertility rate: 5.6 (1987)
Teenage births: no data
Births out of wedlock: no data
Contraception: no data
Government's position on family planning: Population growth is too low, but fertility is satisfactory. No formal policy to modify population size. Government does not promote the use of contraceptives; family planning available only to space births for health reasons. Abortion and sterilization permitted only with approval of the Ministry of Health.

SOCIAL INDICATORS
Life expectancy: 52 yrs. (male: 50; female: 53) (1986)
Infant mortality: 111/1,000 births (1987)
Crude birth rate: 42/1,000 pop. (1987)
Crude death rate: 17/1,000

HEALTH
Access to health services: Primary health care available to approximately two-thirds of the population (1984)
Births attended by trained health personnel: 15% (1974)

HOUSING
Persons per household: no data
Electricity: no data. It can be assumed the rural majority is without.
Access to safe water: 21% (urban: 28%; rural: 20%) (1986)
Source of water (1981)
    Piped inside or out: 3%
    River: 40%
    Dug well: 35%
    Spring: 20%
    Other: 2%
Toilet facilities (1983)
    Sanitation facilities: urban: 13%; rural: 4%
Construction materials: no data
    Bamboo and bush materials

EDUCATION
Literacy: 84% (male: 92%; female: 76%) (1985)
Gross enrollment ratio (1984)
    First level: 91% (completing in 1984–85: 14%)
    Second: 19%
    Third: no data
Educational attainment for pop. 15 yrs. + (1985)
    None: no data
    First level: 81%
    Second: 3.5% (first level: 13%)
    Third: under 1%

ECONOMIC ACTIVITY
Economically active population: no data
Agriculture: 75% act. pop.; 62% of GDP
Mines: 0% act. pop.; 0% of GDP
Industry: 6% act. pop.; 8% of GDP
Services: 19% act. pop.; 30% of GDP
Per capita GNP: US$259 (1985)
National currency: kip
Principal resources: Rice, tin

COMMUNICATIONS
Radio
    Transmitters: 18 (1985)
    Receivers: 104/1,000 pop. (1985)
Television
    Transmitters: 2 (1985)
    Receivers: no data
Newspapers (1984)
    Dailies: 3
    Circulation: no data

Lao People's Democratic Republic

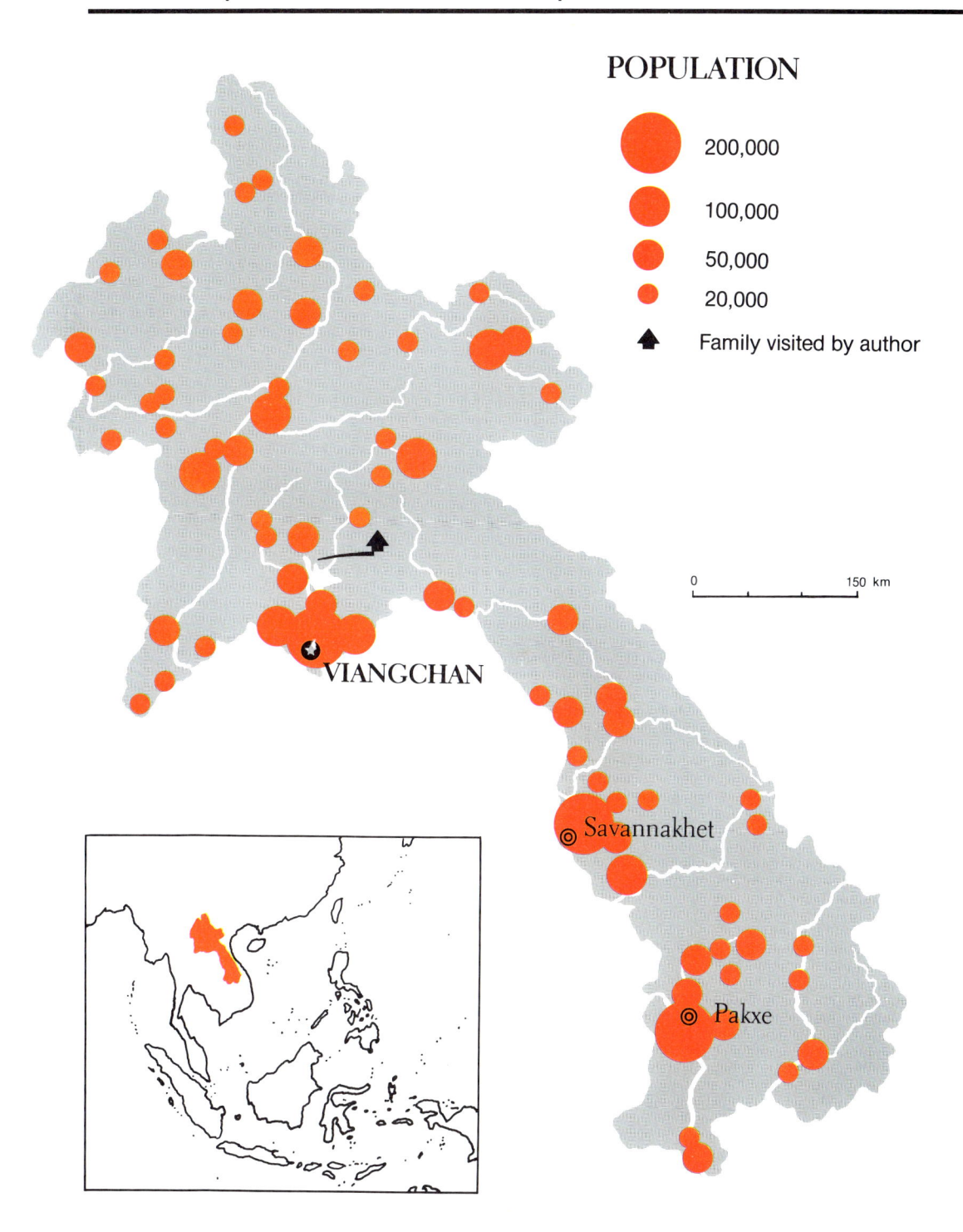

POPULATION

- 200,000
- 100,000
- 50,000
- 20,000
- ▲ Family visited by author

VIANGCHAN

Savannakhet

Pakxe

0   150 km

Malaysia

Sumary's Family

Sumary bin* Sankarjo (Alwi), age 40 (1)
Tuginah binti Kasan, 33 (2)
Salwinah binti Sumary, 14 (3)
Siti Faizah, 12 (4)
Hamimah, 8 (5)
Muhammad Ali bin Sumary, 3 (6)

8 hens and chicks
1 cat

* *Bin* means "son of," and *binti*, "daughter of."

Kampung Jawa Kerling

NOVEMBER 29

5:30 The village mosque broadcasts the *bilal* (Islamic morning prayers) throughout the *kampung*. A few minutes later the boards on the metal bridge over the Kerling River start their clattering as the first motorcycle comes across. The springs of Tuginah's old bed groan as she gets up. She washes, goes to the kitchen to put water on to boil, and comes back to her bedroom to put on her *telekong*, the long white dress in which she prays to Allah. The dress covers even her hands; women must not show any part of their body when praying. Tuginah faces Mecca and bends her head to her prayer carpet.

6:30 Tuginah barely manages to call her sleeping daughters before running outside and throwing up. She is beginning her fifth pregnancy, and on mornings like this she is not sure she agrees with her husband when he says he would like to have twelve children. Feeling a little better, she looks up at the bits of sky that show through the lush garden trees. It has rained during the night, but it seems that the morning will be dry.

Leaving the house to her eldest daughter, Tuginah puts jackfruit bread and hot tea in her bag, climbs on her Honda scooter, and roars down the road from the village. She passes her brother's house and follows the muddy, snaking trail into the rubber plantations. In ten minutes, she reaches a four-acre plot, two and a half acres the family rents, one and a half they own.

Tuginah is a rubber tapper. Before cutting into the bark to release its sap into a little cup which she fixes to the trunk, she carefully checks each of the tall, thin trees. If rainwater from the leaves gets into the trickle of sap, it damages the quality of the rubber; or a cut into a wet tree can destroy the bark and the tree will not be tappable for at least a week. Today there are five hundred trees to be tapped. The five hundred tapped yesterday will be left to rest until tomorrow. The job can be done by one person, but today Tuginah won't be alone. It is the school holidays, so her daughter Siti Faizah will come and help, while Salwinah keeps an eye on her brother Muhammad Ali.

7:00 After his morning prayers and breakfast, Alwi goes to his rubber smokehouse, where his two hired hands are already at work. He prepares a precise mixture of water and acid that will make the rubber sap gel and form slabs in metal trays before being "smoked" dry. Then he opens the doors of the oven, takes out the rubber slabs smoked last night, and stacks them, ready to be picked up by trucks.

Alwi and his wife have worked hard to obtain the little they have. While Tuginah worked the rented land, Alwi employed himself on a big plantation for seven years, saving until he could finally buy their one and a half acres. Then, in a rush of entrepreneurial spirit, he took over the old rubber smokehouse. Nowadays there are few operating smokehouses: trucks pick up the sap and bring it directly to the factories. Still, Alwi's business is doing well, and the ambitious and hardworking couple might just one day be able to own the ten acres of land they wish for.

Alwi's parents died when he was very young, and he was adopted by a poor childless widow. He dreamed that one day he would meet and marry a girl who would inherit lots of land. But that dream never came true. "Rich girls always turn their backs on poor boys," says Alwi. Then he fell in love and was ready to marry, when an old man from the village told him the girl he loved was his own sister, who had also been adopted. It was a few years before Alwi looked at any other girl, and that girl was Tuginah, a poor girl like himself who lived alone with her mother. "She was the only one who understood me," Alwi says. It is to Tuginah that Alwi turns for approval and he entrusts her with his life.

8:00 While their parents work, Salwinah and Siti Faizah clean up the house and prepare the noon meal, with their little brother under their feet. Since he opened his eyes, Muhammad Ali has, as usual, concentrated on annoying his sisters. It works every time. Salwinah turns up the radio to drown him out.

Salwinah is doing the best she can. She does not have much experience in housework. She is usually at boarding school, coming home only during holidays or special weekends. She is waiting for the results of Form 3 exams. Only if she passes can she continue her education. But it will be her choice. Her parents will not force her. Alwi would like at least one of his children to make it to the university, but he is not certain it will be an economic advantage. "There is so much unemployment in the cities that maybe it is better they stay here and work with me," he says.

Hamimah sits passively watching her sisters and then runs out to play. Women's work does not interest her. With her cropped hair and her T-shirt and shorts, she could easily pass for a little boy, which she would prefer. For now, her mother smiles and lets her be, but when Hamimah turns twelve she will have to adopt the Muslim code of dress, covering her head with the veil and her body with a long skirt and blouse. Hamimah will spend this afternoon at religious study, which includes learning Arabic. "This way, she won't spend the days hanging around," says her father. "She will learn something useful."

11:00 Tuginah arrives at the smokehouse with three jerry cans of sap on the back of her Honda. The sap weighs in at fifty-six kilos. One of Alwi's employees takes

Last year Alwi was proud to be able to redo his house's stilt foundation in cement. Now that his family is secure and his house is the way he likes it, Alwi's dream is to make a pilgrimage to Mecca.

a sample to test the quality. Older trees give thicker sap, but moisture and the type of tap cut are also variables. Today, Tuginah's harvest is not of the best quality, and she will be paid accordingly.

2:30 After Tuginah has a simple lunch, she leaves on her Honda with Siti Faizah behind her and Muhammad Ali perched on the bike's front. Salwinah will walk. They are all going to one of the neighboring houses to help prepare the food for the son's wedding. It will take two to three days, but *gotong royong* (community cooperation) is a part of everyone's life. This year, when Alwi re-did the traditional stilt foundation of his wooden house in cement, the whole village helped.

5:30 Tuginah comes back home for a while to wash and pray. Salwinah is trying to wash a crying Muhammad Ali, who protests having a pail of cold water poured over his head.

Alwi finishes putting the rubber into the smokehouse and lights the wood fire to dry the rubber sheets overnight. When the place is clean and the rubber safe behind locked doors, Alwi heads back home. Between the bridge and the smokehouse, on the village green, the young people have started their daily badminton game, *sepak raga*, the traditional Malaysian sport.

In the washroom, the big cement tub is filled and everyone takes turns drawing pails of water to bathe. Tuginah has already washed, prayed, given orders for making dinner, and gone back to the neighbors to help with the wedding preparations for a few more hours.

There is a table in the kitchen where breakfast is sometimes eaten. But the family prefers to eat on the floor, as is traditional.

7:00 Alwi sits at his daughter's desk, the only place where he can open his books. Among the chaos of schoolbooks, he calculates the profits he made for this day.

8:00 The girls have picked up the plates and the tablecloth from the floor, swept the linoleum, and are now laughing at a Malay variety show on TV. By the time his mother returns, Ali has fallen asleep in his father's arms, and he is gently transferred to the floor beside his parents' bed. Alwi loves his son and would like another. The government encourages larger families among the Malays, many of whom would like to have the majority over Chinese and Indian ethnic groups.

Now the rain falls heavily on the corrugated-iron roof, and the thunder roars. Suddenly everything is dark and the TV is off. In a second, Tuginah has lit a nearby candle; power failures are common here. Rubber trees' roots are shallow and not too strong, and nearly every time there is a storm, one falls down on the electrical wires.

The evening is finished in the same soothing light as in the days before electricity. "If you cannot find something to keep busy with at home during the rainy season," Tuginah says, "time passes very slowly and evenings are very boring." Tuginah occupies herself at her manual sewing machine, making new dresses and mending the old ones for her children.

9:30 As everyone settles down for bed, Alwi hears a cracking sound of rifle fire above the pounding rain on the tin roof. "Someone has just killed a snake," he says. "A shot so close means a python was coming for the chickens. Let's hope mine are safe for the night."

The Malaysians

THE NAME: Peninsular Malaysia was called Malaya after the Malay ethnic group until 1963, when it united with Sarawak and Sabah and took the name Malaysia.

GEOGRAPHY

Composed of two non-contiguous regions separated by 643 kilometers (400 miles) of the South China Sea: peninsular Malaysia, which is largely mountainous, with densely forested lowlands on the east; and Sabah and Sarawak, with coastal plains rising to hills.
Max. altitude: 4,100 m. (13,445 ft.) (Mt. Kinabalu)
Area: 330,228 sq. km. (127,502 sq. mi.)
Density: 50 pers./sq. km. (131 pers./sq. mi.)
Arable land: 3% (1985)
Forest: 61%. Deforestation: 1.2% (255,000 hectares) per year (1980s)
CLIMATE: Equatorial tropical climate, characterized by uniformly high temperature, high humidity, and abundant rainfall

CAPITAL: Kuala Lumpur, pop. 937,817 (metropolitan area, pop. 1,250,000) (1980)

LANGUAGE: Bahasa Malaysia (official), a form of Malay. English, Chinese, and Tamil also spoken

RELIGION
Sunni Muslim: 53% (official state religion)
Buddhist: 17%
Chinese religions (Confucianism, Taoism): 12%
Hindu: 7%
Christian: 6%
Other: 5%

POPULATION: Total—16,573,000 (1988)
  Annual growth: 2.6% (401,648) (1985)
  Doubling time: 28 yrs.
  Urban: 38% (1985) (est. for year 2000: 50%)
  Rural: 62%

AGE GROUPS (1984)
14% under 5 yrs.	31% from 20 to 39
38% under 15	14% from 40 to 59
49% under 20	8% 60 yrs. and over

ETHNIC GROUPS (1984)
Malay and other indigenous groups: 60%
Chinese: 31%
Indian: 8%
Other: 1%

HISTORY
The original settlers were Negritos and Proto-Malays and other hunting and gathering tribes
2000 B.C.: Ancestors of the Malays migrate from southern China to what is now peninsular Malaysia. Aboriginal peoples retreat to the highlands
A.D. 100: Malaysia becomes a trading center for China and India, whence Buddhism and Hinduism are introduced
3rd–4th cent.: Many small Hindu–Buddhist states flourish
15th cent.: Islam introduced through Malacca, a major trading center
1511: The Portuguese take Malacca
1641: The Dutch take Malacca
1825: The British take Malacca, making it and Penang part of the Straits Settlements, along with Singapore
1896: Malay states form federation under British advisors
1942–45: Japanese occupation
1948: The Federation of Malaya, a partially independent territory, is formed
Aug. 31, 1957: Federation of Malaya gains independence
1963: Malaya, Sarawak and Sabah, and Singapore unite to form Malaysia, but Singapore soon withdraws

FAMILY
Marital status, for females 10 yrs+ (1980)
  Single: 46.5%
  Married: 47.5%
  Widowed: 5%
  Separated/divorced: 1%
Female head of household: no data
Fertility rate: 3.3% (1987)
Teenage births: 5% / Teenage fertility rate: 26.4/1,000 (1984)
Births out of wedlock: no data
Contraception: 51% (1985)

Government's position on family planning: Reversed policy in 1984; now aims to boost population to 70 million by 2100. Encourages early marriage and large families through benefit programs and tax incentives. Contraceptives legally available, sterilization legal but restricted. Abortion legal only for physical or mental health reasons. Minimum age of marriage is 18 for the non-Muslim population.

SOCIAL INDICATORS
Life expectancy: 68 yrs. (male: 66; female: 70) (1986)
Infant mortality: 24/1,000 births (1987)
Crude birth rate: 29/1,000 pop. (1987)
Crude death rate: 6/1,000

HEALTH
Access to health services: urban: no data; rural: 93% (1979–80)
Births attended by trained health personnel: 87% (1986)

HOUSING
Persons per household: 5.2 (1980)
Electricity: 36% without (1980)
Access to safe water: 69% (urban: 93%; rural: 53%) (1986)
Source of water (1980)
   Piped inside: 47%
   Piped out: 18%
   Without piped water: 35%
Toilet facilities (1980)
   Flush: 26%
   Other: 58%
   None: 16%
Construction Materials
   Wood: 56%
   Cement (concrete/brick): 23%
   Brick and plank: 15%
   Bamboo and other: 6%

EDUCATION
Literacy: 73% (male: 81%; female: 66%) (1985)
Gross enrollment ratio (1985)
   First level: 99% (completing in 1980: 97%)
   Second: 53%
   Third: 6%
Educational attainment for pop. all ages (1970)
   None: 43%
   First level: 30%
   Second: 9%
   Third: no data

ECONOMIC ACTIVITY
Economically active population: 37% (male: 49%; female: 25%) (1980)
Agriculture: 35% act. pop.; 21% of GDP
Mines: 5% act. pop.; 12% of GDP
Industry: 18% act. pop.; 22% of GDP
Services: 42% act. pop.; 45% of GDP
Per capita GNP: US$1,830 (1986)
Population in absolute poverty: urban: 13%; rural: 38% (1977–85)
National currency: ringgit
Principal resources
   Palm oil, natural gas, petroleum, tin, timber. World's leading producer of natural rubber

COMMUNICATIONS
Radio
   Transmitters: 83 (1985)
   Receivers: 424/1,000 pop. (1985)
Television
   Transmitters: 65 (1985)
   Receivers: 101/1,000 pop. (1985)
Newspapers (1984)
   Dailies: 40
   Circulation: 1,670,000 (323/1,000 pop.)

Malaysia

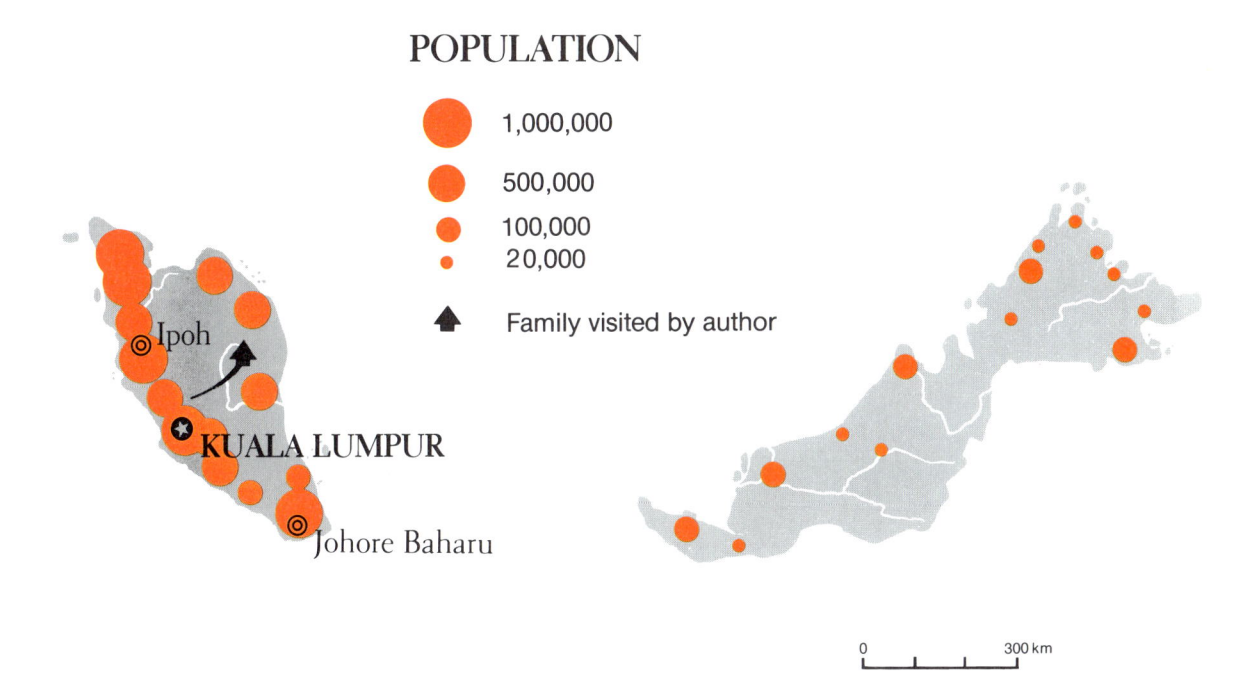

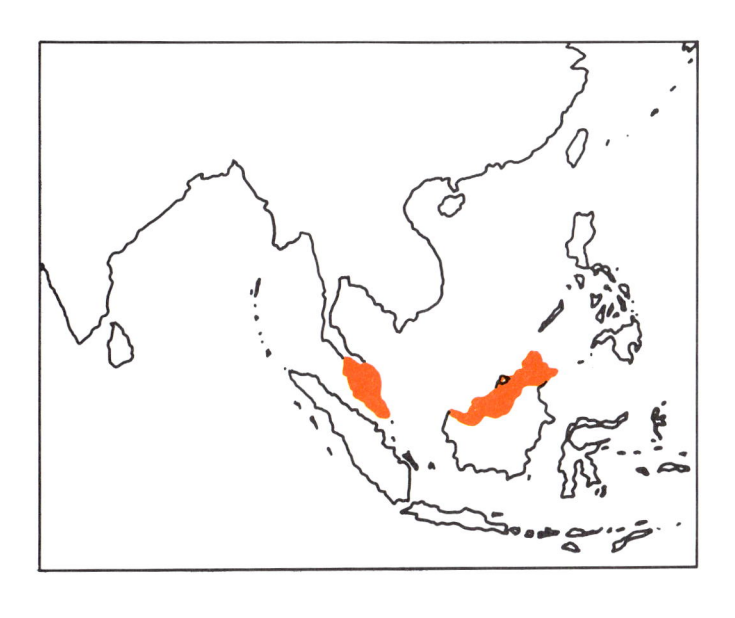

POPULATION

- 1,000,000
- 500,000
- 100,000
- 20,000

▲ Family visited by author

Ipoh

KUALA LUMPUR

Johore Baharu

0   300 km

Union of Myanmar (Burma)

U Maung Gyi's Family*

U Maung Gyi, 42 (1)
Daw Saw Ata, 37 (2)
Ma Myint Myint Yee (My My Ye), 18 (3)
Maung Saw Lwin, 16 (4)
Ma Myint Myint Kyi (My My Ky), 15 (5)
Maung Saw Naing Htun, 12 (6)

3 cows
1 water buffalo

* In Burma, people always refer to each other by the prefix *U* (for men), *Daw* (for women), *Maung* (for young men), or *Ma* (for girls) and the name, unless they are very intimate.

Thandaw

FEBRUARY 14

6:00 The countryside lies still under the morning dew. Out of the fog step saffron-robed monks, earthen jars on their hips, going from house to house to beg their day's food. They beg not because they have to but because people need to give. Buddhists believe this life is but one wedged in among countless past lives and unknown future ones. If one gives in this life, one acquires *kutho* (merits). One's *kan* (destiny) is then strengthened, elevating one's spiritual state and moral balance in order to achieve enlightenment in future lives.

Alongside the two-thousand-year-old wooden footbridge that crosses the dry lake bed, there is already a caravan of bull carts and peasants heading for the busy road to Mandalay. A teahouse at the bridge fills with men having tea before heading for their fields.

In her open-air, thatch-roof kitchen, Daw Saw Ata starts the fire to prepare rice and tea. Before giving to the monks, she first offers some to the Buddha at her home shrine and makes her five daily vows: "I will not kill, I will not steal, I will not engage in sexual misconduct, I will not lie, and I will not cloud the brain with intoxicants."

Daw Saw Ata will always have some food for Buddha and the monks, but at this time of year it will be only a little, as she hardly has enough for her family. The two immense rice baskets, so big they take up nearly a quarter of their home, have been empty since January and will not be filled until the April harvest.

6:30 Out of respect for the elders, the parents have been served before the children. As the first rays of the sun touch the sugar-palm leaves of the village's thatched roofs, U Maung Gyi leaves to tend the fields, bidding his wife goodbye as she sits on the corner of the table in the kitchen with the first of the ten cups of tea she will drink today.

U Maung Gyi has four acres of land in a valley that becomes a large lake during the rainy season. Half is planted with rice; the other half, with greens, tomatoes, and white mustard. U Maung Gyi, his wife, and children plant in September and harvest in April, working with the other families that were apportioned land there by their cooperative. As April nears, the waters can start to rise rapidly and the farmers might have to rush their harvest, losing a significant portion of their crop. Last year's water rose fast and then stayed in the lake for seven months. After giving their quota to the cooperative, the family was four months' short of their year's supply of rice.

My My Ky and her brother Maung Saw Lwin leave for the fields, machetes in hand. Like the rice, the hay from the last harvest is all gone, and they have to weed and collect grasses to feed the cows. First they will stop to water the garden. Their sister My My Ye stays home this morning to do house chores. She does not feel well enough to carry the pails of water from the stream at the center of the dry lake. Once full, the watering cans are heavy, and the children take turns balancing them carefully on their shoulders. They walk up the muddy riverbank without falling, and not a drop is lost. Their feet are used to this: they are large, with toes spread wide like a hand from gripping the mud.

In the cool morning, the village is at its busiest. Children gather animal dung to use for manure; older women sit and talk as they weave baskets or do tapestry or other embroidery. Naing Htun chops up the grass for the cows with a guillotine-like blade that he operates with his foot. The handsome boy is very efficient and pushes the grass under the blade at a stunning speed. Leaning in a neighbor's doorway, a cousin watches him intently, having herself recently lost the tips of the fingers of one hand to the blade.

9:00 As the school bell rings, Naing Htun leaves home with a village friend. The school is close by, in the middle of the village. There are four teachers to educate 250 children in one large room, where there are only benches, not even a blackboard. The parents have decided that, when it is feasible, they will pool their savings to build another school, in hopes of helping their children's performance in the national exams. My My Ye twice failed to pass to secondary studies, and her two siblings never even made it to her standard.

10:30 In front of every kitchen, women and girls are tossing rice on flat bamboo baskets to clean it of stones and debris. While Daw Saw Ata does this, My My Ye cuts cane kindling to start the fire. Mother and daughter squat and rise again and again, each time rewrapping their sarongs around their hips in a motion repeated countless times throughout the day.

11:00 My My Ky and Maung Saw Lwin return sweating from the fields. The noon heat of the dry season is severe. Daw Saw Ata has taken the calves to the cows, leaving My My Ye to scrub the pots and pans with sand to restore their shine. She rinses them at the well and covers them with damp ashes to dry. The ashes will protect the pot the next time it is put on the wood fire, and when washed, it will again look as good as new.

11:30 Morning classes finish, and U Maung Gyi returns from the fields for lunch. Schoolchildren come back with their little embroidered schoolbags on their

The houses of Thandaw sit serene and still behind the village pagoda. Buddhism teaches people to be satisfied with what they have in the world. If life is better for someone else, it is because their kan, *their destiny, dictates it.*

shoulders. U Maung Gyi moves the three cows into the shade and sits down, hungry for his rice, bean soup, and garden vegetables.

Now that the baskets are empty, rice has to be bought, along with oil, soap, sugar, kerosene, and clothing, from the government stores, at subsidized prices but in limited amounts. The family's only source of cash is the sale of the vegetables and the work U Maung Gyi occasionally gets on other people's land.

1:00 U Maung Gyi returns to the fields with his older son, Maung Saw Lwin. The schoolchildren go back for two more hours of lessons, and the women, after a rest in the shade, head for the well near the pagoda, the village Buddhist temple. Daw Saw Ata brings along the dirty dishes, some soap made from pig fat, and a dry sarong. Washing at the well is also visiting time for the women. While they chat, My My Ye draws a tightly woven basket full of water and pours it over her mother. They manage to wash themselves while keeping their bodies covered with a sarong.

2:00 Back home, Daw Saw Ata combs her daughter's hair as they squat on one of the beds in front of a mirror that leans against the wall. They mix their face powder, made from the *tanaka* tree (*Limonia acetisma*) with water. The mixture is clear, but once it dries on the face, it lightens and defines. Fair skin, as close to Buddha's golden complexion as possible, is considered beautiful. The powder also cools and protects them from the sun.

The children return from school yelling boisterously as the heat begins to subside and life returns to the village. A woman peddler stops her bull cart near the house and Daw Saw Ata calls out that she will buy a little sunflower-and-sesame oil.

Naing Htun makes trips to the well to fill the house's four earthen urns. One urn holds the drinking water; another, the cooking water; the other two, the water to wash hands and feet. The waters are never mixed.

4:00   During this scorching season, the vegetables have to be watered two or three times a day. My My Ye is feeling better and goes with My My Ky and a friend to the garden, singing, Naing Htun riding beside them on his water buffalo. Daw Saw Ata smiles; to have had four beautiful healthy children, not to have lost one, is surely good *kan*. "And nature was also good not to have given me one more to feed," she says thankfully.

6:30   The sun has set and a dinner of rice and vegetables is served. Tonight's full moon will help save kerosene. In a corner sits an old car battery that is sometimes used for tiny light bulbs, but only in emergencies.

    Once a week, one of the villagers who has a television and a generator gets videocassettes and lets anyone who pays a small fee gather in his house to watch. But tonight there is a full moon, an auspicious time to make extra vows, and a time for special prayers to Buddha.

9:00   The girls sleep on one bed; the parents on another. The boys sleep in the open kitchen; they don't really need their blankets yet, but keep them near. In the silence of the night, a prayer is said:

> Awgatha, Awgatha . . . In words, deeds, thoughts, in these three things, I have erred. Let me be rid of all anger and passion. I take refuge in Buddha; I take refuge in monkhood; I take refuge in the teachings. To the Buddha I am offering respect. With hands clasped, bowing, adoring, I humble myself in devotion to the Buddha.

The People of Myanmar (Burmese)

THE NAME: As "Burma" represented only one ethnic group, the name was changed in 1989 to Myanmar, an ancient term connoting the general community of ethnic groups in the country.

GEOGRAPHY
Rimmed in the north, east, and west by mountain ranges. Three-fourths of the population live in the central lowlands, which consist of the valleys of the Irrawaddy and Sittang Rivers, and in their river deltas and coastal plains to the south. Max. altitude: 5,881 m. (19,296 ft.) (Hkakabo Razi)
Area: 676,577 sq. km. (261,228 sq. mi.)
Density: 57 pers./sq. km. (148 pers./sq. mi.) (1988)
Arable land: 14% (1985)
Forest: 48%. Deforestation: 0.3% (105,000 hectares) per year (1980s)
Climate: Tropical, greatly influenced by the monsoons of southern Asia. A well-defined rainy season from mid-May to mid-October, a cool dry season from mid-October to mid-February, and a hot dry season from late February to mid-May

CAPITAL: Yangon (Rangoon), pop. 2,458,712 (metropolitan area: pop. 3,000,000) (1983)

LANGUAGE: Burmese (official), related to Tibetan. It is the second tongue to most of the hill peoples, who collectively speak over a hundred indigenous languages.

RELIGION
Buddhist: 89%   Animist: 2%
Christian: 5%   Hindu and other: 0.5%
Muslim: 4%

POPULATION: Total—39,966,000 (1988)
Annual growth: 2.3% (863,512) (1984)
Doubling time: 33 yrs.
Urban: 24% (1985) (est. for year 2000: 28%)
Rural: 76%

AGE GROUPS (1984)
13% under 5 yrs.   29% from 20 to 39
39% under 15   15% from 40 to 59
50% under 20   6% 60 yrs. and over

ETHNIC GROUPS
Burmese: 69% (referred to as Burmans)
Shan: 8.5%
Karen: 6%
Rakhine: 4.5% (referred to as Arakanese)
Mon, Chin, Kachin, and other: 12%

HISTORY
In ancient times, people moved from what is now southwestern China into present-day Burma: the Mon as early as 3000 B.C.; the Pyu at least by the Christian era; and later the Burmans, Chin, Kachin, Karen, Shan, and others
1044: A Burman ruler, Anawratha, assumes the throne at Pagan and unites the region into a single kingdom
1287: A Mongol invasion breaks up the empire
16th cent.: Reunification under the Burman Toungoo Dynasty, which is ended by a Mon rebellion in 1752
1757: Alaungpaya founds the last Burman dynasty
1824, 1852, 1885: Three Anglo–Burmese wars gradually lead to the collapse of the last Burman kingdom and to conquest by the British
1931: A peasant uprising occurs; calls for independence intensify
1937: The British separate Burma from India
1943–45: Japanese occupation
Jan. 4, 1948: Burma gains full independence
1962: Coup led by General Ne Win establishes a Revolutionary Council and creates a socialist system seeking self-reliant development
1973: After eleven years of isolationism, new constitution allows resumption of outside contacts. Socialist Republic of the Union of Burma is proclaimed
1988: Ne Win steps down amid protests against the government, which are suppressed but continue

FAMILY
Marital status, for females 15 yrs. + (1983)
Single: 31%   Divorced: 1%
Married: 59%   Other: 1%
Widowed: 6%
Female head of household: 16% (1983)
Fertility rate: 3.9 (1987)
Teenage births: no data

UNION OF MYANMAR (BURMA)

Births out of wedlock: no data
Contraception: 5% (1985)
Government's position on family planning: Current population growth and fertility rate are satisfactory. No formal policy to modify fertility. Contraceptives are restricted; available at health centers for health reasons only. Abortion and sterilization are illegal except for health reasons.

SOCIAL INDICATORS
Life expectancy: 61 yrs. (1987)
Infant mortality: 71/1,000 births (1987)
Crude birth rate: 31/1,000 pop. (1987)
Crude death rate: 10/1,000

HEALTH
Access to health services: 48% (urban: 100%; rural: 31%) (1980–83)
Births attended by trained health personnel: 97% (1984)

HOUSING
Persons per household: 5.2 (1983)
Electricity: no data. It can be assumed the majority are without access to electricity.
Access to safe water:
   23% (urban: 36%; rural: 21%) (1983–86)
Source of water: no data. It can be assumed the majority do not have piped water.
Toilet facilities (1983)
   Sanitation facilities: 20% (urban: 34%; rural: 15%)
Construction materials (1983)
   Wood and bamboo: 54%
   Bamboo and thatch: 26%
   Wood: 14%
   Pucca (a type of bamboo), semi-pucca, and other: 5%

EDUCATION
Literacy: 77% (male: 82%; female: 71%) (1983)
Gross enrollment ratio (1983)
   First level: 102% (completing in 1980–86: 27%)
   Second: 24%
   Third: no data
Educational attainment for pop. 5 yrs. + (1983)
   None: 48%
   First level: 36%
   Second: 11%
   Third: 4%

ECONOMIC ACTIVITY
Economically active population: 36% (male: 46%; female: 26%) (1983)
Agriculture: 65% act. pop.; 38% of GDP
Mines: 1% act. pop.; 3% of GDP
Industry: 11% act. pop.; 13% of GDP
Services: 23% act. pop.; 46% of GDP
Per capita GNP: US$200 (1986)
Population in absolute poverty: urban: 40%; rural: 40% (1977–84)
National currency: kyat
Principal resources: Coal, tin, lead, zinc, petroleum, natural gas, rice, fish

COMMUNICATIONS
Radio
   Transmitters: 6 (1985)
   Receivers: 81/1,000 pop. (1985)
Television
   Transmitters: 2 (1985)
   Receivers: 0.5/1,000 pop. (1985)
Newspapers (1984)
   Dailies: 7
   Circulation: 511,000 (14/1,000 pop.)

Union of Myanmar (Burma)

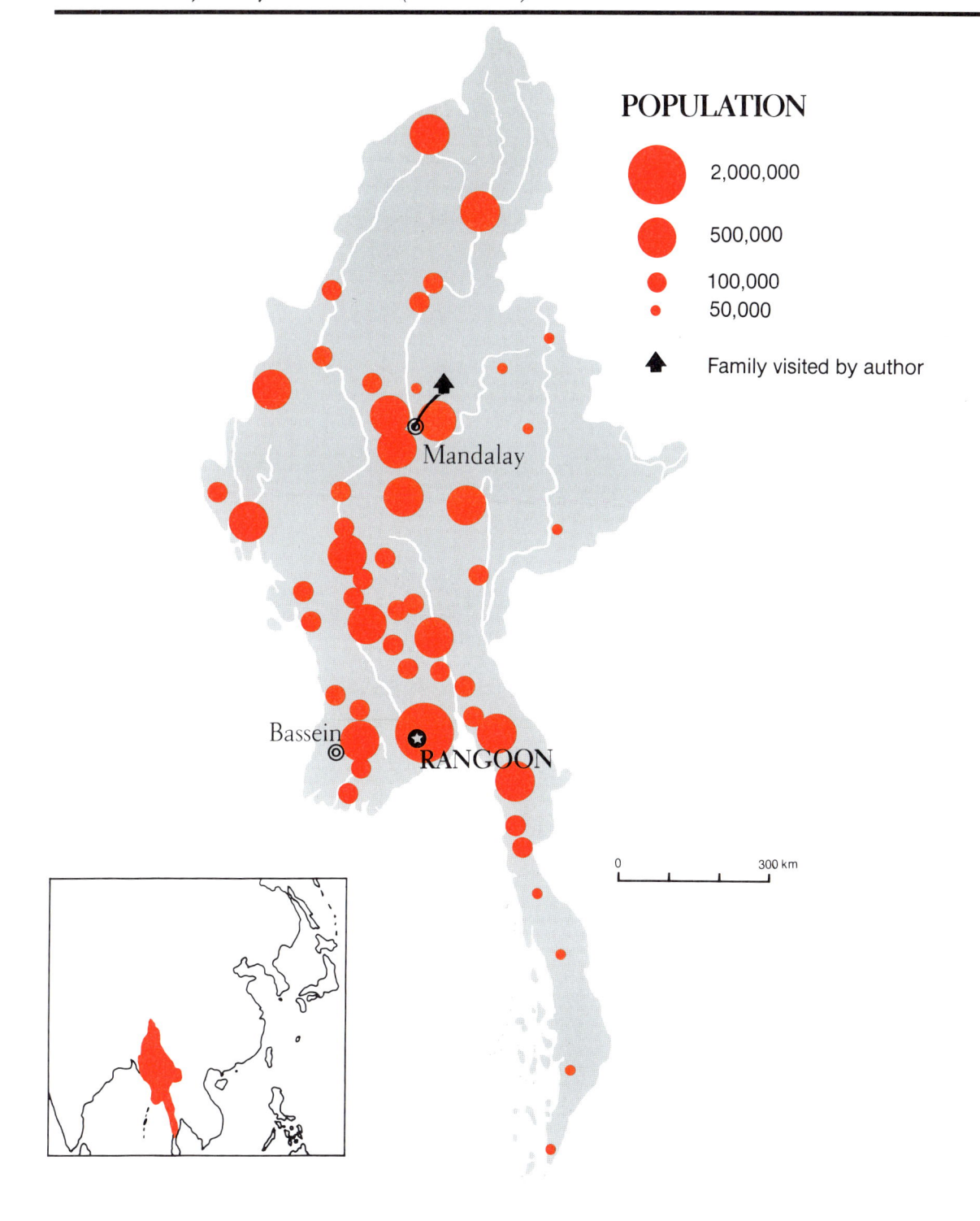

POPULATION

- 2,000,000
- 500,000
- 100,000
- 50,000
- ▲ Family visited by author

Mandalay

Bassein

RANGOON

0　300 km

Philippines

The Tigulo Family

Andres Tigulo, 44 (1)
Miguela Glang Tigulo, 37 (absent)
Enrico, 19 (absent)
Pablito, 17 (2)
Lionara, 15 (3)
Dolores, 12 (4)
Nolilon, 9 (5)
Jimmy, 5 (6)

Maria Lopez Tigulo, 75 (7)
Liwayway Tigulo (aunt), 51 (8)

1 water buffalo
1 sow and piglets
10 hens and chicks
1 turkey
1 dog

Santa Rita

JANUARY 13

3:00   Andres Tigulo can no longer ignore the scratching sounds of the rat feasting on the sack of planting rice in the room where his daughters Lionara and Dolores are sleeping. To save the harvest, he scrambles after the pesty rodent, yelling. The duck farmer from across the road hears the clamor and, knowing that his friend Andres is now awake, comes over with a drink of hot ginger tea. Andres gathers dry branches and rice stalks and starts a fire. One by one his family, and then another neighbor, come and squat beside the two men in the warmth of the fire. This is the cold season, but today the sky is clear and the wind strong, and by midday the sun will be scorching.

4:00   Liwayway, Andres's sister, who has come from Manila to visit their mother, warms herself briefly and heads for the lean-to kitchen shed to start the wood fire and prepare breakfast. She is substituting for Miguela, Andres's wife, who has taken advantage of her sister-in-law's visit to go with her son Enrico to help her aging father on his farm in a nearby district.

5:00   The dark night sky is giving way to blue as the family remains chatting before the warmth of the fire, waiting for the day to begin. A motorbike stops across the rough rural road, to pick up eggs from three duck farmers and bring them to the market. After its departure, the duck boys leave their houses with their two thousand quacking charges. The ducks race into the flooded rice fields to feed on snails and water insects. Raising ducks and selling their eggs is more profitable than tenant farming, and seeing his neighbors' success, Andres has decided to buy twenty ducklings. This morning Pablito will build an enclosure for their new venture.

6:30   The orange sun spills into the water-covered fields, but everyone still moves very slowly. While her grandchildren wash at her splattering tap, Maria Lopez, still very active at seventy-five, sweeps the courtyard between her house and her son's and cleans the pigpen.

On bicycle, one after the other, come the bread boy, the fish boy, the empty-bottle buyer, and the *cobrador*, the lottery man. Twice a day, he takes a few centavos from each peasant, leaving them for twelve hours to dream of what they would do with seven hundred pesos. Aunty Liwayway buys bread to accompany the family's meager breakfast of seasoned rice and duck eggs.

7:30 Pablito leaves for high school; Dolores and Nolilon for primary school. It is impossible for the children to get to school without getting their feet wet. They must cross the river, walk in tricky balance on the rice fields' narrow ridges, and then wade through three more irrigation canals before they even get to the road to school. Each trip is a splashy adventure, but twenty minutes later they will be sitting on wooden benches at long tables inside the rough cement rooms. The front wall of the classroom is covered with optimistic adages written in English, a language they learn but never speak.

Lionara starts the laundry in a basin that she puts on the ground in the yard. The teenager often misses school, as her parents need her help, and expect it of a girl more than of a boy. The chicks rummage about, looking for bits of rice; the sow grunts while her piglets nurse; the hens and the turkey cluck softly as they sit on their eggs. Andres listens to the news on his neighbors' borrowed radio before he goes to the fields. Like all Philippine peasants, he hopes that one day the tinny voice will announce, at last, that "the land reform has begun." But the only news this morning is of a possible typhoon bringing winds up to 190 kilometers an hour. Nearly every year, Andres must rebuild his house. In 1985 the entire house was hurled thirty yards into the rice fields. Andres dreams of a cement home that could withstand the storms.

8:00 Andres goes to the fields, machete in hand, his ever-faithful dog and his young son Jimmy following behind him. Andres's faith in the justice of God is tested every time he sets foot in these fields. His life has never been easy, and he says he does not see any signs of change ahead. He rents the land he now works with his sons. It is the same land his father and he worked together. "I make the same amount of money my father did more than twenty years ago. It wasn't enough then and it is worth even less now," he says.

He can never set aside any savings, not even enough to tide the family over a bad harvest, and the last rice harvest was a disaster. Andres lost nearly three-quarters of it to the strong winds. Now, a month later, the quarter he managed to rescue is all gone, to pay back the loan he had to get to plant that harvest in the first place. It is a never-ending cycle. The Tigulos will survive until the next harvest only by borrowing again from the *capitalistas*, middlemen hired by the landowners. "The owners live richly in the capital and play politics," say the peasants. "We never see them."

Last week Andres borrowed five thousand pesos from his owner's middleman to pay for seeds and insecticides for the new planting. Four months from now, at harvest, he will have to pay back the whole amount plus fifty percent interest. Andres is always a year behind in his payments.

This morning, the father and his five-year-old "helper" repair some *pi-*

Forty years ago, the rice fields were covered with fruit trees. The landowners decided that rice would be more profitable and had the peasants cut down every one, leaving an endless flat expanse.

lalil, ridges between the rice beds, that have been damaged by the plow. In about twenty-five days Andres should be ready for the planting. Although other parts of the province have irrigation systems, the program to build more stopped before it got to the fields Andres works. He taps into the nearby canal and thereby manages a second harvest during the dry season.

12:00 Andres and Jimmy wash the mud off their hands at the water tap, as the schoolchildren appear. Their favorite aunt waits for them with rice and eggs, which they gulp down while gossiping excitedly.

1:00 The children dash back to school, and Andres leaves for a meeting with DIWA, a farmers' organization, which is very important in his life. It was only through their collective efforts in the organization that the peasants finally succeeded in getting some access to low-interest loans, and at least reducing the

PHILIPPINES

This is the table where Miguela has given birth to all her children. Nueva Ecija, one of the central provinces of Luzon Island, is known as the food basket of the Philippines, but sixty-five percent of the local children are malnourished.

grip of the high-interest *capitalistas*. With one of these loans, Andres bought his water buffalo to prepare the rice fields for planting. This afternoon, the peasants spend a long time talking politics, and briefly discuss income-generating projects. To diversify farming is one idea: ducks, chickens, pigs, mushrooms, and fish ponds are all possibilities, but the peasants don't have the money to make the initial investments.

3:30 Jimmy dumps his few old toys out of a small plastic bag, while his sister Lionara rests near him. Aunty Liwayway is with her mother. The arrival of schoolchildren brings life to the small cane house. Births are highly celebrated events in the Philippines, but the Tigulo couple know they can't afford any more children. Since he fell in love with fifteen-year-old Miguela, Andres has struggled to feed her and the six children, and has watched one child die.

4:00 Andres goes to the field to bring the water buffalo closer to the house for the night. Three young neighbors sit on the riverbank cleaning a dozen rice-field rats they have caught for their family meal. The rice fields also provide peasants with frogs and snakes, and the river gives them crabs. At the market, cats and dogs can be bought cheaply when the peasants feel they must have meat. "But I would never eat *my* dog," says Andres fondly.

5:00 The *cobrador* is back with his list of results. Someone down the road has won a few pesos. Everyone gathers again to buy their new tickets. They stay there talking, and the sun is setting when the lottery man rides off on his bicycle.

The air becomes chilled, and everyone dons a sweater. After a dinner of rice and duck eggs flavored with tomatoes, the neighboring men come over to chat, as their women tidy up the kitchens and put the younger children to sleep. One man complains, "We have even less to give our children than our fathers had. What will our children have to give theirs?" Politics is always the favorite and most emotionally charged topic of conversation. Once again, they speak of land reform. "If Aquino does not give us ownership of the land we have been working for generations, we will take up arms." The province of Nueva Ecija has been the cradle of all Philippine revolutions since Spanish colonization. The voices of the farmers reveal that nothing has changed.

Nolilon goes to his grandmother's, and the girls lie down on one of the house's two beds. Pablito stays and listens to the elders. It won't be long before these problems are his.

Philippines

The Balthazar Family

Pablo R. Balthazar, Jr. (Junior), age 34 (1)
Virginia M. Balthazar (Nene), 32 (2)
Jessie, 15 (3)
Jenifer (Daday), 13 (4)
Josephine (Popop), 9 (5)
Gerry, 7 (6)

1 cat and 6 kittens

Manila

JANUARY 28

5:15   The first of the hundred radios that will play all day long blares in the small alley of the San Andres Bukid slum. Nine-year-old Popop comes out from under the mosquito net where she sleeps with her parents and her brother Gerry. She goes to the door to take care of her morning needs in the can that serves as a night pot. Daday is next. She comes down the ladder from the shelf where she sleeps with her brother. In this tiny space (2 × 2 × 1 yard high), the family stores all their belongings, and only a child can lie down.

There is not much more space for the rest of the family. Pablo cannot even stretch his legs on the 2 × 4 yard plywood floor of the family's only room, nor can he stand up. And this house is bigger than their old one. In 1984, a fire destroyed three hundred houses in their dilapidated neighborhood. The government provided the slum dwellers with materials to rebuild their homes, so Pablo was able to give his family a little more space.

6:00   Daday reaches for her school uniform, which hangs from a nail. She props open the door with a paint can full of rocks, and goes to empty the night pot in the public toilet.

Minutes later, Nene gives each of her children a few pesos to buy their breakfast at a neighbor's home store. Her own kitchen is such a tiny corner that Nene is not at all inspired to cook. The children come back with a plate of *soporado* (rice with chocolate, sugar, and milk).

6:30   After Daday finishes her plate, she is off to school. The day has begun for everyone except Pablo, who, in the midst of all this action, is still snoring. He drives a truck at night for five fish salesmen, taking them to the port to get the fresh catch, but he has only been replacing a sick driver. He has heard the man is getting better, so he will soon be out of work again. He is not the type to hang around the house, though, and is always trying to find something to do. The odds are against Pablo; forty percent of the country's population are unemployed. He is considering renting a rickshaw-taxi again to pedal around the streets, but he would be competing with all the others, and he would need to get at least twenty-five fares a day just to pay for the rickshaw.

Nene tries to bring a few pesos home. She will spend all day washing the clothes of the more well-to-do, in pails of water purchased from a neighbor who can afford to have it piped in.

Nene has bought enough water to fill her buckets, and squats in the alley, leaving just enough space for her neighbors to get by. Daytime life in the slum is completely public, as few people stay in their cramped houses.

118   PHILIPPINES

7:00 Popop is also off to work. Her mother gives all the children two pesos a day, but Popop has decided she can earn some herself, as a scavenger. She and her two friends, Christine and Veronique, disappear in the maze of narrow lanes.

They walk the streets with their plastic bags, going from garbage pile to garbage pile, rooting with a stick and picking up all the cardboard, plastic, and glass they can find. A nonprofit group organized to aid the street children was concerned about the children digging in the garbage, and tried to discourage the scavengers. But, as they couldn't offer the children money, they couldn't get them to stop; the best they could do was suggest they use gloves and sticks, and teach them what to look for. Two pesos a day is the girls' average income. They could make more if they went out at night, when most people put out their garbage, but their mothers won't let them. The only time Popop scavenges after dark is when her mother goes with her.

10:00 The girl scavengers are back to bathe and get ready for school. Twenty centavos' worth of water in a plastic basin in the middle of the alleyway will be enough. Gerry is happy to sit there naked, but Popop, getting older and reserved, keeps her panties on.

Nene goes to the kitchen corner to start cooking rice and the fish Pablo has brought back from the market. Feeding her family costs Nene between twenty and thirty pesos a day. Washing clothes brings her only about nine pe-

From the main streets of Manila it is easy to miss the hundreds of alleyways that open as tiny slits between the shops and lead deep into shantytowns. There are 415 slums in Manila. Some are not so well hidden. Seventy percent of this city live below the poverty line and twenty-five percent of the country's urban dwellers live in the same conditions as the Balthazar family, or worse.

A crowded lunch in the family's only room, where Pablo cannot even stand up. Everyone has to step around the house's seven cats. They are always in the way, but nobody puts them out. They keep the rats away.

sos a day, and if Pablo is not working, it is impossible to have enough food. There is just too much to pay, including cooking gas, water, bills sent by the owner whose electrical wires they have tapped into their shack, and finally the one and a half pesos they have to pay every time they use the toilet and shower facilities.

Popop gets a letter from the organization for street children. Because she is a scavenger, Popop is part of their sponsorship program. A family from western Canada pays for her school registration, schoolbooks, and uniform. The organization makes sure that the money is spent properly.

All the schoolchildren have gone except Jessie, who had to quit; his parents can't pay the hundred pesos for his school fees. In a voice that lacks conviction, Jessie says that next year his parents will have the money. With the money he earned from odd jobs, he bought himself seven chickens to raise and sell. They live in a cage hidden under the house. With proud care, Jessie takes them out every two hours for fresh air, a bath, and food.

11:00 Nene is back on the street doing laundry with Daday's help. It's exam week, and Daday is so scared about whether she will pass that she does not want to return to school this afternoon. Her mother lets her stay home. She will probably not have the money to pay tuition for further study, and is happy to have a helping hand.

3:30 Pablo gets up, eats a plate of rice and fish, and is off to help a friend repair his truck. Nene is once again slapping her client's wet clothes with her wooden stick. The wash never ends. Today she is washing for a special client and friend, a woman who has more money than anyone else in the alley. She just came back from working in a nightclub in Japan and now she waits for her papers to go to the United States to marry an American soldier. Her house has a television, a VCR, and a stereo. Nene often visits. If her friend leaves, she will lose a good companion, the video, and a sure income.

5:00 The flies swarm, attracted by the dirty water running down the open gutter. The alleyway loses its daytime calm as those who have been working and those looking for work return. In front of Nene's house there is always action. Meli, who lives across the way, put screened-in shelves in her window and opened a tiny shop—nothing much, only items for a quarter-peso. Women have gathered on Meli's bench to chat and laugh with passersby, and gossip about them when they have gone. A woman goes by and they fall silent; this morning, one of her children died of leukemia.

But mostly they talk about next week's referendum, when they will all have to vote yes or no to the new constitution. Some local leaders have told the women to vote against it. "This government will bring Communism," they say, using a word that alarms them all. The discussion is heated. No one agrees. Nene has been convinced to vote no, but Pablo thinks that life could not be worse than it has been for the last twenty years, and says he will vote yes.

5:30 Pablo wants to wash, but he can't afford a shower. He buys a pail of water and bathes in the house's small entryway, the only space where he can stand.

Nene tells her husband to prepare salad and dress their youngest child. Pablo never contradicts his wife. When he works for the fish salesman, she is the one who collects his salary, and gives him what he needs for his cigarettes and snacks. The couple do not spend wantonly. They allow themselves five cigarettes a day each. "My man, thank God, doesn't drink like many do," says Nene.

Pablo enjoys washing his son. Since they often die young, little children are precious here. Pablo and Nene have lost three children already, and this little boy nearly died on the operating table. They are extremely protective of him, fearful of more anguish. Like his wife, Pablo is doing all he can to keep Gerry a baby as long as possible, even if he is at an age when many children have started to help provide for their family.

9:00 Nene spreads a sheet on the wooden floor, hangs a mosquito net, and lays Gerry down inside it for the night. The rest of the family drift around in the alleyway, waiting for their bedtime. The children play; Nene chats, and then Pablo leaves his family for his night's work. He will not know until later if he will be working tomorrow.

PHILIPPINES

The Filipino

THE NAME: Named in honor of Philip II of Spain, when he was heir apparent

GEOGRAPHY:
Archipelago composed of 7,100 compactly grouped islands of volcanic origin, 2,773 of which are named. There are sixteen main islands; the two largest, Luzon and Mindanao, make up 66% of the territory. The islands are characterized by a rugged and irregular coastline; narrow coastal lowlands, which give way to heavily forested mountain ranges; and interior plains of great fertility.
Max. altitude: 2,954 m. (9,692 ft.) (Mt. Apo)
Area: 300,000 sq. km. (115,831 sq. mi.)
Density: 194 pers./sq. km. (496 pers./sq. mi.) (1988)
Arable land: 15% (1985)
Forest: 38%. Deforestation: 1% (92,000 hectares) per year (1980s)
Climate: Tropical, with a slight variation in annual average temperature. Two seasons: dry, generally from December to May, although the period is shorter in the east; and wet the rest of the year. Typhoons often strike from June through December.

CAPITAL: Manila, pop. 1,630,485 (metropolitan area, pop. 6,800,000) (1980)

LANGUAGE: Pilipino (official), a standardized form of Tagalog
English is widely spoken and is the language of government.
An estimated seventy other languages and dialects

RELIGION
Catholic: 84%
Aglipayan (Philippine Independent Church): 4%
Muslim: 4%
Protestant: 3%
Buddhist and other: 3%

POPULATION: Total—59,456,000 (1988)
Annual growth: 2.5% (1,378,000) (1985)
Doubling time: 25 yrs.
Urban: 40% (1985) (est. for year 2000: 49%)
Rural: 60%

AGE GROUPS (1984)
14% under 5 yrs.
39% under 15
50% under 20
32% from 20 to 39
13% from 40 to 59
5% 60 yrs. and over

ETHNIC GROUPS
Filipino: 95.5% (Hispanicized, of Malay origin)
Other: 4.5% (Igorot groups, Small Negrito, Dumagat, Chinese)

HISTORY
Peoples from the Asian mainland arrive in ancient times. Trade with India and China from the tenth century onward influences society and culture
15th cent.: Islam introduced through Brunei
1521: Magellan, at the head of a Spanish expedition, claims the Philippines for Spain. Conversion to Catholicism begins. Opening of Manila to foreign trade leads to the growth of commercial agriculture; a new landholding class emerges, but there is widespread impoverishment
1896: Revolt for independence quelled by the Spanish
June 12, 1898: Declaration of Independence
1899: Post-war treaty between U.S.A. and Spain cedes the country to U.S.A. After two years of conflict, the Philippines is forced to accept rule by the U.S.A., which proclaims its intention to prepare the Filipinos for self-government
1930: Communist Party established. Organization of peasant unions lays foundation for later nationalist resistance
1942–45: Japanese occupation
1946: Republic of Philippines is proclaimed. In later agreement, U.S.A. retains ninety-nine-year lease on military bases
1949: Rebellion by the Communist-led Hukbalahap organization (established in 1942) in response to social injustices and the need for land reform. Suppression of rebellion followed by attempts at reform under President Magsaysay
1959: In response to increasing Philippine protest, the U.S.A. dismantles several military bases and reduces ninety-nine-year lease to 25 years, to begin in 1967

PHILIPPINES

1965: Ferdinand Marcos elected president
1972: Plagued by a failing economy, political opposition, and diminishing power, Marcos stages an opposition attack on Defense Minister Enrile and establishes martial law
1983: Benigno Aquino, former senator and opposition leader, assassinated upon his return to Manila
1986: Corazón Aquino, widow of Benigno, assumes presidency after Marcos's claim of an election victory leads to revolt. Marcos flees to Hawaii
1987: New constitution approved by referendum vote

FAMILY
Marital status, for females 15 yrs. + (1981)
  Single: 34%
  Married: 59%
  Widowed: 6%
  Divorced: 0.5%
Female head of household: no data
Fertility rate: 4.5 (1986)
Teenage births: 8% (1982) / Teenage fertility rate: 45.8/1,000 (1980)
Births out of wedlock: 6.1% (1982)
Contraception: 44% (1985)
Government's position on family planning: Population growth and fertility are too high. Targets a fertility rate of 3.7 by 1993. Promotes population education and access to family planning

SOCIAL INDICATORS
Life expectancy: 63 yrs. (male: 61; female: 65) (1986)
Infant mortality: 46/1,000 births (1987)
Crude birth rate: 33/1,000 pop. (1987)
Crude death rate: 8/1,000

HEALTH
  Access to health services: no data
  Births attended by trained health personnel: 57% (1983)

HOUSING
Persons per household: 5.9 (1975)
Electricity: 62% without (1981)
Access to safe water: 66% (urban: 83%; rural: 54%) (1987)
Source of water (1980)
  Piped inside or out: 24%
  Developed springs: 11%
  Artesian well: 8%
  Open wells, rainwater cisterns, lakes, rivers and streams: 57%

Toilet facilities (1985)
  Adequate sanitary facilities: 56.5%
Construction materials
  Wood, plywood: 34%
  Bamboo, sawali: 24%
  Mixed tile, concrete, brick, stone, and wood: 17%
  Cogon, nipa (woven grass and palm leaves): 12%
  Tile, concrete, brick, stone: 5%
  Makeshift, salvaged materials: 1%
  Galvanized iron, aluminum: 1%
  Asbestos: 1%
  Other: 3%

EDUCATION
Literacy: 85% (male: 85%; female: 85%) (1985)
Gross enrollment ratio (1985)
  First level: 106% (completing in 1980–86: 64%)
  Second: 65%
  Third: 38%
Educational attainment for pop. 25 yrs. + (1980)
  None: 12%
  First level: 31%
  Second: 19%
  Third: 15%

ECONOMIC ACTIVITY
Economically active population: 63% (male: 80%; female: 48%) (1987)
Agriculture: 45% act. pop.; 25% of GDP
Mines: 3% act. pop.; 3% of GDP
Industry: 18% act. pop.; 25% of GDP
Services: 34% act. pop.; 47% of GDP
Per capita GNP: US$560 (1986)
Population in absolute poverty: urban: 50%; rural: 64% (1977–86)
National currency: pesos
Principal resources: Rice, fish, timber

COMMUNICATIONS
Radio
  Transmitters: 295 (1981)
  Receivers: 65/1,000 pop. (1985)
Television
  Transmitters: 43 (1981)
  Receivers: 28/1,000 pop. (1985)
Newspapers (1984)
  Dailies: 22
  Circulation: 2,022,000 (for 21 dailies)

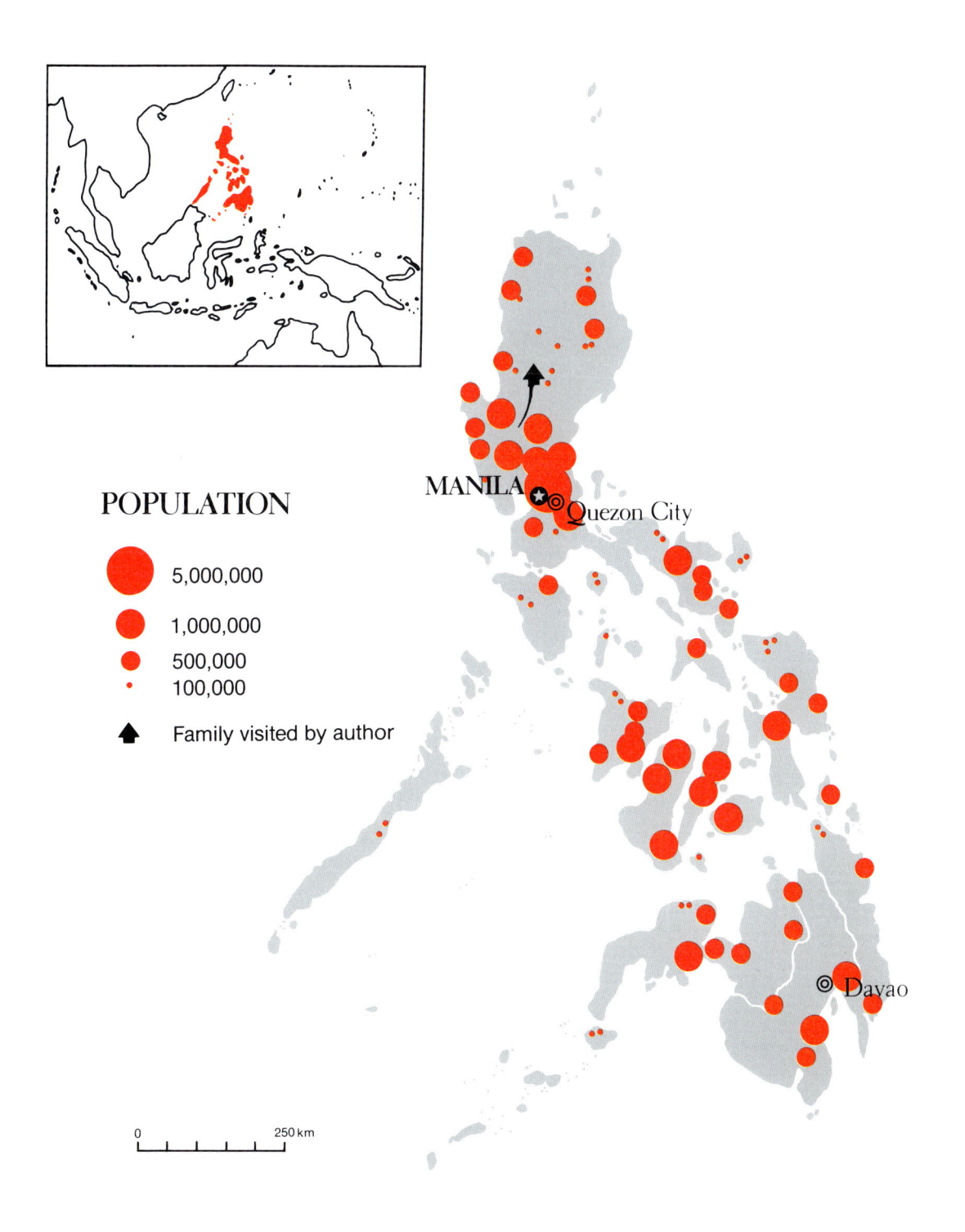

Philippines

POPULATION

- 5,000,000
- 1,000,000
- 500,000
- 100,000

▲ Family visited by author

MANILA
Quezon City
Davao

0   250 km

Singapore

The Tay Family

Tay Ah Soon (Stewart*), age 42 (1)
Seow Boon Keng (Jeannette), 41 (2)
Tay Tien Hee, 14 (3)
Tay Weu Cheng, 13 (4)
Tay Tien Whui, 5 (5)
Tay Eng Kiat, 65 (6)

* Some Singaporeans raised under British influence were given English names.

Singapore

DECEMBER 13

7:00 If one morning Jeannette decided against getting up at this exact time, her five-year-old son Tay Tien Whui would make sure she did. The young man needs his milk bottle. He is a little too old for such a caprice, but that is the only way he will drink milk, and milk is what his mother wants him to drink. With the speed of every employed mother in the world, Jeannette prepares the bottle, gives it to her son, who is still in bed, puts on the electric kettle for coffee, and takes a shower heated by a gas burner. She puts a light touch of pink on her cheeks and combs her hair; gives her older children orders for the day, so that the house will function during her absence; and, at last, puts on her nurse's uniform.

Jeannette is a midwife, but as women in Singapore now have their babies in hospitals, she mainly follows up on mothers who have returned home after giving birth. Today, Saturday, she works a half day and will do the week's shopping during the afternoon. Her husband, Stewart, has stayed in bed, preferring to sleep until the last minute. His aging father, Tay Eng Kiat, reads the newspaper in the living room, while thirteen-year-old Tay Weu Cheng helps tidy up the house. This is the morning routine, and only the most necessary words are spoken.

8:00 Bringing their youngest child to drop off at his sitter, the couple leave their apartment and walk down the fourth-floor balcony to the elevator. This morning a chain saw cutting branches in the trees of the nearby park adds to the clamor of cars and motorcycles leaving the parking lot. In this appearance-conscious city, the Ministry of Parks and Recreation is always tending the greenery. Most of Singapore's trees have been imported, because the native vegetation consists largely of scrub trees and low bushes.

In the intense drive for development since independence, every aspect of life in this city-state is organized as well as the parks. This morning Stewart will attend a residence committee meeting. The high-rise apartment complexes, all similar to the one the Tay family live in, are organized in ten-to-fifteen-block sections, and each has a committee to attend to its needs and complaints.

Singapore has changed under Stewart and Jeannette's feet. They were both raised in what were then rural *kampungs*, tightly clustered groups of wooden houses built on stilts. Today, the spot where their *kampung* stood is only a memory under concrete. The Tays had no choice but to move into a government-subsidized high-rise, along with three-quarters of all Singaporeans.

Jeannette misses the intimate and traditional life of the *kampung*, but she and Stewart are happy with the space their two-bedroom apartment offers them. Less than three years ago, they lived in an identical building, with only one bedroom. They bought this apartment with their gains from selling the first apartment and with funds borrowed from Stewart's retirement money through the Central Provident Fund. Every worker and employer must contribute to the Central Provident Fund, a compulsory savings plan that takes the place of pension or insurance programs. One can withdraw funds for medical needs, housing, or investment, and make a total withdrawal at the age of fifty-five, or if one is unable to work or is emigrating.

Grandfather leaves a few minutes after his son. Partially retired, he supervises the cleaning of one of the big modern buildings on Orchard Road, the downtown main street. The older man cannot stop working, and when he is through with his job, he helps his daughter-in-law around the house.

Tay Tien Hee is still sleeping, and Tay Weu Cheng goes back to bed with a pile of magazines. The teenagers need their sleep, and it is the school holidays.

10:00 The telephone rings. Tay Weu Cheng lies down on the living-room couch with a cushion between her arms and, in the true teenage spirit, begins a long telephone conversation with a girlfriend. The two girls easily select the best word for each thought from their languages: Mandarin, English, and Teochew, a Chinese dialect from Shantou, the home of their ancestors in China. In the complicated educational system necessary in multicultural Singapore, they learn English and Chinese at school. If they were Indian, it would be English and Tamil; if Malay, English and Malay.

11:00 Tay Tien Hee has had breakfast and, hardly saying a word to his sister, comes to sit in the living room to watch a kung-fu video rented for the weekend. Brother and sister spend the next three hours in front of the television. Tay Tien Hee and Tay Weu Cheng take a break only to go get some chicken fried rice for lunch down at the nearby take-out shop.

3:00 Jeannette shops for a present for a nephew's birthday and also buys food for the celebration. With the destruction of the *kampung*, families are often scattered across many different parts of the city. But the importance of family gatherings has not diminished. The new Singapore's large boulevards and transportation system make these reunions easier.

Jeannette buys her family's dinner in a take-out store. People in Singapore were eating out, or taking out, long before it became popular to do so in the West. There are thousands of take-out shops in the city, offering dishes for

Three-quarters of the Singaporean population live in government-subsidized high-rises. Jeannette misses the intimate life of the old kampung *where she grew up. "It is much better now," says Grandfather Tay Eng Kiat. "Before, we were too crowded and the city was dirty. Now it is clean and pretty."*

every Singaporean's taste, whether Chinese from Shantou or Hunan, Malay food, or the huge variety of Indian cuisine.

Before she comes home, she goes by the sitter to get her youngest son. Although Mandarin is Singapore's official Chinese language, Jeannette has actually learned it from her son, because it is the only language of the babysitter who has been caring for him each workday since birth. Jeannette has always worked while raising her children. The two oldest were kept by her mother in the traditional Chinese way, but she was too old to keep Tay Tien Whui.

The rapid change to a modern society has strained relations between parents who were raised to respect authority and children who are growing up in a more diverse and lay culture. Stewart has the most difficulty with Tay Tien Hee. "He does nothing in the house. He could succeed in his studies, but he prefers to play." In a gentler tone, Jeannette excuses her children: "They have grown so big and so fast; often I forget that they are just babies in a grownup skin." Indeed, these children are physically bigger than their parents, the results of a better knowledge of nutrition and hygiene.

7:30 Jeannette has come home, changed into a comfortable cotton dress, heated the food in the microwave, and put everything on the table in a wink. After the meal, Tay Tien Hee leaves for the community center. There he can play squash, basketball, badminton, or ping-pong, but his favorite is carom, a game

Jeannette heats the food in the microwave and puts everything on the table in a wink. She says, "With all the good food we can get from the take-out shops, which offer dishes for everyone's taste, why bother with cooking?"

where checkers pieces are flicked with the finger into corner pockets in a table.

His father leaves for another meeting, this time of the citizens' consultative committee. Stewart is out every night at some community activity. Tonight the elected district representative to the government is there to answer any questions citizens want answered, and to help them. One man does not agree with his electricity bill; an older man cannot fill out a government form; assistants take care of them. The representative invites someone else into his office to deal with a complicated question. It is a long meeting.

10:00 Grandfather Tay Eng Kiat goes to bed. Tay Tien Hee is still out. Tay Weu Cheng has still not tired of television. Jeannette has just finished bringing in, through the windows, the bamboo poles that have been festooned with the daily laundry. She stores the poles on slings along the ceiling, and goes to sit in front of the television.

10:30 A few blocks away, Stewart walks slowly home from the meeting. The streets are well lit and quiet, emptied of colorful clothing and of people. And they are clean. It is against the law to litter, and anyone who spits, or throws a paper or even a cigarette butt on the street, can be fined.

Stewart cuts through an apartment-building underpass used as a recreation area, and stops to chat with a group of men gathered for a traditional bird-singing concert. As in China since time immemorial, each man has brought his favorite singing bird. About twenty cages hang from the beams of the building. The birds, who have been alone all day, suddenly join their repetitive sounds into an orchestra of trilling voices, filling the empty concrete streets with a soft and gentle symphony.

The Singaporeans

THE NAME: From Sanskrit *Singa Pura*, meaning "lion city"

GEOGRAPHY
Consists of the main island and over fifty small islands and reefs. The main island is characterized by low hills and valleys and includes a number of short streams. Much of the coastline has been artificially created by landfill.
Max. altitude: 177 m. (581 ft.) (Bukit Timah Peak)
Area: 620 sq. km. (239 sq. mi.)
Density: 4,274 pers./sq. km. (11,088 pers./sq. mi.) (1988)
Arable land: 3% (1985)
Forest: 5%
Climate: Equatorial, with uniformly high temperatures and relative humidity. Rainfall is fairly evenly distributed throughout the year but is especially heavy December through March and May through September.

CAPITAL: Singapore, pop. 2,559,000 (1985)

LANGUAGE: Malay, Chinese (Mandarin), Tamil, and English are official. Malay is the national language, and English is the language of government.

RELIGION
　　Buddhist and Taoist: 56%
　　Christian, Hindu, Muslim: 44%

POPULATION: Total—2,559,000 (1985)
　　Annual growth: 1.1% (28,149) (1985)
　　Doubling time: 71 yrs.
　　Urban: 100% (1985) (est. for year 2000: 100%)
　　Rural: 0%

AGE GROUPS (1986)
　　8% under 5 yrs.
　　24% under 15
　　33% under 20
　　41% from 20 to 39
　　18% from 40 to 59
　　8% 60 yrs. and over

ETHNIC GROUPS (1985)
　　Chinese: 77%　　Indian: 6%
　　Malay: 15%　　Other: 2%

HISTORY
Populated since prehistoric times
13th cent.: Known as Tumasik, a trading center and outpost of the Sumatran maritime empire of Srivijaya
14th cent.: Controlled by the Javanese Majapahit empire and subsequently by the Ayutthaya kingdom of Siam
late 14th cent.: Internal strife in Tumasik drives out the ruler and his followers
1819: Sir Stamford Raffles establishes the port settlement of Singapore by treaty with the Sultan of Johore; soon becomes part of the Straits Settlements with Penang and Malacca
1867: Straits Settlements become a crown colony, with Singapore as administrative seat
1874: Treaties between the British and the Malay states bring the entire peninsula under British protection
1959: Achieves full internal self-government
1963: Unites with Malaya, Sarawak, and Sabah to form Malaysia
1965: Independence

FAMILY
Marital status, for females 15 yrs. + (1980)
　　Single: 37%
　　Married: 52%
　　Widowed: 9%
　　Divorced: 1%
Female head of household: 18% (1980)
Fertility rate: 1.7 (1987)
Teenage births: 2.5% (1985) / Teenage fertility rate: 8.8/1,000 (1986)
Births out of wedlock: no data
Contraception: 74% (1985)
Government's position on family planning: Having achieved the lowest fertility rate in Asia, it considers population growth and fertility too low. Rather than a two-child family, it now promotes having three children with tax, education, and housing incentives.

SINGAPORE

SOCIAL INDICATORS
Life expectancy: 73 yrs. (male: 71; female: 76) (1986)
Infant mortality: 9/1,000 births (1987)
Crude birth rate: 17/1,000 pop. (1987)
Crude death rate: 6/1,000

HEALTH
Access to health services: 100% (1986)
Births attended by trained health personnel: 100%

HOUSING
Persons per household: 4.7 (1980)
Electricity: 2% without (1980)
Access to safe water: 100% (1986)
Source of water: All piped inside
Toilet facilities (1986)
    Modern sanitation: 95%
Construction materials: All durable housing

EDUCATION
Literacy: 86% (male: 93%; female: 79%) (1985)
Gross enrollment ratio (1984)
    First level: 115% (completing in 1980–86: 90%)
    Second: 71%
    Third: no data

Educational attainment for pop. 25 yrs. + (1980)
    None: 44%
    First level: 38%
    Second: 10%
    Third: 3%

ECONOMIC ACTIVITY
Economically active population: 47% (male: 60%; female: 34%) (1985)
Agriculture: 1% act. pop.; 1% of GDP
Mines: 0% act. pop.; 0% of GDP
Industry: 35% act. pop.; 27% of GDP
Services: 64% act. pop.; 72% of GDP
Per capita GNP: US$7,410 (1986)
National currency: dollars
Principal resources: Manufacturing

COMMUNICATIONS
Radio
    Transmitters: 21 (1983)
    Receivers: 281/1,000 pop. (1985)
Television
    Transmitters: 8 (1983)
    Receivers: 195/1,000 pop. (1985)
Newspapers (1984)
    Dailies: 10
    Circulation: 700,000 (277/1,000 pop.)

Singapore

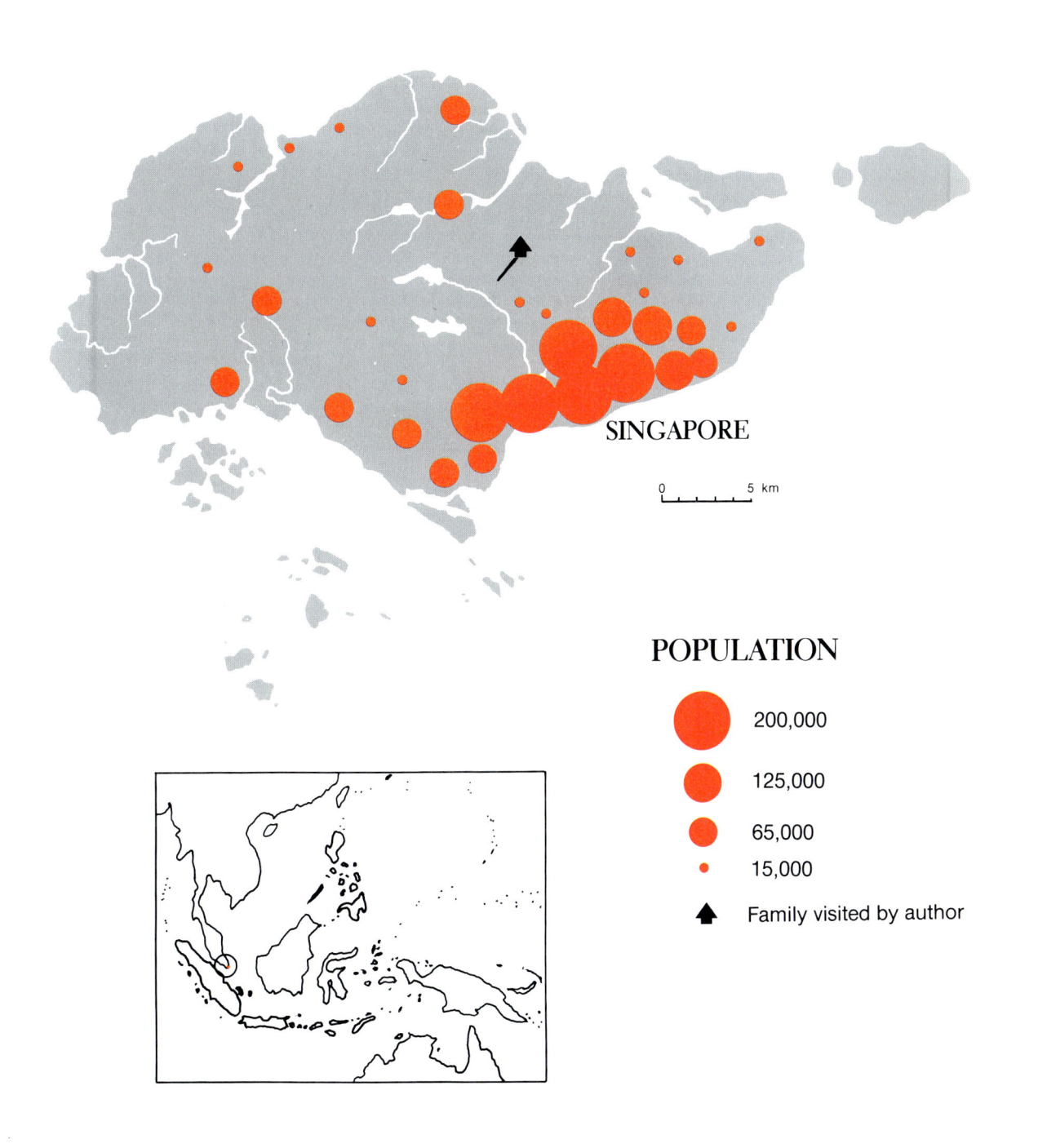

SINGAPORE

0　　　5 km

POPULATION

- 200,000
- 125,000
- 65,000
- 15,000
- ▲ Family visited by author

Thailand

The Sutrong–Yoddumnern Family

    Soan Sutrong, age 63 (1)
    Kao Sutrong, 62 (2)
    Get Yoddumnern (son-in-law), 30 (3)
    Taptim Yoddumnern, 26 (4)
    Kanchai, 7 (5)
    Yukun, 5 (6)
    Chacharin, 8 months (7)

    11 pigs and piglets
    5 ducks
    3 hens
    3 dogs

Hangku

NOVEMBER 15

4:15 In the flatlands at the heart of Thailand, a rooster crows without too much conviction. But that is enough to put the energetic Taptim right on her feet. She crosses the 200-square-meter room, whose space is divided by two mosquito nets that cover the family's two sleeping mats. Her parents sleep on one with seven- and five-year-old Kanchai and Yukun; the other is for Taptim, her husband Get, and their baby. Taptim switches on the light over the kitchen area of the teakwood house. The sounds of her steps, as she lights the charcoal fire, and the pounding of her wooden mortar and pestle, as she grinds the spices for breakfast, dispel the lingering silence of the night and chase the rats back to the rice fields.

5:30 Next door, a baby cries. Taptim's husband starts the first of many trips to the small river nearby to fill up the cement cistern in the back-yard bathing and latrine shed. One year from now, Soan expects to be able to afford running water.

Clouds begin to hide what little blue sky there was to see. The rain they will bring is welcome in this part of the country, where peasants have no irrigation systems. "Unlike the past two years, this year there will be a good harvest and profits for all," say Taptim and Get.

However, the family will have to work hard, for any profit. Soan owns 70 rai (1 rai = 1,600 square meters), three times what most peasants are able to rent from the country's rich landlords, who continue to buy more and more land as peasants move to the cities. Soan decided to buy it thirty years ago, when eighty percent of the country's peasants still owned their own land. "I thought when I was very young that land was the best thing I could buy," he says, proud of his youthful decision.

5:45 Kao crawls out of her mosquito net, shakes her legs, prays to Buddha, and takes one of the many straw baskets hooked to the inside walls. She sits cross-legged, opens a plastic bag from inside her basket, and spreads some white powder and a betel nut on a *bae pu* leaf (a sort of tobacco). She rolls up the leaf and pops it in her mouth to chew. The betel nut is a narcotic which numbs the mouth and was originally Kao's only source of relief for the toothaches she suffered. The daily chewing has stained her mouth permanently red.

6:15 Rice is presented to the Buddha on the family altar. Then the meal Taptim has prepared is put in tiffins, a set of stacked round metal boxes, and secured in straw baskets. Although Taptim and Get own a motorcycle, they rush across the small family hamlet to the road to jump on the back of a farm truck already waiting for them. Other farm workers, mostly friends, cousins, and brothers, have piled in. The small group have hired themselves out to harvest manioc on a larger farm, as there are still about ten more days until the rice harvest. The truck pulls out of the quiet village, passing the monks coming with their begging bowls. As they leave the main district road and head onto dirt roads, the low red sun peers out of the clouds and intensifies the green and gold hues of the fields.

A bumpy half an hour later, the workers jump out of the truck. Men unload the tools, while the women hurriedly lay down a plastic tablecloth and spread out plates and the rice, smoked fish, and hot sauce in their baskets.

Breakfast put away, the women cover their faces with a cloth and put on their *ngob*, a straw hat that perches above their heads on a bamboo frame. Now their faces are protected from the dust and the sun, and the raised hat ingeniously allows air to circulate and cool their perspiring heads.

At home, Soan, a calm and cheerful man with the friendly and hospitable manners attributed to his northeast ancestors, sweeps under the house with a branch broom. While Kao cares for her chubby grandson Chacharin, Soan tears down an old shed. He will use the boards to fortify the pigs' enclosure.

8:30 The neighbor's radio announces the time and Kanchai leaves for school. Kao, with Yukun by her side, ties up the mosquito net, folds the sheets, and rolls the mats. Everything is hung on the wooden walls, to prevent snakes or insects from nestling in the beds and belongings.

9:30 Baby Chacharin rocks in a small bamboo basket hanging beneath the house. Kao swings it at full speed, singing a song only she knows, which usually puts the child to sleep. Chacharin tries to stand and receives a solid whack on his naked backside that convinces him to stay still. Kao cleans the rice for the noon and evening meals, frequently giving the cradle a strong push so it swings at an astounding pace and keeps away mosquitoes and flies.

10:30 The rain falls on the roof and drops into twenty big earthen jars placed around the house to catch it for drinking and cooking.

11:30 Chacharin plays in his doting grandfather's arms while Kao cooks a lunch of rice, cucumbers, pork, and spicy sauce. Kao, Yukun, and Soan will eat whenever they feel like it. Soan puts Chacharin in an infant-walker and guides it under the next house, where all the grandfathers gather to pass the day out of

The house's tin roof makes the midday heat so intolerable inside that most of the day is spent among the ten-foot stilts that also lift the house out of reach of floodwaters.

the sun. All the people in the six houses that form the hamlet are related, or have been friends for so long they are said to be family.

At school, Kanchai finishes his lunch and sets out for a football game during recess. Above the children's chatter and playful yelling comes the pounding of the looms at the workshop where the women weave the colorful cotton cloth they sell for cash. In the fields, the plastic cloths are once again laid down. Lunch is the same as breakfast.

3:00 Chacharin is again unhappy to be in his swinging cradle, but Grandmother's hand wins the struggle once more. Despite the rain this morning, Kao carefully waters her tobacco plants.

Soan, always obliging, comes to rock his sleeping grandson and also prepares and cuts some green vegetables for the pigs. He chops in time with the cradle's rocking, the calm methodic rhythm punctuating the quiet afternoon.

3:30 Calm is never lasting. School finished, Kanchai runs up the steps to drop off his schoolbag, uniform, and shoes. Yukun detaches himself from his grandmother's side and is off to join the youngsters, who now fill the hamlet. The parents hope the two boys will stay in the army after their compulsory service, because further education would be free and could lead to a profitable profession like medicine or engineering.

After fetching water to wash the midday dishes, Kao gets started on dinner. Squatting at the top of the stairs, she cleans a fish, throwing the entrails over the edge for the ducks and chickens to fight over.

5:00   Kao starts a charcoal fire, which she prefers to the small gas stove used mostly by her daughter. The family economizes as much as they can, as there are many things they want to buy. Taptim would like to have a plastic mat to put under their sleeping area to keep the insects away; Get would like to have a car; Kao, a refrigerator. Everyone wants a television set. But no one knows what this year's savings will be. Even now, just a few days before harvest, the price the mills and middlemen will fix for the rice has not yet been determined.

Kao cooks all the dishes on a single fire. She sautés peanuts, puts them on a plate, and roasts the hot green peppers. Mashing both with onions and coarse sea salt, she makes *nam-prik*, a delicious spicy sauce, for the fish.

6:00   Taptim and Get are back from the fields and take turns showering. Refreshed, they dress and come sit on the floor with their family, Taptim in her colorful sarong and handsome Get in his *paakoama*, the less colorful material men wrap around their waist like a skirt. Soan has the job of keeping Chacharin out of the plates that sit on the floor between them.

8:00   Kanchai and Yukun are bored by the conversation going on with an aunt and uncle who have come to sit on the doorstep. They are put to bed by their grandmother.

9:00   Chacharin's bottle of powdered milk has been prepared, and dressed in a cloth diaper for the night, he falls asleep in his father's arms. The young couple follow the elders' example and crawl under their mosquito net. The moonlight filtering through the gaps in the wooden planks transforms the mosquito nets into two white shadowy rooms rising from the large space where the rats are now free to roam.

Let the rats play; a good night's rest is needed. Tomorrow it is Loy Kratong, the Festival of Lights, celebrated since ancient times on the night of the first full moon after the rains stop. Kao will make little *kratongs*, banana-leaf boats, on which she will set small candles and offerings to the goddess of

Yukun learns everything from Khun Yai (Grandmother), including the customary respect for elders. For example, never to stand above an older person's head.

water. Under tomorrow's full moonlight, they will all go to the pagoda and place their *kratongs* on the Mae Nam River. As they watch the hundreds of tiny flames float down the river, they will ask the goddess to pardon them for polluting her waters, and make their personal wishes for a better karma.

Thailand

The Zellon Family*

Zago Zellon, age 74 (1)
Apie Zellon, 71 (2)
Adjo Zellon, 41 (3)
Mechon Zellon, 43 (4)
Atse Zellon, 25 (5)
Bougnhe (daughter-in-law), 20 (6)
Allon, 18 (7)
Bunung (daughter-in-law), 23 (8)
Mide, 15 (9)
Miphaw, 12 (10)
Ate, 5 (11)

1 horse
2 buffalo
17 pigs and piglets
8 ducks
20 chickens
1 cat

* The Zellons belong to the Akha tribe. Along the borders between Southeast Asian countries live whole communities of families with ancient tribal cultures who have been moving back and forth across these borders for many centuries. All governments in the region now seek to assimilate these families into their societies.

Lap Sap Village

NOVEMBER 21

4:30 Somewhere in the small mountain village of Lap Sap a baby cries, and a mother succeeds in calming him. Bougnhe's silver headdress jingles as she stirs, but no one else moves in the Zellons' bamboo-stilt house.

At the rooster's third crow, fifteen-year-old Mide gets up to light the kerosene lamps. Now Bougnhe also rises, and ties a *zdudzan* around her waist. Like all the women, she has slept in a skirt, T-shirt, and knee-length cotton leggings. All she has to do is put on her woven cotton jacket and hook a wedge-shaped silver plate on her head, which indicates she is a married woman.

As Bougnhe fans a fire of bamboo kindling and hardwood, the white cat, blackened by a crazy tomcat's night, comes to huddle near the flames. Bunung appears at the women's door. She has slept with her husband in the *nu za*, the tiny cane hut reserved for intimate meetings between men and women.

4:45 From the yard of every house in the village comes the pounding sound of the treadle-driven rice huskers, and under their house Bunung and Bougnhe take turns operating the heavy treadle. Mide takes the husked grain and sifts it on a woven bamboo tray. The chaff, which is lighter than the rice, separates and falls on the floor; it will be used to fatten the pigs, which bring home much-needed cash. In fact, Adjo will sell some of the pigs today to purchase a new buffalo.

As Atse comes back from his night watch in the family field, his mother, Mechon, puts the rice that has soaked overnight on the woven sieve in the *honsambon*, a large wooden bowl made from a section of a tree trunk. She puts the bowl in an iron pot that sits on the iron tripod of the women's hearth. It will be two hours before the rice is steamed and breakfast ready. Today is Rabbit Day, the first of the Akhas' eleven-day cycle. It is customary once a month to rest on Rabbit Day, as well as on every Tiger Day, the last day, but the three girls choose instead to go collect some more of the rice harvest.

6:30 When they come back with full baskets on their backs, and the horse laden with two more, daylight has arrived. The breakfast rice is ready.

7:00 As it is rice-harvest season, all the family heads out to the field except the grandparents and Adjo, gone to buy his buffalo. Atse, the eldest son, harnesses the horse as the women harness baskets on each other's back. The baskets are

The Zellons have six little huts, three for the couples (Adjo and Mechon, Atse and Bougnhe, and Allon and Bunung), and three for rice and corn storage. In the big house, there are separate sleeping and living areas for men and women, as well as separate hearths.

mounted on a pole across the shoulders and secured with a band across the forehead.

They head down the mountain, following the zigzagging trails. Mountain life has made their short legs strong, and after half an hour they reach their field hut, where the harvested rice is stored to bring home. An estimated 23,000 Akhas now live in Thailand. According to the oral history passed down by generations in songs and poems, theirs has been a long, continuous journey from their ancestral homeland in Central Asia. The Zellon family lived on the Burma border, but their village was becoming too crowded with refugees like themselves and land was too scarce. Seven years ago, with fourteen other families, the Zellons followed a *zdoma*, their headman, walked for three days, and found a place on a mountain slope similar to what they had left. They settled down, cleared fields, and built their traditional houses. This might be the end of the Akhas' long historical journey, for these Thai mountains are on the edge of the large central plain, which Akhas would hesitate to inhabit.

8:00　The Zellons put down their baskets and eat a few papayas. The women take off any jewelry that will interfere with work, put on black pants under their black miniskirts and a hood over their silver headdresses, pick up their long, crooked wooden sticks, and go off to thresh.

In the field, the rice has been stacked. Bougnhe helps Bunung to lay a large plastic sheet on the ground. Then she climbs up on a stack and rolls the rice shafts up in little bunches. She hands these to Bunung, who lays them down in a row. When they have a number lined up, they beat the stalks so the rice detaches itself and falls on the plastic. Mechon has gone to the fields where the family grows vegetables and tobacco. She cuts greens and comes back to the hut to start a fire and prepare lunch for the workers. Ate follows his mother around. At five, he still breast-feeds. Mechon's milk has long dried up. "But he is my last," she says, looking indulgently at her spoiled boy.

Only the noise of the pounding echoing off the mountains breaks the rural silence. People are hurrying to bring the rice to shelter. In a few months, the Zellons will be planting corn. Ideally, the land should rest, as has been the tradition. But there are too many people in the mountains now and deforestation is controlled. New land cannot be cleared, and they must continually plant the already-cleared land in order to grow sufficient crops.

9:00 Grandfather Zago has his morning free, so he joins other elders to watch a neighbor slaughter his pig. The men's talk will be enlivened by rice whiskey. He can drink in peace. Adjo has agreed that the family will live together as long as the old man is still alive. Since their wealth is based on the number of their work force and their diligence, this makes sense, anyway.

Grandmother Apie crosses the house at a slow, steady pace and brings corn to the poultry in the back yard. She makes three trips, then sits on the open veranda to string the green vegetables on a bamboo thread and hang them to dry in the sun. Later this salad will be marinated in water, spices, and salt.

11:00 Grandmother stokes the fire, boils some greens, and eats them with a handful of rice. As Grandpa Zago places a piece of meat beside her, a chicken runs up and snatches it. Grandma yells as Grandpa runs after the bird, rescues the meat, cleans it, and brings it back to his wife. Meat is too precious to waste.

12:40 Grandpa returns to sit with the elders. The sun is out from under the clouds, so the tomcat sleeps in the sun. Grandma takes off her sweater to mend it, letting her old dry breasts flop on her stomach.

1:00 The men return from the fields to attend a meeting at the community center run by the Hill Tribe Welfare Division. It is a way for the government to keep track of the number of refugees entering the country, to integrate those that come, and to teach the peasants to grow other cash crops besides poppies, from which opium is extracted and heroin made. The pretty red flower has made this area, known as the Golden Triangle, famous for violence and bloodshed brought on by the lucrative crop.

4:15 Everyone is home. Atse is washing his clothes at the public standpipe; like all Akha men, he is responsible for his personal belongings. In front of the house,

Every evening, Grandma's betel-nut-stained smile greets the family coming back from the fields. This is the women's side of the dwelling. On the other side of the wall, the men have their cooking hearth and sleeping place.

Adjo excitedly discusses his day's purchase with a group of men. For just a little more money, he bought a male and a pregnant female buffalo. Like a man who has just bought his first used car, Adjo looks for his friends' approval. He has borrowed money that he must pay back in seventeen days if he does not want to pay interest, and hopes the finished harvest will bring that amount.

Grandpa puts a bowl of corn on the veranda and lets out a low squeal. The pigs and chickens know his voice and swarm over the feeding trough as he referees. The girls have carried a last basket of rice from the fields and take turns at the water tap, filling the water gourds and bathing and getting the dust out of their clothing, as the sun prepares to set over the mountains.

5:30

Allon has washed and changed and settles his gun over his shoulder. It is his turn to sleep in the field hut and protect the harvest from animals and thieves. Darkness settles over the house.

Grandpa, Adjo, Atse, and a villager are having dinner on the men's side and are talking buffalo. On the women's side, always more gossipy and lively, the talk is of the day's work, clothing, marriages, embroidery, and the New Year festivities in mid-December. Their dinner finished, the women take off their sweaty, smelly headdresses to scratch their heads with a needle and comb their long black hair. Every three days they wash and polish the silver coins that adorn them. The amount of silver on their body expresses their wealth.

8:30

Mide lays down the bark-fiber sleeping mats and massages her grandmother's old body with all her strength so it will relax and allow her to rest better for the night. And as the other women prepare for bed, Bougnhe lights a torch of grass to make her way to the little house where she will meet Atse.

The Thai

THE NAME: Formerly referred to as Siam, from Sanskrit, meaning both "swarthy" and "gold." Thailand means "land of the free."

GEOGRAPHY
Four natural regions: in the north, heavily forested mountain ranges divided by fertile, steep river valleys; in the northeast, Khorat Plateau, of relatively low elevations; in the center, a low-lying, fertile central plain; and in the south, heavily forested rolling hills and mountains along Malay Peninsula.
Max. altitude: 2,595 m. (8,514 ft.) (Doi Inthanon)
Area: 513,115 sq. km. (198,115 sq. mi.)
Density: 99 pers./sq. km. (255 pers./sq. mi.) (1988)
Arable land: 34% (1985)
Forest: 29%. Deforestation: 2.4% (379,000 hectares) per year (1980s)
Climate: Tropical, monsoonal. Rainy season from May to October; cool, dry season from November to March; hot, dry season from March to May

CAPITAL: Bangkok, pop. 5,174,682 (metropolitan area, pop. 5,900,000) (1984 est.)

LANGUAGE: Thai (official)
Chinese is the second major language. English, Malay, Indian dialects, and tribal languages also spoken

RELIGION: A large majority practice Theravada Buddhism; others are Muslim, Hindu, Sikhs, or Christian. Many of the tribal peoples are Animists.

POPULATION: Total—54,124,000 (1988)
Annual growth: 1.9% (980,476) (1985)
Doubling time: 33 yrs.
Urban: 20% (1985) (est. for year 2000: 29%)
Rural: 80%

AGE GROUPS (1985)
12% under 5 yrs.
36% under 15
48% under 20
15% from 20 to 39
14% from 40 to 59
5% 60 yrs. and over

ETHNIC GROUPS
Thai: 75% Thai Malay: 2%
Chinese: 14% Hill tribes: 1%

HISTORY
Inhabited as long as forty thousand years ago
A.D. 1000: Thai peoples migrate from present-day China to Southeast Asia, where the Mon and Khmer have established civilizations influenced by India. By the 11th century, foreigners refer to the land as Siam
13th cent.: Several small but powerful Thai states emerge, including Sukhothai and Lan Na (Chiang Mai). Thais absorb Buddhism from India, art and architecture from Mon and Khmer culture and create a new alphabet from theirs
1378: Sukhothai falls to Thai kingdom of Ayutthaya, which sets up a state with a hierarchical and centralized system of government
1463: Ayutthaya capital moved north to improve military position, but Ayutthaya fails to conquer Lan Na
early 16th cent.: Lan Sang kingdom flourishes; vies with Lan Na and Sukhothai for leadership of Thais. Portuguese traders and missionaries begin to arrive. Siam manages to remain uncolonized by any European power—the only nation in South or Southeast Asia to do so
1569–93: Burmese forces defeat Thais and dominate the area until Naresuan ousts them
early 17th cent.: Dutch and British establish trading stations. In Europe's eyes, Siam comes to be most important and glamorous nation in Southeast Asia
1688: French bid for power in Siam provokes antiforeign coup that inaugurates 150-year policy of limiting contact with the West
1767: Burmese again capture Siam briefly, putting an end to Ayutthaya period
1782: Chakkri Dynasty, which continues today, established. Capital moves to Bangkok. Relations with West resumed
late 19th cent.: European interest in region increases. Thailand protects independence by playing French and British against each other and conceding Laos (1893), parts of Cambodia (1907), and areas on Malay Peninsula (1909), and making internal reforms

1932: Coup ends absolute monarchy; constitutional regime established. There have been numerous coups since then, and the military has mostly dominated the government, but the king is a revered and stabilizing figure
1939: Renamed Thailand
1941: Government under Phibun agrees to allow Japanese forces passage through Thailand in return for Japan's assurances that it will respect Thailand's independence
1963–73: Intense foreign presence due to Vietnam War brings great social change
1973: Student protest movement leads to dismissal of government leaders and start of elected government
1976: Military forces resume power
1979: Constitution provides for limited democracy; elections take place

FAMILY
Marital status, for pop. 15 yrs. + (1980)
Single: 29%
Married: 59%
Widowed: 9%
Divorced: 3%
Female head of household: no data
Fertility rate: 2.4 (1987)
Teenage births: 12% / Teenage fertility rate: 41.2/ 1,000 (1984)
Births out of wedlock: no data
Contraception: 65% (1985)
Government's position on family planning: Population growth and fertility are too high. Family planning incorporated into schools and adult literacy programs. Minimum legal age of marriage raised from 15 to 17.

SOCIAL INDICATORS
Life expectancy: 66 yrs. (1987)
Infant mortality: 41/1,000 births (1986)
Crude birth rate: 23/1,000 pop. (1987)
Crude death rate: 7/1,000

HEALTH
Access to health services: 70%
Births attended by trained health personnel: 33% (1984)

HOUSING
Persons per household: 5.2 (1980)
Electricity: 76% without (1976)
Access to safe water: 66% (urban: 50%; rural: 70%) (1985)
Source of water (1976)
Piped inside: 12%
Piped out: 2%
Without piped water: 86%
Toilet facilities (1976)
Flush: 0.5%
Other: 50%
None: 49.5%
Construction materials: Traditionally, one large room raised on stilts. Newer homes are being built with concrete and wood, as natural materials become scarce and more expensive.

EDUCATION
Literacy: 91% (male: 94%; female: 88%) (1985)
Gross enrollment ratio (1985)
First level: 97% (completing in 1985: 64%)
Second: 30%
Third: 20%
Educational attainment for pop. 25 yrs. + (1980)
None: 20%
First level: 67% incomplete; 2% complete
Second: 5%
Third: 3%

ECONOMIC ACTIVITY
Economically active population: 53% (male: 55%; female: 51%) (1982)
Agriculture: 66% act. pop.; 23% of GDP
Mines: 3% act. pop.; 1.5% of GDP
Industry: 10% act. pop.; 25.5% of GDP
Services: 21% act. pop.; 50% of GDP
Per capita GNP: US$810 (1986)
Population in absolute poverty: urban: 15%; rural: 34% (1977–85)
National currency: baht
Principal resources: Rice, sugarcane, rubber, tin, natural gas

COMMUNICATIONS
Radio
Transmitters: 207 (1985)
Receivers: 175/1,000 pop. (1985)
Television
Transmitters: 48 (1985)
Receivers: 97/1,000 pop. (1985)
Newspapers (1986)
Dailies: 34
Circulation: 2,390,000

Thailand

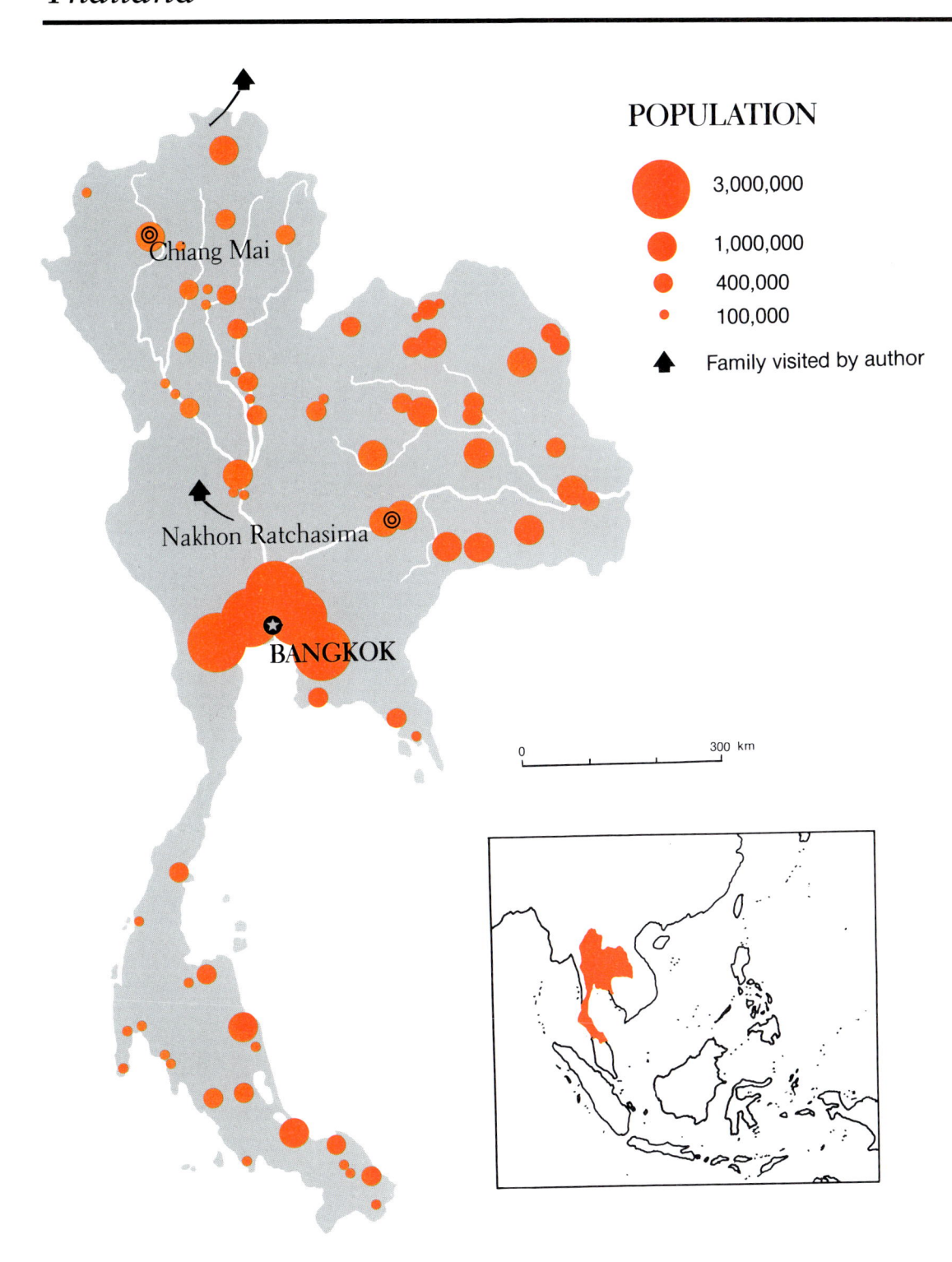

POPULATION

- 3,000,000
- 1,000,000
- 400,000
- 100,000

▲ Family visited by author

Chiang Mai

Nakhon Ratchasima

★ BANGKOK

0   300 km

Socialist Republic of Vietnam

Do Van Thuan's Family

Do Van Thuan, age 50 (1)
Nguyen Thi Thoi, 48 (2)
Do Van Tao, 31 (3)
Le Thi Lam (daughter-in-law), 28 (4)
Do Thi Phuong, 6 (5)
Do Van Taoung, 4 (6)
Do Van Tuy, 2 (7)
Do Thi Thuan, 28 (8)
Dang Van Suc, 4 (9)
Do Van Tien, 25 (10)
Nguyen Thi Xuyen (daughter-in-law), 25 (11)
Do Thi Mingh Phuong, 2 (12)
Do Van Hien, 23 (13)
Do Van Bang, 2 (14)
Do Van Chien, 20 (15)
Do Thi Mien, 17 (16)
Do Van Tuyn, 15 (17)

3 pigs and 9 piglets
30 chickens
10 kilos of fish in the fish pond

Ngoc Dong

MARCH 12

5:00 One, two, three, four . . . A female voice begins the exercises on the national radio broadcast from speakers mounted on posts throughout Ngoc Dong Village. Do Van Thuan, the patriarchal head of the family, ignores the voice. "That's good for city people. Here in Da Ton commune we get enough exercise from farming."

5:30 The commune's propaganda officer now briefs the villagers and announces the national news. Nguyen Thi Thoi fills a kettle at the outside water tank and goes to light the fire in the kitchen shed. In the two brick houses of this overcrowded extended family, each mother cooks for her respective children and husband.

Do Van Thuan opens the house's double wooden doors to the dim morning light. After rinsing his mouth beside the water tank, fifteen-year-old Do Van Tuyn feeds the pigs and chickens. Do Thi Thuan goes to help her mother with tea and breakfast while her brother, Do Van Tien, sweeps the red-tinted cement floor. Everyone has specific chores, which maintains harmony in this large family. Following the adults, the small children wash their mouths and sit down on the cement floor, silently waiting for breakfast. Grandpa demands quiet children in the house.

6:20 The village bell (made from an American aerial bombshell) is rung by the village leader's wife. Over the loudspeaker, her husband asks one member of every family to come to the brigade's office for the day's work needs. Do Thi Thuan goes and reports back to her father that six people have been sent to get mosquito screen; their brigade is in need of corn for planting and farmers who might have any are invited to trade it in for other seed. She then squats around the pot for breakfast with her son, brothers, sisters, and nieces.

7:15 The bell calls the Ngoc Dong peasants to the fields. Before the agricultural reforms of 1981, the six thousand field-workers of Da Ton commune had to work a specific number of hours. Those who worked hard and those who did not received the same share of the harvest. As a result, nobody wanted to work hard, and families put their efforts into raising and selling pigs. Now the land has been divided by family; after a family produce their quota, the rest of the harvest is their profit. The country's production has improved, but Vietnam is still the poorest country in its region and cannot feed all its people.

In fertile Da Ton, they are fortunate because two crops can be harvested yearly. Fields are irrigated, and with the help of foreign aid, water pumps have been installed in the village wells, an important privilege not shared by all Vietnamese. Da Ton is an exemplary commune.

This morning Do Van Thuan's daughter-in-law, Nguyen Thi Xuyen, will weed the family's fields instead of sorting seeds at the seed brigade, but first she must take her two-year-old daughter, Do Thi Mingh, to the day-care center. The little girl says goodbye to her father and grandparents and then nestles in her mother's arms for the short journey to the center, where her mother puts her down at the door, because parents are not allowed inside.

Do Thi Mingh and the other fifteen children sitting on tiny chairs know that there won't be any games, and no one is going to use the center's five precious toys, before all have stopped crying. This is the time in life when children are supposed to learn control. Grandfather Do Van Thuan agrees. "Before," he says, "our children used to play around the village. There was no discipline and they were spoiled." He adds, "Mothers would do everything for their children, even chewing their food. Today they are more active, more intelligent and resourceful."

As she heads for the fields, Nguyen Thi Xuyen is relieved that her daughter wasn't crying, and is happy she is in the day-care center; it can accommodate only twenty-five percent of the village children. She wears a straw hat to protect herself from the sun, but at twenty-five she does not think of herself as a young woman; she accepts her father-in-law's traditional view: "Women are beautiful between eighteen and twenty." On the village's small dirt roads, she joins children slowly heading for school and farmers walking quickly to balance the pole dangling two baskets full of tools and manure on their shoulders.

10:00 At home, Do Van Thuan lights his water pipe and sits on the bed, smoking and watching the children outside, where he can see the green haze of the first apple-tree leaves. In the orange grove, small oranges are also showing. Do Van Thuan goes to the fields only when there is collective work for everyone, even the children, to do, such as plowing, irrigation, and planting.

At the nearby agricultural university, he has learned how to graft fruit trees and, in turn, has taught the technique to his own sons. Together, they earn a significant amount of cash for the family. With that money and the support of his married sons, Do Van Thuan can plan for the future with precise priorities. The first is getting a roof over every one of his children's heads, which means building a third house on his land. The commune requires that he house his sons, as he has the space. Then he must marry his two younger sons. According to custom, he will have to give them beds and kill two pigs so the whole village can share in the wedding feast. That will cost the equivalent of two rice harvests per wedding.

Do Van Thuan's large family is fortunate to have two houses. One was his parents' house, which he helped build at the end of the war, after the old bamboo house was destroyed by a bomb. Now his eldest son lives there with his wife and three children. The second house was finished in 1980, and the brick shelter used for meals is the beginning of the third.

But Do Van Thuan is a hard worker, and he is fortunate. From his parents he inherited more than the 180 square meters of land allotted each family by the commune. He also has a personal garden between the houses, packed tight with apple, lichee, and orange trees, soya beans, green and black beans, and watermelons. There are pigs for very special occasions, and a handmade pond which was stocked with ten kilos of fish ten days ago.

Other families are less fortunate. Do Thi Thuan cannot live with her husband's family because there is no land, or space in the house, for them. The young couple have asked the authorities for land and have been told it might be possible in two or three years. Twelve Ngoc Dong couples want their own home, and this would take land from cultivation. As long as the country lacks food, every new couple in every village faces this trade-off.

11:00 Back from the fields early, Nguyen Thi Thoi squats near her kitchen fire, as a hen sits in the hay in the kitchen to lay an egg. An especially silent woman, the matriarch keeps an eye on her grandchildren as she cooks. Soon the other field-workers will be back home, wanting their midday meal.

2:30 Locking everything as they leave, Nguyen Thi Thoi, Do Thi Thuan, and Do Van Tien head once more to the fields to weed. It is not too hot and tiring in the spring. At the edge of the village, the elderly dig a fish pond, slowly and steadily, carrying small clumps of earth to carts. Last year, their garden and fruit trees brought 150,000 dong (about US$300) to the commune.

Mother and daughter straighten up from weeding, automatically putting

Most Vietnamese like to eat squatting. The whole Do Van Thuan extended family gather in this position at least once a day and stay chatting after the meal.

their hands on their lower backs. This is the field where the family is free to grow what they want, and they have chosen corn and groundnuts.

3:30 Back at home, the women clean rice. Although it's been cleaned by the cooperative, some broken grains always stay in the sheaves. These they laboriously sift through baskets of tighter and tighter weave, saving the chaff to feed the pigs.

5:20 Nguyen Thi Thoi and her daughters are squatting at the fire. Her sons are feeding the pigs, the chickens, and the fish, and sweeping the rice-threshing dust from the front of the house.

The house smells of tobacco. Do Van Thuan is passing the water pipe to a village visitor and his brother-in-law, who have come for tea. Dinner preparations and putting their children to sleep make the evening as busy for the women as is the day. There is little time to chat before exhaustion sets in.

9:30 In one wooden bed, Nguyen Thi Thoi and her granddaughter Dang Van Suc lie down, as always placing their feet toward the head of the bed. Above their heads hangs a picture of one of their ancestors. It would be disrespectful to lie with their feet toward revered ones.

The radio has the last word at night. The propaganda officer announces a long list of members who will attend the annual congress meeting. The village bell rings a last time to call the militia, who make their final rounds of the village, ensuring that all is in order and its citizens are safe. The radio voice continues on and on, and only much later can the frogs be heard in the fish pond.

The Vietnamese

THE NAME: Originally Nam Viet, meaning "kingdom of the southern people"; from *Viet*, the original inhabitants, and *nam*, meaning "south"

GEOGRAPHY
Rugged, forested highlands run from north to south in the west, covering approximately two-thirds of the country. The east is coastal plain; the north, the Red River delta; and the south, the Mekong River delta.
Max. altitude: 3,142 m. (10,312 ft.) (Mt. Fansipan)
Area: 329,556 sq. km. (127,242 sq. mi.)
Density: 195 pers./sq. km. (504 pers./sq. mi.)
Arable land: 19% (1985)
Forest: 40%. Deforestation: 0.6% (65,000 hectares) per year (1980s)
Climate: Tropical monsoon, with cool winters in the north. Rainfall occurs mainly during the summer.

CAPITAL: Hanoi, pop. 819,913 (metropolitan area, pop. 1,500,000) (1979)

LANGUAGE: Vietnamese (official)
French, English, Chinese, and Khmer also spoken, along with the languages of several ethnic minorities

RELIGION: Buddhism and Taoism are traditional and widespread. There are about 3.5 million Roman Catholics.

POPULATION: Total—53,000,000 (1979)
Annual growth: 1.9% (1,007,000) (1985)
Doubling time: 27 yrs.
Urban: 20% (1985) (est. for year 2000: 27%)
Rural: 80%

AGE GROUPS (1979)
15% under 5 yrs.   25% from 20 to 39
42% under 15   14% from 40 to 59
54% under 20   7% 60 yrs. and over

ETHNIC GROUPS
Kinh (Viet): 87%
About 60 indigenous ethnic minorities: 13%

HISTORY
4000 B.C.: People migrate from southern China, followed by the Mon–Khmers and later by the Viets
258–111 B.C.: Au Lac kingdom established under The Thuc, followed by independent kingdom of Nam Viet
111 B.C.: Nam Viet annexed by China; more than ten centuries of Chinese domination ensue in what is today northern Vietnam
A.D. 39: First revolt against the Chinese, led by the Trung sisters. Mahayana Buddhist influence from China
938–16th cent.: Independence; expansion south into Kingdom of Champa and Khmer Funan Empire
1674: Ruled by northern and southern dynasties
1802: Reunited by Nguyen Anh
1857: French seize Saigon. By 1900, France controls Laos, Kampuchea, Tonkin (northern Vietnam), and Annam (central Vietnam) and Cochin China (southern Vietnam) as French Indochina
1930: Indo-China Communist Party formed under Nguyen Ai Quoc (Ho Chi Minh)
1941: League for the Independence of Vietnam (Viet Minh) formed
1940–45: Japanese occupation, with French administration
Sept. 2, 1945: Independence from France under Ho Chi Minh and his Communist-led Viet Minh
1946–54: French Indochina War ends in the defeat of the French in the battle of Dien Bien Phu. Geneva Agreement grants independence to Communist-ruled North Vietnam and U.S.A.-supported South Vietnam
1965: American troops dispatched to assist South Vietnam against North Vietnam
1973: American troops withdraw from the war
April 30, 1975: Saigon captured by Communist forces; South Vietnamese government collapses. Flow of refugees begins
1976: North and South united as Socialist Republic of Vietnam
1978: Vietnam enters Kampuchea; Vietnamese-backed regime established
1979: China invades Vietnam, which turns to the Soviet bloc for assistance
1987: Vietnam agrees to remove its troops from Kampuchea by 1990

FAMILY

Marital status: no data
Female head of household: no data
Fertility rate: 3.9 (1987)
Teenage births: no data
Births out of wedlock: no data
Contraception: 20% (1986)
Government's position on family planning: Population growth and fertility are too high. Promotes delayed marriage, postponement of first and spacing of subsequent births. Parents with one or two children given preference in promotions, bonuses, and opportunities to move to urban areas.

SOCIAL INDICATORS

Life expectancy: 57 yrs. (male: 55; female: 60) (1980)
Infant mortality: 68/1,000 births (1986)
Crude birth rate: 32/1,000 pop. (1987)
Crude death rate: 10/1,000

HEALTH

Access to health services: 75% (1982)
Births attended by trained health personnel: 100% (1982)

HOUSING

Persons per household: 5.0 (1979)
Electricity: Majority without
Access to safe water: 41% (urban: 60%; rural: 32%) (1985)
Source of water: Mostly wells, rainwater, and streams in rural areas
Toilet facilities
  Sanitation facilities: 30% (1983)
Construction materials: In the north, brick; in the south, bamboo

EDUCATION

Literacy: 84% (male: 88%; female: 80%) (1985)
Gross enrollment ratio (1985)
  First level: 100% (completing in 1985: 50%)
  Second: 43%
  Third: no data
Educational attainment for pop. 10 yrs. + (1979)
  None: 14%
  First level: no data
  Second: no data
  Third: no data

ECONOMIC ACTIVITY

Economically active population: no data
GDP: no data
Per capita GNP: US$500 (1983)
National currency: dong
Principal resources: Rice, fish, rubber

COMMUNICATIONS

Radio
  Transmitters: 38 (1985)
  Receivers: 100/1,000 pop. (1985)
Television
  Transmitters: no data
  Receivers: 33/1,000 pop. (1985)
Newspapers (1984)
  Dailies: 4
  Circulation: 545,000

Socialist Republic of Vietnam

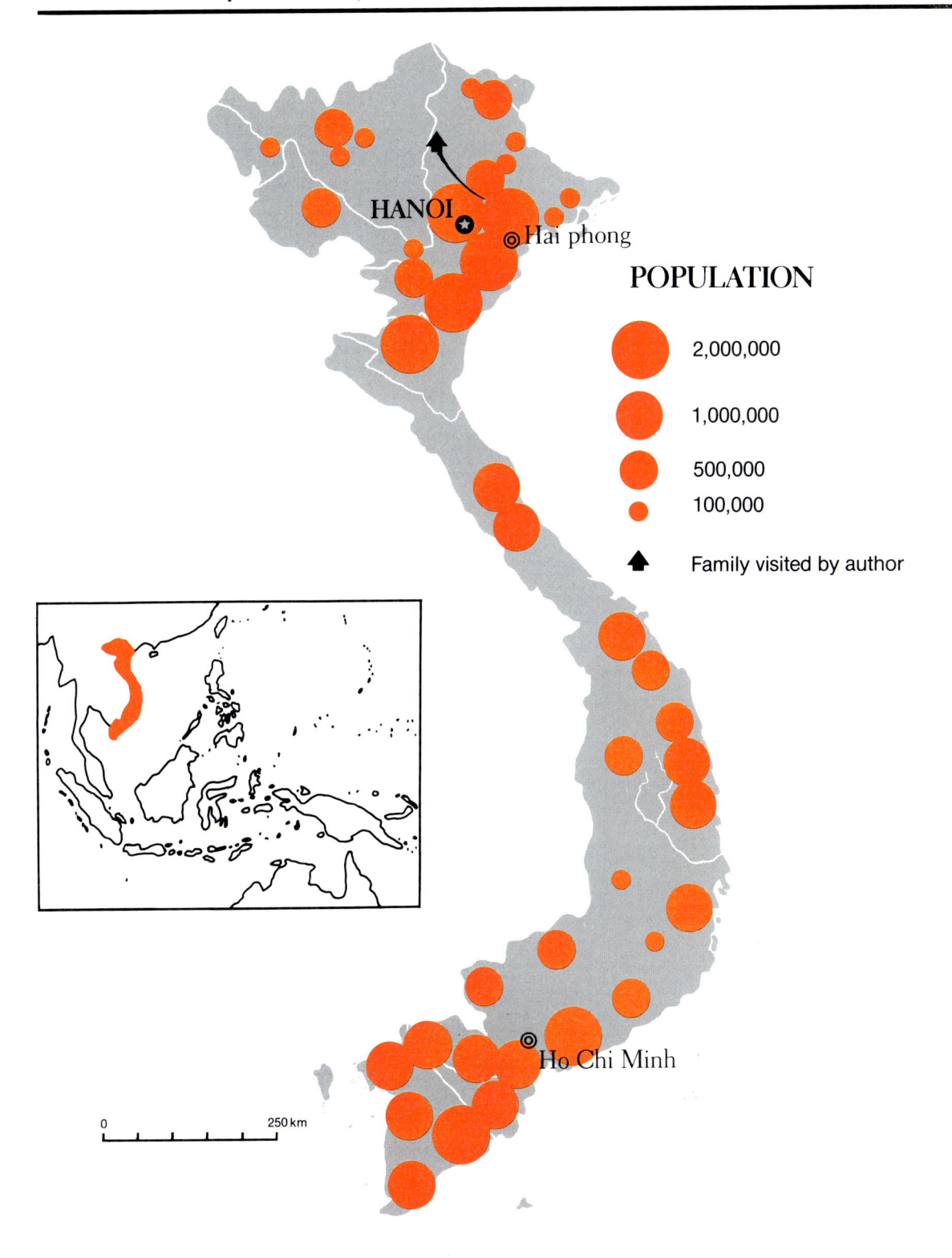

POPULATION

- 2,000,000
- 1,000,000
- 500,000
- 100,000

▲ Family visited by author

0 — 250 km

Refugees and Displaced Persons

The Douch Family*

Douch Vech, age 58 (1)
Douch Vuon, 44 (2)
Douch Muom, 20 (3)
Douch Vout, 15 (absent)
Douch Vhee, 11 (absent)
Douch Vee, 8 (4)
Douch Lean, 5 (5)
Douch Vahn, 8 months (6)

* International and civil wars have created great tides of refugees in Southeast Asia, and neighboring countries have had to accommodate hundreds of thousands of shattered families. The Douches are one such family.

Site 2 *(near Aranyaprathet, Thailand)*
MAY 23

7:00 The senior camp officer of the United Nations Border Relief Operation (UNBRO) and his assistants arrive at the gates of Site 2, one of the nine displaced-persons and refugee camps along the Thai border with Kampuchea. Until they have made their daily security check of the camp's five square kilometers, no other staff from the agencies aiding the camp will be allowed to come in and start their day's work. There are many agencies staffing the camp. They work together to provide medical treatment, education, and social services. They provide for the physical needs of the 173,000 people sheltered in Site 2. The biggest camp on the border, it is the size of a small town. Its inhabitants wait for peace so they can go back home.

7:30 The gong rings for the children to leave for school. Vout, Vhee, and Vee are ready. Their mother, Douch Vuon, has been up for nearly two hours to make sure that they would be. First she breast-fed her baby, Vahn. Then she started the wood fire and prepared rice soup flavored with the string beans she picked from her few plants growing in front of the house. Five-year-old Lean still lies across one of the bamboo beds in the house, waiting for the rice soup to be ready before getting up. After chopping wood, Vout begins the numerous trips to the water tanks necessary to fill the family's water jar. Each row of houses has a row chief who is supposed to see that each individual gets the twenty liters of water a day he or she has a right to, and no more.

It is enough water, and since they came to the camp, the Douches get enough food. From 1974 to 1979 they starved; five of their children starved to death. Talking about that time is not easy. Douch Vech can tell stories about the earlier years when he was a soldier, first in the fifties, when, with Issarak's army, he fought the French colonialists on the Laos border; then with Sihanouk, when he fought the Communists; and later with Lon Nol, when Nol took over from Sihanouk. But of the Pol Pot years he will only say that he survived by hiding the fact that he had been a soldier with the other factions. Those who did not hide their identity died. Then Douch Vech grows silent, and his wife, Douch Vuon, takes over. She is the only one who has the strength to describe how they were forced to work as farm laborers. How they were used as bulls to plow the land. How they worked until they fell in the muddy fields, not getting fed if they did not finish the day's work, or if they couldn't get up the next day. How they were shot if they complained or disagreed.

The Douches have lost all their family on both sides. They only have memories of their dead, and of the beautiful country they remember Kampuchea to have been. Douch Vuon steadies her voice and avoids everyone's eyes, because if she did not, she would start to cry, and rapidly tells how five of her children died. When the Vietnamese attacked the Khmer Rouge, in the chaos she and her husband managed to escape with the three children who were still alive. Word was spreading in the countryside that food was being distributed on the Thai border. With hundreds of thousands of desperate people like themselves, they headed across the Watina Plains to escape Kampuchea.

From the time they reached the camp in 1979, all that Douch Vech, his wife, and the children need has been given to them by the United Nations. Since then, Douch Vech's only dream has been to work for what he and his family need, to work the fertile land back home in Kampuchea. Douch Vech and his family are identified as "displaced persons." They are not considered "refugees," so they cannot be settled in a third country. Douch Vech says that, in any case, he is too old to go live in a foreign land and start all over. "I would never adapt," he says. Going back to Kampuchea to have a piece of familiar land is all Douch Vech and his wife pray for.

7:45

Vout, Vhee, and Vee, in their school uniforms, walk down row 4 of section 3. Fifteen-year-old Vout is heading to one of the three junior high schools, and Vhee and Vee to one of the camp's three hundred primary schools. Vout passes the hospital without thinking that today he could be there himself, adding his name to the list of two thousand crippled men and women who have lost arms and legs to field mines. Yesterday, like nearly every Sunday, Vout and his brother Vhee easily jumped the camp's low fence to go scavenging for wild vegetables. Everyone knows that just two kilometers from the border the fields are full of mines. If ever the doors of the camps were open and the people free to walk back into their country, many would die because the land on the border is so thoroughly mined. The Douches know that, but they prefer to ignore the danger in order to add some taste to the camp's bland rice and canned fish. Traditional Kampuchean cuisine is flavorful, and for a family without a home, eight years of tasteless food becomes an unbearable deprivation.

At this time of day, Site 2 is as alive as a busy city. The streets are swarming with people: the water fetchers, who walk up and down like hens; the bicycle-taxis carrying riders on the fender from one end of the camp to another for less than a penny; the twenty thousand bustling workers whom the camp aid agencies and camp administration employ to maintain their services.

The twenty thousand workers are lucky; they receive rice and fish as their salary, and sell it for cash. Then they can buy a bike, the most prized possession available, and taxi around, earning more money in fares. The Douch

The whole camp is numbered. When asked where they live, the Douch children can only answer, "House 122, row 4, section 3."

family is among the poor; no one has work. The boys are still too young, and the eldest girl, Muom, has just married. The Douches gain some economic independence by selling the surplus of the rice that is distributed to them. As eight- and five-year-old Vee and Lean receive the adult rice ration of five hundred grams a day, more than they need, the family is able to sell the extra rice on the free market to Thai traders. With the money from these sales, Douch Vuon can buy the sugar and spices that are not supplied to her, but nothing more. All that the family has been given—bed, mats, blankets, and mosquito nets—can be carried in their arms and moved away easily. They might have to do this shortly. There are rumors that the southern end of the camp is to be moved to its old site a few kilometers away. Since their arrival at the border, the Douches have rebuilt their house several times with the bush material supplied to them. They always build their house in the fashion of their homeland, but in their minds there is no question, it will never be "home."

10:00 Lean is playing with friends her age around the houses, in the tiny space between the rows where the pit latrines are installed. It is so crowded that Douch Vech's family has to share a latrine with his neighbors. The children are careful. Any incident may start a fight, inside or outside the family. The frustrations of being without a future, without the dignity of work, without the pride of a national identity, burn inside everyone. All the superficial calm in the streets that are slowly emptying as the hot sun rises, and in the passive, contained faces, hides an anguish that often erupts in domestic violence.

All the Douch family owns has been provided to them by the United Nations Border Relief Operation, but what Douch Vech dreams of is to work and provide himself for his family's needs: a man's pride and basic right.

12:00   In the corner of the bamboo house, Douch Vuon rocks her baby in the hammock, waiting for him to fall asleep so she can start cooking lunch. Her children will soon be home from school and hungry. Since her oldest daughter, Muom, married three months ago, she alone does all the housework. Young girls often marry early for security against the sexual pressures of camp life. The Douches received 8,000 baht (US$342) as bride price, a good bit of money. But nearly all of it went for a traditionally lavish Khmer wedding celebration. Douch Vuon lights the wood that she receives as ration along with rice, dry fish, mung beans, salt, cooking oil, and possible fresh green vegetables.

2:00   The afternoon is terribly hot; the children are at school, and parents in the shade. The town has the aspect of a flat Monday. Yesterday there was time to bring alive the culture left behind. Streets were full and a crowd gathered to see a play in the open-air theater of the central square. And, once again, the theme was war, with the Pol Pot fighters dressed in black, the sign of evil.

5:00   The camp officer and his assistants, all connected by walkie-talkie, oversee the exit of all the foreign workers heading to their nearby quarters. Behind them, the gates are closed, and the sun sets outside the fences. Locked for the night, Site 2 is no longer a city, but a camp where no one is allowed in, or out, and where on the stage an actor, dressed in white, wins the battle.

Displaced Persons

DEFINITIONS
Refugee: A person who, owing to well-founded fear of being persecuted for reasons of race, religion, nationality, membership in a particular social group, or political opinion, is outside the country of his nationality and is unable or, owing to such fear, unwilling to avail himself of the protection of that country. (The 1951 United Nations Convention relating to the Status of Refugees and its 1967 Protocol)
Displaced person: One who has been forced to leave his home because of social or political upheaval but is not officially considered a refugee. (There is no official definition of the term "displaced person.")

LOCATIONS: (1988) Approximately forty camps throughout Thailand, Malaysia, Hong Kong, Indonesia, the Philippines, Singapore, Macao, Japan, and Papua New Guinea

REFUGEE POPULATION (1988)
Lowland Laotian: 18,692
Hill-tribe Laotian: 58,390
Kampuchean: 17,625
Vietnamese: 59,932
Irian Jayan: 8,000 est.
Philippine: 90,000 est.

DISPLACED PERSONS POPULATION (1988)
Kampuchean: 300,000 est.

Site 2 Border Encampment

THE PEOPLE: Kampuchean displaced persons

GEOGRAPHY
Area: approx. 5 sq. km.
Density: 39,441 pers./sq. km. (102,179 pers./sq. mi.) (1988)
POPULATION: 197,205 (1988)

HISTORY
In 1975, after the Communist Khmer Rouge forces overthrew the Lon Nol government and Pol Pot took control, 34,000 Kampucheans fled to the Thai border to escape the forced labor and genocide of the new regime. In 1978 the Vietnamese entered and nearly a hundred thousand more Kampucheans fled from Pol Pot and the fighting.

In June 1979 the Royal Thai government, overwhelmed by the number of refugees, sent more than forty thousand back into Kampuchea through a mined border region. The death of thousands of refugees attracted the world's attention. In the aftermath, the Thai government accepted international support and continued to grant temporary asylum to fleeing Kampucheans.

There was a surge of Kampuchean refugees in October of 1979 after a strong Vietnamese advance against the Khmer Rouge. An estimated half of the Khmer Rouge forces fled Kampuchea and arrived, starving, at the Thai border. From October 1979 to early 1980, nearly two hundred thousand people, Khmer Rouge and others, fled the fighting between the various resisting Kampuchean forces and the Vietnamese, and were given shelter in holding centers administered by the Royal Thai government. At one point the largest camp, Khao I Dang, was said to be the largest city of Kampucheans in the world.

In early 1980 these holding centers were closed to new arrivals. The Royal Thai government, along with the international community, considered that the camps had become a magnet drawing people from all over the area. From that time, all new arrivals were given shelter in border encampments and were not eligible for refugee status. Throughout the early eighties, the camps along the border in Kampuchea, run by various Kampuchean resistance forces, were attacked by the Vietnamese. Hundreds of Khmer were killed, thousands wounded, and tens of thousands were uprooted and moved along the border to avoid the fighting. By March 1985, all the displaced persons had been evacuated into camps in Thailand.

These camps have been administered by the United Nations Border Relief Operation (UNBRO), by expatriate Kampuchean forces, and by the Royal Thai government, assisted by a number of voluntary agencies. They have always been considered temporary and the Kampucheans held there have never been given refugee status. Their number continues to grow.

FAMILY: The population in Site 2 has one of the highest birth rates in the world, 47 births per thousand population per year (1988).

FOOD: Dry rations in the form of rice, fish, pulses, and vegetable oil, providing a minimum average of 2,283 calories per person per day, are distributed to eligible beneficiaries. Fresh vegetables, wheat, and salt are also provided. Vulnerable groups receive supplementary feeding.*

WATER: Water for drinking, cooking, and washing, rationed at twenty liters per person per day, is trucked into the camps and is available in centrally located tanks.

HEALTH: Health care, with an emphasis on primary preventive care, is provided to everyone in the camp.

HOUSING: Each family is provided with bush materials and tools to build a house in the style of their homeland.

EDUCATION: Primary education, grades 1–6, and junior high school education, is available in the camp.

---

* UNBRO provides food, water, housing, health care, and education, with the assistance of various agencies.

Refugees and Displaced Persons in East Asia, Southeast Asia, and the Pacific

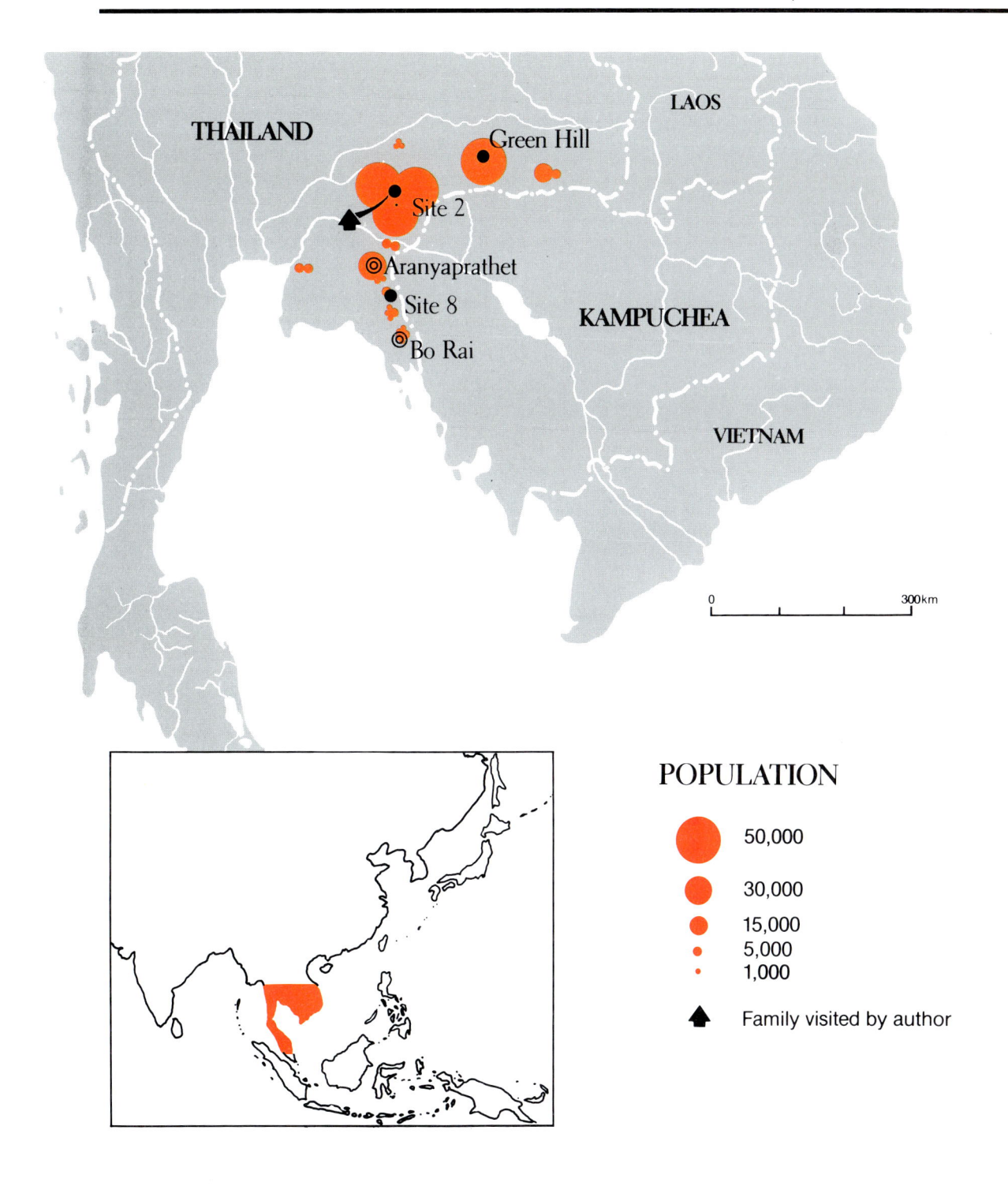

POPULATION

- 50,000
- 30,000
- 15,000
- 5,000
- 1,000

▲ Family visited by author

THE PACIFIC

Australia

The Calleja Family

Stephen Calleja, age 28 (1)
Mary Calleja, 24 (2)
Christopher, 5 (3)
Leah, 3 (4)

1 dog

Melton

APRIL 11

6:15 Mary answers her alarm clock's order and gets up to shower, the only way she can dispel her fatigue. On this cool autumn morning, the hot water quickly fills the bathroom with steam.

Christopher wakes up to his sister Leah's conversation with her dolls. Leah is going through a period of her life where dolls, babies, and playing mother are enough to make her happy. When she hears her parents get up, she pulls her blanket out of the room and rolls in it, lying like a guard dog in the hall between her parents' bedroom, the bathroom, and the kitchen. Whoever moves in the house has to walk over her.

7:00 While his wife is preparing the children's breakfast and the lunch they will bring to the sitter's, Stephen helps his son and daughter dress. "It's impossible to have a cup of coffee in the morning without it getting cold," says Mary, now running to get dressed. It is the trickiest time of year for clothes. In the fall, the Australians say, there are four seasons in a day. Despite the morning cold, it will be very hot by noon. Mary doesn't have much choice in her wardrobe. Since the children were born, she has not had the means to spoil herself. But as of last month, she is back at work at the Australian Eagle Insurance Company, doing computer entry and filing. She looks forward to having room in her family's budget for things they want, as well as things they need.

7:15 "Everybody in the car. Fast! Fast!" cries Stephen. Once again Mary checks the old outfit she has on. "What can you do?" she says, and slams the door. They stop five doors down the street at the family day-care service. Mary brings the kids and their meals to the sitter and runs back to the car. They are now really late, and their 1964 Falcon XM labors to speed to the station. If they miss the 7:30 train, the next will be very crowded, and strap-hanging for the hour-long run to Melbourne's center would be just too much.

Stephen parks his collector's classic in the station parking lot. He keeps his other car, the 1966 Falcon XP, parked in the back yard, for special outings only. Stephen belongs to a collectors' club, and most of his spare time is spent repairing, washing, and talking Ford Falcons.

Husband and wife find two adjacent seats on the train among bleary-eyed fellow passengers still recuperating from the weekend. They talk quietly. In 1981, just five months after their marriage, Mary found herself pregnant, and Stephen was left to meet the financial needs of the family by himself. Today

Mary is glad to go back to work and share this aspect of life with her husband. She earns even more than Stephen, who works as a travel agent, and at first she worried that that would insult him. But, in fact, she says, she feels more like a woman and a wife again. "After Christopher's birth, our lives were separate. Stephen was a worker; I was a mother. Now we spend time together in the train and meet for lunch almost every day. It's like having a new relationship."

Even though it is forty-five kilometers away and has a population of thirty thousand, Melton is still considered a suburb of Melbourne. In the future, the fields that separate Melton from Melbourne will probably be full of houses. For now, the Callejas pass through an immense yellow expanse of Australian outback on their way to work. Stephen does not mind the distance. He likes the open space and the yellow fields stretching to the horizon, to which Mary, a city girl, is only now becoming accustomed.

Moving to an outlying suburb was the only way for the couple to have their own house on Stephen's salary. But, so far, everything is going according to plan; they finished the house and furnished it; the kids are registered for school, and they feel secure and happy with Irene, the children's sitter.

8:20 Irene walks her own son and Christopher to school, bringing Leah and her little girl in a stroller. Irene used to teach, but has decided to stay at home to raise her children. As one salary is not enough for a family to meet Australia's high cost of living, she enrolled to work in the government-run Family Day Care Program. It is professional work: she had to take a special course. She cannot care for more than four children under the age of six, and the house is regularly inspected for cleanliness and security. Only then can she receive special insurance against accidents.

One-third of Mary's salary goes to day care. Every part of the couple's life is counted to the penny. "For the last six years we did not live, we survived," says Mary. With the down payment on the house to save, then the mortgage, then house furnishing, car payments, and taxes, Mary hardly had enough to eat, and no money for pleasure or clothing. The government Family Allowance check was warmly welcomed every month.

Their struggle is all part of "making it in Australia." Owning a home is central to this myth. For years the country has been a magnet for immigrants looking for a place to build a better life. Over twenty percent of the population was born overseas.

Stephen is first-generation Australian. His parents were born on the island of Malta and came to Australia while they were still young, settling and marrying in a Maltese community. Mary's parents are now considered an old Australian family: her mother's British ancestors settled here two hundred years ago, and her father was a Dutch war prisoner who arrived just after World

Melton is full of white couples of European descent who, like the Callejas, are building homes and having 1.9 children. The schools cannot meet the demand; Mary had to register Leah two years in advance to assure her a place in a private school.

War II. For Mary and Stephen, being part of a community is still very important. "If you don't make an effort to meet people in the suburbs," Mary says, "it's like burying yourself." In Melton, she met people through the Catholic church, by volunteering at the community health center and attending church study groups. "This is the community we belong to," she says. "And it's important to fit in." This was the rationale used by many Melton residents recently opposing a Vietnamese community coming into their suburb.

5:00   Daylight prepares to leave "down under," and Melbourne empties of its workers. Mary joins the surge of suburbanites walking briskly toward their trains. Two blocks from her office, she meets Stephen. The couple kiss lightly and rush to the train to find seats. What luck! There in the third car are two seats side by side, and it's non-smoking.

At about the same time, Irene is coming out of the sports center with her four charges. The two girls have just finished their ballet class. Irene buckles the children up safely in her car and heads back to her home, where Leah and Christopher will wait for their parents.

6:20   Mary rings Irene's doorbell. The tired children rush to the door and their mother's welcoming arms, and jump in the car, happy to go home. Eleven hours of games and learning is just a little too much; now they want to be with Mum and Dad.

Dinner is the only time in the week when the family can be together. To meet their goals, the couple must live in a suburb and work in the city, leaving their children for eleven hours each working day.

7:00 As she did this morning, Mary has rushed to the kitchen to prepare "tea" (dinner), and now calls the children to the table. Leah is tired and grumpy. For the last month, she has been making sure her mother will feel guilty about leaving her every day. "She will have to get used to it," says Mary, tired herself after her long day, and trying to be patient with her children.

7:30 Christopher is the last to leave the table. He is pouting and has tears in his eyes. He will not get ice cream for dessert because he has not finished the rice on his plate. Stephen and Mary differ on how children should be educated. Mary, brought up by parents who have lived through more difficult times, is more severe; she believes there are certain rules children should learn. Stephen is less rigid. "There will always be noodles for everyone" was what he learned in his more permissive home. He would like to give his son some ice cream but complies with his wife's decree. Stephen and Mary let each other know their different ideas about things, but have learned to compromise.

7:45 While Mary gives her children their bath and prepares them for the night, Stephen washes the dishes. When his son and daughter are in bed, he goes to kiss them good night. Tonight Leah is sleeping in her own room. Mary would like to put the two children in one room, to use Leah's room for sewing, and Leah prefers to sleep with her brother. But Stephen believes in keeping boys and girls separated. This issue is still under discussion.

With such a race to work and so little time for their family, the Callejas have no time to go out. "I'd feel guilty leaving my children with another sitter after so many hours away from home," says Mary. Often they rent movies at the video club, but tonight is the beginning of a good Australian television series. The week's nights are therefore all planned.

The Australians

THE NAME: From the Latin *Terra Australis* given by early geographers, meaning "southern land"

GEOGRAPHY
The flattest continent (average elevation less than 300 m.) and geologically the oldest. A dry and barren central plain covers more than half the land area. The Central-Eastern Lowlands lie east of the plain. Highlands extend along the eastern rim.
Max. altitude: 2,228 m. (7,310 ft.) (Mt. Kosciusko)
Area: 7,682,300 sq. km. (2,966,155 sq. mi.)
Density: 2.1 pers./sq. km. (5.5 pers./sq. mi.)
Arable land: 6% (1985)
Forest: 14%
Climate: Ranges from tropical (40% of the country) to temperate. The north has hot, humid summers and warm, dry winters; the south has hot, dry summers and mild winters.

CAPITAL: Canberra, pop. 243,450 (1984 est.)

LANGUAGE: English (official)
14% of population do not speak English at home.

RELIGION
Catholic: 26%
Anglican (Church of England): 24%
Other Christian: 24%
No religion: 13%
Not stated: 13%

POPULATION: Total—15,800,000 (1985)
Annual growth: 1.2% (189,600) (1985)
Doubling time: 88 yrs.
Urban: 85% (1985) (est. for year 2000: 86%)
Rural: 15%

AGE GROUPS (1986)
8% under 5 yrs.
23% under 15
32% under 20
32% from 20 to 39
21% from 40 to 59
15% 60 yrs. and over

ETHNIC GROUPS
Majority Caucasian, largely of British, Maltese, Italian, Greek, Dutch, and Polish descent
Aboriginal: 1%

HISTORY
First inhabited by the Aboriginals, a dark-skinned race of hunters and gatherers believed to have arrived from Asia at least 38,000 years ago
1606–44: Dutch explorers claim north as New Holland but do not settle
1688: First Englishman, buccaneer William Dampier, arrives
1770: Captain Cook's visit to fertile east coast results in Britain's taking possession of the eastern part of continent, calling it New South Wales
Jan. 26, 1788: First British settlement established at Port Jackson (Sydney); founded as a penal colony. During the next few decades Australia is used as dumping ground for criminals, bankrupts, and political undesirables transported from the British Isles
1840–68: Permanent colonization replaces penal settlements
1850s: Development of wool industry raises demand for sheep-grazing land. Aborigines pushed deeper into the bush
1851: Discovery of gold brings rapid economic development
Jan. 1, 1901: Commonwealth of Australia proclaimed
April 25, 1915: Australian troops land at Gallipoli in the WWI Dardanelles compaign
1930s: Reserves established for Aborigines
1951: ANZUS security treaty signed with New Zealand and the U.S.A.
1950–70s: Government-financed immigration increases white population, followed by immigration from Asia
1981: Territory in South Australia deeded to Aborigines for the first time

FAMILY
Marital status, for females 15 yrs. + (1986)
Single: 28% Divorced: 4.5%
Married: 58% Separated: 2.5%
Widowed: 6.5%

AUSTRALIA

Single-parent families: 11% (female: 86%, male: 14%) (1986)
Fertility rate: 1.8 (1987)
Teenage births: 5% / Teenage fertility rate: 26.5/1,000 (1983)
Births out of wedlock: 15.5% (1985)
Contraception: no data
Government's position on family planning: Population growth and fertility are satisfactory. Family planning is a personal choice. Government supports information and access to contraception. Abortion and sterilization laws vary from state to state. Minimum legal age of marriage is 16.

SOCIAL INDICATORS
Life expectancy: 78 yrs. (1986) (male: 72, female: 79) (1984)
Infant mortality: 9/1,000 births (1987)
Crude birth rate: 15/1,000 pop. (1987)
Crude death rate: 7/1,000

HEALTH
Access to health services: 98.6% (1982)
Births attended by trained health personnel: 98.6%

HOUSING
Persons per household: 3.0 (1986)
Electricity: 100% with (1986)
Access to safe water: 99% (1982)
Source of water (1986)
   Piped inside or out: 100%
Toilet facilities (1982)
   Adequate sanitary facilities: 99%
Construction materials
   Brick or stone: 62%
   Timber or weatherboard: 22%
   Other: 16%

EDUCATION
Literacy: male: 88%; female: 82% (1981)
Gross enrollment ratio (1985)
   First level: 106%
   Second: 95%
   Third: 27.7%
Educational attainment for pop. all ages (1975)
   None: 0.4%
   First level: 23.7%
   Second: 9.2%
   Third: 3.3%

ECONOMIC ACTIVITY
Economically active population: 60% (male: 75%; female: 46%) (1985)
Agriculture: 6% act. pop.; 7% of GDP
Mines: 4% act. pop.; 9% of GDP
Industry: 23% act. pop; 25% of GDP
Services: 67% act. pop.; 59% of GDP
Per capita GNP: US$11,920 (1986)
National currency: Australian dollars
Principal resources: Petroleum, coal, natural gas, iron and other minerals

COMMUNICATIONS
Radio
   Transmitters: 284 (1981)
   Receivers: 1,274/1,000 pop. (1985)
Television
   Transmitters: 386 (1981)
   Receivers: 446/1,000 pop. (1985)
Newspapers (1984)
   Dailies: 62
   Circulation: 4,588,000 (296/1,000 pop.)

Australia

POPULATION

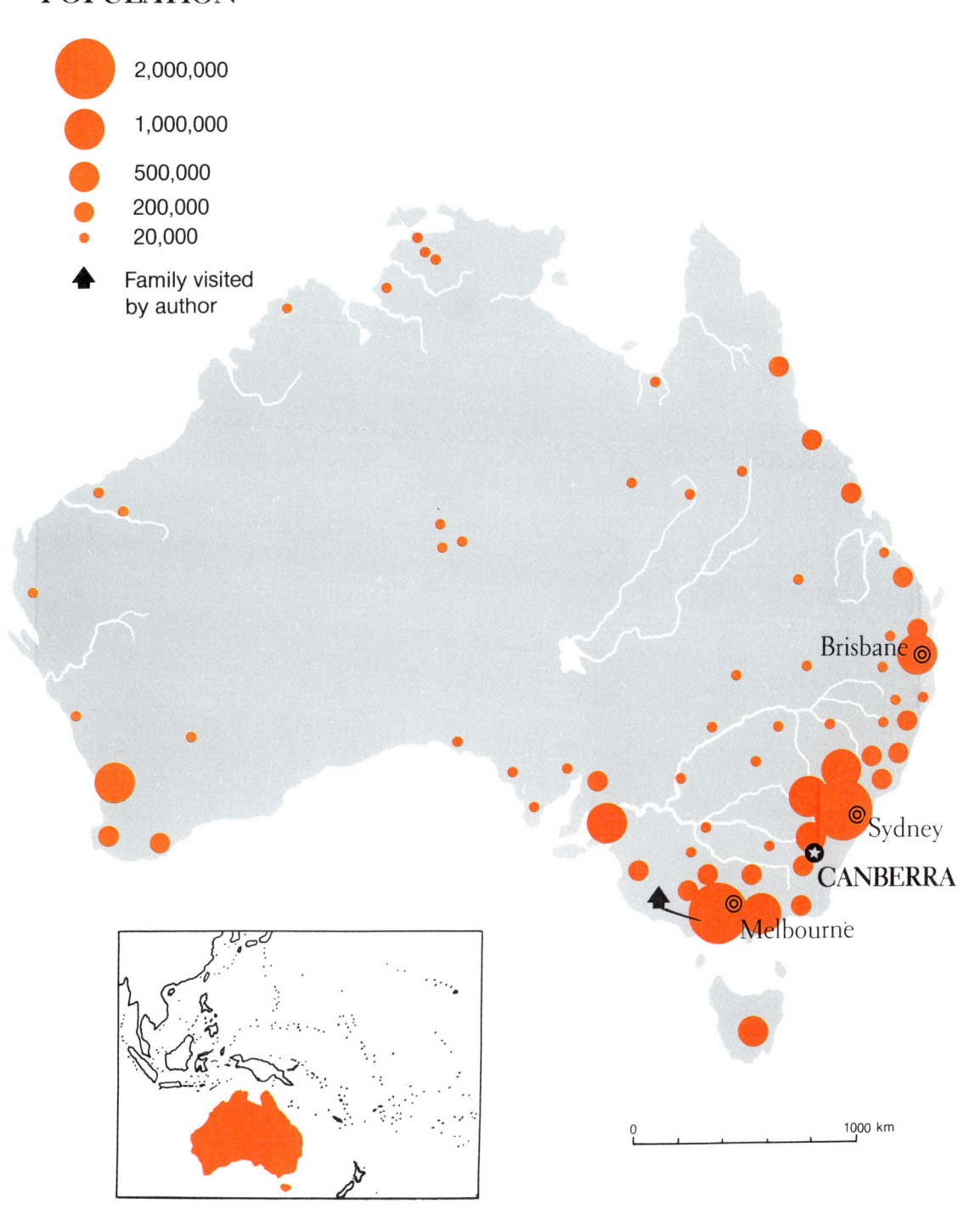

- 2,000,000
- 1,000,000
- 500,000
- 200,000
- 20,000

▲ Family visited by author

Brisbane

Sydney

CANBERRA

Melbourne

Republic of Fiji

Ratu Abele Asaroma's Family*

Ratu Abele Asaroma, age 31 (1)
Silivia Vakaseleasi, 28 (2)
Adi Kubuyana Silivia, 11 (3)
Adi Bilivalu Maria, 9 (4)
Ratu Kalaveti Bebenisala, 7 (5)
Ratu Vilisi Ronaivana (Oscar), 5 (6)
Adi Salote Nayala, 2 (7)

1 cow
5 chickens

* *Ratu* (for men) and *Adi* (for women) are titles given to the descendants of a chiefly family.

Naseuvu Village

NOVEMBER 23

5:00 At the rooster's second crow Silivia crawls from under the mosquito net, leaving her two youngest daughters beneath it; then tiptoes around her husband and three other children sleeping on the floor mat of the *vale-lebo* (sleeping house). She pulls out the tab of wood that serves as a lock and goes to make breakfast in her *vale-kuro* (cooking house) before her children leave for school.

All seems fixed in time. The heavy clouds cling to the mountains of the province of Naitasiri, and their mist settles to the bottom of the valley, giving the impression that the village of Naseuvu nestled there will stay forever between day and night. Only the rushing waters of the Waidina River, and the smoke from the kitchens' wood fires, reveal the activity in the village.

When Silivia steps outside, her foot sinks into the muddy earth. It is the rainy season. Just yesterday, her husband, Ratu Abele, was binding the last leaves on the cooking house's roof, one of the few buildings still made in the traditional style. His father, Ratu Valetino, is so concerned about the loss of tradition that he insists the whole family must know the craft.

In Fijian society, power descends from the paramount chiefs to village chiefs, who distribute the garden space to their villagers, and down to sub-clan chiefs like Ratu Valetino, who represent the needs of their particular tribe.

At the sound of the church's *lali* (a hollow wooden gong), the three older children, dressed for the day after their shower the night before, jump up silently, fold the cotton cloths that have served as bed sheets, pile them in cardboard boxes at one end of the house, where all the family's belongings are kept, then walk across the village. Their first words will be those of the morning's prayers in the small wooden church.

6:15 Adi Salote Nayala, the youngest, her legs still shaky from sleep, is the last to peek out the door, where she discovers her grandmother squatting under an umbrella, washing the dishes at the outside tap that serves the three houses of her husband and her two sons. The child totters toward her father, Ratu Abele, who is going down to the river to milk his father's cow. The milk will serve all sixteen members of the extended family.

7:00 Oldest daughter Adi Kubuyana spreads a long rectangular cloth on the floor of the sleeping house and takes plates from the house's only shelf, singing as she works. She is a happy girl with a magnetic personality. Ratu Vilisi, her brother, who watches her, is just the opposite, often whining and looking for trouble. His nickname is "Oscar," after the cyclone during which he was born, and his family believes that that terrible night influenced his personality.

As Silivia and her oldest daughter bring the *dalo* (a starchy root), the family crawl to their positions around the cloth. No one walks when the father is in the house. Every aspect of their life, including the meal, is guided by tradition. Ratu Abele sits at the upper end of the cloth. He will be served the first and best portions. His two sons are on his left and right, the rest seated by age, with Silivia nearest the door to her kitchen. The meal won't start before grace is said. Children must sit cross-legged, not moving until their plate is finished. It is taboo for them to eat any food from their father's plate, and if they get up to get something, they must clap their hands twice as they sit again, to excuse themselves for having been higher than their father.

The family eats quietly, their silence broken only by the call of a villager blowing the *davui* (conch shell). Today, Monday, is the communal workday. It is this work that has made Naseuvu so beautiful. Women have planted flowers on the village's greens. Men have built sidewalks, a communal house, and the church. Today only the men are called; the dam the villagers have built in the mountain stream is clogged by branches and rocks and the water taps have stopped running. By working together, the men will reestablish the water flow in just a few minutes.

8:00 Ratu Abele has decided not to join the men, as he is anxious to finish the kitchen's hearth. He could not finish it yesterday, since the government, highly influenced by Protestant religious beliefs, prohibits anything but praying, eating, and sleeping on Sunday.

A *lali* rings again, this time from the school on the mountain overlooking the two villages it serves. Children are called early to remove the fallen dry leaves from the school grounds, take care of the flowers, and clean the latrines.

9:00 The *lali* rings once more to tell the school cook and all the villagers the time of day. Silivia lies down all alone in the middle of her house; her pregnancy makes her very sleepy. Her two youngest children are with their father's mother, whose duty it is never to let the children and houses out of her sight. After her nap, Silivia takes a twenty-minute walk to the next village to visit her mother. The dirt road is deserted. A bus travels the road twice a day to bring the villagers to and from the capital's market, and occasionally trucks coming to get the farmers' banana crops.

12:00 Silivia is back from her mother's just as the school gong announces lunch for

All the village kitchens are as new as Silivia's. The fragile buildings must be rebuilt after each cyclone. Ratu Abele has rebuilt both his houses three times. After the last cyclone, the government provided corrugated iron for the roofing, but Ratu Abele decided to rebuild the roof and walls of his sleeping house with the iron, and use bamboo and leaves for the kitchen.

the children. Silivia, her husband, and the two youngest will share the meal cooked by her mother-in-law.

1:30 Machete and fishing pole in hand, Ratu Abele and Silivia walk single-file along the rocky riverbank to fetch vegetables from their garden. Oscar gets to come along, but an upset Adi Salote stays home. From the tone of her cries, she must believe they'll never return.

Ratu Abele, Silivia, and Oscar cross the snaking river twice to get to their garden. All of Ratu Abele's land is near the river. He has planted *dalo*, cassava, banana, breadfruit, and yams. Half of the harvest will feed his family, and the other half he sells at the market once a month. But subsistence living is giving way to a need for cash; now the family needs money for schools, clothing, and the imported canned foods, rice, and spices that they have become accustomed to. The couple do not know, and do not worry about, the size of their plot. They know they could clear as much land as they would need to earn more cash. But the problem is that there is no more land close enough to rivers and roads to get produce out to market.

3:00 Silivia and Ratu Abele's clothes, already damp from crossing the river, are now wet with sweat. After planting new cassava plants, the couple select the best *dalo* leaves, dig up a few yams, and pick bananas. Ratu Abele piles them onto a bamboo raft, which he pulls upriver to the village, with Oscar perched in the middle. Silivia stays behind to fish for tonight's dinner. At the bend of the river, where fishing is plentiful, a dozen villagers already stand in a line along the bank. A daily necessity, fishing is also a time for relaxing. Silivia laughs and jokes and visits with friends, heading back home with seven fish for dinner, long after the *lali* has announced the end of school.

6:00 The sun appears from behind the clouds just before setting, illuminating the greens of the mountainside. The church's *lali* sounds. As her children leave for evening prayers, Silivia goes to her kitchen.

6:30 Back from church, Adi Kubuyana goes to the tap to wash the morning's dishes and then waits, ready to help her mother. While the *dalo* leaves boil, Silivia peels the cassava. In his father's house, Ratu Abele mixes the kava. First he crushes the plant's roots into a fine powder, then wraps it in a thin-spun cloth. He will soak the kava in water in a big wooden bowl used for the nightly "kava ceremony" attended by the men. His father, the chief, sits near the central door in the upper end of the house, where the others lower in rank are not allowed to sit. Ratu Abele's older brother, the chief-to-be, will serve the kava in a half coconut shell. Ratu Abele reaches for the guitar.

8:00 Silivia eats alone with her children. There is more than enough food. Not to have enough would bring shame on the house of Ratu Abele. After the meal, two schoolgirls arrive, to rehearse for the annual year-end show. Adi Bilivalu and her girlfriends practice the traditional songs and the motions of the hands that accompany every word, lulling little Ratu Kalaveti and Ratu Vilisi to sleep. Adi Salote dozes, her head resting on her mother's knees.

9:30 The house is quiet now. On the shelf in a jar used as an oil lamp, a flame is burning and will stay lit all night. Traditionally, it was to keep the bad spirits away, but Ratu Abele's family has forgotten this, and the lamp is now "just the way it has always been." It also makes it easier for anyone to go to the "little house" in the yard during the night.

REPUBLIC OF FIJI 177

Adi Salote won't have the attention as the youngest for long; her young mother is six months pregnant. Although tired of so many pregnancies, Silivia does not interfere with her husband's desire for more heirs. It is her duty to serve and obey the wishes of her husband's family.

11:00 Silivia lies asleep on the doorstep, waiting for her husband's return to serve him dinner. That will be whenever the men have emptied the kava bowl and finished their songs.

Republic of Fiji

The Govind Family

Shiu Govind, age 59 (1)
Ram Devi, 57 (2)
Jagdish Ram Govind, 31 (3)
Prabhasni Devi (daughter-in-law), 27 (4)
Pratish Prasheel Govind, 3 (5)
Premila Wati, 26 (6)
Arishma Kuma, 1 month (7)
Vidya Wati, 22 (8)

3 bulls   50 chickens
3 cows   1 dog
3 goats   1 cat
50 ducks

Olosara

JANUARY 27

4:30   Prabhasni hears the footsteps of her family's hired hand. She rises and serves him a breakfast of tea, bread, and last night's leftover curry, then goes back to her room to lie down near her husband, Jagdish. Pratish Prasheel, their three-year-old son, is sleeping in the bed beside theirs.

5:30   The sun is rising over Olosara, home to the sugarcane farmers, a village of ninety houses stretched over two thousand acres along King's Road. Prabhasni rises for the second time to serve tea to her parents-in-law and her husband, who are joining the hired hand in the field. Since the turn of the century, when their ancestors were brought from India to Fiji by the English colonizers to grow sugar, Shiu's family have been sugarcane farmers. The seventeen acres of land he works, still called "Crown land," is rented from the government.

    Now that the country is no longer part of the Commonwealth, there is talk that the land will again belong to the native Fijians. This worries Shiu. His twenty-one-year lease expires soon, and the rent might triple.

    Since their independence from the plantation owners, the Indians have been working hard to improve their lives and maintain traditions. Originally from separate regions of India with distinct cultures and languages, the Fijian descendants created their own dialect so they could speak to one another, abolished the Indian caste system so they could work and live together, yet kept alive both the Hindu and the Islamic faiths. Their hard work has paid off; the current generation is largely white-collar workers. Shiu's son Jagdish Ram Govind works in a bank; his oldest son is a doctor in the capital; and his daughter, Premila, is a teacher. They have a washing machine and a gas stove, and in the overfurnished living room the VCR has the place of honor. Shiu is a proud man.

    Prabhasni starts cooking breakfast: *roti* (flat bread) and a fresh vegetable curry. She hums while she works, for she likes to cook and, most important, she is satisfied with her new family.

    Her marriage to Jagdish Ram Govind was arranged by telephone. Like all young girls, she was scared to move in with her mother-in-law, knowing she could have been miserable if they did not get along. But, unlike some other families, Ram Devi and her husband allow their daughter-in-law to sit at the table and openly speak her mind. Prabhasni feels lucky to have found such a tolerant family where traditions can be questioned, because she has something to say about everything. Now more women and men are working together and marrying for love. She and Jagdish say: "We have learned to like each other, but it is not the same as marrying for love."

6:30 Premila Wati, Shiu's older daughter, changes her new baby. According to tradition, a woman should be completely inactive the first month after giving birth and should return to her parents' house during this period. Premila, on maternity leave from teaching, enjoys being waited on, hand and foot. Thrilled to have a little girl she can fuss over, she tenderly massages the tiny body with coconut oil. "Massage wakes up a young body that sleeps so much and does not move," she says. She then carefully lines the infant's eyes with kohl (a harmless black coloring) and puts a red dot on her forehead to ward off the evil eye.

7:00 On his thirty-year-old tractor, Shiu brings fertilizer to his newly planted sugar field. In the afternoon he will use his bullock to plow up the weeds between the sugarcane rows. His wife, his employee, and his son Jagdish weed between the plants by hand.

7:45 Jagdish leaves the field to go to his bank work, but first he feeds the ducks and chickens, then showers and breakfasts. A traditional man, Jagdish will always look after his father's land and wishes for more children so he can be sure to have enough helping hands. But the economic situation makes it impossible to give so many children comfortable lives and an education. On his way to work, he will drive his son, Pratish, to nursery school and his sister Vidya to her job at the supermarket in Signatoka.

Shiu sits down at the table. On the wall beside him, color posters instruct him in nutrition. A diabetic, Shiu eats carefully, so that he can continue to work. Only after she finishes milking the cows does Ram Devi come to sit alone at the table's end. Like her husband, she does not want to retire. Shiu is already back in the field and Prabhasni comes to sit beside her mother-in-law.

9:30 The whole family has been served; Prabhasni can now clean her kitchen. Then she sits with the baby while Premila rests. Grandmother Ram Devi washes the diapers in the outside cement sink, hangs them to dry in the hot sun, then squats in the cement shower room, giving the baby a bath in the washtub. She laughs tenderly over the fussing child.

10:30 Premila takes a shower and Prabhasni brings tea and cake to the field for the morning break. When she comes back, she rushes to start the laundry. After nine months of drought, the water reservoirs are nearly empty and the town cuts off the water between eleven and five.

While some dry weather is good for the old sugarcane plants, this year it

Shiu lies on the couch. It is now too hot to be working outside. Premila picks lemons to prepare juice for him, while Ram Devi goes in to soothe her new grandchild, who has broken out in a heat rash. Granny murmurs gently to her, the baby stops crying, and both fall asleep.

is too dry. The first harvest is nearly over and the planting of the new cane has started and it needs rain.

11:30 Jagdish returns his son from nursery school, then drives back to Signatoka for a quick lunch with his colleagues. Pratish's arrival brings an end to the morning peace. The spoiled young boy has this household of adults at his service, and he takes full advantage of it. Especially of his mother. He listens to nothing she says, climbs up on the kitchen counters, and yells if something is not given to him right away. Prabhasni seems overwhelmed by him and leaves it to her sister-in-law to manage him. Contrary to her husband, she would not be upset to have only one child.

1:30 Everyone comes for lunch when they are hungry and Prabhasni serves them. Then everyone naps.

The first house Shiu built for his family is now a shed used to shelter the hired hand. The second he built they now rent to city workers. The one they have lived in for twenty years keeps on growing. After the most recent cyclone, they built a cement addition so Jagdish and his wife would have more space. Shiu's son, the doctor, built himself a room for his visits, and Shiu added on a new gray cement shower room. They have started on a garage, but during the recent political upheavals, all the construction stopped. "First let's see what will happen," says Shiu. Like most of the Indians in Fiji, Shiu does not see much future for his children here. Political instability has undermined all hope, and since he visited his two brothers in America, Shiu is encouraging his children to find work in some other country.

3:00 Ram Devi is off to the field again. Prabhasni, who was sleeping beside her son, starts cooking for the afternoon break.

The kitchen is Prabhasni's domain. As daughter-in-law, she is the homemaker, and the house will be hers, as Jagdish's wife, when her in-laws die. Here the women rule over the affairs of the home; the men are in charge of the land and the harvest.

3:15   Jagdish and Vidya Wati are back from work. Jagdish complains he will have to go to the office tomorrow, although it is Saturday. Since the political coup, so many Indians have emigrated that those who are left in white-collar jobs have to work twice as long. Vidya Wati disappears immediately into her sister's room. Playing with baby is Aunty's passion at the moment. Jagdish changes into his work clothes and joins his parents in the field.

5:45   The sun is setting and the workers are taking their turns in the shower. Delicious odors waft from the kitchen—a rice pilaf, curried chicken, vegetables, and spicy dipping sauces. Prabhasni is responsible for cooking, but Jagdish buys the ingredients. "She is an expensive woman; she always needs foods from all over the world for her cooking," he reprimands indulgently. Prabhasni laughs and turns back to her stove, singing.

   Shiu and his brother, who is visiting from down the road, sit on the front porch to drink kava. They appreciate the Fijian drink but do not perform the ceremony to prepare it. A plastic bowl will do.

7:30   Shiu's daughters eat first; then the men will be served. Prabhasni will serve herself when everyone else has eaten. Vidya Wati is preparing Pratish Prasheel for bed. He is still restless, so she massages his entire body until he is blissfully relaxed.

9:00   The evening entertainment consists of mild conversation on the porch and in the living room. One by one, the family members go to bed. The sun rises as early as it sets.

The Fijians

THE NAME: From *Viti*, the indigenous name of the largest island

GEOGRAPHY
322 islands, some hundred inhabited, scattered over 1,290,000 sq. km. of ocean with some of the world's largest barrier reefs. Larger islands of volcanic origin are mountainous, with fertile coastal plains. The smaller are mostly low coral-reef islands.
Max. altitude: 1,424 m. (4,672 ft.) (Mt. Tomaniivi)
Area: 18,272 sq. km. (7,055 sq. mi.)
Density: 38 pers./sq. km. (99 pers./sq. mi.)
Arable land: 8% (1985)
Forest: 65%. Deforestation: 0.2% (2,000 hectares) per year (1980s)
Climate: Tropical, with uniformly high temperature and humidity. Rainfall is heavy and regular on the southeast (windward) side of island, but the northwest (leeward) side experiences a dry season. Lies in the "cyclone belt." Cyclones occur between December and March.

CAPITAL: Suva, pop. 69,665 (1986)

LANGUAGE: English (official)
The Bau dialect is the most widely spoken Fijian language.
Hindustani, a locally developed form of Hindi, spoken by Indo-Fijians

RELIGION
  Native Fijians
  Methodist: 74%
  Catholic: 14%
  Other Christian: 11.5%
  Other: 0.5%
  Indo-Fijians
  Hindu: 79%
  Muslim: 16%
  Christian: 4.5%
  Other: 0.5%

POPULATION: Total—715,000 (1986)
  Annual growth: 2% (14,300) (1986)
  Doubling time: 31 yrs.
  Urban: 42% (1986) (est. for year 2000: 51%)
  Rural: 58%

AGE GROUPS (1985)
  13% under 5 yrs.
  36% under 15
  47% under 20
  32% from 20 to 39
  12% from 40 to 59
  6% 60 yrs. and over

ETHNIC GROUPS
  Indian: 49%
  Fijian: 46%
  Other: 5%

HISTORY
According to Fijian legend, the great chief Lutunasobasoba led his people across the seas to the new land of Fiji
1250 A.D.: Complex stratified society marked by cannibalism and frequent warfare becomes most materially developed society in the Pacific. Subsequent European forays discouraged by barrier reefs and tales of cannibalism
early 19th cent.: Sandalwood traders, buying boatloads to sell at huge profits for incense in China, deplete forests by 1814
1830s: Missionaries arrive. In 1854, when influential chief Thakombau accepts Christianity, Fijians convert and tribal warfare stops
1857: British consul appointed at Levuka
1860s: Development of Fiji cotton plantations. British consul rules no Fijian can work on European plantations, so laborers are recruited, often forcibly, from other islands
1874: Thakombau is convinced by federation of chiefs to cede his kingdom to Great Britain.
1875: Measles epidemic kills one-third of population
1880s: Development of sugarcane industry, controlled by Australia from 1881 to 1973, brings indentured laborers from India whose descendants stay in Fiji
WWI and WWII: Fijian contingents serve with British forces
1962: Fijians are given the right to vote
Oct. 10, 1970: Independence within the Commonwealth
1987: Following a military coup by Colonel Rabuka to depose newly elected pro-Indian President Bavarda, an independent republic is formed and Fiji breaks from the Commonwealth

REPUBLIC OF FIJI

FAMILY
Marital status, for females 15 yrs. + (1986)
- Single: 57%
- Married: 39%
- Widowed: 3%
- Divorced: 1%

Female head of household: 14% (1986)
Fertility rate: 3.3 (1986)
Teenage births: 11% / Teenage fertility rate: 58.8/1,000 (1985)
Births out of wedlock: no data
Contraception: Fijians: 55%; Indians: 74% (1974)
Government's position on family planning: Population growth and fertility are too high. Promotes community involvement in family-planning programs and supports access to and information on family planning. Sterilization is legal. Minimum age of marriage is 16.

SOCIAL INDICATORS
Life expectancy: 70 yrs. (male: 68; female: 72) (1986)
Infant mortality: 27/1,000 births (1986)
Crude birth rate: 28/1,000 pop. (1986)
Crude death rate: 5/1,000

HEALTH
Access to health services: 100% (1982)
Births attended by trained health personnel: 95% (1984)

HOUSING
Persons per household: 5.8 (1986)
Electricity: 51% without (1986)
Access to safe water: 70% (urban: 100%; rural: 48%) (1986)
Source of water (1986)
- Piped: 78%
- Well: 13%
- Other: 9%

Toilet facilities (1986)
- Flush: 32%
- Pit latrine: 42%
- Other: 25%
- None: 1%

Construction materials (1986)
- Concrete, brick, or cement: 30%
- Wood: 26%
- Durable, tin or corrugated iron: 30%
- Other: 14%

EDUCATION
Literacy: 86% (male: 90%; female: 81%) (1986)
Gross enrollment ratio (1985)
- First level: 129% (completing in 1985: 75%)
- Second: 54%
- Third: 3.0% (1986)

Educational attainment for pop. 25 yrs. + (1986)
- None: 11%
- First level: 36%
- Second: 25%
- Third: 3%

ECONOMIC ACTIVITY
Economically active population: 54% (male: 85%; female: 23%) (1986)
- Agriculture: 40% act. pop.; 23% of GDP
- Mines: 2% act. pop.; 1% of GDP
- Industry: 8% act. pop.; 20% of GDP
- Services: 50% act. pop.; 56% of GDP

Per capita GNP: US$1,810 (1986)
Population in absolute poverty: rural: 15% (1985)
National currency: Fijian dollar
Principal resources: Sugar, copra, coconut oil, ginger, cassava, gold, silver

COMMUNICATIONS
Radio
- Transmitters: 14 (1985)
- Receivers: 579/1,000 pop. (1985)

Television
- Believed to have no television service of its own

Newspapers (1984)
- Dailies: 3
- Circulation: 58,000

Fiji

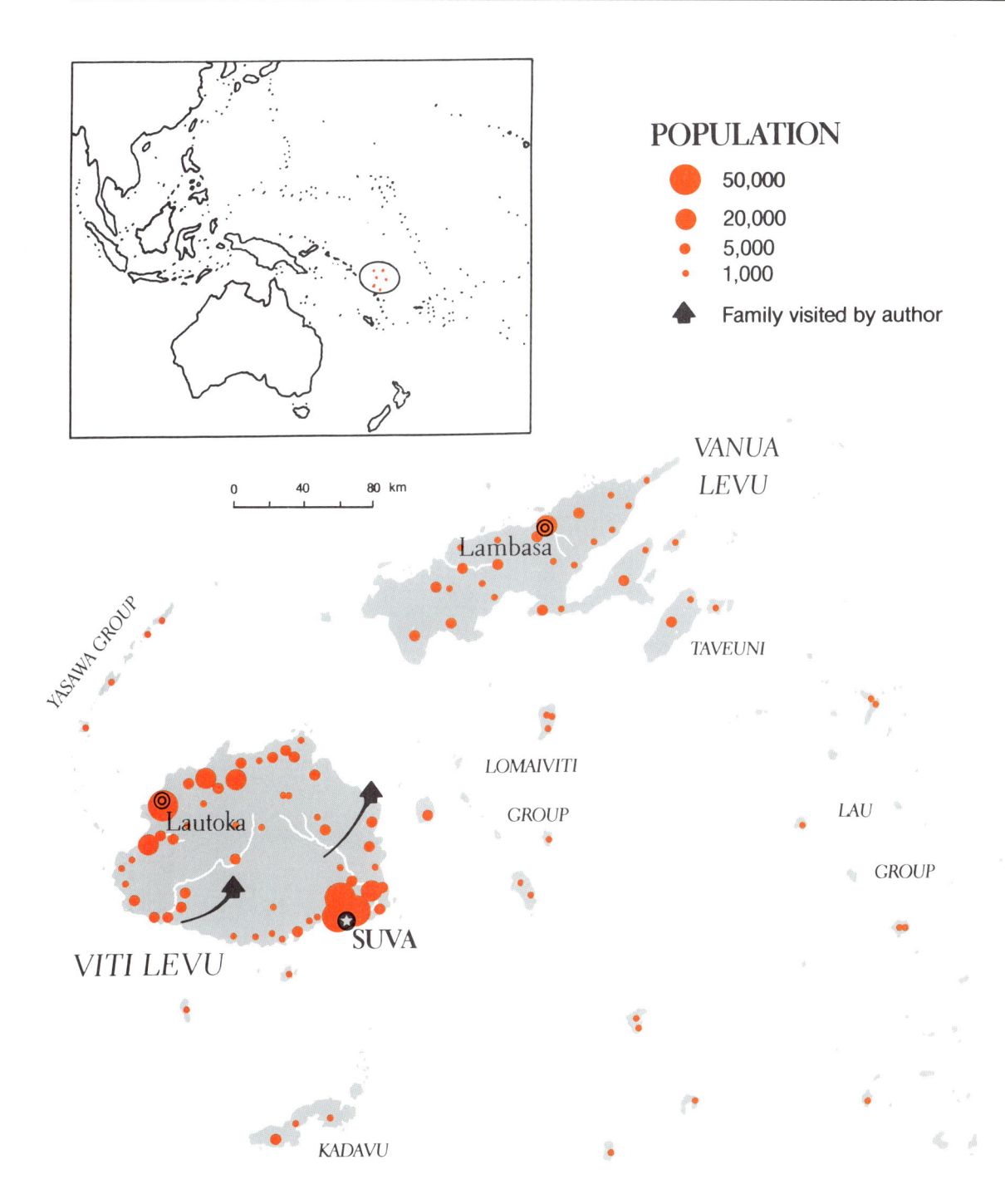

POPULATION

- 50,000
- 20,000
- 5,000
- 1,000

▲ Family visited by author

VANUA LEVU

Lambasa

TAVEUNI

YASAWA GROUP

LOMAIVITI GROUP

LAU GROUP

Lautoka

SUVA

VITI LEVU

KADAVU

Kiribati

Aram Terewati's Family

Aram Terewati, age 34 (1)
Bakea Teteki, 35 (2)
Ritang Aram, 10 (3)
Teteki, 7 (4)
Tabauea, 4 (5)
Teikakee, 11 months (6)
Mimrota, 63 (7)

4 pigs
2 roosters
2 dogs
1 cat

Utiroa Village

JANUARY 9

5:00   Teikakee's short sharp cry is immediately silenced by the breast which his mother, Bakea, lying beside him, puts into his mouth.

6:00   Ritang has slept at her grandmother's house. At ten years old, she already runs the household; at least, it seems not to function without her. "Ritang, do this, Ritang, do that," is heard all through the day. Now she takes a water pail from the bamboo counter in the middle of the yard to fetch water at the nearby well. When she returns, she washes the *teibu*, the empty coconut shells her father will use to collect the *toddy* (coconut-palm sap).

    Bakea ducks out of the mosquito net, reaching for the small basket of tobacco that always sits on the floor of the open-air one-room house. She rolls a cigarette for her husband, Terewati, who is already up and can be heard, like the men in every Utiroa household, sharpening his knife on a rock. He tests it on his hair every so often to make sure it is really sharp; then picks up the coconut shells and leaves, whistling.

    For as long as the oldest person can remember, on the island of Tabiteuea, from one end of the small Pacific atoll to the other, the day begins with men singing. They sing in the morning and evening when they are in the coconut trees fetching *toddy*. The custom is said to have begun to warn any woman using the bush for private matters that there was a man up in the trees who might see her.

    Getting *toddy* is not a simple thing. The nourishing sap is collected from a coconut-palm bud whose young shoot must be bent slowly during several days so that the sap can run down into an empty *teibu*. The bud is cut very carefully, so that the sap will flow for a day but the bud will not be ruined. The quantity of *toddy* depends, not on the size of the bud or the tree, but on the quality of the man's cut. This delicate operation Terewati now performs at the top of tall coconut-palm trees.

7:00   One is always near the sea on the atoll of Tab North, as the twenty-kilometer-long island is no more than one kilometer wide at any point. Bakea walks with her two youngest to the lagoon side of the island, whose coral reefs keep the rough seas calm and whose change of tides over its white sandy bottom turns the sea every shade of blue possible. Bakea joins the other villagers squatting near the water, their backs to the reef. The beach in all its beauty is their toilet.

    Back from the seashore, Bakea squats under the low thatched roof that serves as her kitchen. She starts one wood fire on one side for breakfast; on the other side, she lights a second to dry the copra, the coconut meat. Copra is the Aram family's only source of income. No other cash crops grow on the poor soil of this coral atoll.

Ritang's broom accompanies her father's song. She sweeps the dead breadfruit leaves and dry, empty coconut shells into a pile on one side of the yard. Grandmother Mimrota watches Teikakee. The unprotected well and the sharp coral rock that forms the ground make it impossible to let him go unattended. He is quiet in Grandmother's care, and if necessary, Teikakee will use her old breast as a pacifier.

Bakea believes that she is responsible for making her mother's last days on earth happy and peaceful. Both she and her husband are grateful for the skills their parents taught them: the ability to forecast the weather, navigate by the stars and birds and clouds, build canoes, and cut *toddy*. It is unlikely the couple will now have the time to pass these skills on, as their children will be in school, learning other things.

9:00 "Ritang, take the baby," says Grandmother. She goes to sit in front of her old rotting house and starts weaving pandanus leaves. Her own house badly needs repairs, but the leaves she weaves this morning are for the *maneaba*, the village's large meeting house, where all decisions are made, in the presence of the elders.

Today, except for high-school students, who study on another island, most of the village will meet there. Aram Terewati, however, cannot be with

Bakea sits on a mat to grind coconut. She distributes the juicy white bits into cups. Her husband comes back shortly with the toddy, *and Bakea sets it over the hot fire until it boils. Then she pours it over the coconut and breaks pieces of homemade bread into it—a nourishing and delicious breakfast.*

At night, Bakea unties the mosquito nets from the ceiling and lets them fall, covering the entire floor of the house. Then the roof straw hanging on the sides of the house is untied, and the floor mats attached, to act as venetian blinds.

his people. He has a meeting in another village in the small *maneaba* the Mormons have built to attract converts to their faith. The two missionaries have been on the island only a short time, and the Aram family is their first conquest.

11:00 Bakea goes to the *maneaba* with her neighbor, both women pulling their piece of leaf work for the roof repairs. A week from now, the whole population of Tabiteuea South, the neighboring island, will visit in their canoes, and Tab North is getting ready for the great event. The two islands have a history of violent conflict, and the people are considered the most aggressive and dangerous in the country. Differences are still resolved with bush knives. But on this historic day the islands will compete in sports, forget their differences, and, everyone hopes, begin a new era of peace and friendship.

1:00 Bakea has been too busy to get fresh seafood for lunch, so they'll have smoked fish. While her mother prepares the food, Ritang, who just finished washing the family clothes, walks around with Teikakee on her hip, trying to keep him content. In a few years, she'll take on new responsibilities as a woman. After her first menstrual period, the old women of the village will teach her their skills: cooking, and the intricate weaving patterns used in mats, baskets, and hats.

Sometimes Ritang pouts a bit about having so many duties. She is relieved that this baby is the last sibling she will be taking care of. Her mother is getting contraceptive injections: she does not want any more children.

2:30 Nap time is finished. Grandmother starts cracking coconuts and laying the meat in the sun. Terewati and his wife leave for one of their garden plots. They bring the dry leaves that Ritang swept up to use as fertilizer in one of their six *babai* pits. These large taro-like plants need five to ten years to grow to harvest size. The plants the couple will work on today are intended for their ten-year-old daughter's future marriage.

The starchy root of the *babai* was once the main subsistence food of the islanders, but today they prefer buying rice and canned foods. For this they need cash, and more and more islanders seek jobs to earn money. They work on ships or move to the capital island. With their income, they change their lives. They build with cement, buy stereos and play foreign music, exchange their bicycles for motorbikes. Terewati thinks this is all fine, but not attractive enough to merit working off the island.

4:00 The children have joined their parents—Teikakee, as usual, on his older sister's hip. On their way back, they pass through the garden, gathering the fallen coconuts, which Terewati puts into a bag and carries home. Terewati does not know how much land he has in the five dispersed family gardens. Traditionally, the kin group owns the land. Registration of the land according to individual ownership began under colonial rule, but Terewati, like most I-Kiribati, does not consider it very important. No one ever comes home from the garden empty-handed. The children pick up dry branches for firewood. Hearing impatient crying, Bakea runs the last steps home with her load and pulls up her T-shirt to calm her hungry baby.

5:00 Terewati takes Teikakee in his arms while he sends Ritang to the store with a bag full of coconut as payment for tobacco and tinned fish for the evening meal. Around him, the children pick the coconut meat off the drying mats and put it in bags. In the west, a red sun is setting, while the eastern skies are dark and heavy with the evening rain. Once the ground is clean, each family member will take his turn with the pail to shower.

7:00 Bakea lies with Teikakee, putting him to sleep, and comes back to join her family sitting outside. Tabauea is tired, but there is breadfruit pudding left on the plates and that is a good enough reason to stay awake. When the last bite is taken, she falls asleep, her head on her father's lap.

8:00 The family sits in the dark in front of the house. Suddenly the silence of the night is broken by the wind rising. In less than a minute it is pandemonium. Bakea and her husband run to untie the roof straw hanging on each side of the house and fasten the floor mats to serve as shelter. "Ritang, Ritang"— Grandmother runs to her house, calling her granddaughter to follow. The rain starts.

Terewati sits with Bakea outside the mosquito net while she finishes her meal. Before climbing in beside their children, Bakea turns down the oil lamp. The day surrenders to sleepers' sighs and the sounds of wind and water.

I-Kiribati

THE NAME: From *Kiribas*, the nearest pronunciation in the indigenous tongue to the former name, Gilberts

GEOGRAPHY
Thirty-three low-lying coral atolls and reef islands, many with enclosed lagoons. The atolls lie mainly in three groups, the Phoenix and Line Islands, and the Gilberts, scattered in an area of nearly 3 million sq. km. of the Pacific Ocean. Max. altitude: 87 m. (285 ft.) (on Banaba Island)
Area: 726 sq. km. (280 sq. mi.)
Density: 90 pers./sq. km. (232 pers./sq. mi.) (1988)
Arable land: 52% (1985)
Forest: 3%
Climate: Tropical, with a rainy season from October to March. During the rest of the year, the uniformly high temperatures are moderated by northeasterly trade winds.

CAPITAL: The island of Tarawa, pop. 21,393 (1985)

LANGUAGE: I-Kiribati, formerly called Gilbertese, and English (official)

RELIGION: The great majority are Christians, predominantly Roman Catholic and of the Gilberts Islands Protestant Church. Some traditional beliefs and practices persist.

POPULATION: Total—66,000 (1988)
  Annual growth: 1.7% (1980)
  Doubling time: 41 yrs.
  Urban: 34% (1985) (est. for year 2000: 43%)
  Rural: 66%

AGE GROUPS (1985)
  16% under 5 yrs.
  39% under 15
  51% under 20
  30% from 20 to 39
  13% from 40 to 59
   6% 60 yrs. and over

ETHNIC GROUPS
  Micronesian: 96% (descendants of Melanesians, Moluccans, and Samoans)
  Other: 4% (Polynesians and other Pacific Islanders, Europeans, mixed)

HISTORY
First settled by Austronesian speakers some five thousand years ago, followed by successive migrations of Melanesians, Moluccans, and Samoans
16th–17th cent.: Several European explorers, including Grijalva and Quirós, sight the islands
1788: British commander Gilbert sails through the islands (later named after him)
1840s: First European trading post established; whaling trade flourishes
1857: American Protestant mission established, followed by Catholic priests in 1888; conversion to Christianity begins
1892: Proclaimed a British Protectorate together with Ellice Islands (now Tuvalu)
1916: Becomes a British Crown Colony
1942–43: Japanese occupation
1977: Achieves internal self-government
July 12, 1979: Full independence as the Republic of Kiribati

FAMILY
Marital status, for females 15 yrs. + (1985)
  Single: 29%
  Married: 60%
  Widowed: 7%
  Separated/divorced: 4%
Female head of household: no data
Fertility rate: 4.7 (1982)
Teenage births: 42% (1985) / **Teenage fertility rate:** no data
Births out of wedlock: no data
Contraception: no data
Government's position on family planning: Population growth and fertility are too high. Targets 0% growth by the year 2000. Provides information and access to family planning, and referral services for sterilization. Abortion is legal only if the woman's life is threatened.

KIRIBATI

SOCIAL INDICATORS
Life expectancy: 52 yrs. (male: 50; female: 54) (1978)
Infant mortality: 87/1,000 births (1985)
Crude birth rate: 35/1,000 pop. (1978)
Crude death rate: 14/1,000

HEALTH
Access to health services: 95% (1985)
Births attended by trained health personnel: no data

HOUSING
Persons per household: 6.1 (1978)
Electricity: 78% without (1978)
Access to safe water: 55% (urban: 93%; rural: 35%) (1985)
Source of water (1978)
    Well: 65%
    Tap: 18%
    Rain: 12%
    Delivery: 4%
Toilet facilities (1978)
    Water-seal latrine: 19%
    Flush: 15%
    Reef (pit) latrine: 16%
    None: 49%
Construction materials (1978)
    Bush material for traditional houses: 74%
    Western-style houses: 26%

EDUCATION
Literacy: 100% (1982)
Gross enrollment ratio (1982)
    First level: 91% (completing in 1980: 73%)
    Second: no data
    Third: no data
Educational attainment for pop. 20 yrs. + (1985)
    None: 4%
    First level: 47% (upper primary: 30%)
    Second: 13% (upper secondary: 4%)
    Third: 0.5%

ECONOMIC ACTIVITY
Economically active population: The great majority of the population is involved in subsistence economy.
GDP: no data
Per capita GNP: US$300 (1982)
National currency: Australian dollar
Principal resources: Copra, phosphate

COMMUNICATIONS
Radio
    Transmitters: 10 (1981)
    Receivers: 203/1,000 pop. (1985)
Television
    Believed to have no television service of its own
Newspapers (1984)
    Believed to have no general-interest dailies

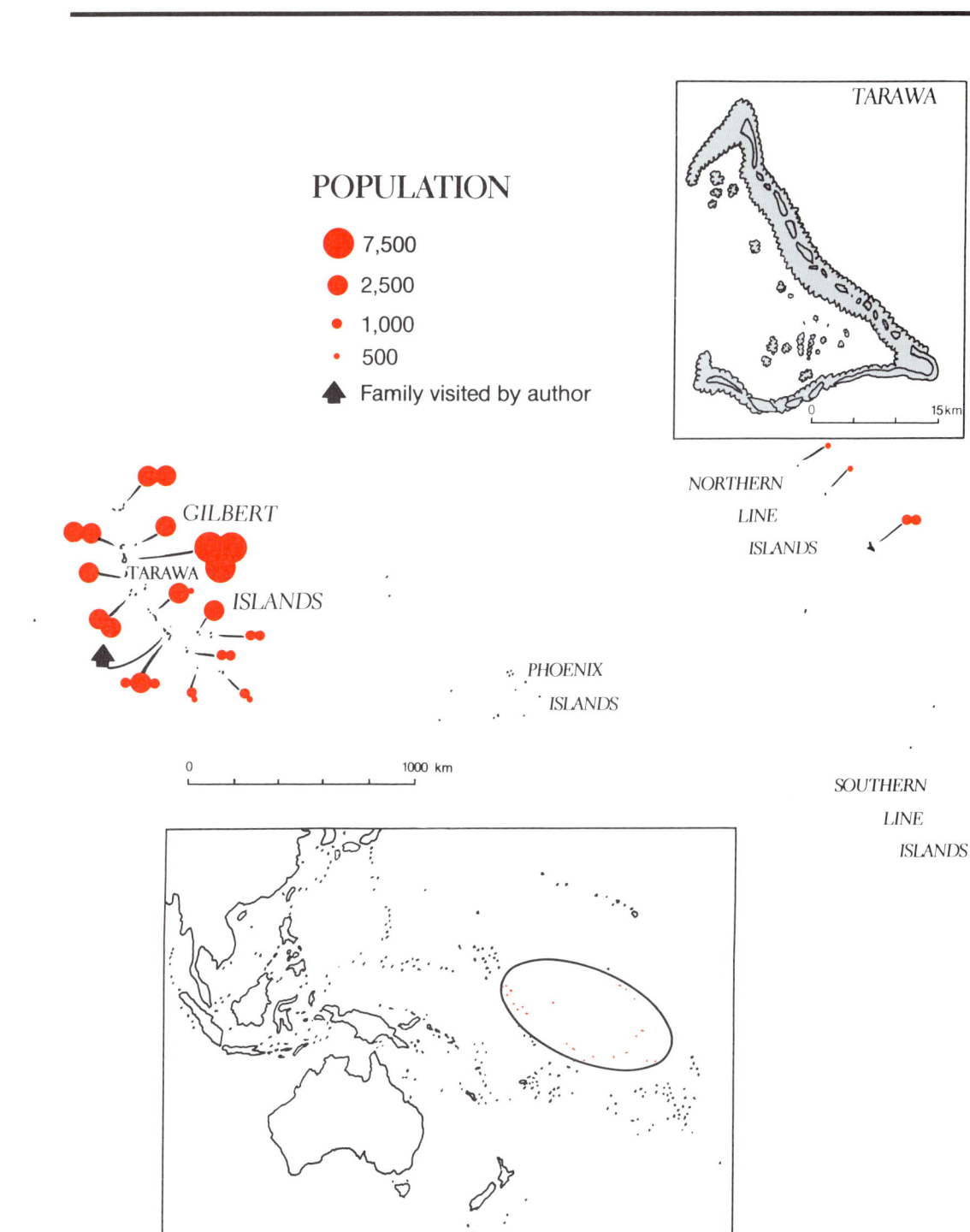

Kiribati

TARAWA

POPULATION

- 7,500
- 2,500
- 1,000
- 500
- ▲ Family visited by author

GILBERT
TARAWA
ISLANDS

NORTHERN LINE ISLANDS

PHOENIX ISLANDS

SOUTHERN LINE ISLANDS

Nauru

The Kun Family

Mark Kun, age 48 (1)
Lise Kun, 43 (2)
Russell, 22 (3)
Annie, 20 (4)
Ruston, 18 (5)
Russ, 12 (6)
Maria, 11 (7)
Tote (daughter-in-law), 32 (8)
Faith Mau, 7 (9)

Uaboa District

JANUARY 19

8:00 Doors click open and bang shut as Ruston leaves his room, takes today's clothing out of the family's large wardrobe in his parents' room, enters the laundry room, and steps into the shower. His mother, Lise, is ready to drive him to the government-office district of Yaren, ten minutes away. His doctor father, Mark, has decided not to work at the hospital this morning, as his allergies are acting up, and his face is swollen.

Although only eighteen, Ruston has a summer job at the Treasury that brings him financial independence for the two months he spends on his home island each year. For the past five years, he has been studying in Australia. Like most of the country's secondary students, he has received a school grant from the government. The Nauruan population is too small to justify varied school curricula and teachers, so they send their high-school students overseas, mainly to New Zealand, Australia, Fiji, and Papua New Guinea.

Nauru is one of the smallest countries in the world; it can all be seen in a forty-five-minute drive. From the sea, the island looks just like an upside-down soup bowl. The round part of the soup bowl is a low plateau of phosphate rocks formed over untold centuries by deposits of marine organisms and seabird guano on coral reefs. Discovered by the colonizers, the phosphate mined from these rocks has been a treasure trove that has brought wealth to Nauru's citizens and government since independence. Nauru supplies Australia's and New Zealand's farmers with the bulk of their fertilizers. But the end is near. It is estimated that by 1995 the phosphate supply will be depleted, leaving Nauruans with an island full of holes, an island where nothing can be farmed and absolutely everything is imported.

9:00 Everyone gets their own breakfast. Annie is sent to pick up some meat. Her sister-in-law, Tote, comes along. Tote is from Western Samoa. Until last month, she was employed as a hostess on Air Nauru, but now that she has married the oldest Kun son, Russell, she is out of work. The airline does not hire married women or women with children, believing them to be unreliable.

Usually a cheerful woman, Tote sometimes finds staying with her husband at his parents' a bit depressing. But getting a house built on the thin strip of land around the phosphate "bowl" is very difficult. Not only is the rim already quite populated, but all houses are pre-fabricated and sent over by boat from Australia. The list of young couples waiting for houses paid for by the Nauruan government is a long one. Tote and Russell will soon move to a house they will rent from a member of their extended family.

At the government-run supermarket, Annie and Tote find the shelves half empty, and choices of different products limited. They leave and go to a private market where the choice is better but things are more expensive. Even here, there are only a few tired vegetables, and not a single fruit. The two young women will have to come back tomorrow if they want produce, which has to be imported. Fresh vegetables and fruits which arrive by plane—on Wednesdays from Fiji and on Thursdays from Australia—are snatched up immediately.

On their way back, Tote wants to stop a few minutes at the run-down house she and Russell will rent. Impatient to have a house she can decorate, she looks at the scrubby dry grass of the yard and dreams of the lush flowery gardens she was used to in Western Samoa. Here, there is drought nearly every year, and the rainwater collected is not enough to water a garden also; during the dry months, only the palms on the island have leaves, and even those are yellow.

Few Nauruans own their land. Mark is part owner of a plot of land called Eatdabudae, and Russell and Tote dream of a new house there. All traditional family land has been registered by the government to enable it to distribute the royalties from the phosphate profits. Nonetheless, using land is very complicated. The Eatdabudae plot on the coastal rim is shared by sixty-one persons who are related one way or another. Mark owns only 1/200th of it, and the piece Russell wants to build on will barely hold two houses. They must approach the sixty other owners for permission; it will take some time.

10:00

Mark appears for the first time, for breakfast in the large family and dining room. A game of Scrabble, just now the favorite family pastime, is all he feels like today. He sits with Lise, and the first game of the day begins.

There have been more exciting days for Mark—days of extravagance when, in the 1960s, his family's phosphate land was mined and they suddenly had large sums of money. Like other Nauruans who had no concept of the future, whose custom was to give and share generously, Mark's father bought him and his three brothers each their own car. Thrift was unheard of then, but now Mark has to be careful with his fixed government salary. Still, he says, "It was a good time and we don't regret a thing." He likes to quote a proverb from one of the many plaques hanging on the wall in the family room: "You can't change the past, but you can ruin a perfectly good present by worrying about the future."

Luckily, the Nauruan government has worried about the future. Its long-term investment of the phosphate profits has assured a secure future for its people. The government will be able to continue paying for medical and dental care, free housing and maintenance, and free education for all Nauruans.

Nauru has very little vegetation; all houses are pre-fabricated and sent over by boat from Australia. The list of young couples waiting for houses paid for by the Nauruan government is long.

11:30 Russ and Maria prepare their own lunch in the microwave and sit down to watch a horror movie. Lise goes to pick up Ruston. After lunch, tempted by the fact that none of the rest of his family is working, Ruston decides he does not want to go back to work for the afternoon. He will be paid, and, anyway, the work will be done. Without the discipline even of farming, Nauruans have not taken easily to regular work, and for every native there is a foreign worker drawn to the island by the country's high salaries.

But even if he is relaxed about work today, Ruston is ambitious. He plans to finish his four years of accounting studies, then two years of computer work, and then come back from Australia to live in Nauru. Like all Nauruans, he likes his country and is impatient to settle down here.

5:00 After an afternoon of Scrabble, Tote goes jogging and Lise takes a long walk, hoping to lose weight. She worries about her health. After car and motorcycle deaths due to alcohol, cardiovascular disease and diabetes are the second greatest causes of premature death. The life expectancy for Nauruan adults is only forty-nine years.

Lise stops halfway through her walk, dripping with sweat and out of breath. She decides against further exercise and returns home. On the roadsides Nauruans are bustling about, and for a special reason: this is the annual cleaning time. All year round, everyone litters freely instead of bringing their garbage to the dump. But, in one week, the country will celebrate its independence, and there will be a contest for the most beautiful district. There will be other competitions as well, including weight lifting, which Russell hopes to win. In preparation, he lifted over four hundred kilos this week.

Everyone eats lunch when they feel like it. Russ, Maria, and a friend have theirs while watching a film on video, captivated by its violence and suspense.

Russell is a fifth-grade and gym teacher and is on holiday. He has slept a large part of the morning, but now leaves for his daily workout. Bodybuilding is his passion, and other than a few words to Tote, he never says much.

6:30 Annie and Lise start preparing dinner, and little Russ is on duty to open the video store that is attached to the house. "It passes the time," says Lise. The meager profits have dwindled, however, since other video stores have opened. Tote, who has taken some shelf space in the store and started a magazine club, follows Russ. When Annie and Lise have the meal ready, the members of the family will take turns tending the shop and coming to sit at the table.

9:00 Russ and Maria close the shop, bringing back *Easy Money*. Russ puts it on and the whole family watches, laughing loudly at all the jokes.

Tote and Russell leave to visit friends from Western Samoa, and Ruston hops in a jeep with some pals. The only evening activity for young Nauruans is to drive around and around the island, drinking numerous beers, until they are tired. But as a member of a born-again Christian family, Ruston is supposed to refuse to take part in this important aspect of Nauruan social life.

11:00 Maria and Russ are off to bed. Their parents are playing another game of Scrabble, but when Ruston returns, they leave the living room to let him sleep. He has to work tomorrow.

12:00 Tote and Russell come in, take the Scrabble board, and go into their bedroom quietly.

The Nauruans

THE NAME: From *Anaoero*, the indigenous name of the island

GEOGRAPHY
Oval island of high coral formation, bounded by a reef exposed to low tide. Central plateau composed of phosphate-bearing rock covers more than three-fifths of the island. It is surrounded by a narrow band (100–300 m. wide) of fertile land, the only cultivatable soil on the island, and sandy beaches.
Max. altitude: 65 m. (213 ft.)
Area: 21 sq. km. (8.1 sq. mi.)
Density: 414 pers./sq. km. (1,074 pers./sq. mi.)
Arable land: no data
Forest: no data
Climate: Tropical. Hot and humid, with wet monsoon season from November to February. Rainfall is irregular from year to year, with frequent droughts. The island is heating up as a result of the intense burning of the sun on the bare phosphate fields; the rainfall is slowly decreasing.

ADMINISTRATIVE CENTER: Yaren district, pop. 559 (1983)

LANGUAGE: Nauruan (official); English widely spoken

RELIGION: Christian, either Nauruan Protestants or Roman Catholics

POPULATION: Total—8,000 (1983) (4,900 Nauruans)
Annual growth: 2.8% (224) (1983)
Doubling time: 18 yrs. (For Nauran population only)
Urban: The population lives around the rim of the island.

AGE GROUPS (1981)
9% under 5 yrs.	22% from 25 to 45
44% under 15	9% from 45 to 65
67% under 25	2% 65 yrs. and over

ETHNIC GROUPS
Nauruan: 62%
Pacific Islander: 26.5%
Asian: 8.5%
Australian, New Zealander, European: 3%

HISTORY
Settled at various times by Polynesians, Micronesians, and Melanesians
1798: British navigator Fearn, first European to visit, names it Pleasant Island
1830s: Whaling industry increases contact with Europeans. Some Europeans settle on Nauru
1878–88: Interclan warfare among Nauruans
1886: Anglo–German convention allocates the island to the Germans and changes name back to original native name of Nauru
1899: Protestant missionaries arrive. Discovery of phosphate deposits brings European companies and Chinese laborers
1914: Australians occupy the island; Germans surrender
1919: Becomes joint Mandate of Britain, Australia, and New Zealand
1940: Germans attack, sinking five phosphate ships
1942–45: Occupation by the Japanese, who deport many Nauruans to the Caroline Islands. About one-third of them survive
1947: Becomes a UN trust territory administered by Australia
Jan. 31, 1968: Independence, making Nauru one of the smallest free states in the world

FAMILY
Marital status: no data
Female head of household: no data
Fertility rate: no data
Teenage births: no data
Births out of wedlock: no data
Contraception: no data
Government's position on family planning: Population growth is too low but fertility rate is satisfactory. No policy. Government supports family-planning services. Abortion is legal for health reasons only.

NAURU

SOCIAL INDICATORS
Life expectancy: 55 yrs. (male: 49 years; female: 62) (1976–81)
Infant mortality: 31/1,000 births (1976–81)
Crude birth rate: 31.2/1,000 pop. (1983)
Crude death rate: 10.5/1,000 (1976–81)

HEALTH
Access to health services: 100%
Births attended by trained health personnel: 100%

HOUSING
Persons per household: 8.5 (1983)
Electricity: It can be assumed that the majority have access to electricity.
Access to safe water: As long as rainwater is clean
Source of water: Majority have rainwater tanks.
Toilet facilities: It can be assumed that the majority have access to modern toilet facilities.
Construction materials: All housing is prefabricated and imported.

EDUCATION
Literacy: no data
Gross enrollment ratio: no data
Educational attainment: no data

ECONOMIC ACTIVITY
Economically active population: no data
GDP: no data
National currency: Australian dollar
Principal resources: Phosphate

COMMUNICATIONS
Radio
    Transmitters: 1 (1985)
    Receivers: 625/1,000 pop. (1985)
Television
    Believed to have no television service of its own
Newspapers (1984)
    Believed to have no general-interest dailies

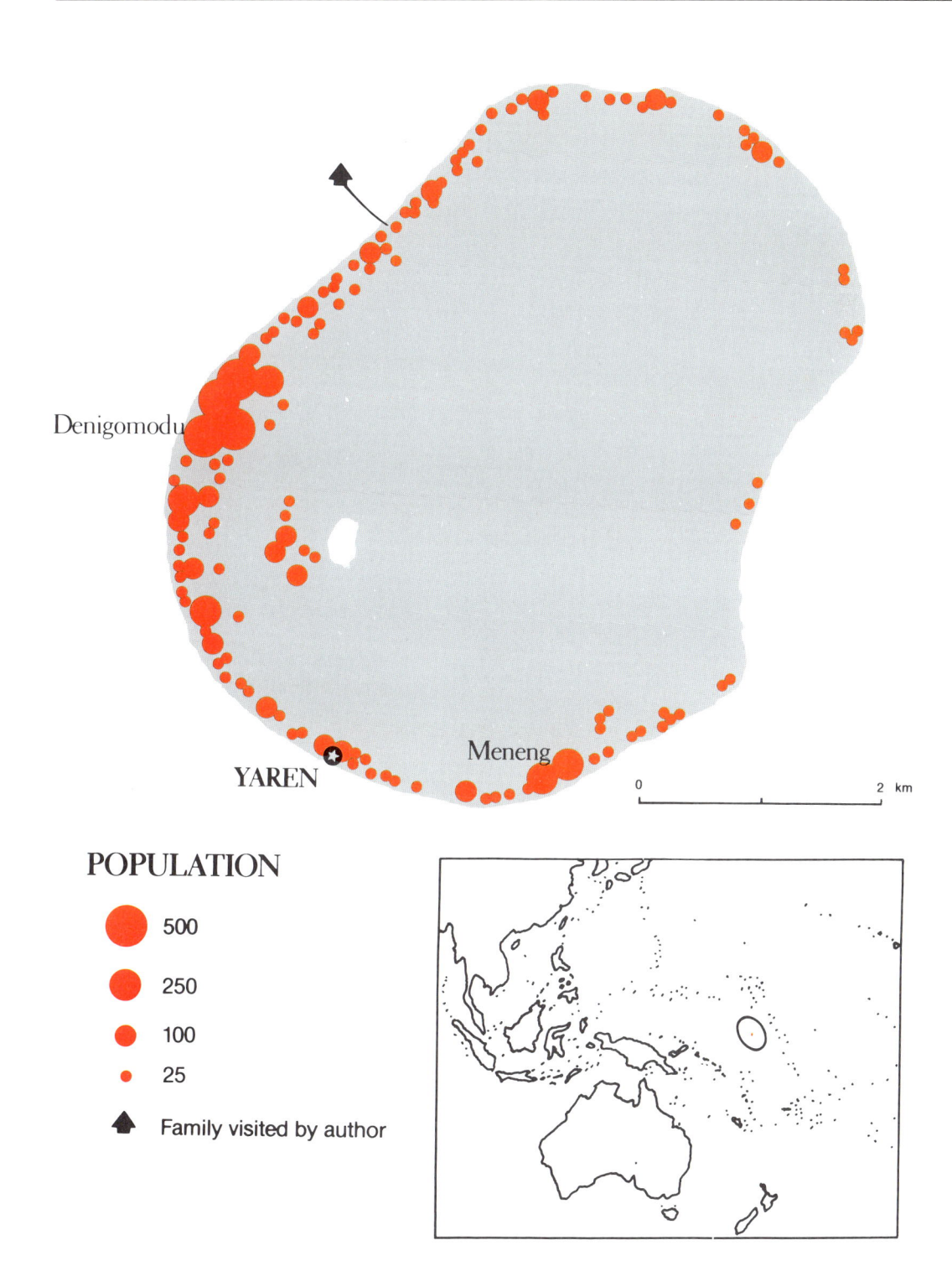

Nauru

Denigomodu

YAREN

Meneng

0 2 km

POPULATION

- 500
- 250
- 100
- 25

▲ Family visited by author

New Zealand

The Benfell Family

Gregory Benfell, age 31 (1)
Diana Benfell, 27 (2)
Stephen, 4 (3)
Nicola, 2½ (4)
Christopher, 6 months (5)

Hamilton

MARCH 7

4:00 Baby Christopher cries. Diana, his mother, is at his side immediately. In the dark, she sits down on her sleeping daughter Nicola's bed and, resting her head against the wall, she gives the baby her breast. Christopher is soon back in his crib, but in less than two hours Diana's night will be over. She gratefully slides back into the water bed beside her sleeping husband.

6:00 Gregory shuts off the alarm clock quickly and gets up. In the next room, Stephen opens an eye, but he has learned to let his mother sleep a little longer, and plays in bed with the dozens of toys that surround him.

Greg takes a shower, grabs a quick cup of coffee and the lunch his wife has prepared the night before, and fifteen minutes after getting up, he is off to work on his bicycle. Three days a week, Diana keeps the car to bring Stephen to kindergarten. Greg likes the quiet morning ride, especially on sunny mornings such as this. He glides down the Fairview Street hill, with its view of the valley and distant mountains, and then follows the Waikato River until he reaches the New Zealand Dairy Cooperative, where two hundred factory workers produce fifty thousand tons of milk powder a day. This means processing 100,000 liters of milk an hour, or 1.6 million liters per day. The Waikato Valley has more cows grazing per acre than any other place in the world and is well known for its dairy products. The richness of its peat soil and the moist, humid climate ensure the continued existence of its lush green pasture. As a mechanical engineer, Greg is responsible for dairy-plant maintenance, a job he finds good and secure. "There will always be work for someone in my field," he says.

6:30 Mother and older son are up now, and it is a matter of minutes before Stephen makes sure his sister is also awake. In the kitchen, Diana pours fruit juice, adds milk to the cereals, and calls her children to the table. After breakfast, the kids go out into the back yard with their miniature world of tables, dolls, and cars. Diana puts a load of wash in the machine.

In contrast to her husband, a first-generation New Zealander, Diana is from a good "old colonial family." Her ancestors were among those who legally purchased an island from the Maori, New Zealand's native people, who still today are putting up a strong fight to get their native land back.

Diana's parents are sheep and cattle farmers farther out in the country. She came to Hamilton for high school and nursing school, and stayed to marry Greg. With a hundred thousand inhabitants, Hamilton is the fourth largest city in New Zealand. Diana misses the vast open spaces where children are free to run. Although they like the site where they live, the Benfells are thinking of selling their house to buy a bigger one. In all the new middle-class developments, however, the houses are bigger but there is less land. The other possibility would be to go back to the country and have Gregory commute. But Greg is a "city boy," and country life does not appeal to him. A solution still has to be found—a compromise, perhaps.

11:15 Stephen and his sister have been playing well together all morning. Diana has taken care of her house, fed the baby, and bathed him. Now she calls in Stephen and Nicola for a small television break.

Until six months ago, Diana had forbidden any television altogether. She did not want to have any excuse for not giving all her attention to her children. But now she spends her nights feeding Christopher and then has three children to care for during the day, so she finally bought a set to give herself a few hours of rest a day. She reviews all new programs, rejects anything violent, and stays vigilant. "Besides," she says, "if I want to keep track of their perceptions and their conversation, I have to watch it with them."

When she does find the time to read, Diana chooses books on child education and parenting. Mothering is very important to her. Still, as a modern woman, she complains about the little public recognition and admiration mothers get from men and the society at large.

In her attempt to be the best mother in the world, Diana follows certain self-made rules. The first is to practice what she preaches. Another is to discuss her children's problems with them attentively and to punish them, so that they will learn from their mistakes. As a result, there is little yelling in the house, and each decision Mother makes has been well reasoned out. However, two-year-old Nicola may let her mother know, with a precocious reserve, "Mother, I am very upset," when she disagrees.

12:30 The children sit down to a bowl of noodles and a piece of watermelon. Greg, at the factory, opens his lunch box. He finds four sandwiches, homemade biscuits, cake, cheese, and fruit. He is the envy of all his colleagues. Diana sees no reason to complain about having to prepare lunch. Greg works hard and has to put in many overtime hours to meet the family's needs. "It's the least I can do for him," she says.

Diana and Greg married six months after they met. "We knew, right away, that we were the partners each was looking for." Their respective families tried to convince them to wait. "But that was a decision that did not need thinking over," they say lovingly. Nineteen months later, the first baby arrived, and the others followed. Three children is all they want, and like most couples in New Zealand, they did not control the spacing between them. Now family planning is a regular topic of conversation. Greg is considering a vasectomy but hasn't committed himself yet.

12:45 Baby Christopher has a new diaper, has napped, is dressed and fed. Stephen has his backpack on and is standing by the door, while Nicola is sliding on her flip-flops. Diana and her troop are ready to go. She belts each one in his individual car seat, and is off in her Toyota to Stephen's nursery school.

While he is there, Diana will visit Judy, a friend with children the same age as hers. Judy lives on an orchard, and while she tends the fruit stand, she and Diana exchange recipes for preserves. The children play by the heavily laden fruit trees; apples, peaches, and pears all grow abundantly in this green country.

Contrary to her husband, who is shy and, besides a few fishing pals, hardly sees anyone other than family friends, Diana is sociable. When she was obliged to stay home with her first child, she felt lonely, so she went looking for friends in the neighborhood by selling Avon products door-to-door. She has long since stopped, but she still has the friends. One of them, Janet, also goes to the same church. Janet will watch Nicola tomorrow while Stephen is at the nursery school. The two women often "swap" children to give themselves some free time.

Six years ago, the Benfells were nearly the first ones on the street. They chose this neighborhood because it was at the top of a hill, giving them a view over the Waikato Valley. Now the house seems too small; the Benfells would like a playroom, and a quiet space for themselves.

Carry-out meals are popular in New Zealand, and the family has them at least twice a week. Diana needs a break from planning meals.

4:00   Diana has picked up Stephen at school. The bathwater is running. At this time, Greg's normal workday is over and he starts his overtime. He works overtime nearly every day. He also works six days a week, and often all weekend. This way, he doubles his salary. He wants to make as much money and get rid of as many debts as possible while the children are still small. When they start school and Diana returns to work, his first priority will shift to his family.

6:00   The children are in their pajamas, ready for "tea," as dinner is called in New Zealand. While they are waiting for their father to arrive with the fish-and-chips—a popular carry-out meal for urban New Zealanders—Stephen and Nicola lie on their sheepskin, watching a cartoon. Diana feeds Christopher.

7:00   Nicola is in bed, with all her stuffed animals around her. Christopher's crib is empty: the baby still hangs on his mother's breast. Stephen is also going to bed; he gathers a car and some other toys to accompany him through the night. While Diana feeds Christopher, Greg reads bedtime stories to the children. Diana lets well-fed Christopher fall asleep in her arms. He is already quite a big baby, and she will miss it when he can no longer fit in one arm and cuddle to her breast. "He is my last, and these moments have to be appreciated to their fullest," says Diana.

9:00   Outside, the rain has started, and the wind is blowing dangerously. The tail of cyclone Bola, in action between Australia and the Pacific island of Tonga, is causing floods and damage in New Zealand.
       Before the television arrived, Greg and Diana would go to bed at this time, but now it depends on the quality of the night's programming.

The New Zealanders

THE NAME: Maoris call it Aotearoa, meaning "land of the white cloud." Named Nieuw Zeeland, New Sea-land, by the Dutch in 1643 after the Dutch province of Zeeland

GEOGRAPHY
Two principal islands, north and south, and a number of small islands, all with an infinite variety of landscapes. The North Island has low mountains, active volcanoes, large lakes, hot springs, and geysers. The South has high mountains on the west coast and plains in the east; much of the countryside is rolling green hills dotted with the country's 71 million sheep.
Max. altitude: 3,764 m. (12,349 ft.) (Mt. Cook)
Area: 268,112 sq. km. (103,519 sq. mi.)
Density: 12 pers./sq. km. (32 pers./sq. mi.) (1988)
Arable land: 2% (1985)
Forest: 40%
Climate: Temperate. Winters are generally mild and, on the South Island, characterized by a high proportion of sunshine. Rainfall is reliable and adequate.

CAPITAL: Wellington, pop. 137,495 (metropolitan area, pop. 325,697) (1986)

LANGUAGE: English and Maori (both official)

RELIGION
Anglican (Church of England): 24%
Presbyterian: 18%
Catholic: 15%
Other Christian: 17%
No religion: 17%
Not stated: 2%
Objected to the question: 8%

POPULATION: Total—3,327,000 (1988)
    Annual growth: 0.8% (1982–87)
    Doubling time: 41 yrs.
    Urban: 84% (1986) (est. for year 2000: 85%)
    Rural: 16%

AGE GROUPS (1986)
    7.6% under 5 yrs.
    24.4% under 15
    33.6% under 20
    31.7% from 20 to 39
    20.0% from 40 to 59
    14.7% 60 yrs. and over

ETHNIC GROUPS
European: 86%
Maori: 9%
Pacific Island Polynesian: 3%
Other: 2% (Chinese, Indian, and Fijian)

HISTORY
Settled by Polynesians before the 15th century. Distinctive Maori culture develops
1768–71: James Cook circumnavigates and charts the two main islands
late 18th cent.: Australian whaling companies establish first small settlements
Feb. 6, 1840: Treaty of Waitangi cedes sovereignty to Queen Victoria; land, forest, and fisheries are secured by Maori chiefs; the Crown alone has right to purchase land
1840–48: Settlers continue to fight Maori for land
1861: Gold discovered on South Island
1860–70: Settlers dislodge Maori from prime land; war again ensues
1867: Four Maori electorates established, with seats in Parliament
1877: Education Act provides for free compulsory education
early 1880s–1895: Severe economic depression, largely a result of war with the Maori
1893: First country to grant women right to vote
1901: Cook and other Pacific islands annexed
1907: Granted dominion status in the British Empire
1920: Western Samoa acquired by the League of Nations mandate
1931: Statute of Westminster gives New Zealand autonomy
1939: Troops participate in WWII
1947: Formal proclamation of independence

NEW ZEALAND

1951: ANZUS security treaty signed with Australia and the U.S.A.

FAMILY
Marital status, for females 15 yrs. + (1986)
- Single: 29%
- Married: 55%
- Widowed: 6.6%
- Divorced: 4%
- Separated: 3.6%

Female head of household: 23.8% (1986)
Fertility rate: 2.0 (1986)
Teenage births: 8.6% (1986)
Teenage fertility rate: 30.6/1,000 (1985)
Births out of wedlock: 27% (1986)
Contraception: 69.5% (1976)
Government's position on family planning: Population growth and fertility rate are satisfactory. Family planning is considered a personal choice. Contraceptive information is available; parental or medical permission required for those under 16. Sterilization is legal. Abortion is legal for health reasons only. Minimum age of marriage is 16, but parental permission is required up to the age of 20.

SOCIAL INDICATORS
Life expectancy: male: 71 yrs.; female: 76.8 (1985)
Infant mortality: 11/1,000 births (1987)
Crude birth rate: 16/1,000 pop. (1986)
Crude death rate: 8/1,000

HEALTH
Access to health services: 100% (1984)
Births attended by trained health personnel: 99%

HOUSING
Persons per household: 2.9 (1986)
Electricity: under 1% without
Access to safe water: 99%
Source of water
- Urban: 100% piped inside
- Rural: majority piped inside

Toilet facilities (1981)
- Flush: 89%
- Other: 11%

Construction materials (1981)
- Wood: 49%
- Stone or concrete: 12%
- Brick: 17%
- Other: 22%

EDUCATION
Literacy: 80–97% (1982)
Gross enrollment ratio (1985)
- First level: 106%
- Second: 85%
- Third: 35.1%

Educational attainment: no data

ECONOMIC ACTIVITY
Economically active population: 66.3% (male: 58%; female: 41%) (1986)
Agriculture: 11.2% act. pop.; 14% of GDP
Mines: 2.0% act. pop.; 2% of GDP
Industry: 30.1% act. pop.; 23% of GDP
Services: 56.7% act. pop.; 61% of GDP
Per capita GNP: US$7,460 (1986)
National currency: New Zealand dollar
Principal resources: Cattle, sheep, iron, natural gas, forestry

COMMUNICATIONS
Radio
- Transmitters: 90 (1985)
- Receivers: 904/1,000 pop. (1985)

Television
- Transmitters: 567 (1985)
- Receivers: 290/1,000 pop. (1985)

Newspapers
- Dailies: 37
- Circulation: no data

New Zealand

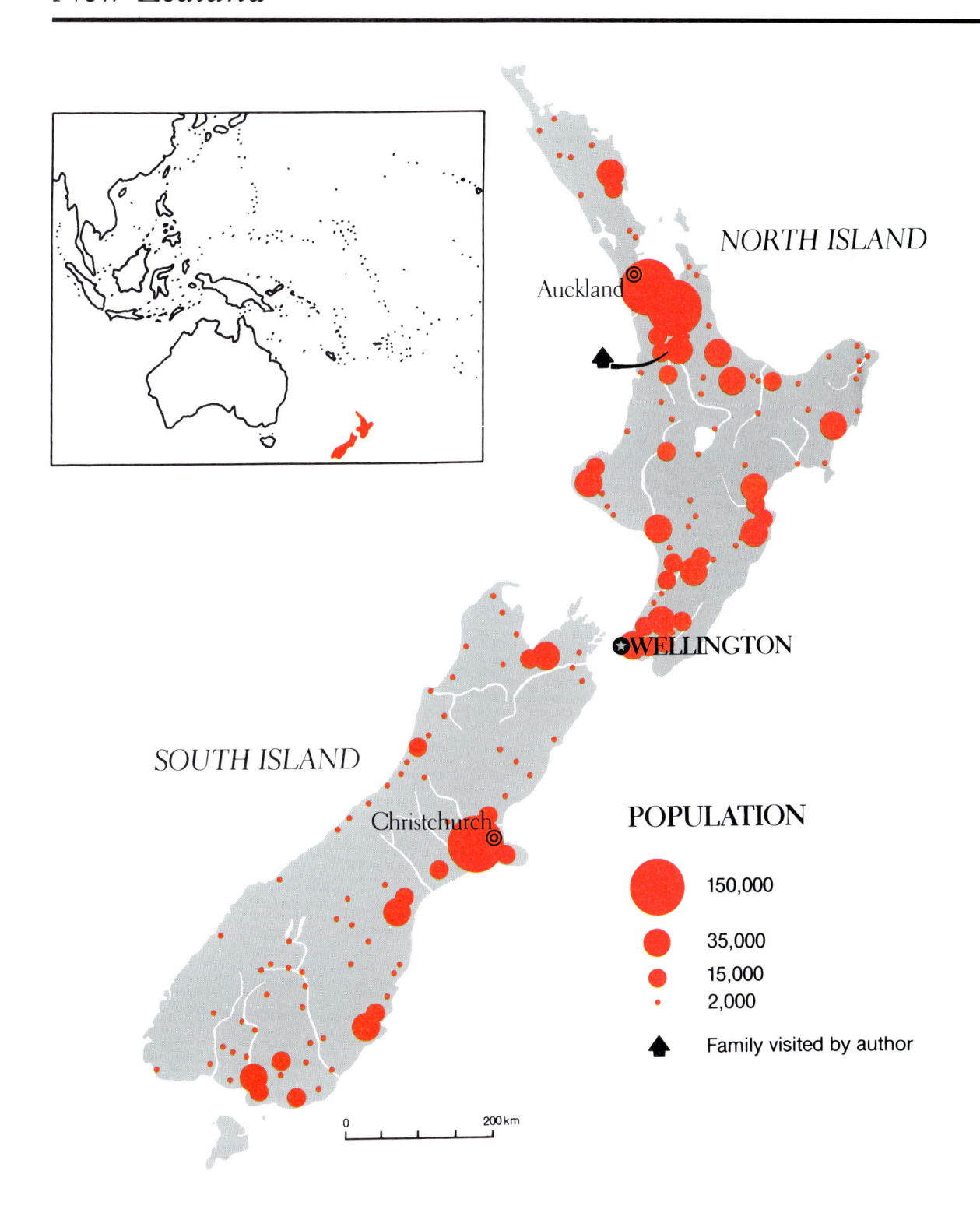

NORTH ISLAND

Auckland

WELLINGTON

SOUTH ISLAND

Christchurch

POPULATION

- 150,000
- 35,000
- 15,000
- 2,000

▲ Family visited by author

0 200 km

Papua New Guinea

Homoko Alembo's Family

Homoko Alembo* (1)
Lunama (Lus) (wife) (2)
Mule Melin (3)
Eralia (Agnes) (wife) (4)
Marira (wife) (5)
Pandai (6)
Akai (7)
Atapa (8)
Apili (wife) (9)
Wawali (10)

Landame (wife) (11)
Her daughter (12)
Her sons (13 and 14)
John (15)
Pirape (16)
Mariam (17)
Piralu (18)

23 cows
14 pigs and 34 piglets

* Homoko Alembo's family do not know their ages; they are members of the Huli people.

Pitapaya

APRIL 25

5:30 The three cane huts that house the five wives of Homoko Alembo are still in darkness. In one, Lus gets up from the elevated cane bed where she has slept with her daughter Mule Melin, blows the embers of last night's fire, then opens the door. At 2,500 meters, it is cold in the morning in the highlands of Papua New Guinea. The three piglets that have slept under Lus's bed scamper outside to join the thirteen kept in the tiny pig shed.

With five wives raising pigs for him, Homoko Alembo is indeed wealthy, but he says: "Prices are going up." Four of his present wives cost nineteen pigs each. He sent back his first six wives to their families because they argued too much. He kept Lus because she always listens to him. In the highlands, the status of a "big man" like him depends on the number of his pigs, and with more land to work and more pigs needed for the feasts, he needs many wives. In other parts of the country, however, men consider additional wives an economic burden rather than an advantage.

Lus brings her pigs into the fields and ties them so that they will turn the earth for the next planting, as they dig with their snouts for leftover sweet potatoes. Then they'll be moved to "plow" another section.

6:30 In the next house, Marira, Apili, and Landame, who share it, feed their seven youngsters and clean their running noses. They all have a cold, and pneumonia is the leading cause of death for children. In the smoke-filled house, there is no ventilation and absolutely no place to move; the sleeping platforms take up all the space.

In the third house, Agnes is alone. She has lost two babies shortly after birth and refuses to try again. Agnes is the youngest and the most rebellious of the wives. Tradition does not allow Homoko Alembo inside his wives' houses. He talks with them at the door; if he wants to meet with them more privately, it is in the forest. Agnes has not been answering her husband's calls; he must run after her, and she disappears, laughing.

Homoko Alembo is a good husband, say his five wives. "He lets us alone and does not call us when the children are small." Abstinence, while waiting for children to be strong and the women able fully to work again, is a rule. "But other men break the tradition," they say. "Some women have one child on the right breast and one on the left and are expected to keep all their children alive, work the gardens, and take care of the pigs."

Homoko Alembo leaves the house he shares with twelve related men and boys to bring his twenty-three cows to graze farther up the mountain, while his sons and relatives prepare sweet potatoes. Men live separately and are responsible for their needs and for teaching boys their most important skills—to protect their land, women, children, and clan with the bow and arrow.

Homoko Alembo does not bother to keep track of exactly how many children he has. Four sons are alive; there are enough girls to sell to acquire more pigs; and he has important things to do. Chief of his clan and chancellor of thirteen clans, he represents the people to other clans and to the district authorities. He relays government agricultural advice to his people and tries to keep peace between clans. The Huli people are the most rebellious of the country's mountain people, and tribal wars are increasing. The government would like to stop them. Already some guns have appeared, and it is feared that the bow and arrow may soon be replaced by more deadly weapons.

8:00 This morning all seems calm; there has not been a war for four months. The clouds are lifting from the mountaintops, assuring another sunny morning; babies pull away from their mothers' breasts with satisfied smiles. It is now time to get going. Marira and Apili will walk for more than thirty minutes to reach their gardens, while Lus, Agnes, and Landame and a few children go to fetch wood and water from the nearby forest. The daily household work requires at least two hours of walking.

9:00 Each living area is protected by trenches up to eight meters deep. Lus, Agnes, and Landame walk between them until they find the exit gates. Outside, they scan trees for dead limbs, climbing up to chop the branch down, then cutting it into smaller pieces on the ground. One hour later, Lus is up a tree when a voice echoes off the mountain. The women stop moving, the children stop yelling, even the baby stops crying. From hilltop to hilltop, the wailing voice brings news which quickly changes the women's expressions. A man of their clan has been killed; there will be war!

"We must go back home and wait for our husband," says Lus. Picking up the wood, they stop only to fill plastic containers with cool water at a mountain spring.

11:00 Marira and Apili have also heard the news while they were in their garden, and have come to Lus's house; the wives feel more secure together. There is panic in each woman's face. Apili says she is scared; Mule is lamenting the killing. Lus is crocheting a new string bag; Agnes sits on a tree trunk, searching for lice in Marira's hair; Marira, in turn, sits between Agnes's legs while she searches her daughter Akai's head below her. They talk and plan how to save the pigs if the men come to fight on their territory.

The house is made of wood covered first with pit pit, *a sort of cane, and then, on the roof, with* kunai, *a tall grass from four to six feet high.*

Suddenly Mule stops crying and smiles. Since there has been a death, there will be a funeral, the opportunity for all women to go and cry together. They will cover their faces with paint, put on their grass skirts and meet along the road, walk together, and yell to the spirit of death to come and help their men get vengeance. All the women now seem happy, and Mule brings out her skirt, washes it, and sets it down to dry on the floor. Then, on her mother's orders, she goes to move the pigs so they will be in the shade. "Our mothers, they tell us what to do: get the wood, the pigs, the firewood. We don't say anything, we do the work. That is the way it is here," explains Mule.

1:30 As on any other afternoon, the clouds come back to cover the sky and then lower themselves to bring the afternoon rain. Lus has started a fire in the unventilated house; she can't stop talking. Some men going by with their bows and arrows call out, "Wait, women, stay silent, do not go out of your gardens, be ready to run and save the pigs." Some of these men live in the cities and work in government offices. But when there is a war and their clan is in danger, they come back and take up their bows and arrows again.

2:00 During the deafening thunder and heavy rain, each woman has gone back to her own fire. In front of Lus, the sweet potatoes are cooking in the ashes. She reads the Bible and sings a "God's song," while her daughter Mule runs through the rain to move the "plowing" pigs to a new part of the field.

4:00 Homoko Alembo stops by his wives' houses to bring them the news. The problem is serious. A week ago, a drunken man of the Ewara clan died in a car accident, but as the Huli believe in sorcery, the clan did not accept the doctor's autopsy verdict. They have accused Homoko Alembo's Pitapaya clan of casting an evil spell on them, and when he tried to talk to the "big men" of the Ewara clan, they refused to hear him—or the police. "They want war," he says, "and in retaliation they killed the son of my brother yesterday, hitting him on the forehead with an ax, and now today an old man with an arrow usually used to kill pigs." Homoko Alembo's clan now also wants battle, because the Ewara clan has broken unspoken rules of war: not to kill children, women, or old people, and never to kill someone by hitting them in the face. So there will be a war, and he tells his wives, "Stay home, women: do not go far; and yes, you must all go to the funerals."

Homoko Alembo then goes off with the men to plan for the war. Tomorrow they will split into gangs and hide throughout the forest to protect their territory.

5:30 The women go get the pigs and bring them in for the night. Lus brings the three piglets near the fire, and Mule happily takes one in her arms while her mother prepares their food.

7:00 It is dark and cold in their houses and the women sit in the smoke on their dirt floors, trying to calm the cries of their hungry children and Lus's three piglets. Outside, Mule calls her mother and Agnes. On the mountain, houses are burning; the Ewara clan is still at work. "I hope they don't come and burn our houses," says Lus. "Last year they did." The fear is justified; the clans have even made a road sign telling the police to stay out of their war.

One of the things Homoko Alembo's first six wives argued about was his distribution of pig meat. Each one wanted the best piece.

9:00 Agnes decides to sleep over. She will feel better not being alone. The piglets are already snoring under the small platform when the three women cram together on it. They fall asleep quickly. With luck, not all rules of war will be broken, and if the warriors come and burn their house, they will wake them and let them out before doing so.

Papua New Guinea

The Momeng Family

Kent Momeng, age 31 (1)
Young Wopit, 28 (2)
Martine Momeng, 8 (3)
Carol, 6 (4)
Doreen, 4 (5)
Deborah, 3 (6)

1 pig
2 ducks
5 chickens
4 dogs
1 cat

Angisi Village, Sepik River

MAY 3

5:30 A child's wail, as he receives his first spanking of the day, blends in well with the wild sounds coming from the forest. Then the guitar music in the church next to Kent Momeng's house calls the villagers to prayer. The whole village is of the same faith. First they were all Catholics, but the missionary left and no one was sent to replace him. So, when a missionary from the Church of Christ arrived, the whole village—altogether, five extended families—changed religion. Kent is the first to arrive. A fervent believer, he dreams of becoming a preacher and goes regularly to the mission to learn the calling. For now, he contents himself with being the assistant preacher.

The mist on the Keram River, one of the tributaries of the Sepik River, rises as Young and her daughter Carol climb down the ladder of branches from their high-perched house to wash their dishes at the river. Young can pray from there, to the sound of her husband's voice as he recites this morning's prayers. Beside her mother, Carol washes her face in the brown river water. Every morning, her eyes are infected, full of pus. Carol says she doesn't know why, and there's nothing to be done about it.

After prayer, there is a meeting on the shore. The villagers are needed for communal work. A teacher's house needs to be rebuilt in Wustsetac, two villages away, where the primary school serves the five neighboring communities. For high-school studies, students must leave to board in towns or Christian missions. That is why there are no young people in Angisi.

6:30 After cooking and serving sego pancakes to her family, Young goes to her canoe with her two younger children, Doreen and Deborah. Always self-effacing, Young does not reveal it, but she is in no condition to work this morning: she is in great pain and has not slept the whole night due to a dreadful toothache. She pushes the canoe offshore toward Bunam Mission, where she will find the *haus sik*, the health center.

Even by motor canoe, Angisi Village is eleven hours up the river from Angoram, a service town where the population living along the Sepik come to sell their products, and where roads begin that lead to cities and airports. Flying is the only way to travel efficiently in the country.

At this time of the morning, the river seems calm like a mirror, but a few minutes after Young has embarked, the sun appears through the clouds. Instantly it reveals the strong current below the surface and brings alive the heat in this region of nearly intolerable humidity, of swamps and of malaria.

Flowing for over eight hundred miles before emptying into the Bismarck

Sea, the Sepik is not a tranquil river. It is constantly changing its course, leaving vast regions of swamps and causing floods. Yet in October there will scarcely be any water in the river.

7:00 Going with the current is easy; Young paddles two or three times, then lets her canoe drift for a while. The shore's wild bush and forest carefully hide the beautiful bird of paradise. Except for the birds' song and Young's paddle as it hits the water, everything is quiet. The first canoe Young meets has a woman paddling, a child feeding at her breast, and another holding the log they are towing home for firewood. The two women nod their heads in greeting.

As she approaches a village, Young sees a fisherman deep in the reeds, searching for the numerous eels that live there. As in Angisi and every Sepik village, the houses are built on stilts and perched at the river's edge. From its shores, yet another canoe appears, laden with garden produce, which the couple paddling are taking to the Angoram market. Their journey will take three days there and back.

7:45 Young ties her canoe to a tree. She has now almost arrived, but still has a half-hour walk cutting through the forest's muddy trails. A shortcut to Bunam, it will save her having to paddle another hour. On her return trip home, she will face the current upriver, and she will need nearly double the time. Deborah is crying and does not want to walk. Young urges her to go faster, only to get sharper cries out of the child. Finally showing her impatience, she brusquely picks her up and hoists her on her back for the rest of the journey.

When she arrives at the mission, she first takes her two young ones to her mother, who lives there. Martine, Young's oldest daughter, greets her sisters. She has been in Bunam over a week. She won't start school until next year, and she has been asked to come and help an aunt who is overwhelmed by too many small children. Young will come back to join them, but first she desperately needs the tooth medication. At the *haus sik* she sits on the stairs, waiting for the nurse to call her. This is where she also came when she and Kent decided they did not want any more children. It was a tough decision, because they only have girls and the traditional inheritance system makes it so important to have a boy; still, the couple decided that four daughters would have to be enough.

The male nurse comes to her, listens to her complaint, and asks her to wait. He soon returns, putting ten aspirins into her hand and telling her that if they do not calm her she should go to Angoram to have the tooth pulled out. Young leaves, looking with hope at the pills. She does not really have the time, or the money, to see a dentist. Her husband is less hopeful about medication from the *haus sik*. "The doctors are not competent and we don't get proper care," he says.

The river is the vital means of transportation for all the Momengs' needs. But it can be very threatening. Just a week ago the water rose so high up the house stilts that canoes could be tied to the veranda. When it receded, the ground around Angisi Village was buried in thick mud and leaves.

2:00 Kent, back from Wustsetac, has eaten a sego pancake and now leaves with a brother and sister-in-law for one of his two gardens on the family land. The one he is going to now is one hour's paddling away. The second is so far that when he works in it he has to sleep there. Often the crops rot before he can go and get them. Just past the village, he turns left into one of the swamp canals, standing in the back of the canoe and paddling slowly. He bends down regularly to avoid branches and quickly veers away when he sees a venomous snake coiled on one of them, waiting.

The two canoes make their way through a very tiny swamp lane in the dense bush. Kent, his brother, and his sister-in-law set to work rapidly. Getting the flour for their staple pancake food from the sego palm tree is a laborious and complicated business that calls for several people. Cutting down a tree, Kent and his brother split the trunk and with home-made pickaxes chop out the soft core until it is half fiber, half powder. Kent's sister-in-law, meanwhile, has made an ingenious bush table out of branches stuck side by side in the ground and bent at neat right angles. She puts the fiber-flour in a basket of loose-woven fronds on the table and pours water through it into a big container of leaves below. The Momengs eat this thick, gluey flour-water mixture either raw or cooked.

4:30 Young is back; the aspirin has given her a little relief. Like many other women, she sits on the veranda of her house, braiding the straw baskets used to filter the sego. These have to be constantly renewed, and weaving is a routine activity for all women of the village. In front of her, her daughters are splashing as they bathe.

The Momeng kitchen is made of woven fronds. The sego-palm flour is the family's staple diet, along with river fish.

6:00   The sun sets, the guitar strings are plucked, and the villagers walk slowly toward evening prayers. After the psalms are sung, the village preacher's voice rises as he yells at the villagers, stressing the necessity of being good Christians, and menacing them with hell if they are not. Then Kent reads the Gospel according to Luke which teaches man that he will become strong through his belief in God, that "he is like a man building a house who dug deep and laid a foundation upon rock." The preacher passionately explains these words to the villagers, but they have never seen anything except muddy, shifting ground, and the crooked trees of the forest, to use as foundations.

7:00   Under the full moon, the river shore now looks like a busy promenade. Kent joins his neighbors walking up and down the village, chatting. His dinner, like everyone else's, is in his hand: a sego pancake and a smoked fish.

8:00   Deborah is put to bed under her parents' mosquito net, and the other girls sit beside their mother on the high balcony, constantly slapping the attacking mosquitoes. Kent joins them with a cousin for the favorite pastime of *tok tok* (chatting). After a while, they take to the guitars to enliven this calm evening. Until bedtime, they will sing "God's songs." With the older generation now dead, they have forgotten their traditional songs; and Kent repeats what he has learned from the missionaries: "It is a sin to sing custom songs."

The Papua New Guineans

THE NAME: From Malay *papuwah*, meaning "frizzy-haired," given by early Portuguese explorers. The Spanish named the island after the Guinea coast of Africa.

GEOGRAPHY
The eastern half of the island of New Guinea is mountainous, with coastal lowlands of marshes and plains, including some of the most extensive swampland in the world. There are several larger outlying islands of volcanic origin; and six hundred smaller, mainly coral-reef islands. Max. altitude: 4,519 m. (14,827 ft.) (Mt. Wilhelm)
Area: 462,840 sq. km. (178,704 sq. mi.)
Density: 7.6 pers./sq. km. (20 pers./sq. mi.) (1988)
Arable land: less than 0.01% (1985)
Forest: 83%. Deforestation: 0.1% (23,000 hectares) per year
Climate: Equatorial, with high heat, humidity, and rainfall. Temperatures are cooler in the highlands. Monsoon season from December through March

CAPITAL: Port Moresby, pop. 136,780 (1985)

LANGUAGE: English (official)
The lingua franca is a Melanesian–English Pidgin; Hiri Motu is also widely spoken on the Papua coast. There are more than seven hundred languages altogether.

RELIGION: In 1966, 93% of the population was nominally Christian, mainly Anglican, Roman Catholic, and Ecumenist. However, belief in magic, taboos, and traditional religious practices remains fundamentally important.

POPULATION: Total—3,804,000 (1988)
Annual growth: 2.5% (87,775) (1985)
Doubling time: 29 yrs.
Urban: 14% (1985) (est. for year 2000: 20%)
Rural: 86%

AGE GROUPS (1985)
15% under 5 yrs.
42% under 15
53% under 20
28% from 20 to 39
14% from 40 to 59
4% 60 yrs. and over

ETHNIC GROUPS
More than 700 ethnic groups, often divided into two broad categories: Papuan, those in the interior and western part of the island of New Guinea; and Melanesian, those in coastal and island areas.

HISTORY
First settled by peoples from Southeast Asia via Indonesia as long as fifty thousand years ago
7000 B.C.: Evidence of irrigated vegetable gardens suggests the highland peoples were some of the world's first agriculturists
A.D. 1000: Contact with Indonesia and China
1545: Spanish explorer Ortiz de Retes names the island Nueva Guinea
1828–1962: Dutch claim western half of New Guinea as part of the Dutch East Indies and administer it until it becomes part of Indonesia as Irian Jaya
1884: Southeastern portion annexed by Britain; northeastern portion annexed by Germany
1906: British New Guinea, under the name of Papua, transferred to Australian administration
1921: Mandate for administration of German New Guinea given to Australia by League of Nations
1930: Previously undiscovered civilization of nearly one million people found in unexplored highlands
1942: Occupation by the Japanese begins. Mainland portion and outlying islands recovered by Australian and American forces in stages
1949: Papua and New Guinea combined under Australian Mandate
Sept. 16, 1975: Full independence within the Commonwealth as Papua New Guinea

FAMILY
Marital status, for females 15 yrs. + (1980)
  Single: 38%
  Married: 56%
  Other: 2%
Female head of household: no data
Fertility rate: 5.4 (1986)
Teenage births: no data
Births out of wedlock: no data
Contraception: 4% (1985)
Government's position on family planning: Fertility rate is considered too high, but no government policy to influence fertility. Family-planning programs promote family well-being and responsible parenthood.

SOCIAL INDICATORS
Life expectancy: 53 yrs. (male: 52; female: 54) (1985)
Infant mortality: 61/1,000 births (1987)
Crude birth rate: 39/1,000 pop. (1987)
Crude death rate: 12/1,000

HEALTH
Access to health services: 93% (1984) within two hours' travel
Births attended by trained health personnel: 34%

HOUSING
Persons per household: 5.6 (1980)
Electricity: Urban: 34% without (1984); rural: no data
Access to safe water: 16% (urban: 54%; rural: 10%) (1983)
Source of water: Mostly wells, rainwater, and streams in rural areas
Toilet facilities (1983)
  Adequate sanitary facilities: urban: 51%; rural: 3.4%
Construction materials: Bush materials

EDUCATION
Literacy: 45% (male: 55%; female: 35%) (1985)
Gross enrollment ratio (1983)
  First level: 69% (completing in 1980–86: 67%)
  Second: 11%
  Third: no data
Educational attainment for pop. 25 yrs. + (1980)
  (Nationals only)
  None: 83%
  First level: 8%
  Second: 4%
  Third: no data

ECONOMIC ACTIVITY
Economically active population: 70% (male: 36%; female: 33%) (1980)
Agriculture: 80% act. pop.; 35% of GDP
Mines: 4% act. pop.; 20% of GDP
Industry: 6% act. pop.; 10% of GDP
Services: 10% act. pop.; 35% of GDP
Per capita GNP: US$720 (1986)
Population in absolute poverty: urban: 10%; rural: 75% (1977–86)
National currency: kina
Principal resources: Gold, copper, silver, coffee, cocoa, coconut

COMMUNICATIONS
Radio
  Transmitters: 54 (1985)
  Receivers: 63/1,000 pop. (1985)
Television
  Believed to have no television service of its own
Newspapers (1986)
  Dailies: 2
  Circulation: 45,000 (8/1,000 pop.)

Papua New Guinea

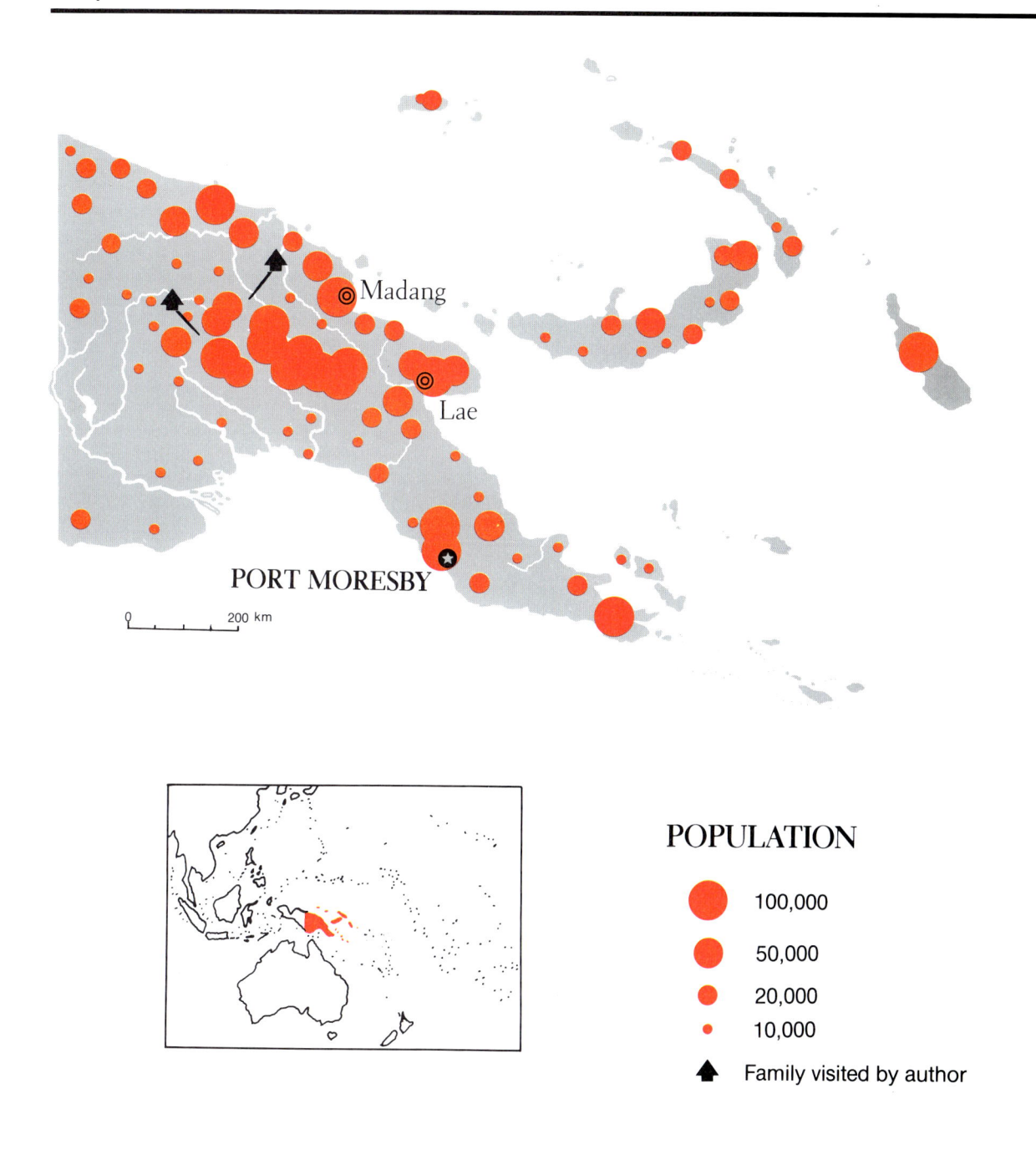

POPULATION

- 100,000
- 50,000
- 20,000
- 10,000
- ▲ Family visited by author

Solomon Islands

The Fihu Family

Selwyn Fihu, age 47 (1)
Agnes Fihu, 40 (2)
Michael, 20 (3)
Jennifer, 17 (absent)
Nash, 13 (4)
Christopher, 7 (5)
Max, 3 (6)

5 pigs
15 chickens

Nareabu

JANUARY 29

6:00 The church keeper beats on an empty gas canister hanging from a breadfruit tree. The Fihu family rise quickly, put on their church clothes, and quietly join the other members of the community crossing the open field in the center of Nareabu Village. In the church, Nareabu's only cement building, one of the women lets out a high, piercing cry, the first note of the morning psalm.

6:30 On his return, Selwyn looks for privacy on the stretch of beach that slopes down from his yard. The beach and the bush are the village's only toilet facilities. Minutes later, a man runs by, shouting: "The boat is coming!" The white silhouette of *Compass Rose 11* is passing the coral reef on its way to the main town of Buala. The ferry has been out of service, and everybody has been waiting for its return.

Michael, Selwyn's oldest son, does not have a minute to lose. He is now two weeks late for the beginning of the school year at college in Honiara, the nation's capital. His sister, Jennifer, managed to get to her school in Honiara before the boat broke down. With his jeans, T-shirt, and earring, Michael already looks like a city boy. Now he rolls his few possessions in his straw sleeping mat and scrambles down the mud slope between his home and the beach, where Selwyn is waiting in his tree-trunk canoe to row him to the reef.

Agnes, his mother, waves her hands to attract the attention of a motorboat taxi racing full-speed toward Buala. The boat, already full of people, swirls around and heads in the Fihus' direction to wait beyond the reef. Michael puts one foot in his father's canoe, then turns. Behind him, Agnes is waiting to say goodbye. They shake hands, avoiding each other's eyes.

Father and son paddle rapidly toward the motorboat. Her skirt trailing in the sea, Agnes stands with Christopher and Max, watching the motorboat disappear around the curve of the land. With today's departures, there are only six young men left in the village.

Agnes knows her son is happy now. Just last night, he again exclaimed: "I can't wait to leave this muddy village. There is nothing for us young people here." He is right. The elders of the village have opposed any special programs or activities for the young, who, they feel, should be content to help their parents work the land. Selwyn does not agree with the old people, and yet he fears for the future of the young who leave for the capital. "What will happen to them if they don't have the land to fall back on?" he asks. Of his son, he says, "This is not the Michael we used to know. He was happy, helpful; now he is never satisfied." But Selwyn knows he has impressed on Michael the need to be a leader if one wants to change things.

Because of their fragile building materials and the cyclones that frequently hit the region, the Fihus have had to build five houses in twenty-three years. Now they are building separate quarters for the boys; the girls will stay in the house with their parents.

7:00   The church gong sounds again. The church and school bells regulate life on Santa Isabel. This one is the call for communal work. A wall must be built inside the school building, to form two classrooms. Some men are needed to weave sego palm leaves together, and others to layer them into a wall.

7:30   The primary-school bell calls the children, who have their own communal work. They pick up dry leaves and sweep the classrooms' cement and dirt floors. Nash and Christopher leave the house, still chewing on their boiled sweet potato. Selwyn starts a fire under the smokehouse to dry copra (coconut meat) and pandanus leaves, which are used to braid mats. Then, bush knife in hand, he strides away, with Max at his heels, leaving Agnes to wash the dishes under the outside water tap. Dense smoke rises through the fruit trees that surround the house, and rays of sunlight filter down, accentuating the peacefulness of the moment.

Selwyn's wife was chosen for him by his uncle. He admits that he was nervous before they were introduced, so he hiked through the forest's plantations up to her mountain to look at her through the branches of the trees. He was happy with what he saw. Agnes has always been very shy and never attended school. Even now, she avoids speaking Pidgin English. Selwyn says, "With an uneducated woman, you are sure you will always have food to eat and a mat to sleep on." But Selwyn insists on education for his sons and daughters, and will let them choose their own marriage partners.

8:00   Agnes prepares to go to one of the family's gardens near Jeevo, her mother's village, a half hour ride away by canoe. In truth, it is her land, as land is inherited on the woman's side. "Women give life, just as the earth does," says

SOLOMON ISLANDS

Selwyn to explain the tradition. Paddling quietly, Agnes sings to give herself rhythm. There are more and more motorboats now. "Once you discover how fast and easy it can be to get from one place to another, the will to paddle leaves you," she says softly.

From this particular garden, she will harvest sweet potatoes. Coconut and bananas grow in another grove. There is enough land for everyone on the island. The Fihus don't even know how much they have. But in spite of the abundance of land, it is difficult this year to find a variety of food to eat. The pineapple planting was not planned well and the harvest is over. Cassava and yams have just been planted, and this year's papaya and cucumber crops were destroyed by seven months of drought.

10:30 Nash runs home during recess to grab a piece of sugarcane. After waiting for his sister to leave, Christopher comes in to serve himself secretly from a cache of dry navy biscuits.

1:00 Selwyn comes home at lunchtime to tend the small shop in the corner of his house, where he sells tobacco, tinned beef and fish, and small sundries. With this income plus the income from the copra that he sells, he just about manages to pay for his children's education. Michael will become a teacher, and Selwyn will pay for Jennifer's schooling for one more year. When she finishes Form 3, she will have to look for a job. He is ready, however, to invest in schooling for Nash. She is the brightest of his children and eager to learn.

Selwyn searches for Max, but the only living thing in the house is a hen laying an egg on the table between the family Bible and some schoolbooks.

The first thing one notices when entering the house is the calendar with which Selwyn plans his family. He follows his wife's menstrual cycle very closely: Selwyn cannot afford any more children.

Max is running around with cousins and friends, and finally his father finds him and gives him a piece of fish and a sweet potato. He is tired and grumpy, so Selwyn ties the child on his back with a cloth, and Max promptly falls asleep.

2:00 Max is still asleep, strapped to his father's strong back as Selwyn cuts bamboo for the boys' new house. Agnes returns, a little excited. Her canoe disappeared while she was in the garden, and she had to ask for a ride back to the village. "Someone must have needed it," says Agnes, not thinking for one minute that it could have been stolen. She asked Jeevo's villagers to tell the borrower to bring her canoe back. She carries the sweet potatoes to the water tap and starts washing them, letting the water fall on her head and body as well. Refreshed, she climbs up the slope to her kitchen, lights the firewood, and starts making *bitis*, a pudding of shredded sweet potatoes and coconut milk.

3:00 The morning was silent, but now children are yelling and laughing. At school, the afternoons are devoted to sports and games. As these activities are finished and the children run home, the sky turns dark gray, the wind gusts, and the tropical afternoon rain starts. Agnes sits on the floor braiding sleeping mats.

5:30 The church gong announces evening prayers. Agnes cannot leave her kitchen, so Selwyn will have to keep Max silent during the service.

6:30 Selwyn pumps the kerosene lamp while the family sit on the floor mat, serving themselves from a plate of fish and sweet potato. There is no rice, no canned food. "Some children now refuse to eat the traditional food, but in this house we will keep on eating the food our garden provides for us," says Selwyn. "It is nature that makes us truly rich."

8:00 The bell rings for the last time to call the schoolchildren to prayers. Once again, they put on their church clothes. They thank God for the day that is ending, sing psalms, and return home to bed.

Christopher and Max, not wanting to miss any of the conversation, fall asleep lying on a mat beside their mother. Agnes will move them into the room she shares with Selwyn when she is ready for bed. At the moment, she is using seashells to decorate a jar, which will serve as a vase at the church.

9:00 The village is now still. It is low tide, and on the empty beach two teenage boys walk hand-in-hand, trying to stretch the day and shorten the night. Like Michael, they say: "In this village, when it is dark, what else is there to do but sleep?"

Solomon Islanders

THE NAME: Named after the wealthy biblical king by Spanish explorers anticipating finding great natural riches

GEOGRAPHY
922 islands extending 1,400 km.: six large volcanic islands in two parallel chains; about twenty medium-sized islands, and countless islets. Two of the country's four active volcanoes are located on the mountainous island chains, covered with dense rain forests.
Max. altitude: 2,447 m. (8,028 ft.) (Mt. Makarakomburu)
Area: 28,450 sq. km. (10,982 sq. mi.)
Density: 10 pers./sq. km. (23 pers./sq. mi.) (1986)
Arable land: 1.4% (1985)
Forest: 90%. Deforestation: less than 1% (1,000 hectares) per year
Climate: Equatorial, with few extremes of temperature. Rainfall occurs throughout the year. From November to April, northwest trade winds bring more rain and occasional cyclones.

CAPITAL: Honiara, pop. 30,413 (1986)

LANGUAGE: English (official)
An estimated eighty-seven indigenous languages; the lingua franca is English–Melanesian Pidgin.

RELIGION
Anglican Church of Melanesia: 34%
Catholic: 19%
South Sea Evangelist Church: 18%
United Church: 11%
Seventh-Day Adventist: 10%
Traditional religion: 2%
Other: 6%

POPULATION: Total—279,000 (1986)
Annual growth: 3.4% (9,486) (1986)
Doubling time: 19 yrs.
Urban: 10% (1986) (est. for year 2000: 14%)
Rural: 90%

AGE GROUPS (1986)
18% under 5 yrs.   25% from 20 to 39
47% under 15   12% from 40 to 59
58% under 20   5% 60 yrs. and over

ETHNIC GROUPS
Melanesian: 94%
Polynesian: 4%
Micronesian: 1%
Chinese, European, and other: 1%

HISTORY
Settled by at least 2000 B.C. by Melanesians
1568: Spanish explorer Mendaña de Neyra reaches the islands. Unsuccessful efforts to settle
1850s: Anglican missionaries arrive
1863–1910: Forcible recruiting of over 100,000 laborers to work plantations in Australia and other islands
1885: Northern islands become German Protectorate; eight years later, southern islands become British Protectorate
1898–99: Northern Solomons ceded to Britain in exchange for its withdrawal from Western Samoa
1920: Bougainville and Buka placed under Australian Mandate by League of Nations
1942: Invasion by Japan. Severe battles during WWII, notably at Guadalcanal. Thousands of islanders volunteer to fight alongside Americans. Island decimated by war
1946–50: First independence movement
1970: New constitution establishes governing council
1976: Granted internal self-government as the Solomon Islands
July 7, 1978: Full independence within the Commonwealth

FAMILY
Marital status, for females 15 yrs. + (1986)
Single: 33%
Married: 61%
Widowed: 5%
Divorced: 1%
Female head of household: no data
Fertility rate: 6.5 (1988)
Teenage births: no data
Births out of wedlock: no data
Contraception: no data
Government's position on family planning: Fertility rate is too high, but no government policy to influence fertility. Promotes awareness of population issues through education

SOLOMON ISLANDS

SOCIAL INDICATORS
Life expectancy: 54 yrs. (male: 54; female: 54) (1976)
Infant mortality: 44/1,000 births (1987)
Crude birth rate: 45/1,000 pop. (1982)
Crude death rate: 12/1,000

HEALTH
Access to health services: 12% (1984–85)
Births attended by trained health personnel: 80% (1983)

HOUSING
Persons per household: 6.4 (1986)
Electricity: no data. It can be assumed the majority is without.
Access to safe water: 50% (urban: 96%; rural: 45%) (1980–83)
Source of water (1984–85)
    Gravity feed, well, or roof tank in village: 38%; outside: 7%
    River or stream in village: 4%; outside: 50%
    Other: 1%
Toilet facilities (1984–85)
    Flush and pit: 27%
Construction materials: Bush materials

EDUCATION
Literacy: 15% (1983)
Gross enrollment ratio (1983)
    First level: 65% (completing in 1985: 49%)
    Second: 49%
    Third: no data
Educational attainment for pop. 25 yrs. + (1976)
    None: 56%
    First level: incomplete: 28%; complete: 12%
    Second: incomplete: 2%; complete: 1%
    Third: 1%

ECONOMIC ACTIVITY
Economically active population: 22% (male: 35%; female: 8%) (1976)
Agriculture: 75% act. pop.; 65% of GDP
Mines: 0% act. pop.; 0% of GDP
Industry: 5% act. pop.; 5% of GDP
Services: 20% act. pop.; 30% of GDP
Per capita GNP: US$346 (1988)
National currency: Solomon Island dollar
Principal resources: Timber, copra, palm oil, fish

COMMUNICATIONS
Radio
    Transmitters: 5 (1985)
    Receivers: 93/1,000 pop. (1985)
Television
    Believed to have no television service of its own
Newspapers (1984)
    Believed to have no general-interest dailies

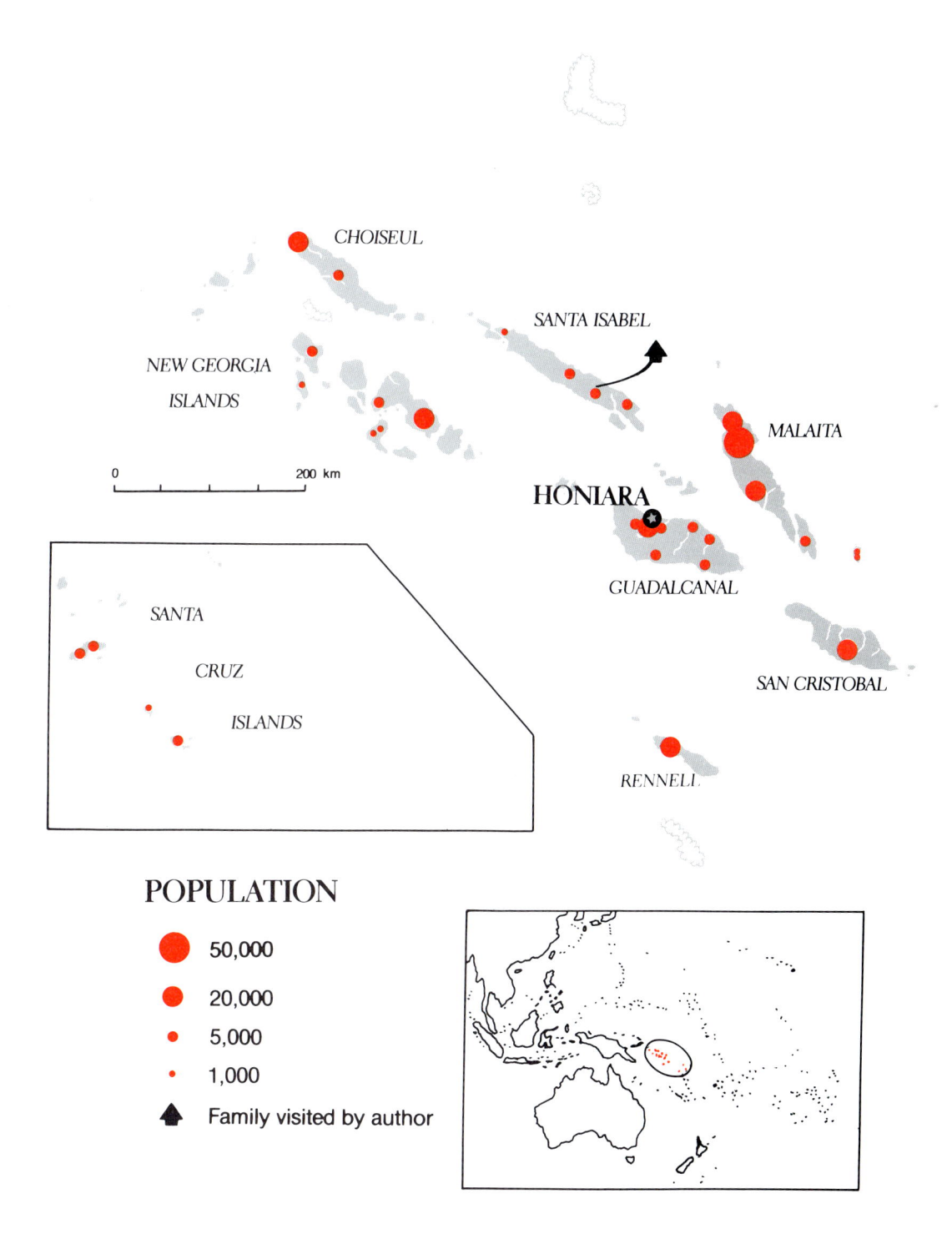

Solomon Islands

POPULATION

- 50,000
- 20,000
- 5,000
- 1,000
- Family visited by author

Kingdom of Tonga

The Manisela Family

Iselili Manisela, age 54 (1)
Ilaisaame Kataii Manisela, 41 (2)
Sulia Mafile, 25 (3)
Epeli, 23 (absent)
Asipau, 21 (absent)
Olalelei (Ola), 20 (4)
Toto Manai, 18 (5)
Anaua Evaloni (Naua), 15 (6)
Betelo (Be), 8 (7)

30 pigs
8 goats
4 chickens
3 dogs
3 cats

Talasiu Village

DECEMBER 4

Because it lies just west of the international dateline, it is said in the Kingdom of Tonga that time begins here and that Tongans usher in each new day. Up before dawn, Sulia Manisela is truly the world's very first riser.

She sits cross-legged in one corner of the dark living room, beside the stereo and an image of Christ in the Garden. This day will start with a prayer, and there will be more prayers before meals and before work and classes. By the light of a tiny lamp, Sulia reads the Bible aloud, so that everyone in bed can hear her.

Sulia is the daughter every Tongan mother dreams of. She is tall and strong, a little plump, and very energetic. She is majestic yet gentle, and is proficient in her native traditions of dancing and weaving. She is also a devout Christian.

6:00 Kataii and Be follow Sulia to the outside bamboo kitchen hut. Be is not Kataii's son. His real mother gave him away when he was not yet two months old. Kataii's father was a Methodist minister, and to honor their friendship and love for him, Be's real parents offered their baby to him and his wife. As the couple were old, they asked their daughter and son-in-law to protect the child. Adoption within a family or a friend's family is common in Polynesian culture.

Be is making enough of a racket to wake his sisters. As a boy he is not allowed to go in the room where his sisters Ola and Naua are sleeping. Those families that still live in houses made of leaves and cane have separate buildings for the boys and the girls. The Maniselas prefer wood over the bush materials, but can only afford one structure, with divided bedrooms. Although men are considered the chiefs in Tongan society, women are highly respected. Be is a high-spirited prankster, but he has learned this well. His sisters always get the best food and do not work in the fields. He knows it is a brother's duty to protect his sister, and never to be disrespectful to her in front of others.

While she cooks, Sulia sings, "Oh, what fun it is to ride in a one-horse open sleigh." Even in the kitchen hut, the music comes in loud and clear over the big speakers in the house. When electricity was installed, a stereo was the first thing the family purchased.

Kataii does not wait for breakfast. Leaving the household chores to Sulia, she goes to church. Today is fund-raising day, when the churchgoers prepare their finest pigs and choicest produce to give to the "Christian Followers" missionaries. Some villagers actually give the church all their yearly savings. Today the missionaries will receive enough gifts to build a bigger church. Kataii is among the earliest to arrive. The first time her family attended the missionaries' ceremony, they were still Methodists, but during the preacher's sermon their polio-stricken son Epeli got up and walked. "He was cured in the middle of the service," says Kataii. Since then, she has never doubted a word the preacher says. Kataii lays coconut leaves on the floor and starts peeling yams. After the missionaries' meal is served, she will come back home.

7:00 Breakfast, like every meal, is substantial: cassava, boiled bananas, yam, a piece of fish. Not one bite is taken before God is thanked. Eating is a joyous act for the Tongans, and offering their food to others is the most generous gesture one can make, the measure of one's well-being. Traditionally, great body size was the standard for beauty among women, and for respect among men. This concept is slowly changing. Even though Kataii's daughters are now attracted to the idea of a tiny waist, not one will leave the kitchen until the plates are empty.

8:30 After breakfast, Iselili and his son Toto, whose name means "Blood of the handsome," leave the village grounds for the family's nearby garden. Iselili's oldest son, Epeli, lives and works as a carpenter in the city of Kulualofa. There is not much work for the farmers at this time. Crops are rotated and a large part of the garden is left fallow. Everything grows in this fertile land: cassava, yam, plantain, papaya, coconut, mango, oranges, breadfruit, watermelon, and other fruits.

Besides farming his garden plot, Iselili is an elected village official and is responsible for the distribution of the eighty acres allocated to the village. In the Kingdom of Tonga's feudal system, all land is the property of the crown, but it is administered by nobles, who allot it to the "commoners." Since 1862, when the king granted the people freedom from the arbitrary rule of minor chiefs, each boy at sixteen has the right to 8¼ acres of land. Many Tongans have emigrated to other countries. Nonetheless, the fertility rate is high and two-thirds of the population live on the island of Tongatapu. Even if the country ranks first in the world for its land under cultivation, some Tongans worry that it might soon be impossible to continue the land policy.

Despite the money he is able to give to the church, the thirty pigs getting fat in his back yard, the richness of his land, and the fact that no one in his family is skinny, Iselili considers himself a poor man. He desires what the members of his family who emigrated to New Zealand, Australia, and America possess: cars, televisions, etc. Iselili's daughter Asipau is married and living in New Zealand and sends her family US$75 to US$100 a month. In 1982, she sent the money to build the wooden house when hurricane Isaac and "the

In most other Tongan yards, pigs are free to roam. The Manisela pigs are in a clean pen.

son of Isaac" destroyed their traditional cane house. Family members working overseas send home an amount equivalent to one-third of the country's foreign aid.

8:45 Sulia leaves for her job at the knitting factory owned by a New Zealand company interested in employing cheap labor. The knitters put together sweaters as fast as they can. Sulia works eagerly and stays apart from her giggling workmates. Paid by the piece, Sulia makes 50 pa'angas (US$36) a week, one of the best salaries one can get with or without an education. Her father earns as much in a month.

While Naua, on her first day of the summer school holidays, tidies up the kitchen, Ola cleans the house to the rhythm of traditional Polynesian music. Tongan dances are stories sung and acted out with movements of the hands and feet. Ola often stops to dance in front of the mirror in the living room. She is practicing the traditional dance for the wedding she dreams of. When she dropped out of school, she wanted to work in a bank, but her application was turned down, and she never looked anywhere else. Now there is a man she wants to marry, and she focuses all her time on this project, dreaming of raising children, and thanking God that in Tonga women do not work in the fields. On her wedding day, in addition to her graceful dancing, Ola's skin must be fair and her legs unmarked. This is why Tongan women wear long, wrap-around skirts.

12:30 Kataii is back in her kitchen, lighting the wood fire for the midday meal. The main meal of the day includes vegetables from the garden and seafood.

3:30 Ola has fallen asleep on the Bible. At the factory, the bell rings for a break. At the pigpen, Toto and his father discuss which pig to kill. The pigs are not for sale; they are either eaten by the family or given away. Today's is for Betelo's

Eating and feasting are joyous acts for Tongans. Offering food to others is the most generous gesture one can make. Cooking is done on the fire but also in a pit oven (umu). Cooking for two hundred people is not a problem; it just means digging a bigger pit.

mother, who has come to the capital for the funeral of one of her daughters.

Toto bleeds the animal, cleans it, fills it with aromatic herbs, and places it on the white-hot stones of the in-ground *umu*. Once on the hot rocks, it is covered with coconut shells and palm leaves, and then with earth. It will cook for two hours.

Toto and his father weed the garden and tease the girls, who sit on a mat outside, welcoming the cooling breeze of early evening.

Kataii heads for the outside shower, then puts on her black mourning dress and wraps her *ta'ovala* (a traditional skirt made of finely woven pandanus leaf) around her waist. The minute the pig is cooked, the parents leave.

7:30 The sky is pink, the day lingers a few more moments, and the children gather around the table for a piece of the steamed raisin pudding their mother has prepared. Their plates empty, Toto and Naua go to watch videos. There is no television station, but several homes in the village have VCRs, so they have a choice of films. Toto chooses *Rambo*; Naua does not know what will be shown where she is going. Brothers and sisters are also not allowed to watch videos together. It would be embarrassing to both if there were provocative scenes.

9:30 Kataii and Iselili have returned. Sulia reads the psalm for the day; then the family sing together. Unlike their parents, Sulia and Ola are not in a hurry to go to bed, so, while they wait for their brother and sister to come back, they sit on the doorstep in the moonlight, trimming each other's hair. Haircuts are best, they say, when the moon is full over the Pacific.

The Tongans

THE NAME: From Samoan *tongatapu*, meaning "sacred garden." It is the name of the mythological Samoan who gave the god Maui a fishhook with which he pulled the islands up from the sea. Tonga also means "south" in some dialects.

GEOGRAPHY
More than 150 islands, thirty-six inhabited, in three main groups: the Tongatapu in the south, with the capital; the Haapai, a far-flung archipelago of low coral islands and soaring volcanoes in the center; and the Vavau, with its immense landlocked harbor in the north.
Area: 699 sq. km. (270 sq. mi.)
Density: 143 pers./sq. km. (370 pers./sq. mi.) (1988)
Arable land: 24% (1985)
Forest: 11%
Climate: Subtropical, cool dry season from April to November and a hot season, with on average two cyclones a year, from November to March

CAPITAL: Nukualofa, pop. 28,899 (1986)

LANGUAGE: Tongan (official), a Polynesian language; English widely used

RELIGION: The majority belong to the Free Wesleyan Church (Methodist); others, to the Free Church of Tonga, the Anglican, Roman Catholic, Seventh-Day Adventist, and Mormon.

POPULATION: Total—95,000 (1986)
  Annual growth: 0.8% (1985)
  Doubling time: 87.5 yrs.
  Urban: 20% (1985) (est. for year 2000: 25%)
  Rural: 80%

AGE GROUPS (1981)
  13% under 5 yrs.
  39% under 15
  52% under 20
  27% from 20 to 39
  15% from 40 to 59
   5% 60 yrs. and over

ETHNIC GROUPS
  Tongan: 98%
  European, part-European: 2%

HISTORY
Inhabited at least three thousand years ago by Austronesian-speaking peoples
10th cent.: Beginning of rule by Tu'i Tonga, a line of sacred kings
1643: Abel Tasman reaches Tongatapu and Haapai island groups
1773: Captain Cook names archipelago the Friendly Islands
1820s: Methodist missionaries arrive. Chief Taufa'ahau converted to Christianity
1845: Tongan archipelago unified, with Taufa'ahau (George Tupou I) as king
1862: King George Tupou I frees Tongan people from forced labor on minor chiefs' estates and grants them land rights
1875: Constitution; over next thirteen years, Germany, Great Britain, and the U.S.A. recognize Tonga's independence
1900: King George Tupou II negotiates treaty with Britain that, upon amendment five years later, makes Tonga a British Protectorate. British agent and counsel appointed, but royal family continues to rule
June 4, 1970: Achieves full sovereignty within the Commonwealth
1972: Group of American millionaires attempts to acquire Tonga's Minerva reef to convert it into a taxless utopian state. The king personally intervenes and ousts them

FAMILY
Marital status, for females 15 yrs. + (1976)
  Single: 39%
  Married: 53%
  Widowed: 5%
  Divorced: 1.7%
Female head of household: no data
Fertility rate: no data
Teenage births: no data
Births out of wedlock: 19.4% (1984)

Contraception: no data
Government's position on family planning: Fertility rate is considered too high. Promotes more effective family-planning programs and education of health-care personnel

SOCIAL INDICATORS
Life expectancy: 60 yrs. (1984)
Infant mortality: 11/1,000 births (1983)
Crude birth rate: 28/1,000 pop. (1983)
Crude death rate: 24/1,000

HEALTH
Access to health services: 80% (1984)
Births attended by trained health personnel: 60% (1984)

HOUSING
Persons per household: 6.5 (1976)
Electricity: 79% without (1976)
Access to safe water: 90% (urban: 91%; rural: 90%) (1985)
Source of water (1976)
Piped inside or out: 61%
Without piped water: 32%
Toilet facilities (1976)
Flush: 42%
Other: 54%
None: 2%
Construction materials (1976)
Wood: 58%   Iron: 10%
Thatch: 22%   Other: 4%
Brick, cement: 15%

EDUCATION
Literacy: 78% (1985)
Gross enrollment ratio (1976)
First level: 70%
Second: 111%
Third: 3%
Educational attainment for pop. 25 yrs. + (1980)
First level: incomplete: 37%; complete: 12.5%
Second: incomplete: 46%; complete: 0.1%
Third: incomplete: 0.3%; complete: 3.5%

ECONOMIC ACTIVITY
Economically active population: 43% (male: 72%; female: 13%) (1976)
Agriculture: 58% act. pop.; 25% of GDP
Half of the population is involved in subsistence agriculture.
Mines: 0% act. pop.; 0% of GDP
Industry: 5% act. pop.; 10% of GDP
Services: 37% act. pop.; 65% of GDP
Per capita GNP: US$740 (1986)
National currency: pa'anga
Principal resources: Coconuts, bananas, vanilla

COMMUNICATIONS
Radio
Transmitters: 2 (1985)
Receivers: 734/1,000 pop. (1985)
Television
Believed to have no television service of its own
Newspapers (1984)
Believed to have no general-interest dailies

Kingdom of Tonga

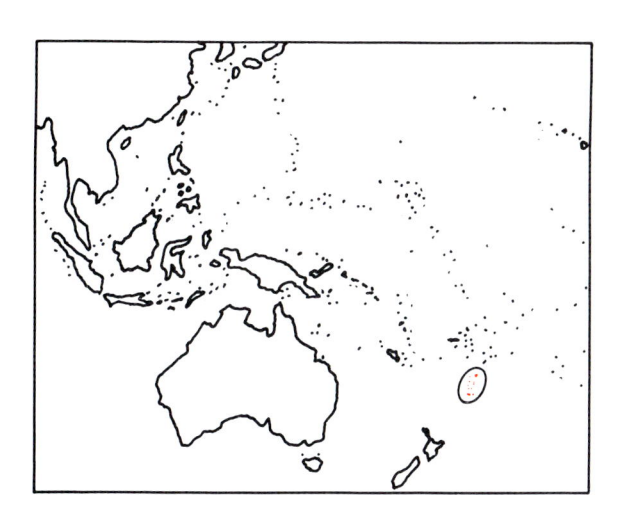

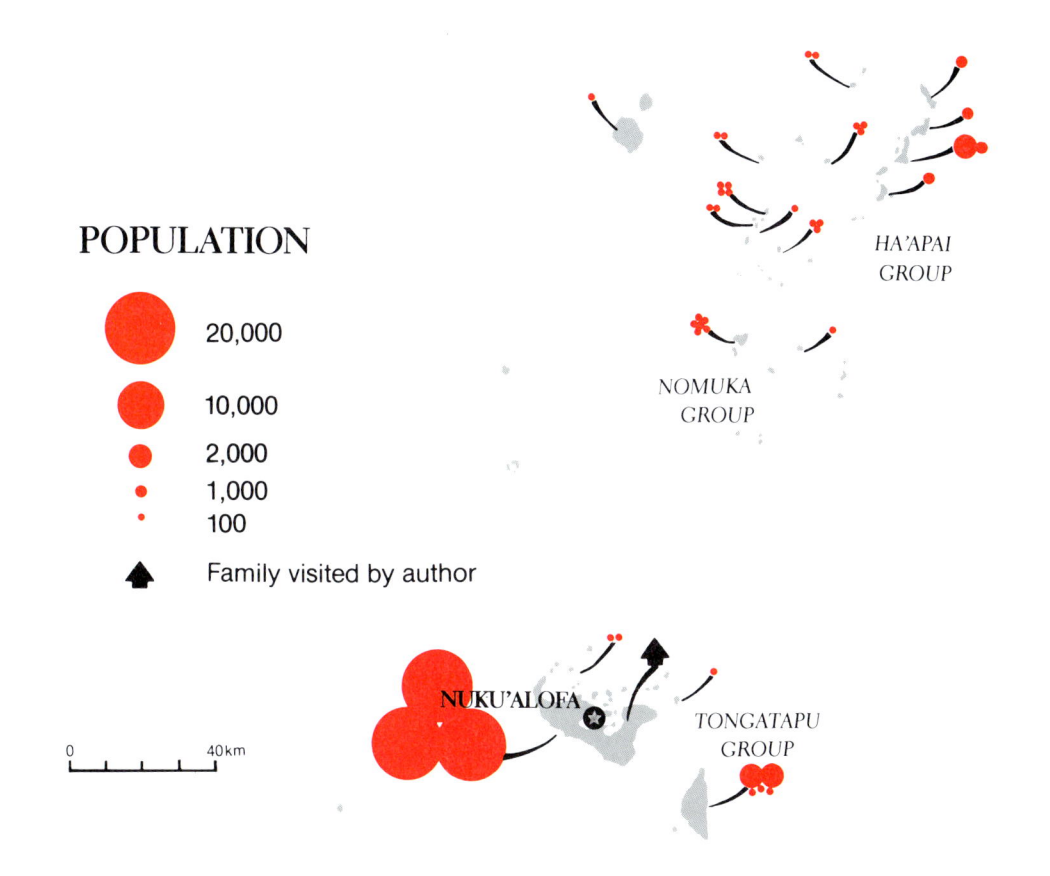

VAVA'U GROUP

HA'APAI GROUP

NOMUKA GROUP

POPULATION

- 20,000
- 10,000
- 2,000
- 1,000
- 100

▲ Family visited by author

NUKU'ALOFA

TONGATAPU GROUP

0 — 40 km

Tuvalu

Vitoli Temou's Family

Vitoli Temou, age 62 (1)
Marao Vitoli, 52 (2)
Talamoni, 27 (3)
Nome, 25 (absent)
Sulufainga (Sulu), 16 (4)
Galuola Talamoni, 2 (5)

10 pigs
87 chickens
2 dogs
2 cats

Funafuti

DECEMBER 29

It is still dark and the moon shines. Vitoli rolls off the side of his open house, grabs his fishing spear, and slings his woven basket over his shoulder. He goes in the direction of Funafuti's only road, which will bring him to the narrow tip of the island, where, he says, fish are numerous. Vitoli knows many ways to fish but will amuse himself this morning with his favorite—spear fishing.

He walks along the quiet road, separated from the calm blue lagoon only by a few coconut trees a hundred meters from the wild Pacific Ocean. There are few houses here. Most of the 2,810 people of the country's capital island live in crowded conditions at the other end, in Tuvalu's only city.

Land is in critical demand in Tuvalu, and especially on Funafuti. In ten years, the population has increased so greatly that there is not enough bush material left to build traditional houses; there is little fresh rainwater (groundwater is not potable); and the soil is tainted by the salt-laden winds, limiting agricultural development. In addition, much of Funafuti's land was excavated by the Americans to build an airstrip during World War II. The huge holes Tuvaluans call "borrow pits" have never been refilled. If they were, as everyone dreams they will be someday, there would be more space for planting.

6:00 Marao, Vitoli's shy wife, lights the fire in the outside kitchen hut to prepare tea, which she will serve with navy biscuits and the fish left over from last night's dinner.

Now her daughter Sulu rises, rolls up the family's sleeping mats, folds the sheets, and puts them away with the pillows on shelves made of tree trunks. Then she takes the coconut-branch broom and sweeps the yard, a daily ritual, as the constant ocean wind scatters the dry leaves of the coconut, breadfruit, banana, and pandanus trees that surround the house.

6:30 Vitoli comes back with six fish and sits down to breakfast. Marao has already finished eating and takes the fish down to the lagoon to clean. Vitoli feeds the hens, while Sulu dresses little Galuola, her older brother Talamoni's illegitimate child, whom the family has adopted.

Sulu is on Christmas holiday, having finished her fourth year of secondary school. Tuvalu's only high school (250 students) is situated on the outer island of Vaitupu, so Sulu boards there most of the year. An intelligent and hardworking girl, she ranks among the first five of her class. Next year will be the last year she can study in her country. Apart from training at the Maritime

School (the money that seamen send back home is of great importance to family income), graduates have few options. Sulu hopes to get a grant to study overseas—in Fiji, New Zealand, or Australia. Vitoli wants his daughter to study medicine. Sulu prefers mathematics. But the government might give her a grant in another field entirely.

While Vitoli pounds coconuts to feed the pigs, Marao scatters grain for the hens. Vitoli has been in the egg business for the last five years. But the hens are not laying well and he is beginning to doubt the quality of his imported feed.

8:30 Talamoni, who has stayed with Galuola's mother in the village, arrives with two cousins to cut the top leaves of the coconut trees to use as decorations for a relative's wedding tomorrow. Vitoli and his son are known in the village for not being easygoing, and they don't get along.

In fact, Vitoli leads a very isolated life and is a strict and intolerant man. "In the village," he says, "they don't like me because I still beat my sons." Vitoli is proud to add that, even at their age, his two sons let him beat them without protesting. He would like his sons to come and care for the hens, so he could rest like a man his age should. But his sons stay away.

Talamoni was an outstanding graduate of the police academy in Fiji but was caught stealing and lost his badge. He has since been in jail many times. Talamoni says he prefers the traditional life, and fishing, to being in the village, but living with his father is too difficult. His brother Nome lives in the village with his wife and rarely comes to see his father. Vitoli's third son committed suicide in 1981.

Only Sulu has escaped her father's severity. "Girls marry and leave to live with their husband's family. It is useless to beat them," says Vitoli.

10:00 Talamoni has gone fishing, and Sulu is gathering firewood with a school friend. Vitoli sits cross-legged, caressing Galuola; all his severity has melted away, and he displays only love for his grandson. By tradition, his son's children belong to his family, so it was important for Vitoli that the child not be raised by anyone else.

11:30 Marao embroiders a pillow for Sulu to take back to boarding school, while Vitoli fills buckets with rainwater from his thousand-gallon storage tank for his chickens. "The minute I stop working, I become restless," says Vitoli, coming back to sit beside Marao, "but a few minutes after I start again, I want to rest." His wife has taken out her old, rusted sewing machine, and Vitoli helps her get it started.

Vitoli lives up to the Tuvaluans' reputation for being adventurous travelers. He left his home island of Nukulaelae with his father in 1936 to go to

This is the season of the west winds, which bring cyclones. In 1972 cyclone Bebe destroyed all houses and trees on the islands. The cement-block houses that now form the capital village were built with relief funds. Vitoli has one of the few traditional houses remaining on Funafuti.

Kiribati and Phoenix Island; and again, during World War II, to go to Canton Island to work as a driver for the Americans. Then he worked in the gold mines of Fiji, and on Christmas Island for the English, who were doing nuclear testing. By then Vitoli had married Marao, the sixth woman in his life. Only the children they have had together have survived. If his other children had lived, Vitoli would have fourteen.

In 1961, Vitoli came back home to care for his aging parents. He would have lost his right to the land and to the title of *matai* (as the oldest son) if he hadn't returned. "Without land and today without education, you just can't live," he says. As the *matai*, Vitoli is responsible for the distribution of the ten plots of land scattered throughout the country to all his family members. The land has been passed down through generations of individuals and family groups, and ownership is very complicated. Land establishes a family's status. Village gossip has it that Vitoli's isolation is due to a family fight over land distribution. Vitoli doesn't talk about it.

3:30 Lunch consisted of tea and small reef fish caught by Talamoni, and now after a siesta during the noon heat, Vitoli goes back to work. He moves the hens' pen and shovels the dried droppings to use as fertilizer for the garden, where he is trying to grow Chinese cabbage and cucumbers.

Sulu and her friend are in the crystal-clear water of the Pacific, snacking on raw fish. They bite into the small fish with relish. Talamoni slips away from the house, carrying his fishing net, his pace quickening as he approaches the ocean. As he tosses his net into the surf, he looks like a free man.

The outer islands still live off the land and the sea, but here on the capital island, shops provide more and more imported products such as rice, canned food, flour, and cooking oil. Vitoli's family's diet has changed considerably.

Besides two planes a week, to and from the capital, travel between Tuvalu's nine islands is limited to one boat, the *Nivaga*. It makes a run of four of the islands north of the capital, stopping a few hours at each, then comes back to Funafuti for a southern run that sometimes brings it down to Fiji. If one goes to an outer island to stay, it could take months to return. When government officials visit the outer islands, the few hours the *Nivaga* stops is all the time they have to speak to their people.

6:30   Sulu has persuaded her friend to go with her to the village to see a film at the community hall. Her father would not have allowed her to bicycle alone, and, in any case, she would not have wanted to; she fears ghosts in the dark. The sun is setting on the lagoon, and night has fallen by the time they reach the village. Their bicycles safely parked at a cousin's house, the two girls walk to the open-walled center. It is already crowded. Women have spread their mats and pillows and laid their babies down to sleep. Men are rolling Gallagher's Famous Irish Cake tobacco in banana leaves to smoke. No one knows what they will see, but any film is welcome.

Young men stretch a large white cloth that looks like a sail between two wooden pillars, but they never do get it taut. Throughout the film, the cloth waves in the wind, adding unplanned movement to the actors in *Our Lady of Fatima*. The eighteen Catholics on the island may know what it is all about, but the others just enjoy a distracting evening.

9:00   Once Sulu and her girlfriend leave the village, there is no more electricity. Sulu's pocket flashlight and the half-moon on the white coral sand are enough to help them avoid the holes in the road. The journey is peaceful. Even the dogs are quiet, and the ghosts have stayed away.

The Tuvaluans

THE NAME: Meaning "eight standing together," in reference to the eight permanently inhabited islands of the group

GEOGRAPHY
Five coral atolls and four reef islands that extend over 560 km. in a winding line from Nanumea in the north to Niulakita in the south. The territory encompasses 1.3 million sq. km. of sea. Max. altitude: 5 m. (16 ft.)
Area: 26 sq. km. (10 sq. mi.)
Density: 327 pers./sq. km. (850 pers./sq. mi.) (1988)
Arable land: no data
Forest: no data
Climate: Tropical, with few seasonal variations; trade winds blow from the east much of the year; occasional cyclones

CAPITAL: Fangafade on the island of Funafuti, pop. 2,810 (1985)

LANGUAGE: English (official); Tuvaluan spoken

RELIGION
    Church of Tuvalu: 97%
    Other (Seventh-Day Adventists, Bahai): 3%

POPULATION: Total—8,000 (1988)
    Annual growth: 1.5% (107) (1983)
    Doubling time: 47 yrs.
    Urban: 21% (1984)
    Rural: 79%

AGE GROUPS (1987)
    12% under 5 yrs.
    31% under 15
    41% under 20
    33% from 20 to 39
    16% from 40 to 59
     8% 60 yrs. and over

ETHNIC GROUPS
    Polynesian: 97%
    Other (Pacific, non-Pacific): 3%

HISTORY
Originally settled by Polynesians from Samoa
1568: Spanish explorer Mendaña sights the island of Nui
mid-19th cent.: Whalers flock to the surrounding waters. European traders and impressment of natives for labor bring social changes
1865: London Missionary Society pastors arrive; conversion to Christianity begins
1892: As the Ellice Islands, made a British Protectorate with the Gilberts
1916: Becomes a British Crown Colony
1942–43: U.S.A. builds air base on Funafuti and moves the six hundred residents to another island while six thousand soldiers take over Funafuti
1975: Ellice group separated from the colony and renamed Tuvalu
Oct. 1, 1978: Full independence
1979: U.S.A. renounces its 1856 claim to four of the islands
1981: First post-independence parliamentary elections

FAMILY
Marital status, for females 15 yrs. + (1979)
    Single: 42%
    Married: 47%
    Widowed: 7%
    Divorced: 3%
Female head of household: no data
Fertility rate: 2.8 (1982)
Teenage births: 6% (1986) / **Teenage fertility rate:** no data
Births out of wedlock: 15% (1986)
Contraception: no data
Government's position on family planning: Fertility rate is considered too high. Government supports information on and access to family planning.

SOCIAL INDICATORS
Life expectancy: 59 yrs. (male: 57; female: 60) (1983)
Infant mortality: 34/1,000 births (1985)

TUVALU

Crude birth rate: 26/1,000 pop. (1983)
Crude death rate: 7/1,000

HEALTH
Access to health services: 100% (1984) within an hour's walk or travel
Births attended by trained health personnel: 100%

HOUSING
Persons per household: 6.4 (1979)
Electricity: 61% without (1979)
Access to safe water: 100% (1984)
Source of water (1979)
    House tank (rain): 85%
    Public cistern: 15%
Toilet facilities (1979)
    Flush: 13%
    Latrine: 58%
    None: 29%
Construction materials (1979)
    Traditional open side: 58%
    Palagi (foreign-style)/local mix: 19%
    Palagi (foreign-style)/glass windows: 22%

EDUCATION
Literacy: 90% (1985)
Gross enrollment ratio (1984)
    First level: 49%
    Second: no data
    Third: no data
Educational attainment for pop. 20 yrs. + (1979)
    None: less than 1%
    First level: 6% (upper primary: 68%)
    Second: 8%
    Third: less than 1%

ECONOMIC ACTIVITY
Economically active population: no data
GDP: no data
National currency: Australian dollar
Principal resources: Coconuts, fish

COMMUNICATIONS
Radio
    Transmitters: 1 (1983)
    Receivers: 250/1,000 pop. (1983)
Television
    Believed to have no television service of its own
Newspapers (1984)
    Believed to have no general-interest dailies

Tuvalu

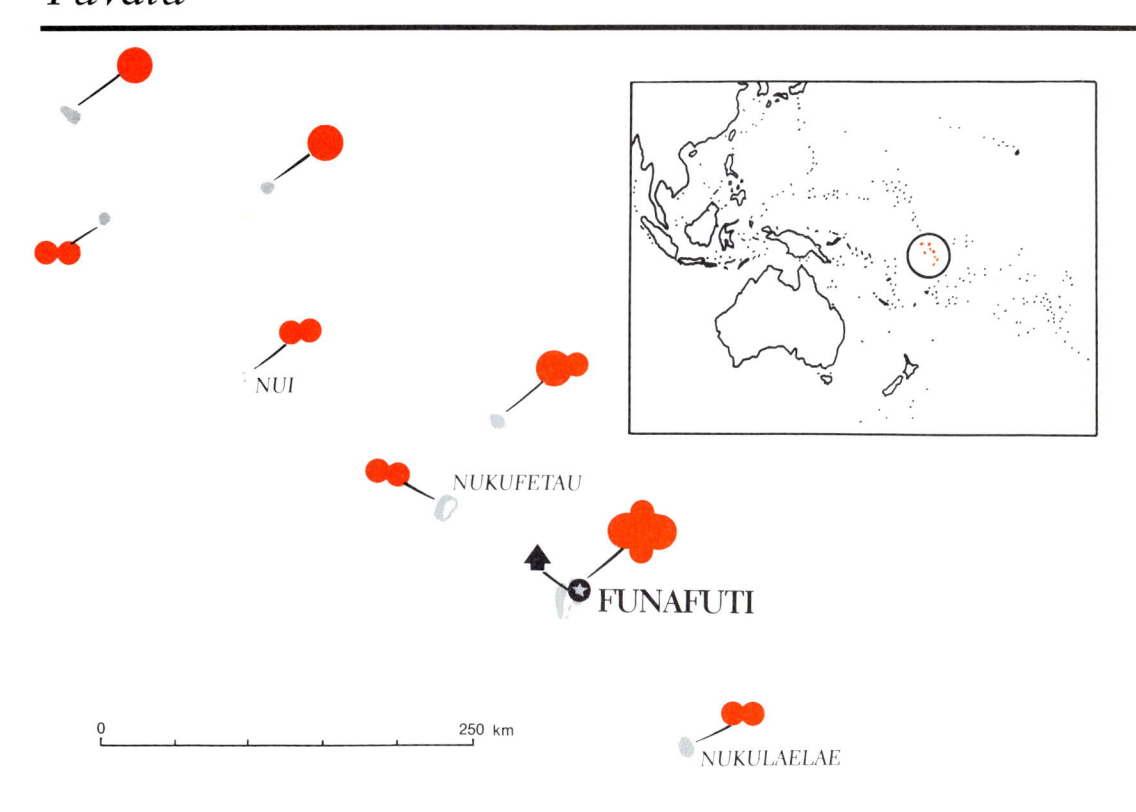

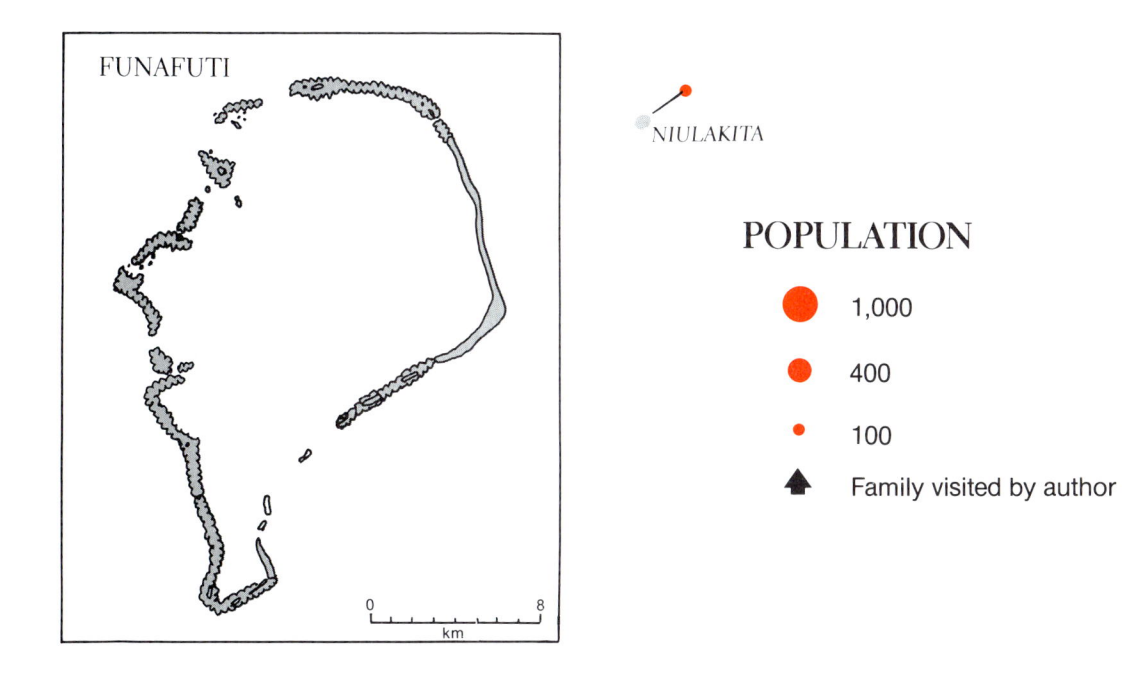

NUI

NUKUFETAU

FUNAFUTI

NUKULAELAE

FUNAFUTI

NIULAKITA

0 250 km

0 8 km

POPULATION

- 1,000
- 400
- 100
- ▲ Family visited by author

Vanuatu

George Loiha's Family

George Loiha* (late 50s) (1)
Wailum (mid-40s) (2)
Anette Nubobo (mid-20s) (3)
John Loa, 22 (he thinks) (4)
Mena Wailum (late teens) (5)
Dugouar Kokarei (mid-teens) (6)
Male (early teens) (7)
Nubobo-Benene, 4 or 5 (8)
Naruagi, 1 (9)
Anette Nubobo's son, 4 (10)

10 pigs
30 chickens
2 dogs
1 cat

* George's family do not know their ages. They establish them in reference to specific events. For example, George was about Kokarei's size when his father went to Vila during World War II, and Naruagi was born after cyclone Umu. Vanuatu is one of the most developed of the Pacific Island nations, and this family does not represent mainstream Vanuatu. It is one of a significant minority of many traditional groups in the midst of such development.

Yakuko

FEBRUARY 7

6:00 The pounding of Kokarei's machete chopping the kitchen firewood echoes through the silent mountain village of Yakuko and his family's hamlet, which lies sheltered by trees and gardens in the lush and hilly landscape of the island of Tanna.

The hamlet consists of four small wild-cane houses and a fifth half-finished one. George wants a chance to sleep alone, without being disturbed by the baby and Benene, who share their mother's bed. His oldest daughter, Anette Nubobo, is married and lives in another hamlet, and Mena and her brothers sleep in the house they have built themselves.

John Loa walks out of his hut. He is of age now and, like all traditional men of his group, always carries his bow and arrows. He will be on the lookout for wild pigeons, often the only meat the family eats. Pigs and chickens are for special ceremonies, and also to pay for John Loa's future bride.

George comes into the kitchen hut and squats, holding a piece of *lepang*, a soft wood that catches fire easily. This he scrapes with another wooden stick. One modern convenience George accepts happily as a gift is matches. All other products of development are refused. "Tradition" is perhaps evoked a little more in Vanuatu than anywhere else in the Pacific countries. The traditional chiefs of the *kastom pipol* (people who preserve traditional customs) have been actively rebelling against the country's development since the 1970s when they closed their area to outside influence.

The tribal elders (the "big men") have refused Christianity and have not allowed their people's children to go to either French or English schools. Only after government pressure did they permit a form of education, which they specified. The *kastom pipol* built their own *kastom skul* (custom-preserving school), in which their elders teach tradition, with one teacher from outside the *kastom* area, who teaches reading and writing, and only to boys. The "big men" regard money and a cash economy as a threat to their tradition. Any payment, whether for taxes or a wife, is made with kava and pigs.

6:30 Squatting in the mist of smoke that he is desperately trying to blow into a flame, George tells his family about last night's meeting of the men. Much of the daily work is done by women, and between harvests, men often journey to other parts of the island, or to the country's other islands. Last night a visitor from a neighboring mountain arrived, bringing fresh gossip. George's news livens up the day for his wife and children.

Wailum, a silent woman, helped by her more exuberant daughter Mena, hangs a pot on a chain attached to a roof beam. Wailum will serve boiled sweet potatoes to her husband and each of her children. Food is scarce now on Tanna. Exactly a year ago, cyclone Umu devastated the island, and the people are waiting for the month of May to harvest their yams, taro, manioc, bananas, and coconuts. For now, there are sweet potatoes three times a day, and an occasional wild pigeon.

9:00 The younger children surround their mother, staying close to the fire and out of the cool morning air. Although this is the place where Wailum spends most of her time, the cane structure was put up hurriedly, the small tree branches and trunks arranged without order or balance. In the kitchen the chickens, dogs, and cat also wait impatiently for food. Mena blows in between the logs, and the smoke gives way to flames. Sitting on the black dirt floor made of the volcanic soil and dust that is strewn over the island by Iasur volcano, a dirty Naruagi tugs at his mother's sagging breast while she tends the fire.

9:30 Mena goes to the mountain spring, carrying the hollowed length of bamboo used as a water container. Her brother Male brings a grasshopper into the kitchen. After letting it jump a bit and catching it, he gets bored and simply stuffs it in his mouth. No one is in a hurry to do anything this morning. George and his son disappear with their bows and arrows, heading for Yaonanen Village, the "big men's" hamlet where the men like to gather. It is the entry to the "*kastom* area." When tourists visit, it is where everyone comes to dance for them. But the "big men" especially like visiting anthropologists, who tell them how right they are to preserve their traditions.

11:00 Wailum waits for her daughter Nubobo. They will go to Nubobo's garden after lunch. That is as far as women are allowed to walk without being accompanied by a man.

12:00 Nubobo arrives. She has inherited a garden on her father's land, and to work it she has to walk down the valley and across the mountain that separates it from her husband's family grounds. Wailum always seems more lively when her beautiful and cheerful older daughter enters the hamlet. Nubobo is followed by a son Benene's age. The two children go off together. When Nubobo has a daughter, she will be given to Wailum and George to raise. Tradition requires that when a family gives a girl away in marriage, her husband's family must "give a girl back." Nubobo squats with her mother and sister near the kitchen fire.

2:00 Wailum, her daughters, and the small children follow the path that brings them to the garden. Each garden plot has a name. The child who will inherit

Western clothing is not allowed; all men and circumcised boys wear only their penis sheaths, and all women wear colorful grass skirts. They are required to put on Western clothing when they go down the mountain to the island capital, but take it off the moment they return to the kastom *area.*

it is often given the same name; thus, land names are passed down from generation to generation. Each member of the family, including every child, has a garden. Using the age-old slash-and-burn method, the women first cut down the trees and bush with their machetes, then burn out the roots to clear a new space. While the women chop the undergrowth, their children play. Everyone takes turns watching Naruagi, who seems determined to use a machete as a walking stick to practice his toddling.

John Loa is in the kava garden, planting fresh tubers. Then he leaves to bathe in one of the mountain streams nearby. Foreign-aid money was offered to pipe in water to the mountain villages, but the "big men" refused, so their women must continue to fetch the water. On his way back, Loa feeds the pigs.

5:00 One hour before sunset, George takes his flashlight and heads for the *nakamel*, a cleared area, surrounded by several banyan trees, used for gathering and dancing during important rituals, including the daily kava ceremony.

Wailum begins once again to boil sweet potatoes. Women are not allowed at the kava ceremony. It is taboo for them to even witness the preparation and the drinking of kava. Once a transgression was punishable by death; today a woman would simply be beaten on the head with a branch. When the food is ready, the women send one of their boys to the *nakamel* with it. After drinking kava, the men like to eat.

John Loa and Kokarei follow their father. Only young men and boys with no sexual experience can prepare the kava powder. First they clean the dirt from the kava root with a knife, then they chew it and spit it out on a wild kava leaf. A handful of this masticated root is placed on a filter made of coconut-

The women have well-defined roles: they prepare food, fetch water, and bear children and take care of them.

palm leaves. This filter is held over a half coconut shell, and while one boy pours water through, another kneads the filter to squeeze out the liquid.

George has had his drink and has gone to sit beside the fire. He is calm and quiet, and speaks in a whisper—one effect of kava. Even those who choose not to participate in the ritual are asked to speak softly, so as not to disturb the others.

The men believe in magic and spirits, and their myths are a hodgepodge of ancient tribal beliefs, influenced heavily by colonialism. There are many cults, like the cargo cult that worships "John Frum," who they say will return in a plane and bring them riches, and the cult that worships England's Prince Philip, who they believe was born on Tanna and will come to die there.

In her kitchen, Wailum and her children sit in the fading light, eating their potatoes. As the sun sets, a long cry is heard; one of the men in the *nakamel* is expressing his state of blissful satisfaction.

8:00 Already sobered, George comes back and sits beside the fire, where sweet potatoes await him. His two youngest have been put to sleep. John Loa has gone to stay with friends in another hamlet. As always, Mena sits in the kitchen beside her mother and listens to her father talk. He is the family's only source of information about the outside world.

The Vanuatuans

THE NAME: From *vanua*, meaning "land" and *tu* meaning "existing forever." Formerly called the New Hebrides

GEOGRAPHY
Consists of twelve principal (93% of area) and some sixty smaller islands, nearly all inhabited, extending 800 km. from north to south. Main islands have rugged mountainous interiors with narrow coastal strips, and there are active volcanoes on several of them. Smaller islands are coral atolls and rocky volcanic outcrops. Max. altitude: 1,877 m. (6,158 ft.) (Mt. Tabwemasana)
Area: 12,190 sq. km. (4,706 sq. mi.)
Density: 9.9 pers./sq. km. (26 pers./sq. mi.)
Arable land: 1.0% (1985)
Forest: 1.1%
Climate: Tropical in the north, subtropical in the south, moderated by trade winds between May and October. The south is subject to devastating cyclones.

CAPITAL: Vila, pop. 14,184 (1986)

LANGUAGE: Bislama (Pidgin English), English and French (official). 115 Melanesian languages, many with several dialects, are spoken. The country has the most languages per capita in the world.

RELIGION: The majority are Christian, including twelve Protestant sects and Catholics. Some follow traditional religious practices.

POPULATION: Total—111,000 (1979)
Annual growth: 3.8% (4,218) (1980)
Doubling time: 21 yrs.
Urban: 25% (1985) (est. for year 2000: 39%)
Rural: 75%

AGE GROUPS (1979)
17% under 5 yrs.
45% under 15
56% under 20
28% from 20 to 39
11% from 40 to 59
 4% 60 yrs. and over

ETHNIC GROUPS
Melanesian: 92%
Other (European, Vietnamese, Chinese): 8%

HISTORY
Inhabited by Melanesian peoples for three thousand years. Numerous autonomous clans, and a remarkable variety of languages and customs
1606: Quirós arrives at the island he names Australia del Espíritu Santo, and claims it and everything south to the South Pole for the King of Spain and the Catholic Church
1774: Captain Cook charts majority of the islands, naming them the New Hebrides after the Scottish Hebrides
1825–65: Sandalwood trade brings wave of European adventurers
1863–1904: Some fifty thousand ni-Vanuatu recruited to work cane plantations in Australia, Fiji, and New Caledonia
1886: Britain and France set up joint naval commission to protect planters' interests
1906: Anglo–French New Hebrides Condominium (joint governing body) established. Each power administers its subjects separately
WWII: Serves as a major Allied air base
1971: Jimmy Stevens leads NaGriamel Party in petitioning UN to stop land sales to American investors. In a turnabout, in 1980, with foreign support, he seeks to declare Espíritu Santo the Independent Republic of Vemarana
1979: Constitution and first free elections
July 30, 1980: Independence as the Republic of Vanuatu
1983: First nuclear-free nation in the Pacific and the first to acquire membership in Non-Aligned Movement

FAMILY
Marital status, for females 15 yrs. + (1986)
Single: 30%
Married: 61%
Widowed: 8%
Divorced: 1%
Female head of household: no data
Fertility rate: 6.5 (1984)
Teenage births: no data
Births out of wedlock: no data

Contraception: no data

Government's position on family planning: Population growth and fertility rates are considered satisfactory. No policy to modify fertility. Supports family and community health services, including family planning

SOCIAL INDICATORS
Life expectancy: 51 yrs. (male: 55; female: 47) (1983)
Infant mortality: 75/1,000 births (1984)
Crude birth rate: 45/1,000 pop. (1983)
Crude death rate: 13/1,000

HEALTH
Access to health services: 80% (1982) within an hour's walk
Births attended by trained health personnel: 61% (1983)

HOUSING
Persons per household: 5 (1979)
Electricity: 12% (urban: 46%; rural: 3%) (1979)
Access to safe water: 66% (1986) (urban: 88%; rural: 25%) (1983) at home or within 15 minutes' walking distance
Source of water (1983)
  Piped: 88% (urban)
  In rural areas, mostly wells, rainwater, and streams
Toilet facilities (1983)
  Urban: 96% (septic tank)
  Rural: 25% (septic tank or pit)

Construction materials (1979)
  Bush material: 61%
  Cement: 14%
  Corrugated iron: 13%
  Wood: 8%
  Other: 4%

EDUCATION
Literacy: male: 57%; female: 48% (1979)
Gross enrollment ratio (1984)
  First level: 87%
  Second: 57%
  Third: no data
Educational attainment: no data

ECONOMIC ACTIVITY
Economically active population: 46% (male: 49%; female: 42%) (1979)
Agriculture: 80% act. pop.; 25% of GDP
Mines: 0% act. pop.; 0% of GDP
Industry: 0% act. pop.; 0% of GDP
Services: 20% act. pop.; 75% of GDP
Per capita GNP: US$620 (1980)
National currency: vatu
Principal resources: Copra, cocoa

COMMUNICATIONS
Radio
  Transmitters: 4 (1983)
  Receivers: 211/1,000 pop. (1985)
Television
  Believed to have no television service of its own
Newspapers (1984)
  Believed to have no general-interest dailies

Vanuatu

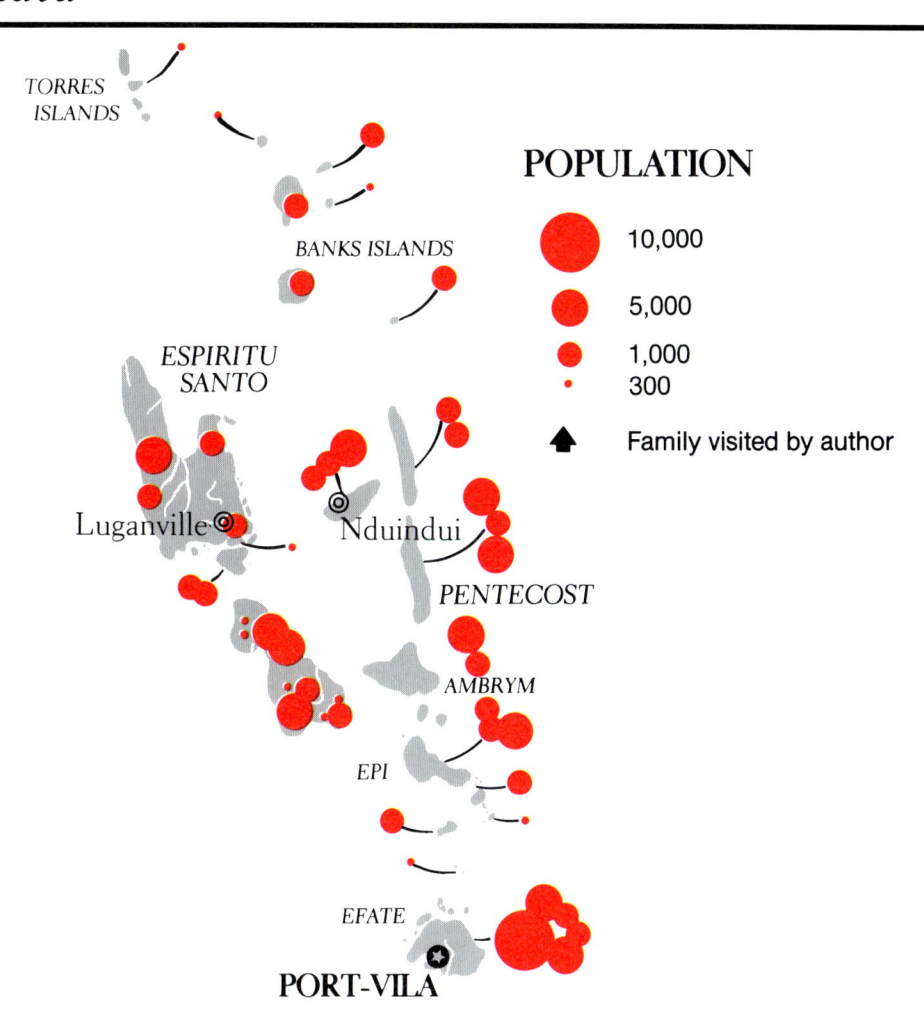

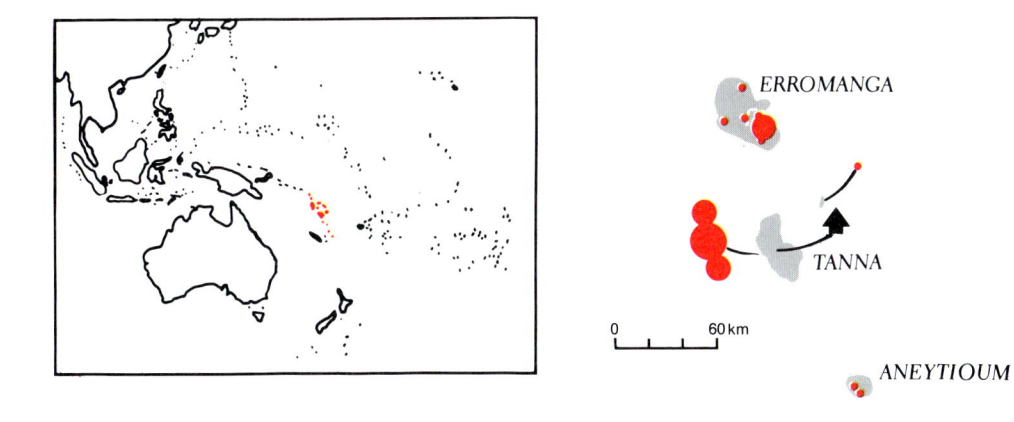

POPULATION

- 10,000
- 5,000
- 1,000
- 300

▲ Family visited by author

TORRES ISLANDS

BANKS ISLANDS

ESPIRITU SANTO

Luganville

Nduindui

PENTECOST

AMBRYM

EPI

EFATE

PORT-VILA

ERROMANGA

TANNA

0 60 km

ANEYTIOUM

Western Samoa

The Sipapa Family

Matautia Sipapa, age 45 *(absent)*
Sasa'e Sipapa, 40 *(1)*
Sulemoni, 19 *(absent)*
Faatupu, 16 *(2)*
Fa'aali, 15 *(absent)*
Molimau, 13 *(3)*
Lafi, 10 *(4)*
Seutaatia, 9 *(5)*
Taliilagi, 7 *(6)*

Lafi Onesemo, 82 *(7)*
Vaoiva Lemusu, 69 *(8)*
Sesilia Lemusu (cousin), 11 *(9)*
Fatuoaiga Lemusu (cousin), 9 *(10)*
Niutuiatua Onesemo (cousin), 7 *(11)*

30 pigs
60 chickens
2 dogs
1 cat

Malaemalu

DECEMBER 15

5:00 Grandfather Lafi Onesemo sits up in bed under his mosquito net and starts the morning prayers. Beside him on the floor of the *palagi-fale* (foreign house), his grandchildren sit up on their mat, their eyes still closed.

Grandfather prays. "Thank you, God, for the food you have given us yesterday and that we will have today. Thank you for giving us the sun and rain and a plentiful garden full of cucumbers, tomatoes, cabbage, banana, coconut, taro, flowers, and the tobacco to sell at the market. Thank you for giving us so much, so that now we have lots to give to others." He then names every single object owned by his family. And he continues. "Thank you, God, for giving us lots of children who are good and strong enough to do all the work." Then Grandfather asks forgiveness for anyone who has been bad but did not mean to be. "And, God, please do not forget to bless Fa'aali, now in prison. Thank you also, God, for bringing us so few worries."

This morning Sasa'e does feel she has been relieved of one worry. Yesterday her fifteen-year-old son, Fa'aali, was tried for manslaughter, and the judge administering *palagi* (foreign) justice sentenced him to five years in jail. She thanks God for the sentence, for she was scared he would go free and do it again.

Fa'aali has created many problems for her and made life in her community difficult. At school and at home, everyone said he was "possessed by the devil." When Sasa'e learned that he had epileptic fits but could be treated, she sent him to Apia, the capital, so he could continue his studies yet see the doctor regularly. Sasa'e's brother took him in for the year, but left him free to watch hours and hours of all sorts of videos from his shop, including violent ones.

Then, during school holidays about four months ago, Fa'aali was sent by his mother to fetch coconuts on the family's grounds. A girl his age was there. Some say she might have been stealing some of the family's coconuts. No one knows. Neither do they know if Fa'aali had a fit, but he raped the girl and slashed her with a bush knife.

During his trial, a social welfare specialist sent a letter to the judge about the effects of videos. In this lush country, where strong temperaments combine with social pressures, violence is part of life. The suicide rate among young people is the highest in the world.

WESTERN SAMOA

6:00 This morning, all is quiet and incredibly beautiful. The flamboyant trees—called Christmas trees—are blooming, as are all the flowers, and the trees are full of fruits. This is a Polynesian paradise.

Sasa'e cooks taro for breakfast. Faatupu is washing last night's dishes at the courtyard tap; the small girls are cleaning the yard; Lafi is feeding the pigs. With Sasa'e's husband away in American Samoa to earn money, her thirteen-year-old son, Molimau, is now the man of the house, with the responsibility to provide for his sisters; he has gone to fetch more coconuts. Coconuts are needed for everything. From the young nut comes a refreshing drink and jelly-like flesh, from the ripened nut comes coconut milk for cooking and oil to rub on skin and hair. From the shell, one makes bowls and spoons and many utensils. From the hairy husk comes rope, fiber for straining, and fuel to make the fire hot; from the fronds, thatch, blinds, mats, and baskets. From the slivered leaf spines come brooms, toothpicks, and reinforcement for the large coiled baskets; and from the trees too old for bearing come house posts, rafters, and canoe paddles.

As Molimau returns, a truck pulls up in the driveway. Sasa'e's uncle will take her and the children farther into the bush to another garden.

The *matai*, the extended-family chiefs, distribute the land in Western Samoa. Modernization has given the *matai* yet another privilege: only they can vote. A *matai*'s word is believed to represent a whole family's thinking, and for this year's election there are some fifteen thousand *matai*. For politicians, the more *matais* the better. For families, that is not so. The more *matais*, the more opinions and family disagreements.

Sasa'e is also a *matai*, reinforcing her position as the head of her own

Grandfather Lafi Onesemo lives in the palagi-fale *(foreign house), built of wood, with a corrugated-iron roof. On either side is a traditional open-walled house with a thatched roof, one for his wife, the other for his daughter and granddaughters.*

In the cooking house, Lafi is bent over the fire, while Molimau prepares the taro to cook in the umu. *Faatupu is washing dishes at the water tap.*

close family. She is a little overwhelmed to be alone, responsible for her children, her old parents, and the three children she adopted when two of her sisters could no longer take care of them. She says she is indifferent to what the title can bring—seniority and prestige in the village, membership in the *fono* (its council), access to certain lands, and the good things of life. Above Sasa'e is the *matai* of the whole *aiga* (clan). He has assigned the lands, and now the only land close to the villages is used as a coconut plantation. The rest of their food has to be grown far in the bush.

Uncle's truck bumps left and right for twenty minutes on a rugged dirt road which can hardly be seen through high grass, until it is impossible for the vehicle to go farther. Then they walk an hour to the family garden, and there is no time for rest, to avoid working in the noon heat. Uncle starts slashing more trees to extend the garden. Sasa'e and Molimau load insecticide sprayers on their backs, and the other children squat together to weed the recently planted taro. They alone chat during this morning of work. Traditionally, the producing and giving of food was a way of expressing respect, but today food is not enough. The church needs money; the government asks the *matais* for financial contributions; subsistence living cannot meet all these demands. More than ever now, Sasa'e will need the money her husband sends because, in addition to the court sentence, traditional Samoan justice has decreed that Sasa'e must compensate the murdered girl's family with an entire coconut plantation, plus pigs, fine mats, and money.

Sasa'e says she will manage, but with Fa'aali in jail, she has been asking herself if she was a good mother. "I think I am too hard on the children," she says. "I love them, but sometimes I am exhausted, I lose patience and hit them." Sasa'e also says that since she had her last child, Taliilagi, she avoids her husband when he visits, as she does not want any more children.

2:30 Young Samoan men are expected to be unruly, whereas girls are expected to care for and honor the family's good name. However, all the Sipapa children are taught never to contradict their mother's orders. This afternoon, Sasa'e has delegated chores. Faatupu brings a basketful of taro to the road for a truck to pick up for export to Samoans in New Zealand. Then she will wash the family's clothes. Sasa'e, helped by Sesilia, will burn coconut shells in a drum to make charcoal. Molimau will strain the milk of ripe coconuts for Sasa'e to cook in young taro leaves wrapped in a breadfruit leaf on the hot stones of the *fumu* (earth oven) to make the favorite Samoan delicacy, *palusami*.

4:00 In the open *fale*, an elderly aunt is braiding mats. She has come to help. Last year, Sasa'e had to contribute twenty *falapapa* (floor mats) and twenty *falalilii* (sleeping mats) to funerals, marriages, school, and various Samoan ceremonies.

5:00 Grandmother, always followed by Niutuiatua, her protégé, is picking up the tobacco she had put out to dry. Her old husband, who has not left his bed during the hot afternoon, now squats in front of his house to weed the green grass.

The sun goes down, its rays piercing the coconut plantations and the smoke that fills the outside kitchen, accentuating once more the beauty of this peaceful family ground. Taliilagi and Seutaatia are singing "God's songs." Maybe someday one of them will marry a preacher—the ultimate goal and a sure road to respectability, the best food, and the biggest house in the village.

6:00 The children are off work. Faatupu switches the batteries from the flashlight to the radio. For two hours, they can hear radio messages sent between families, especially from the outer islands.

6:30 The old couple are served first. Then Sasa'e and Aunty eat their meal. When all the adults are finished, the children, who have been waiting patiently, are served.

7:30 Grandfather walks slowly toward his daughter's *fale* for prayers. Sitting in a circle around the kerosene lamp glowing like one of the stars in the sky, the children have closed their eyes, crossing their arms in front of them, sometimes smiling when Grandfather sings a psalm and is really off-tune. Then Seutaatia bends her head on the mat floor, fighting sleepiness when Grandfather, as in the morning, begins the long list of thanks to God.

The Samoans

THE NAME: Meaning "place of moa," the moa being a now extinct large bird of the ostrich family

GEOGRAPHY
Two large and seven small islands; four of the islands are inhabited. The large islands, Savai'i and Upolu, are rocky and mountainous, with narrow strips of flatland along the coasts. The smaller islands are coral atolls.
Max. altitude: 1,857 m. (6,094 ft.)
Area: 2,842 sq. km. (1,097 sq. mi.)
Density: 7.6 pers./sq. km. (20 pers./sq. mi.)
Arable land: 19% (1985)
Forest: 47%
Climate: Tropical, with two seasons and slight temperature variation. During the wet season, from November through April, there are many cyclones.

CAPITAL: Apia, pop. 163,000 (1986)

LANGUAGE: Samoan and English (official)

RELIGION
Congregational Christian Church: 47%
Roman Catholic: 22%
Methodist: 16%
Latter-Day Saints: 9%
Seventh-Day Adventist: 2%
Other: 4%

POPULATION: Total—167,000 (1988)
Annual growth: 2.1% (3,423) (1981)
Doubling time: 24 yrs.
Urban: 22% (1985) (est. for year 2000: 27%)
Rural: 78%

AGE GROUPS (1981)
14% under 5 yrs.
44% under 15
58% under 20
24% from 20 to 39
13% from 40 to 59
 5% 60 yrs. and over

ETHNIC GROUPS
Samoan: 89%
Other (European, and mixed Chinese, European, Fijian, and Tongan): 11%

HISTORY
1000 B.C.: Settlement by Polynesians
A.D. 950–1250: Tongan invaders rule Samoa. The *matai*, or chief system, is already established
1722: Dutch explorer Roggeveen sights the islands. Other European explorers follow
1830: London Missionary Society establishes a settlement
1850s: German businessmen establish coconut plantations with Chinese and Melanesian labor
late 1800s: Intermittent civil war between chiefly orator groups Pule and Tumua over the four highest ceremonial titles. Rival Europeans side with different factions to gain influence
1878: Treaty grants U.S.A. the right to establish a naval station (on what is now American Samoa) and sets up trade agreement. Similar agreements with Germany and Great Britain follow
1887: Germans stage coup, oust king, and install puppet in his place
1889: U.S.A., Germany, and Great Britain establish tripartite protectorate
1900: Germany annexes Western Samoa
1904: U.S.A. annexes eastern islands (now American Samoa)
1914: New Zealand occupies Western Samoa
1920: League of Nations grants mandate over Western Samoa to New Zealand
1947: Becomes a trust territory with New Zealand as administering authority
1960: Constitution
Jan. 1, 1962: First independent Polynesian nation

FAMILY
Marital status, for females all ages (1981)
Single: 67%
Married: 28%
Widowed: 2.4%
Separated/divorced: 1.6%
Female head of household: 19% (1981)

Fertility rate: 4.4 (1986)
Teenage births: 9% (1980)
Teenage fertility rate: 33.5/1,000 (1977)
Births out of wedlock: 49% (1985)
Contraception: 18% (1982)
Government's position on family planning: Population growth and fertility rates are considered too high. Promotes family planning as part of maternal health programs and plans to integrate family-planning education into school systems

SOCIAL INDICATORS
Life expectancy: 64 yrs. (male: 63; female: 65) (1985)
Infant mortality: 33/1,000 births (1986)
Crude birth rate: 31/1,000 pop. (1986)
Crude death rate: 7/1,000

HEALTH
Access to health services: 100% (1984)
Births attended by trained health personnel: 52%

HOUSING
Persons per household: 5.8 (1971)
Electricity: 62% without (1981)
Access to safe water: 92% (urban: 100%; rural: 90%) (1985)
Source of water (1981)
    Piped inside: 40%
    Piped out: 40%
    Without piped water: 20%
Toilet facilities (1981)
    Flush: 16%
    Pit with septic tank: 54%
    Pit: 21%
    Other: 1%

Construction materials (1981)
    Samoan house (open-walled with thatched roof): 62%
    Wood: 24%
    Brick, concrete: 9%
    Other: 5%

EDUCATION
Literacy: 98% (1985)
Gross enrollment ratio: no data
Educational attainment for pop. 15 yrs. + (1981)
    First level: 3% (upper primary: 26%)
    Second: 27% (upper secondary: 40%)
    Post-secondary: 2%

ECONOMIC ACTIVITY
Economically active population: 26% (male: 43%; female: 8%) (1981)
Agriculture: 58% act. pop.; 30% of GDP
Mines: 0% act. pop.; 0% of GDP
Industry: 10% act. pop.; 12% of GDP
Services: 33% act. pop.; 58% of GDP
Per capita GNP: US$680 (1986)
National currency: tala
Principal resources: Copra, cocoa, timber

COMMUNICATIONS
Radio
    Transmitters: 6 (1981)
    Receivers: 429/1,000 pop. (1985)
Television
    Believed to have no television service of its own
Newspapers
    Believed to have no general-interest dailies (1984)

Western Samoa

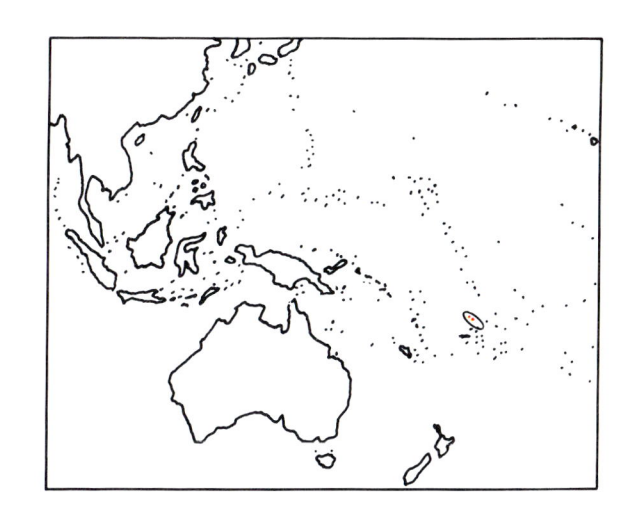

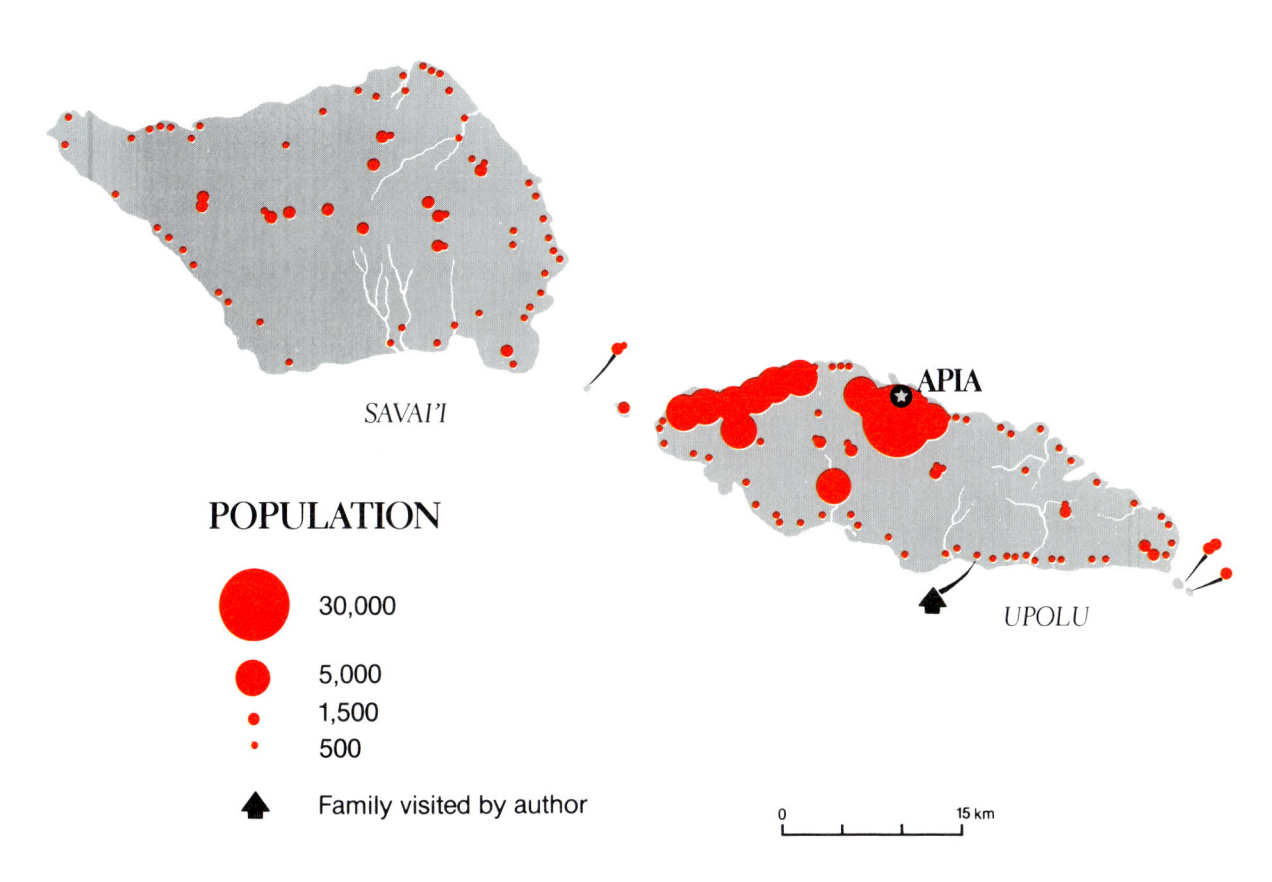

SAVAI'I

APIA

UPOLU

POPULATION

- 30,000
- 5,000
- 1,500
- 500

▲ Family visited by author

0   15 km

SOURCES

Key to Source Notes

1. Area
2. Density
3. **Arable land**—The percentage of land planted with crops, meadows for mowing or pasture, land devoted to market and kitchen gardens (including cultivation under glass), and land lying fallow. Excludes land under permanent crops such as cocoa, coffee, and rubber. The datum is obtained by dividing arable land by the total area of a country, excluding land under inland bodies of water.
4. **Forest**—Land under natural or planted stands of trees. Includes land from which forests have been cleared which will be reforested in the foreseeable future.
5. Religion
6. Total population
7. **Annual growth**—The rate at which a population is increasing (or decreasing) in a given year due to natural increase and net migration, expressed as a percentage of the base population.
8. **Doubling time**—The number of years it would take for a country to double its population size, assuming that the current growth rate is constant.
9. Urban/rural
10. Estimate for year 2000
11. Age groups
12. Ethnic groups
13. **Marital status**—The personal status of women in relation to the marriage laws or customs of the country.
14. Female head of household
15. **Fertility rate**—The average number of children that would be born per woman during her lifetime if she were to live to the end of her child-bearing years and bear children at each age in accordance with the prevailing age-specific fertility rates of a given year. A rate of 2.1 children is necessary for a population to replace itself.
16. **Births out of wedlock**—In certain countries, statistics on births out of wedlock may not be available because of the society's attitude toward sex and marriage. In certain societies, if one becomes pregnant, one gets married to avert criticism, ostracism, or punishment. Those pregnancies will not be considered births out of wedlock.
17. **Teenage births**—The number of live births for mothers aged nineteen years and under as a percentage of live births for women of all ages in a given year.
    Teenage fertility rate—The number of live births for mothers aged nineteen years and under per 1,000 women in that age group.
18. **Contraception**—The percentage of currently married women of child-bearing age using contraception. It generally refers to women between the ages of fifteen and forty-nine who are practicing any form of birth control.
19. Government's position on family planning
20. **Life expectancy**—The number of years a newborn baby can be expected to live if subject to the mortality risks prevailing for the general population at the time of its birth.
21. **Infant mortality**—The number of deaths of infants under one year of age per 1,000 population in a given year.
22. **Crude birth rate**—Number of live births to estimated mid-year total population.
    Crude death rate—Number of deaths to estimated mid-year total population.
23. Health
24. **Persons per household**—The average size of a household or the number of persons living in households divided by the total number of households.
25. Electricity
26. **Access to safe water**—The percentage of the population obtaining water that does not contain chemical substances and microorganisms in concentrations that could cause illness in any form. Such water is considered adequate if obtainable from a facility situated near to or within the household.
27. **Source of water**—Piped water refers to water provided within housing units from community-wide systems or from individual installations such as pressure tanks and pumps. Housing units with piped water more than a hundred meters from the house are defined as without piped water.
28. Toilet facilities
29. **Construction materials**—The predominant materials used in building the outer walls of houses.
30. **Literacy**—The percentage of the population fifteen years of age and over who are able to read and write. Unless otherwise specified, data are UNESCO estimates based on information provided or approved by each country.
31. **Gross enrollment ratio**—The gross enrollment ratio is the total enrollment of all ages divided by the population of the specific age groups which correspond to the age groups of primary and secondary schooling. At the third level, the figures for the population aged twenty to twenty-four years have been used throughout. All ratios are expressed as percentages.
32. **First level**—Completing primary school

33. **Educational attainment**—The percentage of the distribution of the highest educational attainment of the population expressed in levels defined by each country but closely corresponding to the following categories: none, primary, secondary, and university levels.
34. **Economically active population**—Comprises all persons who provide the supply of labor for the production of economic goods and services, as defined by the United Nations systems of national accounts and balances, during a specified time-reference period.
35. **GDP** (gross domestic product)—Measures the total final output of goods and services produced by an economy.
36. **Per capita GNP** (gross national product)—Measures the total domestic and foreign output claimed by residents and is calculated without making deductions for depreciation. The GNP, converted to US$, is divided by the mid-year population to derive the 1988 per capita GNP.
37. **Population in absolute poverty**—The percentage of the population found at an income level below which a minimum nutritionally adequate diet plus essential non-food requirements are not affordable.
38. **Communications**
    Radio transmitters—The total number of radio transmitters in service used for domestic broadcasting to the general public, excluding transmitters primarily used for external broadcasting.
    Radio receivers—The total number of receivers of all types for radio broadcasts to the general public, including those connected to a cable distribution system (wired receivers). The data include such individual private receivers as car radios, portable radio sets, and private sets installed in public places, as well as communal receivers. The datum on receivers is an estimate of the number of receivers in use.
    Television transmitters—The total number of television transmitters operating on a regular basis and used for broadcasting to the general public, regardless of whether the responsibility lies with the broadcasting institution or with other institutions, such as posts and telecommunication. The datum relates to both main and relay transmitters.
    Television receivers—The total number of television receivers representing the estimated total number of receivers in use. Also given is the number of television receivers per 1,000 population.

Sources

EAST ASIA

People's Republic of China

1. *The New International Atlas* (Chicago: Rand McNally, 1987), World Information Table, 1988 revision. Estimates for Jan. 1, 1988, based on official data, United Nations estimates, and other available information.
2. Ibid.
3. *FAO Production Yearbook 1987* (Rome: Food and Agriculture Organization, 1988).
4. Ibid.
5. *1981/82 China Official Annual Report* (Hong Kong: Kingsway International Publications Limited, 1981).
6. *United Nations World Population Chart 1988* (New York: United Nations Population Division).
7. *Social Development Data Base for Asia and the Pacific* (Bangkok: United Nations Economic and Social Commission for Asia and the Pacific, Social Development Division, 1988).
8. *1988 World Population Data Sheet* (Washington, D.C.: Population Reference Bureau).
9. *Statistics on Children in UNICEF Assisted Countries* (New York: UNICEF, 1988).
10. *The Prospects of World Urbanization* (New York: United Nations Population Division, 1984–85 revision).
11. *Demographic Yearbook 1986* (New York: United Nations).
12. *Country Health Information Profile* (Manila: World Health Organization, Nov. 1986 revision).
13. *Demographic Yearbook 1982*.
14. No data.
15. *The State of the World Children 1989*, UNICEF (New York: Oxford University Press, 1989), annex tables.
16. No data.
17. *Statistical Yearbook of China, 1987*.
18. *World Development Report 1988*, World Bank (New York: Oxford University Press, 1988).
19. *World Population Policies*, United Nations Department of International Economic and Social Affairs (New York: United Nations, 1987). To encourage families to have only one child, a series of social and economic measures have been adopted both at the national and at the provincial level which include income bonuses, health-care subsidies, higher pensions, and priority in the allocation of city housing and private vegetable gardens in the countryside to couples having one child. Families exceeding two children will not receive ration coupons for any commodities other than staples and will have ten percent of their monthly wages taxed for welfare payments.
20. *Statistics on Children in UNICEF Assisted Countries*.
21. *The State of the World Children 1989*.
22. A. Laquian, Notes on the Chinese Population Situation, UNFPA Deputy Representative and Senior Advisor on Population, Beijing, China.
23. No data.
24. *Demographic Yearbook 1986*.
25. No data.
26. *The State of the World Children 1989*. Country Health Information Profile (Manila: World Health Organization, Dec. 1985 revision).
27. No data.
28. *Country Health Information Profile*.
29. No data.
30. *Statistics on Children in UNICEF Assisted Countries*.
31. *Statistical Yearbook 1987* (Paris: UNESCO).
32. *The State of the World Children 1989*.
33. *Statistical Yearbook 1987*.
34. *Social Development Data Base for Asia and the Pacific*.
35. *Atlaseco de Poche, Atlas Economique Mondial* (Paris: Les éditions S.G.P., 1988). Data taken from World Bank sources.
36. *World Development Report 1988*.
37. *Statistics on Children in UNICEF Assisted Countries*.
38. *Statistical Yearbook 1987*.

Japan

1. *The New International Atlas* (Chicago: Rand McNally, 1987), World Information Table, 1988 revision. Estimates for Jan. 1, 1988, based on official data, United Nations estimates, and other available information.
2. Ibid.
3. *FAO Production Yearbook 1987* (Rome: Food and Agriculture Organization, 1988).
4. Ibid.
5. *Country Health Information Profile* (Manila: World Health Organization, Dec. 1985 revision).
6. *United Nations World Population Chart 1988* (New York: United Nations Population Division).
7. Ibid.
8. *1988 World Population Data Sheet* (Washington, D.C.: Population Reference Bureau).
9. *Statistics on Children in UNICEF Assisted Countries* (New York: UNICEF, 1988).
10. *The Prospects of World Urbanization* (New York: United Nations Population Division, 1984–85 revision).

11. *Demographic Yearbook 1986* (New York: United Nations).
12. *Country Health Information Profile.*
13. *Social Development Data Base for Asia and the Pacific* (Bangkok: United Nations Economic and Social Commission for Asia and the Pacific, Social Development Division, 1988).
14. *Demographic Yearbook 1987.*
15. *The State of the World Children 1988*, UNICEF (New York: Oxford University Press, 1988), annex tables.
16. *Demographic Yearbook 1986.*
17. Ibid.
18. *World Development Report 1988*, World Bank (New York: Oxford University Press, 1988).
19. *World Population Policies*, United Nations Department of International Economic and Social Affairs (New York: United Nations, 1989).
20. *United Nations World Population Chart 1988.*
21. *The State of the World Children 1989.*
22. Ibid.
23. *Country Health Information Profile.*
24. *Compendium of Human Settlements Statistics 1983* (New York: United Nations).
25. No data.
26. *Social Development Data Base.*
27. *Compendium of Human Settlements Statistics 1983.*
28. Ibid.
29. *Japan Statistical Yearbook* (Tokyo: Statistics Bureau, 1987).
30. *Statistical Yearbook 1987* (Paris: UNESCO).
31. Ibid.
32. *The State of the World Children 1989.*
33. *Statistical Yearbook 1987.*
34. *Social Development Data Base.*
35. *Atlaseco de Poche, Atlas Economique Mondial* (Paris: Les éditions S.G.P., 1988). Data taken from World Bank sources.
36. *World Development Report 1988.*
37. No data.
38. *Statistical Yearbook 1987.*

Republic of Korea

1. *The New International Atlas* (Chicago: Rand McNally, 1987), World Information Table, 1988 revision. Estimates for Jan. 1, 1988, based on official data, United Nations estimates, and other available information.
2. Ibid.
3. *FAO Production Yearbook 1987* (Rome: Food and Agriculture Organization, 1988).
4. Ibid.
5. Korean Ministry of Culture and Information, Seoul.
6. *United Nations World Population Chart 1988* (New York: United Nations Population Division).
7. Ibid.
8. *1988 World Population Data Sheet* (Washington, D.C.: Population Reference Bureau).
9. *Statistics on Children in UNICEF Assisted Countries* (New York: UNICEF, 1988).
10. *The Prospects of World Urbanization* (New York: United Nations Population Division, 1984–85 revision).
11. *Demographic Yearbook 1987* (New York: United Nations).
12. George Thomas Kurian, *Encyclopedia of the Third World*, 3rd ed. (New York: Facts on File, Inc., 1987).
13. *Demographic Yearbook 1982.*
14. *Demographic Yearbook 1987.*
15. *The State of the World Children 1988*, UNICEF (New York: Oxford University Press, 1988), annex tables.
16. *Demographic Yearbook 1987.*
17. *Demographic Yearbook 1986.*
18. *World Development Report 1988*, World Bank (New York: Oxford University Press, 1988).
19. *World Population Policies* and *World Population Trends and Policies: 1989 Monitoring Report*, United Nations Department of International Economic and Social Affairs (New York: United Nations, 1989).
20. *Statistics on Children in UNICEF Assisted Countries.*
21. *The State of the World Children 1989.*
22. Population Statistics Division, Economic Planning Board, Seoul.
23. *Country Health Information Profile* (Manila: World Health Organization, June 1986 revision).
24. *Compendium of Human Settlements Statistics 1983* (New York: United Nations)
25. *Korea Statistical Yearbook, 1987* (Seoul: Economic Planning Board, National Bureau of Statistics).
26. Ibid.
27. *Evaluation of the Strategy for Health for All by the Year 2000* (Manila: World Health Organization, 1986).
28. Ibid.
29. *Korea Statistical Yearbook 1987.*
30. *Statistics on Children in UNICEF Assisted Countries.*
31. Ibid.
32. *The State of the World Children 1988.*
33. *Statistical Yearbook 1987.*
34. *Social Development Data Base for Asia and the Pacific* (Bangkok: United Nations Economic and Social Commission for Asia and the Pacific, Social Development Division, 1988).
35. *Atlaseco de Poche, Atlas Economique Mondial* (Paris: Les éditions S.G.P., 1988). Data taken from World Bank sources.
36. *World Development Report 1988.*
37. *The State of the World Children 1989.*
38. *Statistical Yearbook 1986.*

Mongolian People's Republic

1. *The New International Atlas* (Chicago: Rand McNally, 1987), World Information Table, 1988 revision. Estimates for Jan. 1, 1988,

based on official data, United Nations estimates, and other available information.
2. Ibid.
3. *FAO Production Yearbook 1987* (Rome: Food and Agriculture Organization, 1988).
4. Ibid.
5. *Europa Yearbook, 1988* (London: Europa Publications Limited).
6. *United Nations World Population Chart 1988* (New York: United Nations Population Division).
7. *Social Development Data Base for Asia and the Pacific* (Bangkok: United Nations Economic and Social Commission for Asia and the Pacific, Social Development Division, 1988).
8. *1988 World Population Data Sheet* (Washington, D.C.: Population Reference Bureau).
9. *Statistics on Children in UNICEF Assisted Countries* (New York: UNICEF, 1988).
10. *The Prospects of World Urbanization* (New York: United Nations Population Division, 1984–85 revision).
11. *Statistik des Auslandes, Länderbericht Mongolei 1987* (Wiesbaden: Statistisches Bundesamt). ILO projections.
12. *The Far East and Australasia 1988*, 19th ed. (London: Europa Publications Limited).
13. No data.
14. No data.
15. *The State of the World Children 1989*, UNICEF (New York: Oxford University Press, 1989), annex tables.
16. No data.
17. No data.
18. No data.
19. *World Population Policies* and *World Population Trends and Policies: 1989 Monitoring Report*, United Nations Department of International Economic and Social Affairs (New York: United Nations, 1989).
20. *The State of the World Children 1989*.
21. *Statistics on Children in UNICEF Assisted Countries*.
22. *Health Services: Evaluation of the Strategy for Health for All by the Year 2000* (Manila: World Health Organization, 1986).
Births attended: *The State of the World Children 1988*.
23. *Statistics on Children in UNICEF Assisted Countries*.
24. No data.
25. No data.
26. *Social Development Data Base for Asia and the Pacific*.
27. No data.
28. *Social Development Data Base for Asia and the Pacific*.
29. No data.
30. *Statistics on Children in UNICEF Assisted Countries*.
31. *Social Development Data Base for Asia and the Pacific*.
32. *Statistics on Children in UNICEF Assisted Countries*.
33. *National Economy of the MPR (1924–1984)* (Ulan Bator: Central Statistical Board of the MPR).
34. *Länderbericht Mongolei, 1987*. ILO projections.
35. *Atlaseco de Poche, Atlas Economique Mondial* (Paris: Les éditions S.G.P., 1988). Data taken from World Bank sources.
36. *Statistics on Children in UNICEF Assisted Countries*.
37. No data.
38. *Statistical Yearbook 1987* (Paris: UNESCO).
Other: *Social Development Data Base for Asia and the Pacific*.

SOUTHEAST ASIA

Brunei Darussalam

1. *The New International Atlas* (Chicago: Rand McNally, 1987), World Information Table, 1988 revision. Estimates for Jan. 1, 1988, based on official data, United Nations estimates, and other available information.
2. Ibid.
3. *FAO Production Yearbook 1987* (Rome: Food and Agriculture Organization, 1988).
4. Ibid.
5. Brunei Population Census, 1981.
6. *United Nations World Population Chart 1988* (New York: United Nations Population Division).
7. *Social Development Data Base for Asia and the Pacific* (Bangkok: United Nations Economic and Social Commission for Asia and the Pacific, Social Development Division, 1988).
8. *1988 World Population Data Sheet* (Washington, D.C.: Population Reference Bureau).
9. *Statistics on Children in UNICEF Assisted Countries* (New York: UNICEF, 1988).
10. *The Prospects of World Urbanization* (New York: United Nations Population Division, 1984–85 revision).
11. *Demographic Yearbook 1986* (New York: United Nations).
12. Brunei Population Census, 1981.
13. *Social Development Data Base for Asia and the Pacific*.
14. No data.
15. *1988 World Population Data Sheet*.
16. *Demographic Yearbook 1986*.
17. No data.
18. No data.
19. *World Population Policies*, United Nations Department of International Economic and Social Affairs (New York: United Nations, 1987).
20. *Country Health Information Profile* (Manila: World Health Organization, June 1986 revision).
21. *The State of the World Children 1989*, UNICEF (New York: Oxford University Press, 1989), annex tables.

22. No data.
23. *Country Health Information Profile.* (General medical services are provided through several hospitals, outdoor clinics, traveling dispensaries, and a flying doctor team.)
24. *Social Development Data Base for Asia and the Pacific.*
25. No data.
26. *Social Development Data Base for Asia and the Pacific.*
27. No data.
28. *Social Development Data Base for Asia and the Pacific.*
29. No data.
30. *Statistical Yearbook 1987* (Paris: UNESCO, 1987).
31. No data.
32. No data.
33. *Statistical Yearbook 1987.*
34. *Social Development Data Base for Asia and the Pacific.*
35. *Atlaseco de Poche, Atlas Economique Mondial* (Paris: Les éditions S.G.P., 1988). Data taken from World Bank sources.
36. *World Development Report 1988*, World Bank (New York: Oxford University Press, 1988).
37. No data.
38. *Statistical Yearbook 1987.*

Indonesia

1. *The New International Atlas* (Chicago: Rand McNally, 1987), World Information Table, 1988 revision. Estimates for Jan. 1, 1988, based on official data, United Nations estimates, and other available information.
2. Ibid.
3. *FAO Production Yearbook 1987* (Rome: Food and Agriculture Organization, 1988).
4. Ibid. Deforestation: *World Resources 1988–89*, World Resources Institute (New York: Basic Books, Inc., 1988).
5. *Statistical Yearbook of Indonesia 1984* (Jakarta: Biro Pusat Statistik).
6. *United Nations World Population Chart 1988* (New York: United Nations Population Division).
7. *Social Development Data Base for Asia and the Pacific* (Bangkok: United Nations Economic and Social Commission for Asia and the Pacific, Social Development Division, 1988).
8. *1988 World Population Data Sheet* (Washington, D.C.: Population Reference Bureau).
9. *Statistics on Children in UNICEF Assisted Countries* (New York: UNICEF, 1988).
10. *The Prospects of World Urbanization* (New York: United Nations Population Division, 1984–85 revision).
11. *Demographic Yearbook 1986* (New York: United Nations).
12. George Thomas Kurian, *Encyclopedia of the Third World*, 3rd ed. (New York: Facts on File, Inc., 1987).
13. *Social Development Data Base for Asia and the Pacific.*
14. *Demographic Yearbook 1987.*
15. *The State of the World Children 1989*, UNICEF (New York: Oxford University Press, 1989), annex tables.
16. No data.
17. No data.
18. *World Development Report 1988*, World Bank (New York: Oxford University Press, 1988).
19. *World Population Policies* and *World Population Trends and Policies: 1989 Monitoring Report*, United Nations Department of International Economic and Social Affairs (New York: United Nations, 1989).
20. *Statistics on Children in UNICEF Assisted Countries.*
21. Ibid.
22. Ibid.
23. Ibid.
24. *Compendium of Human Settlements Statistics 1983* (New York: United Nations).
25. *Welfare Indicators, 1986* (Jakarta: Biro Pusat Statistik).
26. *Statistics on Children in UNICEF Assisted Countries.*
27. *Welfare Indicators, 1986.*
28. *Social Development Data Base for Asia and the Pacific.*
29. No data.
30. *Statistics on Children in UNICEF Assisted Countries.*
31. *Statistical Yearbook 1987* (Paris: UNESCO).
32. *The State of the World Children 1989.*
33. *Statistical Yearbook 1987.*
34. *Yearbook of Labour Statistics, 1987* (Geneva: International Labour Office). For pop. 15 years +.
35. *Atlaseco de Poche, Atlas Economique Mondial* (Paris: Les éditions S.G.P., 1988). Data taken from World Bank sources.
36. *World Development Report 1988.*
37. *Statistics on Children in UNICEF Assisted Countries.*
38. *Statistical Yearbook 1987.*

Democratic Kampuchea

1. *The New International Atlas* (Chicago: Rand McNally, 1987), World Information Table, 1988 revision. Estimates for Jan. 1, 1988, based on official data, United Nations estimates, and other available information.
2. Ibid.
3. *FAO Production Yearbook 1987* (Rome: Food and Agriculture Organization, 1988).
4. Ibid. Deforestation: *World Resources 1988–89*, World Resources Institute (New York: Basic Books, Inc., 1988).
5. *Europa Yearbook, 1988* (London: Europa Publications Limited).
6. *United Nations World Population Chart 1988* (New York: United Nations Population Division).
7. Ibid.
8. Calculated from above.
9. *Statistics on Children in UNICEF Assisted Countries* (New York: UNICEF, 1988).
10. *The Prospects of World Urbanization* (New York: United Nations Population Division, 1984–85 revision).
11. 1962 Population Census.
12. George Thomas Kurian, *Encyclopedia of the Third World*, 3rd ed. (New York: Facts on File, Inc., 1987).
13. No data.

14. No data.
15. *The State of the World Children 1989*, UNICEF (New York: Oxford University Press, 1989).
16. No data.
17. No data.
18. *World Development Report 1988*, World Bank (New York: Oxford University Press, 1988).
19. *World Population Policies*, United Nations Department of International Economic and Social Affairs (New York: United Nations, 1989).
20. *The State of the World Children 1989*.
21. Ibid.
22. Ibid.
23. Ibid.
24. 1962 Population Census.
25. UNICEF field office estimate, Phnom Penh.
26. *Statistics on Children in UNICEF Assisted Countries*.
27. UNICEF field office estimates, Phnom Penh.
28. No data.
29. No data.
30. *Statistics on Children in UNICEF Assisted Countries*.
31. UNICEF field office estimates.
32. Ibid.
33. No data.
34. *Yearbook of Labour Statistics, 1987* (Geneva: International Labour Office). For pop. 15 years +.
35. *Atlaseco de Poche, Atlas Economique Mondial* (Paris: Les éditions S.G.P., 1988). Data taken from World Bank sources.
36. *Statistics on Children in UNICEF Assisted Countries*.
37. No data.
38. *Statistical Yearbook 1987* (Paris: UNESCO).

Lao People's Democratic Republic

1. *The New International Atlas* (Chicago: Rand McNally, 1987), World Information Table. 1988 Revision. Population estimates for Jan. 1, 1988, based on official data, United Nations estimates, and other available information.
2. Ibid.
3. *FAO Production Yearbook 1987* (Rome: Food and Agriculture Organization, 1988).
4. Ibid. Deforestation: *World Resources 1988–89*, World Resources Institute (New York: Basic Books, Inc., 1988).
5. *Europa Yearbook, 1988* (London: Europa Publications Limited).
6. *United Nations World Population Chart 1988* (New York: United Nations Population Division).
7. *Social Development Data Base for Asia and the Pacific* (Bangkok: United Nations Economic and Social Commission for Asia and the Pacific, Social Development Division, 1988).
8. *1988 World Population Data Sheet* (Washington, D.C.: Population Reference Bureau).
9. *Statistics on Children in UNICEF Assisted Countries* (New York: UNICEF, 1988).
10. *The Prospects of World Urbanization* (New York: United Nations Population Division, 1984–85 revision).
11. *Demographic Yearbook 1986* (New York: United Nations).
12. *Rapport Périodique de la RDPLao sur l'Elimination de la Discrimination Raciale* (Vientiane: 1987).
13. No data.
14. No data.
15. *The State of the World Children 1989*, UNICEF (New York: Oxford University Press, 1989), annex tables.
16. No data.
17. No data.
18. No data.
19. *World Population Policies*, United Nations Department of International Economic and Social Affairs (New York: United Nations, 1989).
20. *Statistics on Children in UNICEF Assisted Countries*.
21. *The State of the World Children 1989*.
22. Ibid.
23. *Health Services: Evaluation of the Strategy of Health for All by the Year 2000* (Manila: World Health Organization, 1986).
Births Attended: *Statistics on Children in UNICEF Assisted Countries*.
24. No data.
25. UNICEF field office estimates, Vientiane.
26. *Statistics on Children in UNICEF Assisted Countries*.
27. UNICEF field office estimates, 1981.
28. WHO Health Statistics Annual, 1985.
29. No data.
30. *Statistics on Children in UNICEF Assisted Countries*.
31. *Statistical Yearbook 1987* (Paris: UNESCO).
32. *Statistics on Children in UNICEF Assisted Countries*.
33. *Statistical Yearbook 1987*.
34. No data.
35. *Atlaseco de Poche, Atlas Economique Mondial* (Paris: Les éditions S.G.P., 1988). Data taken from World Bank sources.
36. *LAO PDR Report on the Economic and Social Situation, Development Strategy and Assistance Needs* (Vientiane: April 1986).
37. No data.
38. *Statistical Yearbook 1987*.
Other: *Social Development Data Base for Asia and the Pacific*.

Malaysia

1. *The New International Atlas* (Chicago: Rand McNally, 1987), World Information Table, 1988 revision. Estimates for Jan. 1, 1988, based on official data, United Nations estimates, and other available information.
2. Ibid.
3. *FAO Production Yearbook 1987* (Rome: Food and Agricultural Organization, 1988).
4. Ibid. Deforestation: *World Resources 1988–89*, World Resources Institute (New York: Basic Books, Inc., 1988).
5. *1980 Population and Housing Census* (Kuala Lumpur: Department of Statistics, 1983).

SOURCES

6. *United Nations World Population Chart 1987* (New York: United Nations Population Division).

7. *Social Development Data Base for Asia and the Pacific* (Bangkok: United Nations Economic and Social Commission for Asia and the Pacific, Social Development Division, 1988).

8. *1988 World Population Data Sheet* (Washington, D.C.: Population Reference Bureau).

9. *Statistics on Children in UNICEF Assisted Countries* (New York: UNICEF, 1988).

10. *The Prospects of World Urbanization* (New York: United Nations Population Division, 1984–85 revision).

11. *Demographic Yearbook 1986*, United Nations.

12. *Yearbook of Statistics 1984* (Kuala Lumpur: Department of Statistics).

13. Population and Housing Census of Malaysia, 1980.

14. No data.

15. *The State of the World Children 1989*, UNICEF (New York: Oxford University Press, 1989), annex tables.

16. *Demographic Yearbook 1986*.

17. No data.

18. *World Development Report 1988*, World Bank (New York: Oxford University Press, 1988).

19. *World Population Policies*, United Nations Department of International Economic and Social Affairs (New York: United Nations, 1989).

20. *Statistics on Children in UNICEF Assisted Countries* (New York: UNICEF, 1988).

21. *The State of the World Children 1989*.

22. Ibid.

23. *Monitoring the Strategies for Health for All by the Year 2000, 1988 Report* (Kuala Lumpur: Ministry of Health).

24. *Social Development Data Base for Asia and the Pacific.*

25. *Compendium of Human Settlements Statistics 1983* (New York: United Nations).

26. *Statistics on Children in UNICEF Assisted Countries.*

27. *Compendium of Human Settlements Statistics 1983.*

28. Ibid.

29. 1980 Census of Population and Housing.

30. *Statistics on Children in UNICEF Assisted Countries.*

31. *Statistical Yearbook 1987* (Paris: UNESCO).

32. *The State of the World Children 1989.*

33. *Statistical Yearbook 1987.*

34. *Social Development Data Base for Asia and the Pacific.*

35. *Atlaseco de Poche, Atlas Economique Mondial* (Paris: Les éditions S.G.P., 1988). Data taken from World Bank sources.

36. *World Development Report 1988.*

37. *Statistics on Children in UNICEF Assisted Countries.*

38. *Statistical Yearbook 1987.* Television receivers: number of licenses issued or sets declared per 1,000 pop.

Union of Myanmar (Burma)

1. *The New International Atlas* (Chicago: Rand McNally, 1987), World Information Table, 1988 revision. Estimates for Jan. 1, 1988, based on official data, United Nations estimates, and other available information.

2. Ibid.

3. *FAO Production Yearbook 1987* (Rome: Food and Agriculture Organization, 1988).

4. Ibid. Deforestation: *World Resources 1988–89*, World Resources Institute (New York: Basic Books, Inc., 1988).

5. 1983 Population Census of the Socialist Republic of the Union of Burma.

6. *United Nations World Population Chart 1988* (New York: United Nations Population Division).

7. *Social Development Data Base for Asia and the Pacific* (Bangkok: United Nations Economic and Social Commission for Asia and the Pacific, Social Development Division, 1988).

8. *1988 World Population Data Sheet* (Washington, D.C.: Population Reference Bureau).

9. *Statistics on Children in UNICEF Assisted Countries* (New York: UNICEF, 1988).

10. *The Prospects of World Urbanization* (New York: United Nations Population Division, 1984–85 revision).

11. *Demographic Yearbook 1986* (New York: United Nations).

12. 1983 Population Census.

13. Ibid.

14. Ibid.

15. *The State of the World Children 1989*, UNICEF (New York: Oxford University Press, 1989), annex tables.

16. No data.

17. No data.

18. *World Development Report 1988*, World Bank (New York: Oxford University Press, 1988).

19. *World Population Policies*, United Nations Department of International Economic and Social Affairs (New York: United Nations, 1987); *World Population Trends and Policies: 1989 Monitoring Report*, United Nations Department of International Economic and Social Affairs (New York: United Nations, 1989).

20. *Statistics on Children in UNICEF Assisted Countries.*

21. *The State of the World Children 1989.*

22. Ibid.

23. *Statistics on Children in UNICEF Assisted Countries.*

24. 1983 Population Census.

25. No data.

26. *Social Development Data Base for Asia and the Pacific.*

27. No data.

28. *Social Development Data Base for Asia and the Pacific.*

29. 1983 Population Census.

30. Ibid.

31. *Social Development Data Base for Asia and the Pacific.*

32. *The State of the World Children 1989.*

33. 1983 Population Census.

34. Ibid. For pop. 10 years +.

35. *Atlaseco de Poche, Atlas Economique Mondial* (Paris: Les éditions S.G.P., 1988). Data taken from World Bank sources.
36. *World Development Report 1988.*
37. *The State of the World Children 1989* (UNICEF field office).

Philippines

1. *The New International Atlas* (Chicago: Rand McNally, 1987), World Information Table, 1988 revision. Estimates for Jan. 1, 1988, based on official data, United Nations estimates, and other available information.
2. Ibid.
3. *FAO Production Yearbook 1987* (Rome: Food and Agriculture Organization, 1988).
4. Ibid. Deforestation: *World Resources 1988–89*, World Resources Institute (New York: Basic Books, Inc., 1988).
5. *Country Health Information Profile* (Manila: World Health Organization, Dec. 1985 revision).
6. *United Nations World Population Chart 1988* (New York: United Nations Population Division).
7. *Social Development Data Base for Asia and the Pacific* (Bangkok: United Nations Economic and Social Commission for Asia and the Pacific, Social Development Division, 1988).
8. *1988 World Population Data Sheet* (Washington, D.C.: Population Reference Bureau).
9. *Statistics on Children in UNICEF Assisted Countries* (New York: UNICEF, 1988).
10. *The Prospects of World Urbanization* (New York: United Nations Population Division, 1984–85 revision).
11. *Demographic Yearbook 1986*, United Nations.
12. *Country Health Information Profile.*
13. *Social Development Data Base for Asia and the Pacific.*
14. No data.
15. *Social Development Data Base for Asia and the Pacific.*
16. *Demographic Yearbook 1986.*
17. Ibid.
18. *World Development Report 1988*, World Bank (New York: Oxford University Press, 1988).
19. *World Population Trends and Policies: 1989 Monitoring Report*, United Nations Department of International Economic and Social Affairs (New York: United Nations, 1989).
20. *Statistics on Children in UNICEF Assisted Countries.*
21. *The State of the World Children 1989.*
22. Ibid.
23. *Statistics on Children in UNICEF Assisted Countries.*
24. *Social Development Data Base for Asia and the Pacific.*
25. *Philippine Statistical Yearbook, 1983* (Manila: National Economic and Development Authority, National Census and Statistical Office).
26. *The State of the World Children 1989.*
27. *Philippine Statistical Yearbook, 1983.*
28. *Social Development Data Base for Asia and the Pacific.*
29. *Philippine Statistical Yearbook, 1984.*
30. *Statistics on Children in UNICEF Assisted Countries.*
31. *Statistical Yearbook 1987* (Paris: UNESCO).
32. *Statistics on Children in UNICEF Assisted Countries.*
33. *Statistical Yearbook 1987.*
34. *Yearbook of Labour Statistics, 1987* (Geneva: International Labour Office).
35. *Atlaseco de Poche, Atlas Economique Mondial* (Paris: Les éditions S.G.P., 1988). Data taken from World Bank sources.
36. *World Development Report 1988.*
37. *The State of the World Children 1989* (UNICEF field office).
38. *Statistical Yearbook 1987.*
Other: *Social Development Data Base for Asia and the Pacific.*

Singapore

1. *The New International Atlas* (Chicago: Rand McNally, 1987), World Information Table, 1988 revision. Estimates for Jan. 1, 1988, based on official data, United Nations estimates, and other available information.
2. Ibid.
3. *FAO Production Yearbook 1987* (Rome: Food and Agriculture Organization, 1988).
4. Ibid.
5. *Country Health Information Profile* (Manila: World Health Organization, Sept. 1987 revision).
6. *United Nations World Population Chart 1987* (New York: United Nations Population Division).
7. *Social Development Data Base for Asia and the Pacific* (Bangkok: United Nations Economic and Social Commission for Asia and the Pacific, Social Development Division, 1988).
8. *1988 World Population Data Sheet* (Washington, D.C.: Population Reference Bureau).
9. *Statistics on Children in UNICEF Assisted Countries* (New York: UNICEF, 1988).
10. *The Prospects of World Urbanization* (New York: United Nations Population Division, 1984–85 revision).
11. *Demographic Yearbook 1986*, United Nations.
12. Department of Statistics, Singapore.
13. *Social Development Data Base for Asia and the Pacific.*
14. *Census of Population, 1980* (Singapore: Department of Statistics).
15. *The State of the World Children 1989* UNICEF (New York: Oxford University Press, 1989), annex tables.
16. *Demographic Yearbook 1986.*
17. No data.
18. *World Development Report 1988*, World Bank (New York: Oxford University Press, 1988).
19. *World Population Trends and Policies: 1989 Monitoring Report*, United Nations Department of International Economic and Social Af-

fairs (New York: United Nations, 1989).
20. *Monitoring the State* (Singapore: Ministry of Health).
21. *The State of the World Children 1989.*
22. Ibid.
23. *Monitoring the State.*
24. *Compendium of Human Settlements Statistics 1983* (New York: United Nations).
25. Ibid.
26. *Country Health Information Profile.*
27. No data.
28. *Country Health Information Profile.*
29. No data.
30. *Statistics on Children in UNICEF Assisted Countries.*
31. *Statistical Yearbook 1987* (Paris: UNESCO).
32. *The State of the World Children 1989.*
33. *Statistical Yearbook 1987.*
34. *Social Development Data Base for Asia and the Pacific.*
35. *Atlaseco de Poche, Atlas Economique Mondial* (Paris: Les éditions S.G.P., 1988). Data taken from World Bank sources.
36. *World Development Report 1988.*
37. No data.
38. *Statistical Yearbook 1987.*
Other: *Social Development Data Base for Asia and the Pacific.*

Thailand

1. *The New International Atlas* (Chicago: Rand McNally, 1987), World Information Table, 1988 revision. Estimates for Jan. 1, 1988, based on official data, United Nations estimates, and other available information.
2. Ibid.
3. *FAO Production Yearbook 1987* (Rome: Food and Agriculture Organization, 1988).
4. Ibid. Deforestation: *World Resources 1988–89*, World Resources Institute (New York: Basic Books, Inc., 1988).
5. *Europa Yearbook 1988* (London: Europa Publications Limited).
6. *United Nations World Population Chart 1987* (New York: United Nations Population Division).
7. *Social Development Data Base for Asia and the Pacific* (Bangkok: United Nations Economic and Social Commission for Asia and the Pacific, Social Development Division, 1988).
8. *1988 World Population Data Sheet* (Washington, D.C.: Population Reference Bureau).
9. *Statistics on Children in UNICEF Assisted Countries* (New York: UNICEF, 1988).
10. *The Prospects of World Urbanization* (New York: United Nations Population Division, 1984–85 revision).
11. *Demographic Yearbook 1986*, United Nations.
12. George Thomas Kurian, *Encyclopedia of the Third World*, 3rd ed. (New York: Facts on File, Inc., 1987).
13. *Demographic Yearbook 1987.*
14. Ibid.
15. *The State of the World Children 1988*, UNICEF (New York: Oxford University Press, 1988), annex tables.
16. *Demographic Yearbook 1987.*
17. No data.
18. *World Development Report 1988*, World Bank (New York: Oxford University Press, 1988).
19. *World Population Trends and Policies: 1989 Monitoring Report*, United Nations Department of International Economic and Social Affairs (New York: United Nations, 1989).
20. *The State of the World Children 1989.*
21. *Statistics on Children in UNICEF Assisted Countries.*
22. *The State of the World Children 1989.*
23. *Statistics on Children in UNICEF Assisted Countries.*
24. *Compendium of Human Settlements Statistics 1983* (New York: United Nations).
25. Ibid.
26. *Statistics on Children in UNICEF Assisted Countries.*
27. *Compendium of Human Settlements Statistics 1983.*
28. Ibid.
29. No data.
30. *Statistics on Children in UNICEF Assisted Countries.*
31. *Statistical Yearbook 1987* (Paris: UNESCO).
32. *The State of the World Children 1989.*
33. *Statistical Yearbook 1987.*
34. *Yearbook of Labour Statistics, 1986* (Geneva: International Labour Office). For pop. 15 years +.
35. *Atlaseco de Poche, Atlas Economique Mondial* (Paris: Les éditions S.G.P., 1988). Data taken from World Bank sources.
36. *World Development Report 1988.*
37. *Statistics on Children in UNICEF Assisted Countries.*
38. *Statistical Yearbook 1986.*
Other: *Social Development Data Base for Asia and the Pacific.*

Socialist Republic of Vietnam

1. *The New International Atlas* (Chicago: Rand McNally, 1987), World Information Table, 1988 revision. Estimates for Jan. 1, 1988, based on official data, United Nations estimates, and other available information.
2. Ibid.
3. *FAO Production Yearbook 1987* (Rome: Food and Agriculture Organization, 1988).
4. Ibid. Deforestation: *World Resources 1988–89*, World Resources Institute (New York: Basic Books, Inc., 1988).
5. *Country Health Information Profile* (Manila: World Health Organization, Dec. 1985 revision).
6. Population Census 1979.
7. *Social Development Data Base for Asia and the Pacific* (Bangkok: United Nations Economic and Social Commission for Asia and the Pacific, Social Development Division, 1988).
8. *1988 World Population Data Sheet* (Washington, D.C.: Population Reference Bureau).
9. *Statistics on Children in UNI-*

SOURCES

CEF Assisted Countries (New York: UNICEF, 1988).
10. *The Prospects of World Urbanization* (New York: United Nations Population Division, 1984–85 revision).
11. Population Census 1979.
12. Ibid.
13. No data.
14. No data.
15. *The State of the World Children 1989*, UNICEF (New York: Oxford University Press, 1989), annex tables.
16. No data.
17. No data.
18. *World Development Report 1988*, World Bank (New York: Oxford University Press, 1988).
19. *World Population Trends and Policies: 1989 Monitoring Report*, United Nations Department of International Economic and Social Affairs (New York: United Nations, 1989).
20. *Statistics on Children in UNICEF Assisted Countries*.
21. *The State of the World Children 1989*.
22. Ibid.
23. *Country Health Information Profile*.
24. Population Census 1979.
25. No data.
26. *Statistics on Children in UNICEF Assisted Countries*.
27. No data.
28. *Social Development Data Base for Asia and the Pacific*.
29. No data.
30. *Statistics on Children in UNICEF Assisted Countries*.
31. *Statistical Yearbook 1987* (Paris: UNESCO).
32. *The State of the World Children 1989*.
33. *Statistical Yearbook 1987*.
34. No data
35. *Atlaseco de Poche, Atlas Economique Mondial* (Paris: Les éditions S.G.P., 1988). Data taken from World Bank sources.
36. *Statistics on Children in UNICEF Assisted Countries*.
37. No data.
38. *Statistical Yearbook 1987*.
Other: *Social Development Data Base for Asia and the Pacific*.

Refugees and Displaced Persons

Locations: United Nations High Commissioner on Refugees (UNHCR), Geneva.
Total populations: Ibid.
Site 2 population: United Nations Border Relief Operation (UNBRO), Bangkok.
Birth rate: UNBRO
Food: UNBRO
Water: UNBRO
Health: UNBRO
Housing: UNBRO
Education: UNBRO

THE PACIFIC

Australia

1. *The New International Atlas* (Chicago: Rand McNally, 1987), World Information Table, 1988 revision. Estimates for Jan. 1, 1988, based on official data, United Nations estimates, and other available information.
2. Ibid.
3. *FAO Production Yearbook 1987* (Rome: Food and Agriculture Organization, 1988).
4. Ibid.
5. *1986 Census of Population and Housing*, Bureau of Statistics (Canberra: Bureau of Statistics).
6. *Social Development Data Base for Asia and the Pacific* (Bangkok: United Nations Economic and Social Commission for Asia and the Pacific, Social Development Division, 1988).
7. Ibid.
8. *1988 World Population Data Sheet* (Washington, D.C.: Population Reference Bureau).
9. *Statistics on Children in UNICEF Assisted Countries* (New York: UNICEF, 1988).
10. *The Prospects of World Urbanization* (New York: United Nations Population Division, 1984–85 revision).
11. *1986 Census of Population and Housing*.
12. Ibid.
13. Ibid.
14. Ibid.
15. *The State of the World Children 1989*, UNICEF (New York: Oxford University Press, 1989), annex tables.
16. *Demographic Yearbook 1986*, United Nations. For under 16 and 16–19 years, as appropriate.
17. Ibid.
18. *World Development Report 1988*, World Bank (New York: Oxford University Press, 1988).
19. *World Population Policies*, United Nations Department of International Economic and Social Affairs (New York: United Nations, 1987).
20. *World Development Report 1988*.
male–female: *Country Health Information Profile* (Manila: World Health Organization, Dec. 1985 revision).
21. *The State of the World Children 1989*.
22. Ibid.
23. *Country Health Information Profile*.
24. *1986 Census of Population and Housing*.
25. *National Energy Survey* (Canberra: Australian Bureau of Statistics, 1985–86).
26. *Country Health Information Profile*.
27. *National Energy Survey*.
28. *Country Health Information Profile*.

29. *National Energy Survey*. Excludes mobile or improvised, high- or low-rise dwellings.
30. *Country Health Information Profile*.
31. *Statistical Yearbook 1987* (Paris: UNESCO).
32. No data.
33. *Families in Australia* (Rosebery, Australia: University of New South Wales, 1983).
34. *Social Development Data Base for Asia and the Pacific*.
35. *Atlaseco de Poche, Atlas Economique Mondial* (Paris: Les éditions S.G.P., 1988). Data compiled from World Bank, the *Asian Yearbook*, and the *Far Eastern Review*.
36. *World Development Report 1988*.
37. No data.
38. *Statistical Yearbook 1987* (Paris: UNESCO).

Other: *Social Development Data Base for Asia and the Pacific*.

Republic of Fiji

1. *The New International Atlas* (Chicago: Rand McNally, 1987), World Information Table, 1988 revision. Estimates for Jan. 1, 1988, based on official data, United Nations estimates, and other available information.
2. Ibid.
3. *FAO Production Yearbook 1987* (Rome: Food and Agriculture Organization, 1988).
4. Ibid. Deforestation: *World Resources 1988–89*, World Resources Institute (New York: Basic Books, Inc, 1988).
5. 1986 Census of Population.
6. Ibid.
7. Ibid.
8. *1988 World Population Data Sheet* (Washington, D.C.: Population Reference Bureau).
9. *Statistics on Children in UNICEF Assisted Countries* (New York: UNICEF, 1988).
10. *The Prospects of World Urbanization* (New York: United Nations Population Division, 1984–85 revision).
11. *Demographic Yearbook 1986*, United Nations.
12. 1986 Census of Population.
13. Ibid.
14. Ibid.
15. Ibid.
16. *Demographic Yearbook 1986*.
17. *Social Indicators for Fiji* (Suva: Bureau of Statistics, 1980).
18. No data.
19. *World Population Policies*, United Nations Department of International Economic and Social Affairs (New York: United Nations, 1987).
20. *Statistics on Children in UNICEF Assisted Countries*.
21. Ibid.
22. Ibid.
23. *Country Health Information Profile* (Manila: World Health Organization, 1986 revision).
24. 1986 Census of Population.
25. Ibid.
26. *Statistics on Children in UNICEF Assisted Countries*.
27. 1986 Census of Population.
28. Ibid.
29. Ibid.
30. *Statistics on Children in UNICEF Assisted Countries*.
31. *Statistical Yearbook 1987* (Paris: UNESCO).
32. *Statistics on Children in UNICEF Assisted Countries*.
33. *Statistical Yearbook 1987*.
34. 1986 Census of Population.
35. *Atlaseco de Poche, Atlas Economique Mondial* (Paris: Les éditions S.G.P., 1988). Data taken from World Bank sources.
36. *World Development Report 1988*, World Bank (New York: Oxford University Press, 1988).
37. *Statistics on Children in UNICEF Assisted Countries*.
38. *Statistical Yearbook 1987* (Paris: UNESCO).

Other: *Social Development Data Base for Asia and the Pacific* (Bangkok: United Nations Economic and Social Commission for Asia and the Pacific, Social Development Division, 1988).

Kiribati

1. *The New International Atlas* (Chicago: Rand McNally, 1987), World Information Table, 1988 revision. Estimates for Jan. 1, 1988, based on official data, United Nations estimates, and other available information.
2. Ibid.
3. *FAO Production Yearbook 1987* (Rome: Food and Agriculture Organization, 1988).
4. Ibid.
5. *Country Health Information Profile* (Manila: World Health Organization, Dec. 1986 revision).
6. *United Nations World Population Chart 1988* (New York: United Nations Population Division). Includes Canton and Enderbury Islands.
7. *Statistics on Children in UNICEF Assisted Countries* (New York: UNICEF, 1988).
8. Ibid.
9. *Statistics on Children in UNICEF Assisted Countries*.
10. *The Prospects of World Urbanization* (New York: United Nations Population Division, 1984–85 revision).
11. 1985 Census of Population.
12. Ibid.
13. Ibid.
14. No data.
15. *Country Health Information Profile*.
16. 1986 Census of Population.
17. No data.
18. No data.
19. *World Population Policies*, United Nations Department of International Economic and Social Affairs (New York: United Nations, 1989).
20. *Statistics on Children in UNICEF Assisted Countries*.
21. Ibid.
22. Ibid.
23. *Country Health Information Profile*.
24. No data.
25. 1986 Census of Population.

26. *Statistics on Children in UNICEF Assisted Countries.*
27. 1978 Census of Population and Housing.
28. Ibid.
29. Ibid.
30. *Statistics on Children in UNICEF Assisted Countries.*
31. Ibid.
32. No data.
33. 1986 Census of Population.
34. No data.
35. No data.
36. *Country Health Information Profile.*
37. No data.
38. *Statistical Yearbook 1987* (Paris: UNESCO).

Other: *Social Development Data Base for Asia and the Pacific* (Bangkok: United Nations Economic and Social Commission for Asia and the Pacific, Social Development Division, 1988).

Nauru

1. *The New International Atlas* (Chicago: Rand McNally, 1987), World Information Table, 1988 revision. Estimates for Jan. 1, 1988, based on official data, United Nations estimates, and other available information.
2. Ibid.
3. *FAO Production Yearbook 1987* (Rome: Food and Agriculture Organization, 1988).
4. Ibid.
5. *Europa Yearbook 1988* (London: Europa Publications Limited).
6. Census of Population, 1983.
7. Ibid.
8. Ibid.
9. *Statistics on Children in UNICEF Assisted Countries* (New York: UNICEF, 1988).
10. *The Prospects of World Urbanization* (New York: United Nations Population Division, 1984–85 revision).
11. *Nauruan Mortality 1976–1981* (Noumea, New Caledonia: South Pacific Commission, April 1983).
12. Census of Population, 1983.
13. No data.
14. No data.
15. No data.
16. No data.
17. No data.
18. No data.
19. *World Population Policies,* United Nations Department of International Economic and Social Affairs (New York: United Nations, 1989).
20. *Nauruan Mortality 1976–1981.*
21. Birth: *Europa Yearbook 1988;* Death: *Nauruan Mortality.*
22. *Nauruan Mortality.*
23. Ibid.
24. Census of Population, 1983.
25. No data.
26. No data.
27. No data.
28. No data.
29. No data.
30. No data.
31. No data.
32. No data.
33. No data.
34. No data.
35. No data.
36. *Atlaseco de Poche, Atlas Economique Mondial* (Paris: Les éditions S.G.P., 1988). Data taken from World Bank sources.
37. *Europa Yearbook 1988.*
38. *Statistical Yearbook 1987* (Paris: UNESCO).

Other: *Social Development Data Base for Asia and the Pacific* (Bangkok: United Nations Economic and Social Commission for Asia and the Pacific, Social Development Division, 1988).

New Zealand

1. *The New International Atlas* (Chicago: Rand McNally, 1987), World Information Table, 1988 revision. Estimates for Jan. 1, 1988, based on official data, United Nations estimates, and other available information.
2. Ibid.
3. *FAO Production Yearbook 1987* (Rome: Food and Agriculture Organization, 1988).
4. Ibid.
5. *1986 New Zealand Census of Population and Dwellings* (Auckland: Department of Statistics).
6. Ibid.
7. *Social Development Data Base for Asia and the Pacific* (Bangkok: United Nations Economic and Social Commission for Asia and the Pacific, Social Development Division, 1988).
8. *1988 World Population Data Sheet* (Washington, D.C.: Population Reference Bureau).
9. *Statistics on Children in UNICEF Assisted Countries* (New York: UNICEF, 1988).
10. *The Prospects of World Urbanization* (New York: United Nations Population Division, 1984–85 revision).
11. *1986 New Zealand Census of Population and Dwellings.*
12. Ibid.
13. Ibid.
14. *Demographic Yearbook 1987,* United Nations.
15. *Monthly Abstract of Statistics* (Auckland: Department of Statistics, January 1988).
16. Ibid.
17. *Vital Statistics* (Auckland: Department of Statistics, January 1986).
18. United Nations Population Division, New York. Married women 15 yrs. + considered at risk of pregnancy.
19. *World Population Policies,* United Nations Department of International Economic and Social Affairs (New York: United Nations, 1989).
20. *1986 New Zealand Census of Population and Dwellings.*
21. *The State of the World Children 1989.*
22. *Monthly Abstract of Statistics,* Jan. 1988.
23. *Country Health Information Profile* (Manila: World Health

Organization, Dec. 1985 revision).
24. Department of Statistics, Auckland.
25. Ibid.
26. Ibid.
27. *Evaluation of the Strategy for Health for All by the Year 2000* (Manila: World Health Organization, 1987).
28. Department of Statistics, Auckland.
29. *1981 New Zealand Census of Population and Dwellings.*
30. *Country Health Information Profile.*
31. *Statistical Yearbook 1987* (Paris: UNESCO).
32. Ibid.
33. No data.
34. *Yearbook of Labour Statistics,* 1987 (Geneva: International Labour Office). For population 15 yrs. +.
35. *Atlaseco de Poche, Atlas Economique Mondial* (Paris: Les éditions S.G.P., 1988). Data taken from World Bank sources.
36. *World Development Report 1988,* World Bank (New York: Oxford University Press, 1988).
37. No data.
38. *Statistical Yearbook 1987.*
Other: *Social Development Data Base for Asia and the Pacific* (Bangkok: United Nations Economic and Social Commission for Asia and the Pacific, Social Development Division, 1988).

Papua New Guinea

1. *The New International Atlas* (Chicago: Rand McNally, 1987), World Information Table, 1988 revision. Estimates for Jan. 1, 1988, based on official data, United Nations estimates, and other available information.
2. Ibid.
3. *FAO Production Yearbook 1987* (Rome: Food and Agriculture Organization, 1988).
4. Ibid. Deforestation: *World Resources 1988–89,* World Resources Institute (New York: Basic Books, Inc., 1988).
5. *The Europayear Book 1988* (London: Europa Publications Ltd).
6. *United Nations World Population Chart 1987* (New York: United Nations Population Division).
7. *Social Development Data Base for Asia and the Pacific* (Bangkok: United Nations Economic and Social Commission for Asia and the Pacific, Social Development Division, 1988).
8. *1988 World Population Data Sheet* (Washington, D.C.: Population Reference Bureau).
9. *Statistics on Children in UNICEF Assisted Countries* (New York: UNICEF, 1988).
10. *The Prospects of World Urbanization* (New York: United Nations Population Division, 1984–85 revision).
11. *Demographic Yearbook 1987,* United Nations.
12. *Country Health Information Profile* (Manila: World Health Organization, Dec. 1985 revision).
13. 1980 National Population Census.
14. No data.
15. *Social Development Data Base for Asia and the Pacific.*
16. No data.
17. No data.
18. *World Development Report 1988,* World Bank (New York: Oxford University Press, 1988).
19. *World Population Trends and Policies: 1989 Monitoring Report,* United Nations Department of International Economic and Social Affairs (New York: United Nations, 1989).
20. *Statistics on Children in UNICEF Assisted Countries* (New York: UNICEF: 1988).
21. *The State of the World Children 1989,* UNICEF (New York: Oxford University Press, 1989), annex tables.
22. Ibid.
23. *Country Health Information Profile.*
24. 1980 National Population Census.
25. National Statistical Office, Port Moresby.
26. *Country Health Information Profile.*
27. No data.
28. *Country Health Information Profile.*
29. No data.
30. *Statistics on Children in UNICEF Assisted Countries.*
31. *Social Development Data Base for Asia and the Pacific.*
32. *The State of the World Children 1989.*
33. *Statistical Yearbook 1987* (Paris: UNESCO). Nationals only.
34. 1980 National Population Census.
35. *Atlaseco de Poche, Atlas Economique Mondial* (Paris: Les éditions S.G.P., 1988). Data taken from World Bank sources.
36. *World Development Report 1988.*
37. *The State of the World Children 1989.*
38. *Statistical Yearbook 1986* (Paris: UNESCO).
Other: *Social Development Data Base for Asia and the Pacific.*

Solomon Islands

1. *FAO Production Yearbook 1987* (Rome: Food and Agriculture Organization, 1988).
2. 1986 Population Census (Honiara: Statistical Bureau).
3. *FAO Production Yearbook 1987.*
4. Ibid. Deforestation: *World Resources 1988–89,* World Resources Institute (New York: Basic Books, Inc., 1988).
5. 1986 Population Census.
6. *Social Development Data Base for Asia and the Pacific* (Bangkok: United Nations Economic and Social Commission for Asia and the Pacific, Social Development Division, 1988).
7. Ibid.
8. *1988 World Population Data Sheet* (Washington, D.C.: Population Reference Bureau).
9. *Statistics on Children in UNICEF Assisted Countries* (New York: UNICEF, 1988).

SOURCES

10. *The Prospects of World Urbanization* (New York: United Nations Population Division, 1984–85 revision).
11. 1986 Population Census.
12. Ibid.
13. Ibid.
14. No data.
15. *1988 World Population Data Sheet.*
16. No data.
17. No data.
18. No data.
19. *World Population Trends and Policies: 1989 Monitoring Report*, United Nations Department of International Economic and Social Affairs (New York: United Nations, 1989).
20. *Statistics on Children in UNICEF Assisted Countries.*
21. *The State of the World Children 1989*, UNICEF (New York: Oxford University Press, 1989), annex tables.
22. *Statistics on Children in UNICEF Assisted Countries.*
23. Access to health services: Village Resources Survey, 1984–85 (Honiara: Statistics Office). Percent of households with access to clinic or aid post.
Births attended: *Statistics on Children in UNICEF Assisted Countries.*
24. 1986 Population Census.
25. No data.
26. *Statistics on Children in UNICEF Assisted Countries.*
27. Village Resources Survey, 1984–85.
28. Ibid.
29. No data.
30. *Statistics on Children in UNICEF Assisted Countries.*
31. Ibid.
32. Ibid.
33. No data.
34. *Social Development Data Base for Asia and the Pacific.*
35. *Atlaseco de Poche, Atlas Economique Mondial* (Paris: Les éditions S.G.P., 1988). Data taken from World Bank sources.
36. *Solomon Islands Trade Directory 1988.*
37. No data.
38. *Statistical Yearbook 1987* (Paris: UNESCO).

Other: *Social Development Data Base for Asia and the Pacific.*

Kingdom of Tonga

1. *The New International Atlas* (Chicago: Rand McNally, 1987), World Information Table, 1988 revision. Estimates for Jan. 1, 1988, based on official data, United Nations estimates, and other available information.
2. Ibid.
3. *FAO Production Yearbook 1987* (Rome: Food and Agriculture Organization, 1988).
4. Ibid.
5. *Country Health Information Profile* (Manila: World Health Organization, Dec. 1985 revision).
6. Population Census 1986.
7. *Social Development Data Base for Asia and the Pacific* (Bangkok: United Nations Economic and Social Commission for Asia and the Pacific, Social Development Division, 1988).
8. Ibid.
9. *Statistics on Children in UNICEF Assisted Countries* (New York: UNICEF, 1988).
10. *The Prospects of World Urbanization* (New York: United Nations Population Division, 1984–85 revision).
11. *Country Health Information Profile.*
12. George Thomas Kurian, *Encyclopedia of the Third World*, 3rd ed. (New York: Facts on File, Inc., 1987).
13. *Social Development Data Base for Asia and the Pacific.*
14. No data.
15. No data.
16. No data.
17. *Demographic Yearbook 1986*, United Nations.
18. No data.
19. *World Population Trend and Policies: 1989 Monitoring Report*, United Nations Department of International Economic and Social Affairs (New York: United Nations, 1989).
20. *Country Health Information Profile.*
21. Ibid.
22. Ibid.
23. Ibid.
24. *Compendium of Human Settlements Statistics 1983* (New York: United Nations).
25. Ibid.
26. *Statistics on Children in UNICEF Assisted Countries.*
27. *Compendium of Human Settlements Statistics 1983.*
28. Ibid.
29. *1983 Statistical Abstract* (Nukualofa: Statistics Department).
30. *Statistics on Children in UNICEF Assisted Countries.*
31. *1983 Statistical Abstract.*
32. Ibid.
33. Ibid.
34. *Social Development Data Base for Asia and the Pacific.*
35. *Atlaseco de Poche, Atlas Economique Mondial* (Paris: Les éditions S.G.P., 1988). Data taken from World Bank sources.
36. *World Development Report 1988*, World Bank (New York: Oxford University Press, 1988).
37. No data.
38. *Statistical Yearbook 1987*, (Paris: UNESCO).

Other: *Social Development Data Base for Asia and the Pacific.*

Tuvalu

1. *The New International Atlas* (Chicago: Rand McNally, 1987), World Information Table. 1988 Revision. Estimates for Jan. 1, 1988, based on official data, United Nations estimates, and other available information.
2. Ibid.
3. *FAO Production Yearbook 1987* (Rome: Food and Agriculture Organization, 1988).
4. Ibid.
5. *Country Health Information Profile* (Manila: World Health Organization, Dec. 1985 revision).
6. *United Nations World Population Chart 1988* (New York: United Nations Population Division).

7. *Country Health Information Profile.*
8. Ibid.
9. Ibid.
10. No data.
11. Integrated Island Development Office.
12. *Census of the Population of Tuvalu, 1979.*
13. Ibid.
14. No data.
15. *Country Health Information Profile.*
16. Tuvalu Birth Summary, 1986 (Funafuti: Ministry of Social Services).
17. Ibid.
18. No data.
19. *World Population Trends and Policies: 1989 Monitoring Report,* United Nations Department of International Economic and Social Affairs (New York: United Nations, 1989).
20. *Statistics on Children in UNICEF Assisted Countries* (New York: UNICEF, 1988).
21. Ibid.
22. *Country Health Information Profile.*
23. Ibid.
24. *Census of the Population of Tuvalu, 1979.*
25. Ibid.
26. *Country Health Information Profile.*
27. *Census of the Population of Tuvalu, 1979.*
28. Ibid.
29. Ibid.
30. *Statistics on Children in UNICEF Assisted Countries.*
31. Ibid.
32. No data.
33. *Census of the Population of Tuvalu, 1979.*
34. No data.
35. No data.
36. No data.
37. No data.
38. No data.
Other: *Social Development Data Base for Asia and the Pacific* (Bangkok: United Nations Economic and Social Commission for Asia and the Pacific, Social Development Division, 1988).

Vanuatu

1. *The New International Atlas* (Chicago: Rand McNally, 1987), World Information Table, 1988 revision. Estimates for Jan. 1, 1988, based on official data, United Nations estimates, and other available information.
2. Ibid.
3. *FAO Production Yearbook 1987* (Rome: Food and Agriculture Organization, 1988).
4. Ibid.
5. *Country Health Information Profile* (Manila: World Health Organization, Dec. 1986 revision).
6. 1979 Population Census.
7. *Statistics on Children in UNICEF Assisted Countries* (New York: UNICEF, 1988).
8. *1988 World Population Data Sheet* (Washington, D.C.: Population Reference Bureau).
9. *Statistics on Children in UNICEF Assisted Countries.*
10. *The Prospects of World Urbanization* (New York: United Nations Population Division, 1984–85 revision).
11. 1979 Population Census.
12. George Thomas Kurian, *Encyclopedia of the Third World,* 3rd ed. (New York: Facts on File, Inc., 1987).
13. *Demographic Yearbook 1987,* United Nations.
14. No data.
15. *Social Development Data Base for Asia and the Pacific* (Bangkok: United Nations Economic and Social Commission for Asia and the Pacific, Social Development Division, 1988).
16. No data.
17. No data.
18. No data.
19. *World Population Trends and Policies: 1989 Monitoring Report,* United Nations Department of International Economic and Social Affairs (New York: United Nations, 1989).
20. *Country Health Information Profile.*
21. Ibid.
22. Ibid.
23. Ibid.
24. *Vanuatu Facts and Figures, 1987* (Port-Vila: Statistics Office).
25. 1979 Census of Population (Port-Vila: National Planning and Statistics, 1983).
26. *Statistics on Children in UNICEF Assisted Countries.*
27. *Country Health Information Profile.*
28. Ibid.
29. 1979 Census of Population.
30. *Social Development Data Base for Asia and the Pacific.*
31. *Statistics on Children in UNICEF Assisted Countries.*
32. No data.
33. No data.
34. *Social Development Data Base for Asia and the Pacific.*
35. *Atlaseco de Poche, Atlas Economique Mondial* (Paris: Les éditions S.G.P., 1988). Data taken from World Bank sources.
36. *Country Health Information Profile.*
37. No data.
38. *Statistical Yearbook 1987* (Paris: UNESCO).
Other: *Social Development Data Base for Asia and the Pacific.*

Western Samoa

1. *The New International Atlas* (Chicago: Rand McNally, 1987), World Information Table, 1988 revision. Estimates for Jan. 1, 1988, based on official data, United Nations estimates, and other available information.
2. Ibid.
3. *FAO Production Yearbook 1987* (Rome: Food and Agriculture Organization, 1988).
4. Ibid.
5. Census of Population and Housing, 1981, Department of Statistics, Apia.
6. *United Nations World Population Chart 1988* (New York: United Nations Population Division).

SOURCES

7. *Social Development Data Base for Asia and the Pacific* (Bangkok: United Nations Economic and Social Commission for Asia and the Pacific, Social Development Division, 1988).
8. *1988 World Population Data Sheet* (Washington, D.C.: Population Reference Bureau).
9. *Statistics on Children in UNICEF Assisted Countries* (New York: UNICEF, 1988).
10. *The Prospects of World Urbanization* (New York: United Nations Population Division, 1984–85 revision).
11. *Demographic Yearbook 1987*, United Nations.
12. Census of Population and Housing, 1981.
13. Ibid.
14. Ibid.
15. *Social Development Data Base for Asia and the Pacific.*
16. *Demographic Yearbook 1985.*
17. Department of Statistics, Information from Birth Notification.
18. *World Development Report 1988*, World Bank (New York: Oxford University Press, 1988).
19. *World Population Trends and Policies: 1989 Monitoring Report*, United Nations Department of International Economic and Social Affairs (New York: United Nations, 1989).
20. *Statistics on Children in UNICEF Assisted Countries.*
21. Ibid.
22. Ibid.
23. Ibid.
24. *Social Development Data Base for Asia and the Pacific.*
25. Census of Population and Housing, 1981.
26. *Statistics on Children in UNICEF Assisted Countries.*
27. Census of Population and Housing, 1981.
28. Ibid.
29. Ibid.
30. *Statistics on Children in UNICEF Assisted Countries.*
31. No data.
32. No data.
33. Census of Population and Housing, 1981.
34. *Social Development Data Base for Asia and the Pacific.*
35. *Atlaseco de Poche, Atlas Economique Mondial* (Paris: Les éditions S.G.P., 1988). Data taken from World Bank sources.
36. *World Development Report 1988.*
37. No data.
38. *Statistical Yearbook 1987* (Paris: UNESCO).

Other: *Social Development Data Base for Asia and the Pacific.*